Praise for *The Reproach of Hunger*

"[Rieff's] unflinching analysis is an invaluable corrective to the happy-clappy unreality of much of our current thinking on hunger. A forceful critique of the ideology that has captured many transnational institutions in recent decades, *The Reproach of Hunger* is a substantial work of political thought."

—John Gray, *New Statesman*

"David Rieff reminds [us] that hunger is a war not won. Rieff, a veteran thinker on development issues, spent six years researching the nexus of population, food commodification, and persistent poverty for this critical analysis. Scathing about the alarmist or over-optimistic pronouncements of development officials, agribusiness multinationals, and philanthropic nabobs, he notes that any issue involving billions of humans cannot be neatly engineered. Thoughtful, trenchant, and bracingly skeptical."

—*Nature*

"Hunger, [Rieff] writes, is a political problem, and fighting it means rejecting the fashionable consensus that only the private sector can act efficiently."

—*The New Yorker*

"An erudite and well-researched analysis of the problem of world hunger and the challenges associated with international development. . . . [The book] exposes the contradictions of the philanthrocapitalist dogma currently in vogue and challenges readers to reexamine the causes of growing development inequality among countries."

—*Philanthropy News Digest*

"A stinging indictment of modern philanthropy and development theory's capacity to resolve the pressing issues of poverty and hunger. In the wake of so many books rehashing the same arguments about how to help the developing world, readers will be grateful for a different (and impeccably researched) perspective. This is a stellar addition to the canon of development policy literature."

—*Publishers Weekly* (starred review)

"A realistic examination of the world's ability to solve the global food crisis."

—*Library Journal*

Praise for *A Bed for the Night: Humanitarianism in Crisis*

"A withering, thought-provoking study."

—*The Wall Street Journal*

"Hardheaded, sophisticated, and urgent."

—*The New York Times Book Review*

Praise for *Slaughterhouse: Bosnia and the Failure of the West*

"Rieff writes with a knowledge so thorough, an intelligence so keen, a passion so scalding, and a morality so vigorous that one cannot come away from reading this without despair for mankind."

—*The Advocate*

"It is David Rieff's shocking conclusion . . . that we have reached the point where to bear witness is the remaining alternative to losing hope in the face of unchecked crimes against humanity."

—*The Baltimore Sun*

ALSO BY DAVID RIEFF

Against Remembrance

Swimming in a Sea of Death: A Son's Memoir

At the Point of a Gun: Democratic Dreams and Armed Intervention

A Bed for the Night: Humanitarianism in Crisis

Slaughterhouse: Bosnia and the Failure of the West

Exile: Cuba in the Heart of Miami

Los Angeles: Capital of the Third World

Going to Miami: Exiles, Tourists and Refugees in the New America

THE
REPROACH
OF
HUNGER

Food, Justice, and Money in the
Twenty-First Century

DAVID RIEFF

• SIMON & SCHUSTER PAPERBACKS•
New York London Toronto Sydney New Delhi

This book is for Judith Thurman

Simon & Schuster Paperbacks
An Imprint of Simon & Schuster, Inc.
1230 Avenue of the Americas
New York, NY 10020

First Simon & Schuster trade paperback edition October 2016

SIMON & SCHUSTER PAPERBACKS and colophon are registered
trademarks of Simon & Schuster, Inc.

For information about special discounts for bulk purchases,
please contact Simon & Schuster Special Sales at 1-866-506-1949
or business@simonandschuster.com.

The Simon & Schuster Speakers Bureau can bring authors to
your live event. For more information or to book an event contact
the Simon & Schuster Speakers Bureau at 1-866-248-3049 or visit
our website at www.simonspeakers.com.

Interior design by Lewelin Polanco

Manufactured in the United States of America

10 9 8 7 6 5 4 3 2 1

The Library of Congress has cataloged the hardcover edition as follows:

Rieff, David.
  The reproach of hunger : food, justice, and money in the twenty-first century
/ David Rieff.
    pages cm
  Includes bibliographical references and index.
  1. Food supply. 2. Hunger. 3. Social justice. 4. Money. I. Title.
HD9000.5.R53 2015
363.8—dc23
                                                2015007343

ISBN 978-1-4391-2387-4
ISBN 978-1-4391-2388-1 (pbk)
ISBN 978-1-4391-4859-4 (ebook)

But we don't see or hear those who suffer, and the horrors of life go on somewhere behind the scenes. Everything is quiet, peaceful, and only mute statistics protest: so many gone mad, so many buckets drunk, so many children dead of malnutrition. . . . And this order is obviously necessary; obviously the happy man feels good only because the unhappy bear their burden silently, and without that silence happiness would be impossible. It's a general hypnosis. At the door of every contented, happy man somebody should stand with a little hammer, constantly tapping, to remind him that unhappy people exist, that however happy he may be, sooner or later life will show him its claws, some calamity will befall him—illness, poverty, loss—and nobody will hear or see, just as he doesn't hear or see others now.

ANTON CHEKHOV, "GOOSEBERRIES"

Poor nations are hungry, and rich nations are proud; and pride and hunger will ever be at variance.

JONATHAN SWIFT

Plenty is at our doorstep, but a generous use of it languishes in the very sight of the supply. Primarily this is because the rulers of the exchange of mankind's goods have failed, through their own stubbornness and their own incompetence, have admitted their failure, and abdicated.

Practices of the unscrupulous money changers stand indicted in the court of public opinion, rejected by the hearts and minds of men. . . .

The money changers have fled from their high seat in the temple of our Civilization. We may now restore that temple to the ancient truths. The measure of the restoration lies in the extent to which we apply social values more noble than mere monetary profit.

FRANKLIN DELANO ROOSEVELT, FIRST INAUGURAL, 1933

Contents

Contents

Introduction

It was the crisis that was not supposed to happen. If you had asked most mainstream development experts in the year 2000 to name those factors they thought would most imperil their efforts to substantially reduce poverty globally in the new millennium, it is highly unlikely they would have mentioned a sudden, radical spike in the price of the principal agricultural commodities, and the staple foods made from them, on which the poor of the world literally depended for their survival. What seems obvious in hindsight—that the long period in which food prices had steadily declined would come to an abrupt end—seemed anything but obvious at the time. As Rajiv Shah, the then-administrator of the US Agency for International Development under President Barack Obama, put it, "by the late 1990s, global food security had mostly fallen off the world's agenda." The reasons for this were partly empirical (even if, self-evidently, in retrospect not empirical enough) and partly ideological, even in what was supposedly a post-ideological age. The empirical part was based on what seemed to be a secular rather than temporary decline in the price of food staples, which, by 2000, were at an all-time low. The ideological part lay in the presumption that, in Shah's words, "the success of the Green Revolution [in agriculture] had helped hundreds of millions of people in Latin America and Asia avoid a life of extreme hunger and poverty. Governments—developed and developing alike—assumed this success would spread and cut their investments in agriculture, allowing them to turn their attention elsewhere."[1]

They could not have been more wrong. At the end of 2006, the price of wheat, rice, corn, and soybeans—the four food staples that nearly three billion people who live on less than two dollars a day principally depend on not just as one element among several of their diets (as is the case in the rich world), but as the foodstuffs they almost exclusively depend on to avoid going hungry—began to rise vertiginously on world markets. By the time they peaked in early 2008, the price of corn had gone up by 31 percent, of rice by 74 percent, of soybeans by 87 percent, and of wheat by 130 percent, compared to what they had been in early 2007 at the beginning of what came to be known as the global food crisis.[2] In many parts of the globe, the brutal secondary effects on the prices of food available to ordinary people in the market were almost immediate. In Egypt, for example, the price of bread doubled in a matter of months. In Haiti, the price of rice increased by 50 percent, while in South Africa, the price of maize meal increased by 28 percent. By some estimates, taken in aggregate the food bill for the world's poor rose by 40 percent, while what soon came to be known as the global food crisis added 25 percent to the food import bills of many poor countries. And in thirty of the worst-affected countries across the globe, from Ethiopia to Uzbekistan, food riots broke out.

The significance of these riots was subsequently somewhat exaggerated. As every college student learns in freshman statistics, correlation is not causation. These were spasmodic episodes of civil unrest, not insurrections, let alone revolutions. And given the enduringly dire social and political conditions of the poor in those countries, to claim that the food crisis was the principal underlying cause of the conflicts seems too much like special pleading. But it is undeniable that the price spikes galvanized the poor in many countries in different regions of the world to a degree that, however briefly, seemed to be a genuine and at least potentially uncontrollable threat to the status quo.

And to the poorest of the global poor, the so-called bottom billion of the world's people who try to survive on less than a dollar a day, the threat was literally existential. For several billion more, any hope of "food security," the term of art in the development world meaning that one can depend on getting enough—as well as the right things—to eat throughout the year, seemed to be evaporating before their eyes. And it was not only those who had joined in the food riots, but also the vastly larger number of people who despaired in silence who worried for their survival and the prospect of any better future for their children. To put it another way, what the food crisis meant for the poor was the very real prospect of going hungry, not because there would not be enough food, but because they would no longer be able to afford to buy it. The anger that this crisis produced is one that has, across the centuries, proven to be the most dangerous form of anger of all: anger in the belly.

In the rich world, there were many who reasoned that because the worst effects of the crisis were occurring in parts of the world where there had been huge population increases, brute demography had been at the root of what had taken place. But this was a fundamental misunderstanding of what had occurred; however counterintuitive the thought may be, it was wrong. Instead, what had in fact taken place was not the "population bomb" finally exploding, to use the phrase coined by the neo-Malthusian American biologist and demographer Paul Ehrlich, leading inexorably to famine. For despite the fluctuating relationship between food consumption and food production, when the crisis began to unfold in 2007 there was (as there is as of this writing in 2015) more than enough food being produced to feed everyone alive. In the two decades preceding the 2007 crisis, global population increased by an average of 1.5 percent per year, and food production rose by 2 percent over the same time. If there was confusion about this among the general public, it was in considerable measure. The preponderance of media reports about hunger, at least those to which the general public in the rich world are exposed, focus on famines in the Horn of Africa or, in more sophisticated narratives, on hunger in rural India. This focus understandably gives the false impression that there are important food shortages, but in actuality the problem is food affordability, not availability.

But, important though it is, pointing out what the food crisis was not does little to explain how and why the global food system could have seized up to such an extent in 2007–2008. Nor does it shed much light on how even most agricultural experts and both governmental and nongovernmental development agencies throughout the world could have been taken by surprise in this way. In other words, if the effects of the global food crisis were obvious, its causes were much harder to get right. In part this was because, if anything, there were too many causes that could be credibly held out as having contributed to the disaster, and figuring out which had played major roles and which had played minor ones proved to be enormously difficult.

One key driver of the crisis beyond dispute was the rising price of oil which, beginning in late 2006, had a secondary effect on the price of the fertilizers needed for industrial agriculture. This type of farming has increasingly become the norm not just in the rich world but in much of the poor world as well, far more to the detriment of its masses of smallholder farmers. Another factor, seemingly episodic rather than systemic, was the severe weather in many parts of the world during 2006, ranging from drought in Australia, the world's second-largest producer of wheat, to Cyclone Nargis, which hit Myanmar hard in the spring of 2008 and devastated that country's rice production.[3] In the rich world, the practice of diverting grain from feed for livestock to the production of biofuels (40 percent of US corn now goes to ethanol production) certainly played a role, as did the virtual takeover of the world's commodities markets by speculators whose entry radically increased the volatility of these markets, causing wild price swings in the costs of food staples. In short, viewed as a discrete event, the 2007–2008 global food crisis had been, as the cliché goes, a perfect storm.

But while storms dissipate eventually, in the crisis's wake in 2008, even after the prices of agricultural staples had declined sharply, it soon became clear that far from having been an anomalous event, the price rises were a more extreme but still emblematic manifestation of what, to borrow the image of the money manager Bill Gross about the post-2007 crash of the financial markets, was likely, over the long term, to be a "new normal" of secular price increases of agricultural staples. This supplanted the "old normal" in the last quarter of the twentieth century, which had been a process beginning with the establishment of price stability and then of price decline. And while he was admittedly extrapolating from a very short period, the senior World Bank official Otoviano Canuto was reflecting a broad consensus when he observed that this "new norm of high prices seems to be consolidating [in the second decade of the twenty-first century]."[4]

Hunger and poverty are inseparable, and despite the many real successes in poverty reduction in many parts of the Global South, it is highly unlikely that these gains will be sustainable if rises in the price of staple foods significantly outstrip the rise in incomes of the poor as a result of sound development policies. That is why, at least assuming Canuto's now widely accepted conclusion is correct, it is not too much to say that the entire global food system is gravely ill, and that the central question is how to reform it, if, indeed, it is not too late to do so.

But while there is wide disagreement about what needs to be done, there is surprisingly wide agreement that most, if not all, of the assumptions that undergirded the system in the later part of the twentieth century had either been wrong to begin with or simply no longer applied in the first decade of the new century, above all the conviction that food prices were likely to continue to decrease. Simply put, the evidence for the new secular trend toward higher food prices has accumulated to the point that it now seems all but irrefutable.[5]

The trajectory is clear. After having fallen in 2008, food prices rose again, almost as sharply, in 2010 and 2011, then fell back and rose once more toward the end of 2012 and into 2013, at which point prices for corn on the world market were higher than they had been at the height of the 2007–2008 crisis. These subsequent rises in the cost of cereal grains and the realization among development specialists that the prices of food staples have not diminished all that much since 2007 have not received the same amount of attention in the global media. That does not make them any less ominous. In Mexico, for example, the price of tortillas, the most basic foodstuff in the diets of most poor people, was 69 percent higher in 2011 than it had been in 2006. In Indonesia, the average national price of rice reached a record in February of 2012. And it should be remembered that both Mexico and Indonesia are what the World Bank calls "middle income" countries. In much poorer nations like Guatemala, Haiti, Niger, Yemen, and Afghanistan, the effects of this "new normal" of high food prices have been more damaging still to the lives of the poor and the life chances of their children.

That is the bad news, and it is, indeed, very bad news. But even the most dyed-in-the-wool pessimist would have to concede that it is by no means the whole story. As the British development economist Charles Kenny has argued, there is no reason to believe that global misery is so intractable a problem that it cannot be relieved. Even if one doesn't agree with Kenny and like-mindedly optimistic colleagues that things are getting better and, barring environmental catastrophe, will continue to improve in ways that were all but unimaginable half a century ago, they are right to insist that there has been a considerable amount of good news as well, above all in the extent of the progress that has been made over the past three decades. "The biggest success in development," Kenny has written, "has not been making people richer but, rather, has been making the things that really matter—things like health and education—cheaper and more widely available."[6]

Overall, the percentage of the poor in the global population has decreased steadily, even if in some of these countries, notably India, the number of those who have not benefitted from these changes is far greater than those who have. There are now hundreds of millions of people in countries as varied in their political systems, the condition of their economies, and their approaches to chronic hunger as Brazil, China, Mexico, Vietnam, and India who are now eating more and usually, though not always, better (as the rapidly rising obesity rates in the developing world demonstrate) than previous generations ever did. Whether this has been the result of development aid or the economic growth and prosperity created in much of Asia and parts of Latin America over the past thirty years remains a subject of bitter dispute. The scope of this transformation, not simply the reality, is what cannot be denied—it is unparalleled in human history in terms of its effects on so many over such a relatively short period of time. By comparison, the general prosperity eventually created by the Industrial Revolution in Europe took far longer and affected far fewer people.

If one is being optimistic, it is possible to say that the 2007–2008 crisis taught us at least to ask the right questions about hunger. But whether countries—rich, developing, or poor—will be able to come up with the right answers is another matter altogether. The optimists—and given my own pessimism on these questions, it is important to be clear that they include many of the most brilliant people now working in government, philanthropy, the NGO world, and in science—are convinced that it is now possible, perhaps for the first time in human history, to reform the global food system and make sustained global agricultural development an enduring reality. Indeed, many of these men and women have become increasingly drawn to timelines that posit "ending hunger" by some date certain in the coming decades. This belief is anchored in the undeniable fact that the "international community" (an unfortunate intellectual "tic" of the aid and development world is its reliance on largely unexamined, pious clichés about global governance) is once again paying attention to agriculture. Investments are being made, and, perhaps most importantly, the emphasis is now on the smallholder farmers and their families instead of on industrial agriculture; it's on those who make up the overwhelming majority of the people who work the land in the poor world. As a former head of the US Agency for International Development (USAID), Rajiv Shah has argued, "the world is once again delivering a global commitment to strengthening food security."[7]

Are such hopes warranted? In some cases, such as whether the agricultural foundations on which this new prosperity in Asia and Latin America rests will endure or whether they will prove chimerical, the answer is unknowable, and it would be foolish to pretend otherwise. In contrast, it is clear that barring the global catastrophe that some of the more militant members of the green movement have been predicting and that were it to occur, would lead to such global immiseration that even to talk about markets would be to paint too rosy a scenario, the underlying causes of the secular rise in the prices of food staples are unlikely to change. Global population continues to rise, while powers such as China and Brazil have been finding it increasingly hard to maintain the growth rates on which their initial surge in prosperity rested. It seems improbable that such difficulties will decrease anytime in the foreseeable future. Meanwhile, extreme weather events, whether or not these are related to climate change, seem to be increasing rather than stabilizing, putting further pressure on the global food system. And there is little doubt about the role played by climate change in exacerbating the desertification of significant parts of the world.

That is the situation on the ground in much of the Global South. At the same time, the structure of the global commodities markets in the Global North continues to reward rather than discourage speculation on the future prices of food staples, thereby all but ensuring continued price volatility. And every year, despite the questions that are increasingly being posed about the wisdom of the practice, a sizeable percentage of the world's corn harvest continues to go to ethanol used in gasoline rather than to be made into foodstuffs or to be employed as feed for livestock. By now the inefficiency and, in global terms, even the danger to the world's food supply of this is all but undeniable. On average, it takes approximately ten pounds of feed corn to produce one pound of beef. The writer Michael Pollan summed up the situation well when he wrote that "there would be plenty of grain for everyone if we actually ate it as food and didn't use it to make meat."[8] At the same time, much of the world's corn continues to be diverted to the manufacture of ethanol-based fuels. And while this policy has come under increasing attack over the past decade, so far, at least, the ethanol lobbies in Europe and the Americas have been relatively successful in maintaining this extremely wasteful status quo.

Given these realities, it is hardly a surprise that worldwide food consumption has outstripped food production for six of the eleven years between 2001 and 2012. Critics of the current global food system, such as Pollan, have suggested that stresses put on the system not just by ethanol but by the increasing demands for meat in countries that have seen the greatest increases in their middle-class populations, notably China and India, are to blame. Again, as with suggestions that the 2007–2008 food crisis "caused" the riots, correlation is not causation, and many food experts point to data that imply that such suggestions remain far-fetched. For example, Timothy Wise, the policy director of Tufts University's Global Development and Environment Institute, has flatly denied that increased demand for meat in India and China has been "the main driver" of the food crisis,[9] even if over the longer term it is difficult to see how a vast increase in the number of people who eat meat daily would not tax global grain supply beyond its capacity to adapt, and that assumes the production increases the optimists are predicting in these staples prove to be sustainable.

It should come as no surprise that just as there has been no single cause for what has happened since 2007, there is no one solution for it either. And again, for now at least, the world is still producing enough cereal grains so that in terms of supply alone everyone on the planet *could* have enough to eat. But even assuming this, with droughts and other extreme weather events seemingly becoming more and more common, and with the diversion of corn to ethanol, on a year-to-year basis the margin of error is getting smaller and smaller. In 2002, most countries had approximately 107 days of food reserves. Today, the figure is 74 days. As Abdolreza Abbassian of the UN Food and Agriculture Organization (FAO) has put it, this leaves "no room for unexpected events."[10] And yet if the droughts and floods that have come to seem more and more the norm in many parts of the world persist, it is difficult to see how such extreme events will *not* take place on a fairly regular basis.

The increasing insecurity of supply that has accompanied the rise in the price of food staples is a global problem. But as with almost every other significant global challenge,[11] what has become a problem even for most people in the rich world is now a catastrophe in the making for the poorest among us, the three billion living on less than two dollars a day. Starkly put, if the price of food staples on the world market continues to rise, the ability of the poor to afford the food they need to feed themselves properly will become increasingly tenuous. And even if prices were to stabilize at the current high levels, the chances of reproducing past levels of success in bringing more people out of poverty will greatly diminish. For to expect people who have not gotten enough to eat as children to flourish as adults, no matter what economic system they live under, is the purest magical thinking about a global food system that already suffers from a steadily worsening crisis of access, one that shows no sign of abating. And the results are entirely predictable: they will guarantee that the divide between global haves and have-nots in terms of access to the most basic human needs—food and potable water, from which everything else derives—will grow ever wider, and that an unjust world will grow more unjust still.

Terrible as it is, though, deepening injustice is scarcely the worst thing we have to fear. If significant changes to the global food system are not made, a crisis of absolute global food supply could occur sometime between 2030 and 2050, when, according to the most conservative estimates, the world's population will have risen from seven billion in 2012 to nine or perhaps even ten billion. Cicero wrote somewhere that he did not understand why, when two soothsayers met, they both did not burst out laughing, and bearing his sensible admonition in mind, it is important to be cautious. In reality, the data are nowhere near as clear as they are generally presented, both by the optimists and by the pessimists. The Irish economic historian Cormac Ó Gráda, whose work on the history of famine has been enormously important in the field, has written that current "forecasts of future food output are unreliable and conflicting."[12] This is true even with regard to climate change, where there remains considerable disagreement among experts as to how effectively farmers will be able to respond to the changed conditions that already confront some of them and will soon confront many more—one of the few facts that, American climate denialists to the contrary notwithstanding, can be predicted with confidence.

If this crisis of absolute supply does indeed occur in the coming decades, whether this is the result of population growth alone or population growth interacting in malign synergy with the likely rising in both global temperatures and global sea levels resulting from anthropogenic climate change (of which population increase itself is an important driver), the effect on the poor will be incalculably more devastating in everything from public health to mass migration. To take only one obvious example, it has become a psychosocial and political commonplace that many people in the rich world increasingly feel engulfed by mass migration from the Global South. But one does not need to be a soothsayer to have a pretty good idea of what they will feel when confronted by the predictable movements of people from those parts of the world where drought becomes the norm and where sufficient quantities of food can no longer be produced.

The current migratory flows have been unprecedented and have steadily gathered momentum in the wake of the NATO overthrow of the Gaddafi regime in Libya, which had impeded the migrants' departures. Today it is common for armadas of literally thousands of migrants from sub-Saharan Africa and from Syria to land on the Italian island of Lampedusa or along the Sicilian coast at one time. This flow is unlikely to abate in any usable time frame. Well over two hundred thousand made the crossing in 2014 (the previous high had been seventy thousand in 2011, at the height of the Libyan Civil War), and the consensus view is that the number will continue to rise for the foreseeable future. At the very least, as one experienced official from the German refugee NGO, Günther Bauer, put it to a reporter from *Der Spiegel*, "The strain from Africa will remain constant."[13] But even this flood will seem like a trickle by comparison if people are fleeing toward Europe because they literally don't have enough to eat—something which in the overwhelming majority of so-called sender countries is not the case today—not simply because they wish to secure a better future for themselves and to support their extended families back home (remittances from immigrants now considerably outstrip all official development aid worldwide).

But even if one assumes that the development optimists' far more cheering predictions about imminent and ongoing radical reductions in absolute poverty rates in the Global South turn out to be correct, it in no way implies that there will be a concomitant reduction in inequality. And this is the dispositive point. For as Branko Milanovic, formerly the chief research economist at the World Bank, has demonstrated in a number of important papers as well as in his book, *The Haves and the Have-Nots: A Brief and Idiosyncratic History of Global Inequality*, inequality is one of the most important, if not *the* most important, drivers of migration, the other being the unprecedented familiarity—courtesy of globalization in general and the new communications technologies in particular—among people in the poor world about how people in the rich world live. As Milanovic put it in his book, "In an unequal world where income differences between countries are large, and information about these income differences is widespread, migration . . . is simply a rational response to the large differences in the standard of living."[14]

For the past several decades, the rich world has been experiencing something of a slow-motion nervous breakdown about mass immigration from the developing world. It is not difficult to predict with reasonable confidence what the reaction would be if this migration doubled or tripled, as it very well may do over the coming decades. And to focus on migration is in some ways to present a false picture, since the real catastrophe will take place in the Global South. According to "The Geography of Poverty, Disasters and Climate Change in 2030," an October 2013 paper for the United Kingdom's Overseas Development Institute, disasters linked to climate change, "especially those linked to drought, can be the most important cause of impoverishment, canceling progress on poverty reduction" for what the report identified as the "325 million people [who will be] living in the 49 most hazard-prone countries in 2030, the majority in south Asia and sub-Saharan Africa."[15] The report does not need to add that the rate of population increase in this group of nations was, at the time the report was written, among the highest in the world and was likely to remain so for the forseeable future.

Were this doomsday scenario to pan out, there would be nothing apocalyptic about the fear that Thomas Hobbes's vision of a breakdown of society both in the Global South and in the Global North would usher in the war of all against all. In such circumstances—what Marx once called "a general negation"—injustice would almost certainly come to seem like the least of the world's worries, and human rights a luxury that a world torn apart could no longer afford to take much notice of. For all that human rights activists tend to describe as inevitable what the Canadian writer and politician Michael Ignatieff has called a "revolution in moral concern"—which began with the creation of the United Nations system in the aftermath of the Second World War and finds much of its practical as well as normative expression in the global human rights movement—such high expectations about its "inevitability" in fact depend on, at a minimum, the continuation of the present global system in either a better or at least the same conditions that now define it. But it would be the sheerest wishful thinking to expect it to survive the kind of global economic and political crisis that the grimmer climate-change scenarios would engender. In that case Hobbes would be right, and as the American philosopher, Thomas Nagel, has written, "If Hobbes is right, then global justice is a chimera." If this is true, then to hope for a significant global reduction in poverty—not to speak of its elimination, as the World Bank, the UN Secretariat, USAID, the British government's Department for International Development (DFID), and countless NGOs and philanthropies now routinely argue is feasible—is more chimerical still.

To sketch out this dystopic prospect is emphatically not the same thing as arguing that it is inevitable. Many of the smartest and best-informed people in politics, science, and the aid and development world who are thinking about hunger today believe human beings now have the scientific knowledge to transform agriculture to such an extent that even if global warming turns out to be even more severe than the consensus view now anticipates it will be, they remain cautiously optimistic that not only can enough food be produced to feed a world of nine billion people but it will also be possible to secure much greater access to it for the bottom three billion while creating conditions for much improved livelihoods for the farmers, above all smallholders, who produce the food but for now are themselves barely getting by. These critics of this mainstream view are equally intelligent, passionate, and well-informed. They don't believe technology to be the answer. On the contrary, for them the key to resolving the crisis of the global food system is to view the access to food as a human right. Where the mainstream call is for food security, which is a fundamentally apolitical, technical concept, the critics call for food sovereignty and insist that no durable solution can be based on the current global food system, which they view as too dependent on profit and on global commodities markets that are beyond the control of anyone except a business and technocratic elite.

But while advocates of the mainstream view and their critics differ on what political and social changes are required and what technical innovations have to be deployed, the idea that, assuming people have enough will and money, human beings would *not* flourish in the coming world of the nine billion is almost never mentioned by specialists and activists as a serious possibility.[16] Instead, the debate is full of jargon-laden idealism that gives rise to papers with titles such as "Strategies for Adapting to Climate Change in Rural Sub-Saharan Africa," and hortatory declarations such as the statement by the former president of Ireland, Mary Robinson, that, "We must minimize loss and damage, [and] put steps in place to address it and seek ways to avoid it," as if it were simply a fact that everyone knows what to do. But while it is true that there is a wide consensus within the development world that a sufficient degree of "resilience," to use one of its reigning cliches, can be built into the global food system to nullify or at least dramatically mitigate the worst effects of climate change, since no one actually yet knows how bad these effects are going to be, such confidence has much less empirical basis than is generally assumed.

Many development workers and human rights activists counter that without such an optimistic perspective, whether about the future of the global food system or any of the other great causes of the time, they simply could not do their jobs half so well, by which they mean that unless the public believes the NGOs have the answers, people are unlikely to go on supporting them. For them, the question is almost always "What kind of world do we want?" rather than "What kind of world can we realistically expect to have?" In a sense, this represents a kind of globalization of what historically has been the kind of utopianism associated with the United States, where, at least in more self-confident times, it was commonplace to hear politicians use the phrase "Living the American Dream" as if it were not an oxymoron. As Tom Bradley, a former mayor of Los Angeles, once put it, "If we can dream it, we can make it happen."

But this unyielding hopefulness about finding a lasting solution to the crisis still coexists with a great deal of confusion about what the nature of the crisis actually consists of. Famine is routinely conflated with chronic malnutrition; absolute food supply is confused with access to food both in terms of availability and cost; and, on an ethical level, food as a human need is too often spoken of as if food were a commodity little different from any other, a view that has the effect of eliding the essential moral difference between needs and wants that most people may not be able to formulate in philosophical terms but understand perfectly well just the same. After all, no one in his or her right mind thinks human beings have the same right to a Rolex watch that they do to potable water. These may be cynical times, an era of ever-widening inequality, but they are not that cynical. What remains to be seen is whether or not they are as hopeful as the mainstream view would lead one to believe.

The history of development has been one in which the belief that the correct formula to rid the world of poverty had been found has alternated with despondency, as model after successive model failed to live up to the lofty hopes that were riding on it. If the development world were a human being, one would say it had lived a life marked by extraordinary mood swings.

Despite the challenges posed by the global food crisis and the current dysfunction of the global food system of which it is the emblem, by the population explosion, and by anthropogenic climate change, even by the standard of development's "highs," the present moment is one of exceptional optimism. What is at issue in the debate—and it is difficult to think of anything more important—is whether such hopes are actually warranted. The consensus in the development world is that the early twenty-first century really marks the "end time" for extreme poverty and hunger, and the radicalism of such claims can often seem like a secularized version of the Messianic Era of the Abrahamic faiths, in which swords would be beaten into ploughshares. The end of hunger was central to that vision. As Maimonides foresaw it in his Mishneh Torah, it would be a time "when there will be no hunger or war" and in which "the good will be plentiful, and all delicacies as available as dust."

A modern, secular version of this vision is Francis Fukuyama's argument in 1992 that the triumph of democratic capitalism over its communist rivals marked "the end point of mankind's ideological evolution and universalization of Western liberal democracy as the final form of human government."[17] The appeal of this view for those seeking to end extreme poverty and hunger is obvious: if everyone agrees on the broad outlines of what human society should look like and how it should be constituted, then there is no longer any need to debate first principles. And if that is the case, then all the remaining problems in the world are essentially technical rather than moral. Moral problems are perennial: in the deepest sense, they may change form, but they never go away. In contrast, if every problem, even one as historically central to the human condition as hunger, is in essence technical and thus amenable to a lasting solution, then of course there is absolutely no reason why humanity should resign itself to continue having to endure it.

But is this right? Can the seven billion people now living all be assured they will be properly nourished? And can this promise be extended to the nine or ten billion who will inhabit the earth in 2050? Or have we mistaken our wishes for realities, overestimated the promise of our science, and made a fundamental error in assuming there to be a global ideological and moral consensus? It is no exaggeration to say that the future of the world in the most basic and existential sense is riding on the answer.

· 1 ·

A Better World Finally within Reach?

In order to properly understand what the food crisis is, it is essential first to understand what it is not. Unfortunately, it often seems from their public statements as if officials charged with coping with the food crisis and developing plans for reforming global agriculture are as mystified as the general public. Instead of asking hard questions, these officials frequently seem content to fall back on pat answers and development boilerplate. A particularly egregious example of this occurred in April 2008, when Josette Sheeran, then executive director of the World Food Programme (WFP) and an official widely admired in the world of relief and development, described the global food crisis of the previous year as a "silent tsunami," and declared that it presented the WFP with "the greatest challenge in its 45-year history." Such over-the-top rhetoric, an amalgram of apocalyptic worst-case scenario building and shameless institutional self-aggrandizement, is not peculiar to responses to the global food crisis. To the contrary, it has been more often the rule

1

than the exception in the development world at least since the days of Fritjof Nansen, whose pioneering efforts on behalf of refugees in the early twentieth century served as an inspiration for the current humanitarian relief system. In this sense, Sheeran's statement was unremarkable, a standard-issue iteration not simply of the rhetorical but of the ideological furniture of relief and development work.

However they are communicated, whether in speeches by senior officials, in press conferences and briefing materials for the media, or on the organizations' websites, such appeals almost invariably start with a lurid, oversimplified account of a particular crisis and end with a fund-raising pitch that usually either states or at the very least implies that if donors will just fork over, the agency in question is ready, willing, and able to save the day.

In fairness, Sheeran was only fulfilling one of the principal institutional demands that went with her job. Her predecessors were certainly no better. Four years earlier one of them, James Morris, had called the Asian tsunami of December of 2004 "perhaps the worst natural disaster in history." And in the immediate aftermath of the 2010 earthquake that devastated Port-au-Prince, Elizabeth Byrs, the spokeswoman for the UN Office of Humanitarian Assistance (OCHA), one of the WFP's sister agencies, stated flatly that the UN had "never been confronted with such a disaster," which she characterized as being "like no other."

Morris's claim was absurd—nonsense on stilts, to use Bentham's inspired phrase. Only someone historically illiterate, or at least a person whose historical imagination did not reach much further back in time than 1961, when a UN General Assembly established his agency, could have seriously advanced such a claim, and it is of course entirely possible that Morris, who was a cultivated man, knew better but felt constrained (just as Sheeran may well have done) to adhere to the familiar script. But Byrs's assertions were not much better. Was the Haitian earthquake truly a greater challenge and a more profound human tragedy than the refugee emergency that followed the Rwandan genocide of 1994 or the outbreaks of famine in North Korean in the 1990s—in both cases, human disasters that involved the relief and development arms of the United Nations? Perhaps a moral philosopher could have adjudicated the hierarchy of these horrors, but surely it was above the moral pay grade of an international civil servant such as Byrs, or Morris, or Sheeran (or, for that matter, of a writer like me). But even in the context of the shameless hyperbole that has been the common coin of humanitarian agencies since the refounding of modern humanitarian action that can be dated to the work of the so-called French Doctors in Biafra between 1967 and 1969, and the specific special pleading of WFP agency, Sheeran's image of the global food crisis as a silent tsunami was particularly ill judged. It was not an assault of nature for which, at least in the case of earthquakes or tsunamis, it is possible to prepare but that human beings can do nothing to prevent. If anything, the food crisis is the diametrical opposite of a natural disaster such as a tsunami or an earthquake, and is instead the product of the current world system. In other words, it is the result of such things as the current relations of force between haves and have-nots, on how world markets work, on what technologies we use (and the moral and political assumptions behind those technologies)—when all is said and done, about what kind of world we want to live in, about the world order that now exists and the world order that might one day exist. There is nothing "natural" about it.

To posit matters in such starkly ideological terms is commonplace in the Global South. But it tends to disturb mainstream opinion in the Global North, where most economic and political power still resides, both on the center-right and on the center-left. There it has been widely assumed, and with increasingly hegemonic authority since the end of the Cold War, that throughout the world, enlightened people agree on how global society should be organized. It is a view championed first and foremost by the human rights movement, and it has percolated through global institutions, above all the UN system. It might have been thought that the rise of China would of itself serve to undermine such millenarian fantasies. For the moment, however, it has not. And yet it is the persistence of ideology that helps explain why, despite the "zero-sum game" quality of much of the debate that the global food crisis has engendered, intelligent people can disagree so comprehensively and passionately both about the causes of the price rises of 2007–2008 and about how, in its wake, the world's food system can be successfully reformed or even almost entirely remade so that even if hunger persists, the number of hungry people begins finally to diminish.

If we do not agree on how societies should be ordered, we are unlikely to agree about how poverty can be alleviated and hundreds of millions of poor people can enjoy at least a measure of what development experts call food security. Is capitalism the answer or the root of the problem? Can there be nutritional transformation without political transformation? Are the challenges to the global food system analogous to an engineering problem that one can expect to be largely solved by technical innovation, scientific innovation, and of course money, accompanied by some lashings of "good governance" and "transparency" (to use two "default" expressions favored by those in the mainstream for whom the concept of ideology is an intellectual atavism that stubbornly and incomprehensibly refuses to sign on to the humane global consensus that democratic capitalism is asserted to be)? Or is greater social justice what matters most, and with it the need to stop thinking of food as a commodity like any other and start thinking of it as a human right?

On the antiglobalization side of this "dialogue of the deaf," as the French often call such mutual incomprehension, the conviction is strong that the food crisis is first and foremost the inevitable product of what one briefing paper from Food First, the think tank based in Oakland, California, that has produced much of the best analysis of the current global agriculture and broader food system from a radical perspective, describes as a "dangerous and unjust global system."[1] Leave that system standing, this argument goes, and no matter how many reforms are put in place, the world will lurch from food crisis to food crisis, because, on this view, systematic injustice is the root cause of hunger, and the only steps that can ever make a lasting difference are those that lead to its removal—a transformation that, to be effective, could not be restricted to poor farmers and their families but would have to include all poor workers, rural and urban alike.

On the other side of the ideological divide, a consensus most powerfully articulated by the World Bank has developed around the view that the crisis had three central causes. The first was the insufficient global attention paid to agriculture during the three decades before the crisis. The second was the failure to increase the production of vegetable staples. And in diametrical opposition to the food rights campaigners' claim that the dire situation of smallholder agriculture has been the inevitable result of the deepening of a global regime of free trade, the mainstream view is that on the contrary, the real problem was the failure to open markets completely during the 1980s and 1990s. This is despite the fact that this was the era of the so-called Structural Adjustment Program (SAP), a free-market economic prescription for developing countries whose adoption was a prerequisite for further loans or guarantees. But, unlike at the WFP, neither officials of the World Bank nor their food activist adversaries have ever suggested that the crisis of global agriculture was anything other than man-made. Indeed, in a number of interviews, Robert Zoellick, who became the World Bank's president in 2007—after the brief and troubled tenure of Paul Wolfowitz, former US deputy secretary of defense in the George W. Bush administration—and served until the summer of 2012, was quite explicit. He flatly rejected the tsunami image outright, instead calling the global food crisis "a man-made catastrophe that must be fixed by people."

The point would seem to be self-evident. That is what makes it so difficult to fathom why someone as knowledgeable as Josette Sheeran, whose tenure at the WFP has been viewed favorably even by a surprising number of the institution's many critics on the left (this despite the fact that her political roots were in the American right, hardly a place where commitment to the UN system has ever been in ample supply), could think it appropriate to speak of a silent tsunami. And as if the natural disaster image was not bad enough, the image of a "silent" crisis was even more wildly off the mark. For if the global food crisis so quickly provoked, as it did, the extreme degree of alarm within an international policy elite that literally for decades was comfortable to the point of complacency in ignoring the predicament of agriculture in the poor world, it is precisely because the manifestations of the crisis have been so, well, noisy, which is to say, so potentially destabilizing to the status quo. Tsunamis or earthquakes provoke fear, but also a large measure of resignation, and appropriately so, since human beings have no means of preventing them, only of doing a better or worse job at rescue and at mitigating their long-term effects. It is only when the effectiveness of the emergency relief and subsequent development efforts is found wanting that the anger arises—again, appropriately so. In contrast, the anger that the global food crisis provoked among the poor of the Global South, who have been its principal victims, and activists north and south who support them, has had an entirely different quality to it.

It is probably the case that in the late twentieth and early twenty-first centuries, what remains of the global left has a weakness for grasping at straws, too often seeing the constituent elements of a new global revolutionary moment in almost every eruption by an urban *jacquerie*—from the Los Angeles riots of 1992 to the London riots of 2011—as well as in various episodes of student wrath—from the student protest in France in 2005, through the student riots in Santiago de Chile in 2011 and 2013, and on to the so-called Occupy movement that began on Wall Street in the fall of 2011 and soon spread to many parts of the world before slowly fizzling out. In reality, though, none of these events ever posed a serious challenge to the global system as it is currently organized. In contrast, historically, time and time again food riots actually have been the catalyst for revolutions.

It is a commonplace that a rise in the price of bread was at least as important a catalyst to the French Revolution as taxation or Enlightenment ideas. Less well known is the fact that the failed revolutions that broke out across much of Europe in 1848 followed hard on the heels of a series of lethal droughts that had provoked a significant number of food riots. And all but forgotten in twenty-first-century America were the widespread food protests by poor women in New York City almost one hundred years ago. These began in February 1917, lasted for almost two months, and quickly spread to Philadelphia and Boston. The parallels with the current global food crisis are startling. Just as in 2007–2008, the women were confronted not by food shortages but by food prices they simply could no longer afford. The protests centered on a successful mass boycott of the pushcart peddlers from whom the urban poor bought most of their staples, though at one point it also led to the storming, not of the Bastille this time, but of the Waldorf Astoria hotel.

Historically, it should come as no surprise that global food crises should have global political and social ramifications, perhaps most lastingly in the Islamic Middle East. For while it is important to avoid overstating the influence of the global food crisis on the genesis of the so-called Arab Spring, it is not unreasonable to assume that the further immiseration of the poor of the Maghreb that the events of 2007–2008 engendered played at least some role, even if they were secondary to other, largely more conventionally "political" and religious grievances and hopes. A comprehensive report by the US think tank the New England Complex Systems Institute would appear to demonstrate a correlation between sharp rises in food prices and social unrest. For example, it is true that the rioting that swept thirty countries in 2007–2008 virtually ceased once food prices had dropped to precrisis levels at the beginning of 2009. But they began to break out again in the Middle East at the end of 2010 and the beginning of 2011 as prices once more started to rise—in other words, at more or less the same time as street protests began in earnest first in Tunisia and then in Egypt.

It is impossible to prove this, of course, and, to paraphrase Au-gust Bebel on anti-Semitism, conspiracy theories are the political understandings of fools. Nevertheless, it hardly seems likely that the major rich-country governments and international and intergovern-mental institutions that had been so passive (to put it charitably) in their previous responses to the problem of global hunger should have reacted as swiftly as they did in 2007 and 2008 had the dangers to the current global system of inaction not been apparent. After all, while it is true that that the price spike directly or indirectly caused at least one hundred million more people to go hungry (though nei-ther of two familiar demographic responses—famine or a reduction in the birthrates of the affected populations—resulted), somewhere between eight hundred and nine hundred million people were *al-ready* hungry when prices were lower, and it was broadly assumed that prices either would remain stable or continue to trend lower as they had done during the previous thirty years. What made the hunger of a billion or so people a crisis when the hunger of eight hundred million had been the factual backdrop for business as usual? It is not as if the major international donors, the World Bank, or the IMF had been in the dark about the prevalence of hunger and malnutrition before the 2007 crisis. To the contrary, international NGOs with a particular interest and expertise in food—notably Ac-tion Against Hunger, Concern Worldwide, Save the Children, and Oxfam—and a few Western governments—above all the Republic of Ireland because of the importance of the famine of 1847 in its history and in its collective memory, that is to say its constructed and politicized imaginative political geography—had been sounding the alarm for years. But while some initiatives were taken, they had never before succeeded in garnering the support needed from those institu-tions and governments to have any lasting effect at the macro level.

Again, why this was the case is anything but clear. A hundred years from now, it will probably seem incomprehensible that it took a radical rise in the price of food in the first decade of the twenty-first century for those who wield power and influence, in what we so self-regardingly and stipulatively persevere in calling the "international community," to stop sweeping the broader crisis of global agriculture under the development carpet and finally start to think about it seriously after a more than a thirty-year hiatus. To say that it may be too late for the international food system to be reformed in such a way as to prevent it from lurching from crisis to crisis would be to give in to an unwarranted despair. Even if one is skeptical about the extent to which the governments of the major aid donors in the Global North and the World Bank and the IMF will follow through on the new commitments they have made, there are too many smart, committed, and influential people working diligently on rethinking global agriculture to condemn the enterprise to failure as of this writing. But by the same token, it would be foolish indeed to assume, just because these people have dedicated themselves to finding solutions, that these solutions are there for the finding. It is at least possible that like the rising tide of global migration from the poor to the rich world, the crisis of the world's food system is unlikely ever to be "solved," but, rather, the best that can be hoped for is that it will be managed intelligently. Given the many grave mistakes that have been made in the past, errors that are likely to haunt policy makers and activists alike for a long time to come, this would already represent considerable progress.

The political cliché that "a crisis properly made use of is an opportunity" would seem to describe establishment responses since 2007. These include a wide range of initiatives ranging from new seed technologies, through women's rights (the majority of smallholder farmers are women, just as the majority of the poor are women: in that sense, women's development *is* development), to a renewed emphasis on proper nutrition for pregnant women and children from gestation through the first one thousand days of life. And it is simply an empirically verifiable historical fact that hope can be a powerful catalyst for reform and for social transformation. But what is less often pointed out, in an age where hope and optimism are often presented as the only morally licit stance for any person of conscience and goodwill to take, is that hope can also be a denial of reality and "solutionism" a form of moral and ideological vanity. One does not have to go as far as Nietzsche and insist that "hope in reality is the worst of all evils, because it prolongs the torments of man." But one reality that is not in question is the extent of the damage done to global agriculture, above all to smallholder farmers in the Global South, in the three decades before the 2007–2008 crisis. As the Filipino sociologist and food rights activist Walden Bello has put it—and it is a sentiment that many people who could not be further from sharing his political views about what measures need to be taken and what sort of society brought into being to avert disaster would endorse—whether this damage "can be undone in time to avert more catastrophic consequences than [the world] is now experiencing remains to be seen." Of course, this should be obvious. If it is not, again it is because hope has become the default position of our age, and realism (never mind pessimism!) is now widely considered to be a moral solecism and almost a betrayal of what it should mean to be a compassionate human being.

But whether one looks at the ongoing crisis of the global food system from an optimistic perspective or a pessimistic one, food has increasingly become a Rorschach blot for humanity's highest hopes and greatest fears. There is nothing surprising about this. Napoleon famously said that an army marches on its stomach, but in fact it is all of human civilization that does so. More than half a century of plenty in the rich world—a time when expenditures on food as a share of a family's budget just kept diminishing and diminishing—and, over the past twenty years, the adoption of the opulent (and not particularly healthy) diet of the rich world by middle-income countries from China to South Africa allowed at least the privileged among us to lose sight of this. It could hardly be otherwise, since rising incomes invariably increase the demand not just for food and access to an improved diet but also for more expensive food, meat above all. The change in European and North American diets from the 1930s to the current day is one illustration of this. Another is the rapidly growing Chinese middle class, which passed in two generations from fearing famine to coping with obesity and obesity-related ailments. And unless or until the prediction in Matthew 20:16 that "the last will be first, and the first will be last" actually comes to pass, it is the interests of these privileged groups that will determine the global agenda.

This is not to say that this agenda either was or is immovable. The world is full of cruelty, but there is a surprising amount of altruism around as well, whose power it would be a great mistake to underestimate. One may legitimately question the wisdom of their strategies, but whatever else can be said about the leaders of many countries in the Global North that give development aid, mainline development NGOs like Oxfam or World Vision, philanthropies like the Bill and Melinda Gates Foundation, and, somewhat surprisingly given its past history, the World Bank, their commitment to reducing poverty is genuine and deep. To lay my own cards on the table, the shift in the thinking at the World Bank that began when James Wolfensohn assumed the presidency of the institution in 1995, and which emphasized global poverty reduction or, to use the current term of art, "pro-poor growth" (rather than, as it had done previously, economic growth at virtually any cost, including the exacerbation of poverty) still seems to me to have been nowhere near sufficient. And every so often, one will be reminded that the "new World Bank," with its shiny new slogan, "Working for a World Free of Poverty," hasn't moved quite as far as it claims to have done. For example, the maverick development economist William Easterly discovered in the course of writing his book *The Tyranny of Experts: Economists, Dictators, and the Forgotten Rights of the Poor* that officials of the bank are forbidden to use the word *democracy* because, by its charter, the bank can't engage with politics (hence the weak replacement, "good governance"). But I see absolutely no basis for doubting Wolfensohn's commitment or his sincerity, or that of his successors.

Similarly, for reasons that I will go on to lay out in some detail in this book, I have been and remain extremely critical of the Gates Foundation, both in terms of what I view as its excessive emphasis in its grant-making and lobbying and public relations activities on technology-based solutions to the global food crisis and the foundation's increasing ability to dominate the debate and shape the policies of the UN system and major donor governments on agriculture. But whatever one's differences with him, not only could Bill Gates have spent his money on other things than HIV/AIDS, education, and smallholder agriculture, but one only has to listen to him to understand his moral seriousness. And this is equally true of Melinda Gates, whose role in moving the foundation to concern itself with certain issues has been at least the equal of her husband's.

Would it be a better world if the fate of hundreds of millions of smallholder farmers, especially in sub-Saharan Africa, did not depend so heavily on what are essentially decisions made unilaterally, and certainly with no democratic accountability whatsoever, by the richest couple in the world, whose foundation, as Bill Gates wrote unashamedly in his 2013 annual letter, "picks its own goals"? In my view, it would be a far better world. But given the reality of how decisions are made and power is exercised in the world as it actually exists in the early twenty-first century, would these smallholder farmers or, indeed, the rest of us be better off without the Gates Foundation? In my view, even though I do not subscribe to the idea that capitalism (and most especially either its American or East Asian variants) is the best form of social organization that we can aspire to, the answer is still, we would not. To appropriate Donald Rumsfeld's admittedly self-exculpating but nonetheless unforgettable remark about the preparations or lack of them that the Pentagon made on the eve of the Second Gulf War, you fight hunger in the context of the economic system you have, not the one you wish you had.

In any case, the Gateses' altruism, if that is indeed the right name for it, is anchored in the conviction that the world is witnessing what economists Abhijit Banerjee and Esther Duflo, using language far more modest than Gates's, have called the "quiet revolution" of sustainable progress. Gates has said that with regard to most global problems, "time is on our side."[2] But it is far from clear that he is right. For even if a consensus could be reached over what changes needed to be made, they may prove to be so radical—a drastic restriction in the amount of meat that will be available for human beings to consume being an obvious example—that it will be politically and culturally impossible to achieve them. If that turns out to be the case, then, indeed, it is entirely possible that the Hobbesian dystopia of the war of all against all will prevail rather than the Kantian order of perpetual peace in a global commonwealth—the philosophical bedrock on which the UN system, the human rights movement, and the project of the Gates Foundation ultimately rest. But for all that is getting worse in the world—above all, climate change, which, if the pessimists are right, may render discussion of anything else moot[3]—humanity has scored some major victories as well. Probably the greatest of these have been the steady decline in interstate war and the taming of famine, without an understanding of which the nature, scope, and significance of the contemporary crisis of the global food system is extremely difficult to get right. In the main, my own views are pessimistic. But I not only accept, I insist that it is entirely possible that twenty years from now, it is the optimists who will have proven to be right. Caveat lector.

But while I believe that these dualities of optimism and pessimism need to be kept in mind, I also want to make it clear to the reader that I would not have written this book had I only aspired to play Cassandra, which is itself not the least culpable species of vainglory. Between 1992 and 2004, I worked as a kind of war correspondent, first in the Balkans, then in Rwanda and Congo, and finally in Israel-Palestine, Afghanistan, and Iraq. My "beat" was not these wars themselves, not the horrors of the front line, nor the political breakdown that had set the torch to the pyre, nor the politics that eventually brought peace or, if not peace, at least an open-ended silencing of the guns.

Instead, I mostly followed what we have all come, somewhat misleadingly, to call the "humanitarian" dimension of these conflicts. I spent my time in refugee camps, with the internally displaced, and with the UN agencies (above all, the Office of the UN High Commissioner for Refugees [UNHCR]) and relief NGOs (above all the International Rescue Committee and Médecins Sans Frontières). At the time—particularly in the 1990s, before 9/11 put an end to the era in which the United States, France, and Britain could imagine that the principal role their militaries would play would be as global policemen, intervening, though only when they chose (Rwanda. Rwanda!), to prevent mass atrocities—these conflicts got far more attention in the media and, arguably, at times at least, in the UN system as well than all the ongoing efforts, whether they were effective or not, to alleviate the grinding poverty of so many hundreds of millions of people in countries and regions that were *not* at war. "If it bleeds, it leads," and all that.

I do not presume to judge whether this was right or wrong. What I am certain of, though, is that despite the overthrow of the Gaddafi regime in Libya, uncertainty about the outcome in Sudan, the French intervention in Mali, ethnic cleansing and massacre in the Central African Republic, and the horrors of the Syrian Civil War, which grind on unstaunched as I write, the age of humanitarian war is largely over. The question is whether the end of poverty looms as well. When I first heard it suggested that the answer is "yes," by a wide range of influential public figures ranging from pop stars such as Bob Geldof and Bono, by economists such as Jeffrey Sachs, and by a cohort of journalists and writers lauding the transformative power of what they called "philanthocapitalism," I could not believe that they were serious. For me, the biblical insight that the poor would always be with us seemed a far more reliable true north. But I was quite wrong. As I would learn, and as I will go on to narrate in this book, Jeffrey Sachs's conviction that it was perfectly feasible, as long as rich countries provided the money needed—money Sachs insists is trivial by the standards of the US military budget or even the bonus culture of Wall Street and the City—to end extreme poverty by 2025 had become the received wisdom of the entire development world.

Not everyone agrees. Some development skeptics, such as William Easterly and Dambisa Moyo, whose work is routinely dismissed as too "anti-aid" by the global food and development establishment (Gates has attacked Moyo with an especially acrid vehemence), have argued that it is capitalism, and not official development aid or philanthropy, that will bring people out of poverty. At the same time, there are many people and organizations on the antiglobalization left who are firmly convinced that any major progress in poverty reduction, let alone the end of poverty itself, will be impossible to sustain as long as the current capitalist order prevails. Since the Gates Foundation is the product and in many ways the apotheosis of this order, they are simply skeptical of the idea that such institutions, and the governments with which they collaborate more and more closely, can be the source of the major changes that are needed. It is one thing for capitalists to be philanthropists, they say, but quite another to expect the Gateses and Buffetts of the world to commit class suicide.

When the global food crisis erupted in 2007, revealing the general crisis of the world's food system of which it was only a symptom, I imagined that those who were so confidently predicting that extreme poverty would soon be an artifact of the past would at least modify their views and ratchet down their expectations. But rather than ratchet down, they have doubled down. The UN and World Bank officials, the senior staff of the major development NGOs, and figures such as Bill and Melinda Gates and Bill Clinton continued to insist not only that progress has been made, which at least in some regions of the world is unquestionably true, but that this progress is for all intents and purposes unstoppable. This view is exemplified by Charles

Kenny's *Getting Better*, the full title of which includes: *Why Global Development Is Succeeding—And How We Can Improve the World Even More*, a book that has been lavishly praised by Bill Gates. As far as Kenny was concerned, there was no doubt that the world was, as he put it, "winning the war on human suffering," and his view very much reflects the mainstream consensus. Writing to me in response to a question I posed to him on Twitter two years after his book was published, Kenny remarked that if anything, he felt he had not been optimistic enough, even though, to his great credit he conceded that there was some element of faith in his belief that the threat of global warming would be seriously addressed.

Assuming for the sake of argument that Kenny is correct about the present trends, even "impatient optimists" like himself and Bill Gates (the expression is also the name of the Gates Foundation's website) presumably would concede that the victory will be a Pyrrhic one unless the global food system—which, again, even the global food establishment acknowledges is largely broken—can be reconstructed in such a way that will provide food security to the almost one billion poor people in the world who have no such guarantee today. Gates knows this, of course, which is why he has committed so much of his foundation's resources to agriculture. An optimist he may be, but Gates is a sensible "poverty optimist" who understands as well or better than anyone that extreme poverty cannot be ended while hunger endures. And he may well be right. But what if the future doesn't cooperate?

My purpose in this book is precisely to try to understand why that might be the case, and if indeed this optimistic framing of the future by the mainstream of the development world is at least partly mistaken, what alternatives exist to their vision of what can and needs to be done? Is the program of militant peasant groups such as Via Campesina and, more broadly, of the antiglobalization movement, with its vision of supplanting the reigning capitalist system both in terms of production and consumption, a viable alternative? Or does the rights-based approach championed by Olivier de

Schutter—the Belgian lawyer who is the UN's special rapporteur for food and whose most sophisticated and developed expression is to be found in the Right to Food movement in India, which insists on the universal legal obligation of governments to provide sufficient nourishing food for all—have the greatest potential for transforming what critics of the food establishment, and even at least some people within it, view as an increasingly dysfunctional global food system?

These two visions of what that system can and should be could scarcely stand further apart. To acknowledge this is not wholly to rule out the possibility of finding common ground. Indeed, unlike his predecessor, the Swiss politician and writer, Jean Ziegler, Olivier de Schutter made many attempts during his tenure as special rapporteur to facilitate meetings between the two sides to precisely this end. At the same time, though during his tenure as special rapporteur de Schutter did not always make the point explicitly, his vision of the "transformative potential of the right to food" was a call for the radical transformation not just of the global food system but of the global order in its totality. "The normative content of the right to food," he wrote, "can be summarized by reference to the requirements of availability, accessibility, adequacy, and sustainability, all of which must be built into legal entitlements and secured through accountability mechanisms."[4] The difficulty with this, as de Schutter doubtless knew, was that norms are not realities, although the international human rights community often seems to prefer to act as if it believed otherwise. "All democratic revolutions begin with human rights," de Schutter wrote.[5] Even if he was correct, this begged a question that while doubtless not popular at the UN Human Rights Council that had appointed him, was in reality the salient one: Was there any basis for thinking that the early twenty-first century was a revolutionary epoch, democratic or otherwise?

Supporters of current efforts at reform of the type that the Gates Foundation has played so central a role in promoting do not have this difficulty. To the contrary, for all its tragedies (which they of course acknowledge and lament) the past two centuries have been an era of unprecedented progress in science, in technology, and, as Jeffrey Sachs has put it, "in fulfilling human needs."[6] That is why the mainstream view is that while reform is very much needed, in some areas even urgent, it makes no sense to repudiate a system that for two centuries has seen the continued upward trajectory of global living standards and the reduction of the proportion of poor people in the global population. And according to Sachs, Gates, and many other extremely intelligent, thoughtful defenders of reform but not revolution, the sunny uplands of a world free of extreme poverty are firmly in sight—no more than thirty years off, according to the World Bank's president, Jim Yong Kim—and, if we all put our shoulders to wheel, could be within our grasp even sooner.

Where does this leave us? The antiglobalization movement slogan, which, it is worth noting, is a great deal more modest than Jeffrey Sachs's "End of Poverty," is "Another World Is Possible." To which the most sensible if not the most inspiring reply is, "Yes, it is indeed possible. What it is not is likely." But surely the activists are right about one thing: in the future, food and water shortages, whether they prove to be absolute or relative, and the political and social crises that will ensue from them are more likely than not to pull the world down into the bloody muck of a war of all against all unless some historic compromise, to use the term Italians once used for the bargain struck in the 1970s between their country's Communist and Christian Democratic parties, can be found between the rich and poor worlds. At the time of this writing, it is obviously impossible to know in which direction things will go. It is very early innings yet, and I will certainly no longer be alive when the final outcome does become clear. If I had to bet, I would opt for the war of all against all, but it is only a bet. And it is one on the subject of which I very much hope Jeffrey Sachs, Bill and Melinda Gates, Hillary Clinton, Bono, and all those whose views are close to theirs are right and I am nonsensically wrong.

· 2 ·

The Wages of Optimism

Six centuries before the beginning of the Common Era, the prophet Ezekiel declared hunger to be the shame of nations. By hunger, he first and foremost meant famine, the hunger that kills. And for most of the 2,600 years since Ezekiel's time, in virtually every part of the world, his words have continued to ring as true as when he wrote them. Famine has been a constant in human history, its appearance as regular and dependable as the arrival of each of the four seasons and as inexorable as the life cycle. Historically, it has known no geographical boundaries, even if at different periods, different countries and regions of the world have been particularly associated with it.

For example, today we think of Africa as the center of famine in the world, although the reality is that well through the middle of the last century, its locus was actually in Asia. Thus, writing in 1946, the great Brazilian diplomat-scholar, Josué de Castro, who was the gray eminence behind the founding of the UN Food and Agriculture

19

Organization (FAO) in 1943 and whose pathbreaking book, *The Geography of Hunger*, though now somewhat dated, inspired several generations of agronomists, could state matter-of-factly that "Asia, more than any other continent, is the land of man, and the land of hunger. Nowhere else has man carved the evidences of his presence so deeply into the earth, and nowhere else has hunger left such profound marks on the structure of human society."[1]

In both India and China, particular famines themselves and the failure or success of the state in mitigating their effects have exerted a huge influence politically and socially. Given the regularity of famines—only war has been a more dependable event in human history, the norm rather than the exception—this is entirely logical. For example, in India, though the evidence for the famines that occurred in preclassical and classical times is often derived from myths, somewhere on the order of ninety major famines are thought to have occurred during these two and a half millennia. In China, the precise number of famines is equally difficult to state with certainty, but the figure is not likely to have been significantly lower than that of India. In her definitive study, *Fighting Famine in North China*, the historian Lillian Li cites with approval a book called *China: Land of Famine* that was published in 1926 by American traveler Walter H. Mallory, because, as she puts it, "no other civilization has had such a continuous tradition of thinking about famine."[2]

The frequency of famines in the Americas, Europe, and the Near East has been broadly similar. Nor is there much doubt about what caused the overwhelming majority of them. As the great Irish economic historian and specialist in famine, Cormac Ó Gráda, has described it, until relatively recently, the late seventeenth century at the earliest, most famines were mainly linked either to "extraordinary natural events" or to "ecological shocks." To be sure, for most of human history, there was ample justification for thinking that a society might successfully organize itself to palliate the effects of a given famine. There are also some historical examples of polities doing this over an extended period of time, notably the three emperors of the Qing dynasty between 1662 and 1796. Ó Gráda has rightly emphasized many more examples of poor people seeing famine as an event the rich and powerful had the means to mitigate had they only chosen to do so.[3] But if palliation was considered an obligation on which the legitimacy of states could depend, until the twentieth century no one seriously thought that famine would ever become a thing of the past. One could fantasize about such a utopia—indeed, like immortality, it was impossible not to yearn for it—but it was understood to be out of reach. And rightly so, for as a practical matter, there was no basis other than grief leavened by hope to believe that there would ever be an end to famine as a perennial event in the lives of human beings this side of the End of Days.

And yet, during the second half of the twentieth century, precisely what theretofore had been an unattainable utopia increasingly seemed to be like an entirely attainable, eminently practical goal. Throughout the world, famines began to decline both in deadliness and in frequency. Fifty years is most of a human life, but in historical terms it is a negligible period of time, and in retrospect, the speed of this transformation was breathtaking. It was Lenin, of all people, who said that, "There are decades when nothing happens; and there are weeks when decades happen." In the case of global hunger and nutrition, it is fair to say that there were not just centuries but millennia when little changed and years and decades when the possibilities for positive change came to seem boundless. The first half of the twentieth century was an era when little or nothing changed. Famines came and went as they always had, wreaking the havoc they had always wrought. There were some changes in the ability, at least intermittently when other reasons of state did not trump humanitarian concern, of governments to alleviate the effects of famine, notably the so-called famine codes developed by the British colonial administration during the 1880s, which with reason have been called the first modern reaction to famine. But otherwise a fatalistic attitude regarding the perennity of famine remained the norm.

The beginning of the twentieth century, a period in which a great many multinational organizations were formed (the most notable of which was the precursor to the League of Nations, the International Parliamentary Union), did see the creation of the first clearing house for the collection of global agricultural statistics. The International Institute for Agriculture (IIA) was the brainchild of David Lubin, a Polish-Jewish immigrant to the United States who settled in Sacramento, California, and started a dry goods business before eventually buying a fruit ranch. There was something of Henri Dunant, founder of the Red Cross movement, in Lubin's single-minded determination to create an institution with a remit that was largely unprecedented. Lubin and his son Simon returned to Europe in 1896 and campaigned fiercely for the project. In 1904, they succeeded in gaining the attention of King Victor Emmanuel of Italy. The king gave his support to the project, donating a building in Rome to serve as its headquarters[4] and underwriting it financially after its establishment in 1908. The IIA was a genuinely international body, and by 1919 it included representatives from fifty-three countries. However, when the League of Nations was founded in the immediate aftermath of the First World War, neither the IIA itself nor some other body concerned with agriculture in general was attached to the League, though a great deal of research on nutrition was done under the League's auspices.

The contrast between this indifference of the League and the commitment of the United Nations during the Second World War, when the League's successor was still in embryonic form, could not be more complete. Almost a year before the United States entered the war, in the State of the Union address of January 1941 that would come to be known as the Four Freedoms speech, President Franklin Delano Roosevelt had proposed freedom from want, very much including hunger, as being, along with freedom of speech, freedom of worship, and freedom from fear (that is to say, from tyranny), one of the fundamental freedoms people everywhere in the world should be able to enjoy. Five months later, Roosevelt convened the first National Nutrition Conference for Defense. The principal motivation for this was in fact that the United States would soon enter the war, and American military planners had been shocked by the high levels of malnutrition they discovered to be common among prospective recruits. But there were more idealistic motivations as well, incarnated in one of the conference's final resolutions. There it was set out that one goal of democracies should be to conquer hunger, which, presciently, the delegates understood to mean "not only the obvious hunger that man has always known, but the hidden hunger revealed by modern knowledge of nutrition."

Agriculture was also emphasized from the first as the nascent UN system took shape. Indeed, the first formal UN conference to be held on any subject was in the meeting on food and agriculture that President Roosevelt convened in Hot Springs, Virginia, in late May 1943, a full two years before the UN's actual founding. The Hot Springs conference drew delegates from forty-five countries, including the Soviet Union, and its importance in thinking about how to remake the postwar world was well understood at the time. In its coverage of the meeting, *Life* magazine reflected what was rapidly becoming the consensus view about the centrality of food questions. Its story stated as if it were simply a statement of obvious fact that not only had food become "the United Nations' most potent political weapon not only in winning the war but also in preserving the peace," but went on to say that the conference—two years before Germany surrendered—"was the first great test of whether or not the United Nations could operate as effectively over a peace table as over a battle terrain."[5] If the National Nutrition Conference for Defense gave rise to the bureaucratic structures, above all the Food and Drug Administration (FDA) and, perhaps, more important to the computational mind-set of calories and supplements that has remained essential to the orthodox understanding of nutrition ever since, the

Hot Springs conference was the direct precursor of the UN's Food and Agriculture Organization, which has been at the heart of the global food system ever since.

It is important not to exaggerate the farsightedness of the Hot Springs conferees. At the moment the conference was taking place, the famine in West Bengal was becoming more and more catastrophic, even though it would reach its peak only in early November of that year. And there was no analysis of famine as a fundamentally socioeconomic and political event rather than as mainly the result of weather. Yet even though for most of human history climate and subsequent crop failure had been essential drivers of famine, since the Great Irish Famine of 1847 the role of politics had become central. During the last quarter of the nineteenth century, somewhere between thirty-two and sixty-one million people are thought to have died as the result of famines in China, India, and Brazil. The American writer Mike Davis wrote a highly regarded book about these "imperialist famines" that he quite simply called *Late Victorian Holocausts*. In Davis's view the combination of droughts associated with the so-called El Niño Southern Oscillation weather pattern in Asia and the tropics and the new economic order being imposed on the colonial world led to human disasters that Davis believes to have been as severe as the so-called Black Death, the epidemic of bubonic plague that swept across Europe in the middle of the fourteenth century. And Davis is convinced this catastrophe could have been avoided had the colonizers not destroyed the ability of peasant societies to cope. Tremendous care must be taken here. As the great Indian economist and political philosopher Amartya Sen, whose work on famine quite literally transformed the way it is understood and who has highly praised Davis's work, has cautioned, there have been other terrible famines besides those that can be laid at the doorstep of the European colonial powers. What is beyond debate, though, is that by the beginning of the twentieth century famines were first and foremost the product of politics, whether the politics in question were those of imperialism or socialism, war or revolution.

West Bengal in 1943 was the last of the imperial famines—"man-made," as Sen has put it—in India. That it was the result of wartime social conditions and economic changes is now beyond dispute. It is noteworthy that there has not been a famine in India since independence in 1947.[6] But at the time, in Sen's words, what had served as the "detonator" of the disaster was a "rise in aggregate demand [that] was very large in the war economy of Bengal, leading to a sharp rise in the price of rice and the starvation of those left behind in the boom economy."[7] It was not that the food supply had fallen all that much in absolute terms, even if there were shortages due not only to price increases and increases in demand but also to the determination of Raj officials to continue to send foodstuffs out of India in aid of Britain's war effort. The imperial authorities were correct in understanding that there was still sufficient food in West Bengal, and that actually made a terrible situation far more terrible. Sen has characterized this as "the imperial confusion [which had tied] the causation of famines entirely to supply conditions (and in particular to the decline of food availability), ignoring the influence of demand and of the distribution of purchasing power, which led to the death of millions."[8]

In Cormac Ó Gráda's view, the issue of food availability was a key one, as was the underlying cause that wartime Britain had other priorities. The famines in Europe during that same wartime period were man-made. Greek history books describe the "Great Famine" of 1941–1942, during which some three hundred thousand people out of a total population at the time of a little under 7.5 million perished. This famine was a result of wholesale plunder by the German occupiers but also caused by a British naval blockade of Athens. It was so severe that even in the draconian moral climate of a total war, it so shocked British public opinion that campaigners led by the group of Oxford professors who in response had founded Oxford Famine Relief (the organization that would become the global relief and development NGO now known as Oxfam) were able to persuade Churchill to relent and order the partial lifting of the blockade. The last European famine during the Second World War was the so-called Hunger Winter of 1944–1945 that occurred in those parts of the Netherlands still under Nazi occupation and was the product of an exceptionally harsh winter and German punitive measures against the civilian population (though some scholars argue that excess mortality was even higher in the nonfamine parts of the Netherlands because they were a combat zone). One inescapable lesson to draw from this is that while there have been famines in times of peace, there have been few major wars without famine. It is estimated that somewhere between fifty and seventy-two million people died during World War II. But the roughly twenty million of those deaths that were in fact due to hunger, more than half of these in the Soviet Union, equal the roughly twenty million estimated to have died in actual combat.

To the extent that one can legitimately view the last part of the nineteenth century as the age of imperialist famines, it is equally appropriate to view much of the twentieth century as the age of socialist ones. The worst of these by far and, in absolute numbers (though not proportionally; the Irish famine of 1847 claims that dreadful honor), probably the most lethal single event in human history was the Chinese famine of 1958–1962. Though nature played a role, as it almost always does even in "man-made" famines, the catastrophe was caused mainly by Mao Zedong's disastrous farm and food policies which abolished private cultivation and collectivized Chinese agriculture and his equally disastrous strategy for national development, whose emphasis on industrialization had led to millions of farmers being sent to the cities.

Mao's political famine was hardly unique. To the contrary, its precursors were those that had occurred in the Soviet Union: the first under Lenin in 1921, which reached throughout most of the Western USSR, and the second under Stalin in Ukraine in 1932 and 1933, the event Ukrainians know as the "Holodomor." The last of these Soviet famines occurred in 1946 and lasted into 1948, taking place in Moldova, though it touched the Ukraine and Belarus as well. It seems to have been precipitated by a severe drought in grain-growing regions whose effects were made vastly more severe by the havoc wrought by the war.

Since the 1960s, though, famine has steadily retreated, all but disappearing from the Asian heartland (with the exception of North Korea, though even there it is anything but clear how reliable media reports about very high mortality rates actually are), and subsequently from every continent except Africa, which today is famine's last redoubt. And even in sub-Saharan Africa, despite recurring tragedies in the Horn, above all in Somalia and Ethiopia, and in the Sahelian countries—Mali, Chad, the Central African Republic, and above all Niger—famine has also diminished very substantially. At long last this good news has started to reach the general public. Certainly we have come a long way from 2000, when the *Economist* ran a cover that read "The hopeless continent," set above an image of a young fighter holding a rocket-propelled grenade launcher inset into a map of Africa. Indeed, in December 2011, the weekly would print an apology in an issue whose title was, "Africa Rising." Still, for all the optimism about Africa that one now regularly hears from Western politicians such as Hillary Clinton, who gave it particular emphasis during her tenure as Barack Obama's secretary of state, and that one encounters in the business press, where the continent is viewed as the next emerging market (a view shared, though in a far more nuanced way, in parts of the development world), the fact that famines still regularly occur there has had an outsized influence on forming the perspective of the general public in the Global North—a pessimism that is particularly curious given the fact that as a number of Pew polls have shown, Africans tend to be more optimistic about their future than inhabitants of every other continent.

One does not have to subscribe unwaveringly to some form of Christian or secular progress narratives to find in this vanquishing of famine in so much of the world an indisputable instance of real progress. In some parts of the world, Asia in particular, it has been as radically transformative as the abolition of slavery in most (though not all) of the world and the emancipation of women, at least in Europe, much of northeast Asia, much of Latin America, and among the upper classes on the Indian subcontinent. Cormac Ó Gráda makes the essential point when he writes that "for economic historians, today's world is remarkable for its near absence of catastrophic famine," and that those famines that have occurred "have been small and short-lived by historical standards."[9]

What was unimaginable in the middle of the twentieth century is increasingly taken for granted in the early twenty-first, and those who celebrate the end of famine are right to do so. But is the corollary to this equally undeniable? Or, to put it another way, is the progress toward ending global hunger just as unstoppable? Eleanor Roosevelt once described wishful thinking as one of America's "besetting sins." Where hunger is concerned, has it become the world's besetting sin as well? In its fidelity to that quintessentially American variant of millenarianism in which it is assumed that we can remake the world as we want it to be, we come face to face with at least one sense in which the worldview of globalized capitalist modernity seems to have become more rather than less of an American construct writ large, despite the fact that by many measures the early twenty-first century has been an era of at least relative decline for the United States. Wittingly or unwittingly, the rhetoric of the development world in particular seems to recapitulate the prototypically American view that in the words of Henry Ford, "history is more or less bunk," at least insofar as the progress that can reasonably be expected in the near future is concerned. What the American anthropologist James C. Scott has called the future's "radical contingency" in his book, *Seeing Like a State: How Certain Schemes to Improve the Human Condition Have Failed*, is an idea that seems to have no place in the current development consensus.

In the nineteenth century, Nietzsche could call one of his most important books *The Birth of Tragedy*. These days, it often seems that were he to want to find any audience at all for his views, a twenty-first-century Nietzsche would have to assign himself a very different task, and instead write a book called *The Death of Tragedy*. For better or for worse, that is how far we have come in a time when the dominant view is one that combines Michael Ignatieff's "revolution of moral concern"—which he argued began with the creation of the United Nations system at the end of the Second World War and came to maturity with the success of the human rights movement—with Bill Gates's faith in technological innovation and scientific discovery as all but guaranteeing that the world will continue to progress from poverty to prosperity.

Ignatieff's work has largely been focused on the human rights revolution, up to and including the dilemmas of humanitarian action in emergencies and up to and including military interventions on human rights grounds. He has paid scant attention to development. But it would have been interesting had he done so, for, if anything, the radicalism of contemporary thinking about poverty and hunger is even more extreme. Indeed, in that context Ignatieff might have been widely viewed as having been overcautious in his claims. Certainly, his admonition in his 2000 Tanner Lectures that human rights at its best was a form of politics but always ran the risk of becoming a form of idolatry—"humanism worshipping itself," as he put it—would not sit well with the many campaigning groups with names such as The World We Want Foundation, End Poverty 2015 Millennium Campaign, and Make Poverty History that have had such an outsized influence on what development in the early to mid-twenty-first century is expected to accomplish. For them, all doubt about the eventual outcome, though obviously they concede that great challenges will be encountered along the way, is either mad or bad or both.

To the extent that the nexus of human rights and development has come to seem like a secular religion, it is like no religion that has preceded it, as a cursory look at the way in which the major faith traditions have thought about poverty and hunger will demonstrate. For example, in most mainstream understandings of Hinduism, the rigidity of the caste system and the moral judgments about why people find themselves in the material circumstances that they do have always served to confirm the "unendingness" of poverty. Hinduism's offshoot, Buddhism, also takes poverty as one of the givens of the human condition. And echoing and amplifying Moses in Deuteronomy 15:11 that "For the poor will never cease out of the land," Jesus instructs his disciples in Matthew 26:11 that "For you always have the poor with you, but you will not always have me." But in only a little over half a century, this age-old view of every major faith tradition seems to have been supplanted by the idea that we stand on the threshold of making poverty and hunger "history," to use the catchphrase that was originally popularized by the Irish pop singer Bono in 2005.

In fact, we have been here before. Already in 1974, an FAO-sponsored World Food Conference in Rome adopted what it called "A Universal Declaration on the Eradication of Hunger and Malnutrition." The title was clearly intended to echo the 1948 UN Universal Declaration of Human Rights, which sets out the basic principles of the human rights movement. At the conference, Henry Kissinger, then US secretary of state, declared that "within a decade no child will go to bed hungry . . . no family will fear for its next day's bread, and . . . no human being's future and capacities will be stunted by malnutrition." To be sure, given that he was an unreconstructed international relations realist, it is difficult to believe Kissinger believed anything of the sort. And in the 1970s, Ignatieff's revolution of moral concern was still in its infancy.

The situation is entirely different in the second decade of the twenty-first century. For example, when Bill Gates writes an entry on his blog praising the so-called Millennium Development Goals (MDGs), those "dreams with a deadline," as he called them, which consist of eight goals agreed to by the UN General Assembly in 2000, ranging from halving extreme poverty rates through halting the spread to HIV/AIDS, there is no reason to doubt either his commitment or his sincerity. And Gates is anything but alone. To the contrary, the assumption that poverty and hunger can be abolished if only the world can muster the determination and the money to make it happen is now the central "framing" mechanism for the way poverty is understood within the world of international development, private and governmental alike. As for those who might still argue that in fact "abolishing" poverty once and for all is beyond the capacities of human beings, no matter how committed they were, no matter what political backing they received, and no matter how much money they had at their disposal, such persons tend to be viewed with the same pitying incredulity that a conference of astronomers would give to someone blundering into their midst insisting that the earth was flat or that the sun revolved around it.

Can a religion be anti-metaphysical? Bill Gates, who is on record as saying that "just in terms of allocation of time resources, religion is not very efficient,"[10] and that "there is a lot more I could be doing on a Sunday morning," does not even appear to have considered that such doubts might be inspired by a moral intuition rather than a strictly practical one. Gates does acknowledge that some do indeed question his view. But this he has attributed almost entirely to the complexity of the problem. That for him is the beauty of the MDGs: they "cut through that complexity."[11] For as his good friend and collaborator, Bono, put it in an interview in 2004, "Let's be honest. We have the science, the technology, and the wealth." He conceded that for the moment the world did not have the collective will to eliminate poverty, but he added that this was "not a reason that history will accept."[12]

Even more than Gates, and much like Jeffrey Sachs, Bono's own long-standing activism has also increasingly been grounded in the idea that the first part of the twenty-first century is when extreme poverty and hunger will be ended. This became clear with the original Make Poverty History campaign, which had played a key role in campaigning for development to be priority when Britain assumed the presidency of the G8 in 2005. In 2013, as the UK once more assumed this role, most of the major international development NGOs, with Bono still serving as the frontman but this time backed heavily by the Gates Foundation, again banded together to promote what they began by calling Make Poverty History 2, but which they eventually launched with the more euphonious title of the IF Campaign, whose slogan was that the world has enough food for everyone, and that hunger was totally preventable everywhere on earth if donor governments would take some simple steps—specifically, living up to the aid commitments they had already made, making additional investments to help small-scale farmers and in nutrition programs, helping to finance the adaptation of global agriculture to climate change, assuring that multinationals paid their taxes in full, protecting farmers from being forced off their land, stopping the diversion of corn to ethanol (that is, being used for fuel instead of food), and pushing governments and businesses to be transparent about their affairs. Do this, they insisted, and the world could start "ending hunger during 2013."

What was striking about this was the campaigners' apparent assumption that governments could fulfill these demands without radically changing the global system. In this essential sense, theirs was and remains an antipolitics—a vision of the world based on technology, above all on the limitless promise of technological innovation that when deployed in the context of Ignatieff's revolution of moral concern, is commonly held to be unstoppable. As Kate Nash of Goldsmiths College pointed out in her brilliant paper analyzing the 2005 campaign, Make Poverty History was "an anti-poverty campaign, not anti-capitalist or anti-globalization." To the contrary, it presupposed "that structures of capitalist global governance [were what made] the goal of ending poverty possible for the first time."[13] And yet, as Nash pointed out, while some of the demands of the 2005 campaign, such as canceling the debts of some of the most heavily indebted poor countries and increasing aid, cost rich donor countries comparatively little, the trade justice that the Make Poverty History campaign called for, and that is also present, albeit in a somewhat different form and with important differences in emphasis, in the IF Campaign[14] raised profound issues of conflict of interest between the Global North and the Global South, and, more fundamentally still, ignored the fact that as Nash puts it, working through existing international institutions could never succeed because these institutions are "structured to benefit rich and powerful states."[15]

It is perfectly understandable and indeed laudable that any well-intended person confronted by the brutal realities of hunger in the poor world would want to feel that, as the famous formula goes, they are "part of the solution, not part of the problem." What is less understandable is why slogans such as "In the next fifty days, you can change the world for good [by participating in Make Poverty History]" seemed so compelling, even taking into account the undoubted appeal of what Nash calls "global citizenship as show business." Part of the answer almost certainly derives from the fact that the late-twentieth and early twenty-first century world is a place in which pessimism (public pessimism, anyway) is increasingly viewed as moral solecism. There has come to be something almost impious in denying that *all* societies and all human problems this side of mortality can be radically made over and suffering brought to an end. And by definition, in a progress narrative, the good eventually triumphs and the bad is defeated. In this universe, perhaps more emotional (not to say narcissistic) than it is moral in any proper sense, it is almost an assertion of one's membership in the party of the good *not* to treat skeptically the claims that the world is on the cusp of being made anew that are routinely made by development and aid officials from major Western governments, which, in any case, remain the source of most development aid globally.

In this vast choir, so vast that it does not seem to occur to those singing in it that any decent person could disagree, one also finds virtually the entirety of the United Nations system, not just the secretary general and his secretariat, but the specialized agencies such as the World Food Programme (WFP), the World Health Organization (WHO), and the UN's development arm, the UNDP. One also finds global philanthropies, above all the Gates Foundation, whose hegemony in the philanthropic world has come to mirror (troublingly so for those who do not see it as desirable, let alone as the natural order of things) the hegemony of the United States in the global political system. The increasingly central role occupied by these institutions in the global aid system has been transformative, even though the long-established roster of mainline international relief and development NGOs continues to wield great influence.

It is as if the undeniably very mixed results of more than half a century of global development efforts count for nothing. What F. Scott Fitzgerald said of his fellow citizens, that "there are no second acts in American lives," now seems to characterize the world of international development as well. A skeptical observer might inquire why members of these campaigning groups appear to be so reluctant to ask themselves more often whether, by painting a picture of the foreseeable future in terms that in any other era would have been described not just as millennial but as millenarian, they have gotten into the bad habit of mistaking the nobility of their intentions for the feasibility of their goals. But either they consider this question asked and answered (positively) or else they consider it to be a moral solecism even to pose it in the first place.

How could it be otherwise when the received wisdom of the age is not simply that it will be possible to end extreme global poverty permanently sometime in the future—itself an extraordinarily radical claim in historical terms—but rather the certainty that if the world puts its collective shoulder to the wheel, this can be done within a period of one or two decades? The fact that this has become the consensus within the international system and an article of faith with a great many well-intended people throughout the world has served to obscure the radicalism of the claim that is being made: in half a century, roughly from the establishment of the United Nations in 1945 to the adoption of the MDGs in 2000, the world's great and good have moved from the belief that the poor would always be with us to the confidence that what has been deemed impossible for all but a temporal flake of human history is now deemed to be not only imaginable but inevitable. This consensus is so entrenched that it is difficult to imagine, whatever the results on the ground prove to be, any sort of climbdown. Instead the UN system, the Bretton Woods institutions, and most mainline international NGOs and philanthropies have been united in viewing the MDGs and the Sustainable Development Goals (SDGs) as the central organizing principal of development and poverty reduction. Having headed the UN Millennium Project, the experts' panel charged with the MDGs' implementation, Jeffrey Sachs was obviously an interested party. But he was absolutely right to insist that "to the extent that there are any international goals, they are the Millennium Development Goals."[16]

This party-line optimism about development has effectively marginalized criticism of the current development expectations, whether that criticism comes from the free-market right or the anti-globalization left. And the adoption of the MDGs and the focus on the so-called SDGs that are planned to succeed them have essentially institutionalized this moralization of hope. This has certainly been done with the best of intentions. Nonetheless, by conflating realism and pessimism and arriving at understanding that in reality both are largely smoke screens for an immoral cynicism, the mainstream of the development world has turned what should have been a productive debate between its vision and some of the opposing or at least critical worldviews into a discussion in which the only debate seen as worth having seems to be when the world will finally reach the slopes of what, without irony, was called in the old Soviet Union the "radiant future."

· 3 ·

Malthus Only Needs to Be Wrong Once

Whether it was wise to elevate the MDGs to such a pedestal, as the Canadian lawyer and public health expert Amir Attaran has described it, is anything but as clear as their proponents have claimed. This is because, by 2015, along with more realistic projects like combating AIDS and promoting gender equality, those who had designed them held out the promise, doubtless offered with perfect sincerity, that extreme poverty and hunger would be "eradicated" (the use of a word associated with conquering diseases was emblematic of the entire mind-set behind the project), while also insisting that environmental sustainability would be assured and universal child education would be achieved (though the actual details of what the content and quality of that education would be was left an open question). When critics like Attaran questioned if the success or failure of some of the MDGs could even be measured accurately, then-deputy UN secretary general Louise Frechette ignored the evidence of her own statisticians and declared that UN meetings "should not be distracted by arguments over the measurement of the MDGs," because "any changes would only distract from the result we would like to achieve." And instead of asking the essential questions, which were whether the MDGs should be the locus of the collective goals of the international system, and, more concretely, if a number of the MDGs could not be measured accurately, was it not worth at least considering whether the MDGs were in reality an achievable program or an act of collective global hubris? Former secretary general Kofi Annan seems to have preferred to deepen the UN's commitment, declaring publicly that the MDGs were not ultimate feasible goals but rather a minimum from which, once accomplished, the world needed to set for itself and then move on to fulfilling still more ambitious goals. "Achieving the MDGs," Annan wrote at the time, "is only the first step."[1]

If one reads a representative sampling of the statements of senior UN officials, the leaders of most governments (whether in the rich or the poor worlds), NGO and development workers, and those who oversee the major global philanthropies, one discovers that Annan actually has been one of the more cautious and nuanced campaigners for the MDGs. The more common view is one of a kind of steely, euphoric confidence that if all the relevant actors will just pull together, poverty will soon be just as much an artifact of the past in most of the world as slavery became in the nineteenth century, and as so many of the worst epidemic diseases like smallpox and polio became in the twentieth. The danger of overpromising inscribed on this kind of millennial thinking is obvious, as some radical food activist groups, militant peasant organizations, and environmentalists, alarmed by the extent to which the claims for MDGs became wilder and wilder, attempted to point out. A prime example of such overpromising was a book called *The End of Poverty: Economic Possibilities for Our Time* that Sachs published in 2005. According to Sachs, if the rich countries would simply contribute 0.7 percent of their Gross National Product to lifting poor countries out of poverty, this would suffice. As Bono wrote in his foreword to the book, Sachs had written "a handbook on how we could finish out the job [of ending poverty for good]." What "the professor proposes here," Bono concluded, is that "we can choose to shift the paradigm."

Sachs is hardly the first economist to put his faith in what one of his most distinguished predecessors, Irving Fisher, had called "human improvability." Eighty years earlier, Fisher had written in a 1925 journal article that "political economy is no longer the 'dismal science,' teaching that starvation wages are inevitable from the Malthusian growth of population, but is now seriously and hopefully grappling with the problems of abolition of poverty." For Fisher, economics needed to be dragged out of the fatalism that had marked it and instead find inspiration in the limitless confidence of the biologists.

Just as in the first age of scientific medicine in the eighteenth and nineteenth centuries, physicians had imagined there would eventually be a remedy for every illness,[2] so Fisher thought that economic changes could bring about the end of poverty. Sachs is very much Fisher's inheritor in this sense (though he of course could not be farther from Fisher's belief in eugenics). But the historical comparison that Sachs draws in *The End of Poverty* is not with Fisher but instead with the other great economist of the Depression era, John Maynard Keynes. In 1930, Keynes had written an essay called "Economic Possibilities for Our Grandchildren," in which he, too, foresaw the end of poverty in Britain and the other countries of the developed world. In an important sense, Sachs's argument is simply the extension of this prediction to the developing world. As he writes confidently in his book, "Keynes got it just right, of course: extreme poverty no longer exists in today's rich countries, and is disappearing in most of the world's middle-income countries." And, he concluded, "Today we can invoke the same logic to declare that extreme poverty can be ended not in the time of our grandchildren, but in *our* time."[3] The problem is that in this homage to Keynes, Sachs ignores a crucial aspect of Keynes's argument—one on which much of his confidence about the future depended. Keynes does seem to have been correct about what would happen in the rich world, though the human and material consequences of the savage austerity the IMF and the EU imposed on Greece in 2011 suggest how he might one day still turn out to have been wrong even there. But Keynes was careful in his essay to add an important caveat to his irenic scenario that in a hundred years the problem of poverty might very well have been solved. "I draw [this] conclusion," he wrote, "assuming no important wars and no important increase in population."[4] Given that by the time Sachs wrote his book he was entirely aware that population had not just increased but exploded (a lurid verb, but an entirely appropriate one just the same), and in much of sub-Saharan Africa, it would continue to grow very fast well into the middle of the century, one might have expected this to have tempered his optimism. For example, the current population of Tanzania is roughly forty-nine million. Kenya has roughly forty-five million inhabitants. At a conservative estimate, both are expected to more than double by 2050. Historically, a third East African country, Uganda, has had a smaller population than its neighbors. At thirty-five million this is still the case. But according to many demographers, it will not hold true for long, and some leading demographers believe that Uganda, which already has one of the world's highest population growth rates, may have 104 million people by 2050.[5]

Sachs certainly knows these figures as well as anyone. But while he acknowledges them in *The End of Poverty*, he insists that if nations take the relatively simple steps he outlines, there is no cause for alarm. This is hardly Sachs's view alone. To the contrary, and not just about Ethiopia, optimism remains the reigning view in the development world, even though human rights activists view things quite differently. Sachs's confidence rests on the idea that technological progress "enables us to meet basic needs on a global scale and to achieve a margin above basic needs unprecedented in history." And even though Africa's population continues at least for now to grow at the dizzying rates demographers have been tracking and reporting, Sachs seems to think that the right investments, particularly in women and girls in rural Africa, will not only produce declines in fertility over the medium and long terms, but, as he puts it, "will produce a rapid and decisive drop in fertility rates over a short period of time."[6]

In fairness, Sachs has since conceded in an interview that he had "wanted to simplify the problems by putting aside the rich world's issues and so forth and [focus] on extreme poverty. But it's all interconnected."[7] And he has always been perfectly well aware that if the rate of population increase in countries like Uganda and Ethiopia does not start to come down fast, there will not be an end to global poverty but a severe aggravation of it. For example, in an interview he gave to the British journalist Peter Gill about Ethiopia, Sachs admitted that, "Unless the fertility rate comes down sharply I'm running out of ideas." And when Gill told him that Ethiopia's population was likely to be nearly 160 million by 2050, Sachs's response was anything but sanguine. "It is absolutely unmanageable," he said, "beyond any of our [development] tools right now."[8]

And Ethiopia is generally considered in the development world to be a positive example. Since the MDGs were adopted, the country has cut infant mortality, built schools, improved nutrition, and even launched an ambitious program of solar powered generation in the countryside. The fact that Ethiopia—like another African poster child for the MDGs, Rwanda—is a dictatorship rarely earns a mention. To the contrary, not just Sachs but Bill and Melinda Gates and Tony Blair have also praised its government's antipoverty and health programs to the skies, with Melinda Gates going so far as to note on her blog that "Ethiopia is one of my favorite places, because it proves the world can get better—a lot better, very quickly—with the right kind of leadership."[9] The problem here is that many dictatorships have been successful in reducing poverty, improving public health, and making their societies work more efficiently. The Nazis made considerable improvements in public health. And Mussolini really did make the trains run on time. In the case of the communist world, pointing to social improvements, particularly in education and public health, has been a standard reply by supporters of these regimes to accusations of human rights violations, repression of free speech and of the press, and the like. (Cuba is the obvious case in point, and, more recently Venezuela.)

For those who believe, as William Easterly does, (and with him virtually the entire global human rights movement), that successful development almost invariably depends on democratic freedoms— that is, that authoritarian development is not only bad morally but ineffective economically, at least in the long run—taking a stand against repressive regimes like those in Rwanda and Ethiopia is a straightforward matter. But this is not the mainstream view in the development world, where the consensus is that there is no necessary connection between successful development and democracy. And for those of a technocratic cast of mind (and if Bill Gates is anything, it's that), despotisms that are genuinely concerned with their citizens' material welfare are in fact easier to deal with and often freer to make the kinds of economic changes that major Western donors and philanthropies such as Gates and Rockefeller believe to be necessary in order to end extreme poverty and hunger. Still, by the standards of what the Gates Foundation, USAID, the Clinton Global Fund, and DFID wrote about Ethiopia in 2013, for Sachs to have admitted to a journalist to a feeling of helplessness was (comparatively) an act of the bleakest pessimism. And in most of his work he has been unwilling to concede even the possibility that the end of poverty is something beyond the powers of human beings to accomplish, assuming, of course, that enough money is made available and enough political will can be mobilized, let alone that at least in some parts of the world, it may already be too late. Sachs is certainly no vulgar determinist. This book, he writes in his introduction, "is not a forecast." And yet three sentences later, he insists that "our generation can choose to end that extreme poverty by the year 2025,"[10] which while not a forecast about the political chances of his strategy being adopted is indeed a forecast about what can be accomplished if the will to do so can be mobilized.

One can admire Sachs's missionary zeal in putting forward his formulas of economic salvation for the poor, even if his seeming determination to present himself as a kind of anti-Malthus seems more than a bit grandiloquent, particularly given what he told Peter Gill. And, to put it charitably, his curt dismissal of economic analyses and understandings of the world that do not coincide with his own do him little credit, particularly when contrasted with his own seeming inability to admit to ever having made a mistake that was actually his own fault rather than a failure of his interlocutors to do what he had recommended.

The question as to whether the rapid rise in population in countries like Ethiopia really can be halted in time is only one problem with the optimistic formula Sachs puts forward. Another is his highly questionable claim that extreme poverty is disappearing from middle-income countries. To be sure, it is beyond dispute that many countries such as Thailand, Chile, and Brazil have radically reduced both the number and the proportion of their poor people. But there are other countervailing claims that are at least as noteworthy. In 2013, fewer than 10 percent of the poor lived in what development economists call "fragile low-income countries."[11] In a 2011 paper, Andy Sumner of the Institute for Development Studies at Sussex University in the UK described this shift, estimating that 70 percent of the global poor now lived in middle-income countries.[12] In some of these countries, there has been no correlation between achieving high economic growth rates and joining the ranks of middle-income states, and sharply reducing poverty, malnutrition, and food insecurity. The textbook case of this is India, which, given that it will soon overtake China as the most populous country in the world (one in seven human beings alive today is an Indian), can hardly be described as an outlier. And this does not take into account the fact that because the world's population is now increasing by approximately 70 million per year, what this means in practical terms is that it is possible to reduce the proportion of malnourished people without lowering their absolute numbers.

Despite all this, Sachs remains convinced that Keynes's claim that "the dramatic march of science and technology and the ability of advances in technology to underpin continued economic growth at compound interest would eventually end poverty and hunger in the rich world" applies equally to the poor world and therefore makes "the end of all poverty a realistic possibility by the year 2025."[13] In his own career, where he has moved from being a believer in economic shock therapy involving rapid transition to unrestrictive free markets for Russia in the early 1990s to his current stance as an apostle for massive foreign aid to Africa, Sachs has often seemed vulnerable to that same cast of mind that informed the weakest elements in Keynes's thought, his wild oscillations between optimism and pessimism. In *The Economic Consequences of the Peace*, written in 1919 in the immediate aftermath of the Versailles Treaty, Keynes had looked at continental Europe and thought he discerned "the fearful convulsions of a dying civilization."[14] Eleven years later, in "Economic Prospects for our Grandchildren," he thought he saw of future of untrammeled prosperity. Sachs also shares Keynes's belief that most problems are fundamentally technical. As Sylvia Nasar has put it, Keynes was convinced that "once the problem was correctly diagnosed, there was a solution—if only the authorities had the *conviction* to act."[15] In this regard, she might as well have been describing Sachs, for this is precisely the assumption that underpins the argument he makes in *The End of Poverty*.

Historically, this confidence in technological solutions to all the world's problems goes back beyond late-nineteenth-century biologists like Pasteur and Koch to the Positivists and to the writings of Henri de Saint-Simon and Auguste Comte. John Gray has succinctly summed up what he calls this positivist "catechism" as being based on three tenets: "History is driven by the power of science; growing knowledge and new technology are the ultimate determinants of change in human society. Second, science will enable natural scarcity to be overcome; once that has been achieved, the immemorial evils of poverty and war will be banished for ever. Third, progress in science and progress in ethics and politics go together; as scientific knowledge advances and becomes more systematically organized, human values will increasingly converge."[16] And as Gray pointed out, "The problem with the secular narrative is not that it assumes progress is inevitable (in many versions it does not). It is the belief that the sort of advance that has been achieved in science can be reproduced in ethics and politics."[17]

In Sachs's particular case—and here, again, Irving Fisher comes to mind—this scientism has a medical cast to it. Again and again in his book, Sachs relies on medical metaphors to explain what needs to be done and how it can be done successfully. Starry-eyed in some ways, he is steely in others, and repeatedly emphasizes the impediments that have to be overcome to end poverty and makes the commonsense observation that each poor country would have its own particular challenges. It is here that Sachs deploys the most important of these medical metaphors. "The challenges facing economists advising poor countries," he writes, share "many of the same challenges as clinical medicine," particularly in the need to make a "differential diagnosis."[18] In order to respond effectively to them, the global response must be based on what he calls "clinical economics."[19]

Those who remembered Sachs's enthusiasm in the 1990s for economic shock treatment in the former Soviet Union might have been tempted to murmur "physician, heal thyself" under their breath. Sachs remains personally a controversial figure in the development world. Even George Soros, whose $50 million gift to Sachs's Millennium Village Project was by far the largest it received, conceded to the journalist Nina Munk that "there's a certain messianic quality about [Sachs], and it needs to be kept under critical control."[20] Off the record, many other colleagues of Sachs in the academic and philanthropic worlds are far more scathing. And yet whatever the mainstream development world's reservations about Sachs the man, his view that poverty can be ended relatively soon is its conventional wisdom. The medical analogy he employed has now become almost as much of a development commonplace. For example, on assuming the leadership of the World Bank in 2012, Jim Yong Kim, who had spent most of his career as a physician with a specialty in public health (he was one of the founders of the Harvard-based international medical relief and development group, Partners in Health), declared that, "I want to eradicate poverty." His model for how to achieve this also was a medical one based on the campaign he had led a decade earlier to greatly increase the number of poor people receiving treatment for HIV/AIDS.

Almost no one seized by the metaphor of poverty as a sort of disease that could be wiped out just as epidemics have been in the past seems to have looked very hard at the question of whether such models and metaphors were the appropriate ones. It is not just that the "disease of poverty" is any more a disease than, as my late mother argued so passionately, the effort to find cures for cancer can appropriately be called a war. The point may seem like a comparatively trivial one. And yet no one should underestimate the distorting effects of inaccurate language on any thinking worthy of the name, as, if it taught us nothing else, the rhetoric of the communist world should have shown us. In the particular case of the poverty-epidemic disease analogy, there is an even more serious problem. Once vaccines had been developed, wiping out smallpox and polio were entirely achievable medical goals. It was perfectly reasonable for Carl-Wilhelm Stenhammar—the chairman of the board of Rotary International, which had raised more than $1 billion for global polio eradication—to insist in an interview that "we have the power to eradicate polio—we have the vaccine." To the extent that problems remained, he added it was because "there's still a funding gap, so it's a question of money, but it can be done."[21]

At best, he was only partly right. For as we have since learned to our cost, in wiping out diseases, political consent is at least as important as vaccines. At the turn of the millennium, public health officials were indeed confident that polio would be wiped out within a decade or so. What they had not anticipated was the fierce, sanguinary resistance to these vaccination programs that would be put up by Jihadi groups, particularly in Pakistan and Afghanistan, and by Boko Haram in northern Nigeria. Their willingness to kill health workers doing the vaccinations has meant that at best, hopes for a polio-free world have had to be deferred. At least as worrying has been the return of polio to Syria, where the civil war has made vaccination impossible in many areas and which has also led to the return of the disease to Iraq, where it had also not been present for many years. In light of all this, perhaps the medical model is not entirely sound even with regard to medical matters.

But even if one sets aside the degree to which Stenhammar's assumptions about ending polio have proved to be flawed, the fact that they are almost identical to Sachs's about ending poverty is not reassuring. The problem is that the challenges posed by an epidemic disease are fundamentally different. Assume, for the sake of argument, that Sachs, Dr. Jin, and other members of the international development mainstream for whom the medical metaphor makes sense are correct when they claim that with enough money, poverty can be eliminated; unlike polio or smallpox, there is actually no guarantee that it will not come back. There are innumerable examples throughout history of rich countries becoming poor and poor countries rich, and no guarantee of how long the social and historical circumstances will prevail that have led Sachs and many of his colleagues to believe poverty can be "made history." In other words, unlike a disease against which people can be permanently inoculated with a vaccine, there can be no vaccine against poverty, and thus it is no more appropriate to speak of ending poverty than it is of "ending" mortality. Yes, technological progress and accumulated scientific knowledge are, on the whole, irreversible, but to believe the contrary assumes far more than this. It means proceeding on the working assumption that there will be no more terrible wars, no new epidemics on the model of HIV/AIDS, no mutations because of which existing treatments are no longer effective, as seems to be the case with a particularly virulent, artemisinin-resistant strain of malaria that has already spread from Southeast Asia to Myanmar, and may well spread into India, causing the Indian health authorities to warn that such a development might wipe out the gains their country had made in reducing both malaria cases and deaths. Nor do these optimistic assumptions properly factor in the possibility of irreversible catastrophic environmental developments. To cite only one example, number seven of the eight MDGs is titled "Ensure Environmental Sustainability." It is divided into four parts, the third of which calls for "Halv[ing], by 2015, the proportion of the population without sustainable access to safe drinking water and basic sanitation." And yet, as a recent story in the *Guardian* chronicled, the Yemeni capital Sana'a, which is a city of almost two million people whose population continues to grow rapidly, may soon become the first world capital in the world to run out of a viable water supply. In 1970, its water table was thirty meters below ground level. Today, it is now 1,200 meters down in some parts of the city.

The water crisis in Sana'a is anything but an outlier. To the contrary, it is only one of the most extreme examples of the numerous water crises already well underway in many parts of the world—part of the rolling disaster that is climate change. Given this reality, the suggestion that we will escape the tragedies of wars (above all, resource wars that diminishing water supplies in many of the great cities of the Global South are virtually certain to produce), new epidemics, and environmental disasters seems improbable to the point of absurdity. It is this that makes the grandiose promises of the development elite ring so terribly morally off key. If even some of these apprehensions about the future are warranted, then these claims do not embody hope; they make a mockery of hope.

Even with regard to conditions as they now exist, the careful listener or reader will soon find that at places in what may appear at first glance to be the monolithically upbeat public pronouncements about the MDGs by institutions such as the World Bank and by Bill

Gates, who, in this matter at least, can be said to speak for "philanthrocapitalists" as a group, it is well worth reading the fine print. There, one finds more realistic assessments that, were they more widely known, would presumably have called into question or at least led to some reconsideration of the prevailing consensus of unyielding optimism. The evidence is there, but what is missing, it seems, is the willingness to take a fresh look that this evidence would seem to call for. This is in many ways odd, since Bill Gates in particular has been a huge proponent of the need for looking closely at hard, measurable data when evaluating programs. But as Andy Sumner pointed out in his paper, the fact that the majority of the poor live in middle-income countries "will place far more importance on external actors understanding the political dimensions of development."[22] For all their technical expertise, this is precisely what neither Sachs nor the Gates Foundation has shown much ability to undertake—witness Melinda Gates's hymn of praise to an Ethiopian government that has one of the worst human rights records in Africa.

Nor is the underlying macroeconomic analysis much more reliable. For example, in a 2010 World Bank paper called "Unfinished Business: Mobilizing New Efforts to Achieve the 2015 Millennium Development Goals," after listing the progress to date in reaching the MDGs (and highlighting the bank's role in it), the authors listed the challenges the effort faced. First among these was the assertion that "achieving the MDGs requires a vibrant global economy, powered by strong, sustainable, multi-polar growth, underpinned by sound policies and reform at the country level."[23] If the bank really believed this, then its report should have been far more cautious. For by 2010, it was already fairly obvious that growth rates in Europe and North America had stagnated and were likely to continue to do so for some time. It took no great expertise to see that if the economies of these OECD countries would not be expanding, China's own economy, so dependent on exports to these markets, could not grow at the stratospheric levels it had attained in the previous decade.

More broadly, by 2010, no one in his or her right mind—not even the cheerleader-journalists on business cable channels that over the past decade seem to have proliferated as if by parthenogenesis— from London to Delhi and Johannesburg to Sao Paulo would have dared to describe the global economy as "vibrant." If this was what was required to achieve the MDGs, then given that these conditions were unlikely to occur by 2015, surely the only sober inference to draw was that the MDGs were not going to be achieved or, at the very least, not only not going to be achieved on schedule but would take far longer than even the most cautious experts involved in the project had predicted. And in 2012, a UN report entitled "The Global Partnership for Development: Making Rhetoric a Reality"[24] conceded that the millennium goal eight was not living up to expectations. Goal number eight had focused on the role and obligations of rich countries to foster poverty reduction in the poor world through increases in official development aid (ODA) and through reform of the international trading system that almost everyone agreed was so unfavorable to the Global South. Instead, the report predicted that because of the economic crisis, ODA would almost certainly stagnate, while, having preached free trade to the developing world for so long, "the current economic situation has lured Governments [of rich countries] back into using protectionist trade policies."

Nonetheless, supporters of the MDGs have not backed away from their claims of success on the other seven millennium goals. Progress in poverty reduction, education, and access to medical treatment, they argued, was ahead of schedule. It was only when one read some of the detailed reports issued regularly by the UN, the World Bank, the IMF, and the British government's Overseas Development Institute that a different picture emerged. For example, the opening paragraph of the UN's 2011 Millennium Development Goals report states that while "more work lies ahead, the world has cause to celebrate" the accomplishments to date of the MDGs. A few paragraphs later, however, the report concedes that the conditions in

South Asia, above all the "shortage of quality food and poor feedings practices, combined with inadequate sanitation" that had given the region the dubious distinction of having the highest childhood un-dernutrition in the world before the MDGs, remained unaffected by the MDGs, at least among children in the poorest households.[25] The only progress that had been made between 1995 and 2009 was among children in the richest 20 percent of families. And given the enormous number of poor people who had joined the ranks of the Indian middle class during this period, it hardly seemed likely that the MDGs could be credited with having played a central role.

Advocates of the MDGs might insist that the world was well on track to meet the goal of halving extreme poverty. But again, a care-ful look at the geographical breakdown of that accomplishment told a very different story. According to the same UN report, between 1990 and 2005, absolute poverty had indeed gone from 60 percent to 16 percent in East Asia (a geographical designation that for all intents and purposes actually meant China), from 39 percent to 19 percent in Southeast Asia (Thailand, Vietnam, Laos, Cambodia), and from 49 percent to 39 percent in India. In contrast, the sub-Saharan African rate had dropped only from 58 percent to 51 percent, the rate in the Caribbean from 29 percent to 26 percent, and the rate in Latin America from 11 percent to 7 percent. And rates had actually gone up in Central Asia and the Caucasus, rising from 6 percent to 19 percent. Dani Rodrik, professor of social science at the Insti-tute for Advanced Study in Princeton, New Jersey, drew the essential conclusion: if the goal of halving extreme poverty was indeed going to be achieved ahead of schedule, he wrote, this was "largely thanks to China's phenomenal growth."[26] This seemed to confirm the criti-cisms made by development skeptics like William Easterly, who has argued in a review of Sachs's *The End of Poverty*[27] that less ambitious exercises than the MDGs, combined with sensible national strategies for economic growth, were far more likely to achieve the desired re-sult. Rodrik was categorical, writing that there was little evidence to suggest that China's success, without which the claims for the MDGs' success in reducing absolute poverty could not even have been advanced, "were the result of the MDGs themselves." The reason for this, Rodrik added, was that "China implemented the policies that engineered history's greatest poverty eradication prior to, and independently from, the Millennium Declaration and the MDGs."[28]

Faced with increasingly mixed news, above all, skepticism concerning the degree to which rich nations have been willing to follow through on the commitments they signed on to when they endorsed the Millennium Declaration, many advocates of the MDGs began emphasizing how the eight goals had focused attention and raised awareness about extreme poverty. This fallback position was hardly new. Indeed, the story of Pollyanna is just as relevant a cautionary tale to development as the story of the Boy Who Cried Wolf is to the humanitarian relief organizations whose media releases too often err in predicting the most apocalyptic possible outcome in any given crisis. In the long run, overpromising, which the claim in the MDGs that poverty can be eradicated by 2015 has already proven to be, can only engender cynicism regarding the many real successes there have been globally in reducing poverty—a danger that all the upbeat conferences outlining what the UN is now describing as "what happens after the MDGs" should not be allowed to obscure.

It is important not to stray too far in the opposite direction either. It is one thing to point out the hubris of assumptions on which the MDGs are based—assumptions that continue to echo down the development food chain to specialists in subjects as different as nutrition and environmental sustainability, as when the head of the Institute for Development Studies at the University of Sussex wrote in the aftermath of the 2012 Olympics that a new slogan for campaigners for better nutrition should be "No stunting by the 2032 Olympics." But this does not mean that there has been and can be no progress in reducing poverty. And in the specific case of the global food system, there is the example of what is probably the most stunning success to date: the real prospect of ending famine. To be sure, the process is still not inevitable. To his great credit, after he stepped down as UN secretary general, Kofi Annan tried repeatedly to raise the alarm over the fact that the sedulous failure of various international conferences to cobble together a workable environmental policy to limit the rise in global temperatures meant that the most catastrophic global warming scenarios simply could not be excluded. The threat that it would pose to food supplies in the most vulnerable parts of the world, whether through drought (parts of sub-Saharan Africa) or rises in sea levels (mostly obviously in the Bay of Bengal), could herald a new age of famine. But there is reason for hope as well. For if the global warming that is already occurring and that is now far too late to reverse can be held to the lower end of the projections of temperature rises, then, for the reasons that Cormac Ó Gráda has outlined, the end of famine may prove to be a world-historical shift rather than an unsustainable interregnum.

Just as the misperception on the part of the general public in the Global North has been extremely difficult to dislodge, the worldwide good news about famine, including in much but not all of Africa, has been, if anything, even harder to shake. But this is largely because the perceptions of most nonspecialists, at least in the rich world, continue to be in the thrall of the view first propounded by the eighteenth-century English divine, Robert Thomas Malthus, often called the "father" of modern demography, who propounded the view that famine was nature's ultimate way of reducing human populations when every other means failed. There is no question that the tremendous rise in the world's population over the past seventy-five years, particularly in regions of the world such as the Horn of Africa, the Sahelian countries, and in parts of the Islamic Middle East where hunger remains an endemic problem, has engendered fears of engulfment and despair over poverty in much of the rich world. Faced with these developments, it should hardly come as a surprise that Malthus's proposition, in all its apocalyptic neatness, has retained its appeal. For as the German essayist Hans Magnus Enzensberger once quipped, the apocalypse is "one of the oldest ideas of the human species," historically accompanying utopian thought "like a shadow."[29] Surely, given the fact that in our era utopianism has for all intents and purposes been institutionalized as the moral conventional wisdom, it should hardly be surprising that these apocalyptic shadows retain their psychic currency and stubbornly refuse to be dispelled.

At least, barbaric though it is, the apocalypse offers a kind of solution to the population crisis. The problem is that, at least so far, Malthus has been wrong in his apocalyptic prediction that food supply would never be able to keep up with population increase. In advancing this argument, Malthus made several errors, but the principal one lay in his not having been able to imagine the tremendous progress in agricultural methods, not all of which, it should be pointed out, are the product of new technologies, as the agricultural multinationals would like to convince us all that they are. Again, in fairness to Malthus, it is by no means clear whether he will always be wrong or whether those who rely on the falsity of his claim are in the position of the man in the joke about someone falling from a one-hundred-story building, who, fifty floors down, is asked how he's doing and replies: "So far, so good." The stark fact is that to avoid famine recurring throughout a world that now has seven billion people and will almost certainly add two billion more by 2050 and possibly another billion in the two decades after that, agricultural production has to increase unceasingly. And while the gains that have resulted from the MDGs are real in some sectors (though, as Gates himself has conceded, less for the poverty-reduction goal than for any other), whether they can be maintained is anything but clear. Saying, à la Bill Gates, that you are an impatient optimist, or à la Sachs, when in 2005 in the company of Angelina Jolie he visited the first of his Millennium villages and insisted here was "a village that's going to end extreme poverty," is evidence of one's benevolent state of mind and of one's hopes for the future. But to claim that one actually has a good idea as to how that future is going to play out is not optimism—it's hubris.

To put it starkly, Malthus only has to be right once. To say that he has been proven wrong so far about food production being unlikely to keep up with population increase over the long term is beyond dispute. He would have been dumbfounded by the ability of countries like Burkina Faso and Niger, where populations continue to grow at 3 percent per year, to keep the wolf of hunger from the door. But assume for the sake of argument that the great strides in agricultural crop yields, those that both supporters of genetically modified organisms (GMOs) like the Gates Foundation and those on the left who adamantly oppose them and favor what they call an agroecological solution, indeed continue to take place above all in countries where population growth remains stubbornly high. This still does not support the claim that no set of environmental or political facts could have such a limiting effect on global food supplies to demand that there will always be enough to adequately feed the world's people. That would be as dangerously triumphalist an extrapolation of the past into the future as Malthus's predictions were dangerously apocalyptic ones. The most judicious evaluation of these demographic, agricultural, and, above all, moral cross currents may well have been made by Walden Bello, whose own systematic critique of the global food system from the antiglobalization left could not be further from Malthusianism. As he has written, "One can certainly criticize Malthus's extreme pessimism and that of many of his contemporary disciples. But it is difficult to entirely reject their admonitions. For if we do not take the necessary measures to limit our population, our consumption, and our carbon emissions, nature will indeed find much less pleasant ways of re-establishing the equilibrium between herself and us."[30]

· 4 ·

The Food Crisis of 2007–2008: A Turning Point?

I n "Innovation with Impact: Financing 21st Century Development," his report to the G20 leaders for the 2011
Cannes summit, Bill Gates wrote that "people who are pessimistic about the future tend to extrapolate from the present in a
straight line. But innovation fundamentally shifts the trajectory of
development." Malthus had made just such a flat-line extrapolation
from the world he observed all around him, a world in which population rise was quick and easy (the only way to assure that fertility
rates remained low, he thought, was to keep people in penury), but
adding to food supply was slow and difficult. Over the course of the
twentieth century, world population grew from 1.5 billion to a little
under 7 billion. On Gates's account, this enormous and, in historical
terms, unprecedented population rise (which, while slowing somewhat, is still continuing in the twenty-first century) created conditions that should have inexorably led to a new age of global famine.
But far from this occurring, something almost diametrically opposite

took place: famine began to disappear, first from South Asia, then East Asia. As I observed earlier, at the time of this writing it is everywhere in retreat, including in sub-Saharan Africa, even if this would not necessarily be clear to someone who relied on the nonspecialist media for his or her information.

In other words, where famine is concerned, the intellectual descendants of Malthus have been wrong and optimists in the mold of Bill Gates have been entirely correct. In large part thanks to new seeds and improved techniques of cultivation that Gates has championed and in many cases underwritten, agricultural production has kept pace with and at times even outstripped population growth. The poster child for this extraordinary record of success has been the so-called Green Revolution, which transformed agriculture first in Latin America and then in much of Asia in the 1950s and 1960s through a combination of higher-yielding wheat varieties combined with Western-style agricultural production techniques. And yet, when Norman Borlaug, the American agronomist generally considered to have been the animating spirit of the Green Revolution and who in 1970 won the Nobel Peace Prize for his work, was pioneering these new methods of plant breeding meant to be undertaken in tandem with new farming methods, the general consensus was neo-Malthusian. Indeed, from the late 1940s through the early 1960s there had been something of a Malthusian revival, with writers and activists such as William Vogt, who at one point was the national director of Planned Parenthood, and Fairfield Osborn, an important figure in mid-twentieth-century American conservationism, writing books that simply took the Malthusian future as a given unless radical efforts were made first to curb the huge demographic increases the post–World War II world was witnessing and eventually to enduringly reduce global population.[1] These works, and others like them, with titles such as Hugh Everett Moore's 1954 pamphlet "The Population Bomb!" and William and Paul Paddock's 1967 book, *Famine, 1975*, provide the background to the most influential post–World

War II statement of the Malthusian position, Paul and Anne Eh-rlich's *The Population Bomb*, first published in 1968 and periodically republished in revised editions into the twenty-first century.

Whether one considers their unshakeable confidence in their pre-dictions a virtue or a case study in stubbornness, the Ehrlichs have stuck to their beliefs ever since, to the point that in a 2009 interview, they insisted that "the most serious flaw [in *The Population Bomb*] was that it was much too optimistic about the future." The reality, how-ever, is that while there has undoubtedly been a population explosion, the population *bomb* that they warned of has so far not exploded. A world in which there are fewer famines than ever before can hardly be considered preapocalyptic, however much the Ehrlichs and their followers passionately insist that one day history will absolve them. And in fairness, Norman Borlaug himself was extremely worried by the modern vectors of population increase. In his 1970 Nobel lecture, he warned that "most people fail to comprehend the magnitude and menace of the 'Population Monster.' . . . Where will it all end?"[2] But while he seems to have had his moments of Ehrlichian angst over the threat population increase posed to human survival, he remained con-vinced that new seed technologies and improved farming techniques would save humanity. Borlaug put it in a lecture in 2000: "I now say that the world has the technology—either available or well advanced in the research pipeline—to feed on a sustainable basis a population of ten billion people. The more pertinent question today is whether farmers and ranchers will be permitted to use this new technology? While the affluent nations can certainly afford to adopt ultra-low-risk positions, and pay more for food produced by the so-called 'organic' methods, the one billion chronically undernourished people of the low income, food-deficit nations cannot."[3] And, again, so far at least, he has been proven to be right, and so has Bill Gates, who is by orders of magnitude Borlaug's most powerful and influential disciple and inheritor. One can question the role that development aid—whether dispensed by governments in rich countries, by the UN system, or by private philanthropies of which the Gates Foundation is by far the largest, richest, and best organized—has played in the improvements over the past half century in the lives of hundreds of millions of poor people. Maverick economists such as William Easterly have argued that most of this progress is more accurately attributed to capitalist development, above all in China, India, and Vietnam. Easterly's observation, while beyond dispute, is also too partial an account. The difficulty is that the mass prosperity that has been created in these societies and that he rightly praises (even if, to me, he seems far too confident that the terrible costs exacted from the very poor and from the physical environment that have accompanied them will be transient) has been largely an urban phenomenon. In the countryside, especially in many parts of rural India, poverty and malnutrition have not been substantially lowered, and population increase continues to outstrip the migration of the rural poor to the cities. And where agriculture is concerned, increased prosperity has done little or nothing to improve the lives of smallholder farmers and farm laborers, even though in certain areas larger farmers have indeed become more prosperous.

That said, the reality of these improvements, *including* in the countryside, is simply indisputable and can easily be demonstrated by a whole series of social indicators from maternal mortality to education. The salient question, though, is not whether progress has occurred, but rather whether that progress, barring some truly apocalyptic event, can be treated as a new baseline that can be safely assumed to be an enduring minimum highly unlikely to be undone and from which the development world can go on to make still greater strides in reducing extreme poverty and hunger. It was this confidence that led virtually the entire development establishment— the UN system, both donor governments and beneficiaries, NGOs in both the rich and poor worlds, and of course philanthropies—to describe the 2015 deadline for the MDGs as an opportunity to extend progress through the vehicle of a new initiative that came to be called the Sustainable Development Goals (SDGs). A major UN conference held in Rio in 2012 offered up a kind of first draft of what the SDGs should look like in a document with the title "The Future We Want."[4] The fact that the document in no way accurately described the world "we" were living in seemed not to daunt any of the participants in the slightest. To the contrary, it seemed as if the participants assumed that to want something noble meant that one could surely have it.

To be sure, "The World We Want" contained the discreet concession that progress in poverty reduction had been, as the report chastely described it, "uneven" progress and that there had been "setbacks" since the Earth Summit twenty years earlier at which many of these goals had first been formulated. The report also acknowledged the danger of climate change but seemed to assume that presuming its call for "urgent action" was heeded, there was no reason to worry that far too ambitious goals were being proclaimed. And the political transformation that it called for was utopian in the narrowest and strictest sense of the word *utopia*, the first definition of which in Merriam-Webster's dictionary is of "an imaginary place in which the governments, laws, and social conditions are perfect."

In an age of steadily deepening inequality, ecological nihilism (Brazil, the host country of the Rio+20 conference, was at the same time failing to stop, if not actually encouraging, the destruction of the Amazon rain forest), and the emergence of an authoritarian capitalism that was illiberal in every sense except the right accorded to elites to get very, very rich, the authors of the report wrote the following: "We acknowledge that democracy, good governance and the rule of law, at the national and international levels, as well as an enabling environment are essential for sustainable development, including sustained and inclusive economic growth, social development, environmental protection and the eradication of poverty and hunger. We reaffirm that to achieve our sustainable development goals, we need institutions at all levels that are effective, transparent, accountable and democratic." To follow their logic, or rather their wishful thinking, extreme poverty and hunger could be ended once and for all by 2030, and that new world could be made sustainable, but on condition that climate change was curbed, inequality lessened dramatically, and good governance and the rule of law established globally in the same time period. That this was indeed the world they wanted and, for that matter, the world that most decent people wanted is obvious. Why was it not equally obvious to those signing on to the report that it was also a world they could not have?

This was where the deterministic confidence (the greatest proselytizers of which, applied to development, were Bill and Melinda Gates) came in: that innovation will *always* give the world's people the means to meet any challenge. Why such unshakeable conviction? For the global food establishment generally and particularly for the Gates Foundation, with its enormous role in shaping that establishment's understanding, the example of the Green Revolution was dispositive and was also the model for the future successes that technological innovation was bound to bring about. That what seemed to Gates an emblem of future success looked very different to many critics of development, particularly among Right to Food activists and among many militant peasant organizations influenced by the antiglobalization movement, was of course predictable. For them, at best it presented a much more mixed picture of success and failure at once, and at worst it had been an unmitigated disaster both for farmers and for the environment. And even Gates has conceded that the Green Revolution did considerable ecological damage, above all through water pollution from nitrogen-based fertilizers, and in some places benefitted large farmers but not smallholders, though Gates's claim that these inequities were largely resolved by the Green Revolution's second decade would certainly not ring true to most Indian food activists. But clearly, in Gates's view, these were in effect the teething pains of one of the great victories over hunger in human history. Certainly, nowhere in his copious speeches and writings is there any evidence that he views innovation in any other way than as a *deus ex machina* in exclusively the positive sense. The idea that it might be a double-edged sword whose negative side, once identified, is not susceptible to a technical fix is simply alien to his engineer's mind.

It is easy to see why Bill Gates considers these to be inspirational times, a view that even a quick look at the Twitter feeds of mainstream food activist groups will show is widely shared. In an age of fierce nominalism, a time when Samantha Power, the US permanent representative, commenting on a UN report regarding rape in war, could say that "we are crushing it on the normative front" (as if a change in norms almost always heralded a change in realities), the fact that Gates's tweets are fiercely nominalist should come as no surprise. A skeptic may question whether repeating the mantras of "we are the generation that is going to end hunger for good" and "we are the generation that is going to end extreme poverty for good" over and over again, in one form or another, makes these outcomes any more likely to be realized. Notwithstanding these cyber pep rallies, the fine old Scottish verdict "Not Proven" would seem the more sensible conclusion about such proclamations of imminent victory. But to say this, or even think it, is simply to demonstrate how out of sync one is with the spirit of the age.

Gates and those who share his view point to the fact that famine does indeed appear to have been conquered, but again, past victories are no guarantee of future ones. Mainstream activists know this, of course, but their rhetoric rarely if ever overlaps with such knowledge. It is tempting to account for this by the fact that the link between optimism and morality has become so well established that even to entertain the possibility of failure is viewed as a moral solecism. Lest this claim seem hyperbolic, consider that in 2012, Dr. Jim Yong Kim, only two months after assuming the leadership of the World Bank and on his first visit to Africa, told an interviewer, "For me, optimism is a moral choice." And he added, "If you are a person who is privileged, has resources, and you go into a situation where you are working with people who are very poor, if you are cynical and pessimistic and negative, that is absolutely deadly for poor people." Two years later, in a speech he gave to Sojourners, a US-based NGO that defines itself as "a national Christian organization committed to faith in action for social justice," Kim was even more categorical. "Optimism," he declared, "is your moral duty in working with the poor."

In fairness, Dr. Kim was only conforming to the political style of the age, one that all but requires chief executives, whether they lead countries, NGOs, philanthropies, the World Bank, or the IMF, to assume the role of "optimist in chief." Kim's insistence that only optimism would do reflects a culture in which it is generally assumed that even good deeds have to be branded and then publicized as if what was being sold was a particular make of car or a fast-food restaurant. After all, when you are selling something, you are not expected to say, "Oh, but then again, our product may not live up to your expectations." Add to that the fact that those in the development world who dumb down their messages in this way believe they are doing so for a great cause, the end of poverty and hunger, and indeed that they must keep things simple anyway in order to engage the general public, which they seem to believe craves uplifting stories rather than reality in all its chastening complexity. There are inward-looking motivations as well, with many believing that to do otherwise, indeed for some even to *think* otherwise, can only demoralize and sow confusion. Given such premises, operational and moral alike, it is easy to see why other, less exuberantly positive stances have come to seem almost morally illicit, and no distinction is made between pessimism and cynicism, optimism and hope, even if in reality they mean very different things.

And hunger *is* confusing. As Jean-Hervé Bradol, the former head of the French section of Médecins Sans Frontières (MSF), has put it, too often when an alert is sounded about hunger, the message "conflates 'those who are hungry' with 'those who are dying of hunger.'"[5] Leaving the propaganda wars to one side for a moment, it is entirely reasonable to be guardedly optimistic about the end of famine. But again, if one can get past the white noise of the millenarian sales pitches, things look very different. Bill Gates is convinced that just as with famine, there will be similarly transformative good news about relieving the suffering of the more than a billion people who are not starving and not suffering from acute malnutrition but still chronically malnourished—that is to say, either don't get enough to eat, or else don't get the essential vitamins and nutrients that human beings, above all very young human beings, need if they are to lead reasonably healthy and productive lives.

So is Bill Gates right to be optimistic, not just about famine but about chronic malnutrition and undernutrition as well? On the positive side of the ledger, the number of chronically malnourished people as a proportion of global population has been diminishing steadily for some time. But if one moves from percentages to actual numbers, one uncovers a very different story. For example, one of the boasts of the development world is that between 1999 and 2010, the levels of absolute poverty have declined from 58 percent to 48 percent in sub-Saharan Africa. The problem with this is that, because of population growth, the actual number of people living on less than $1.25 a day there has increased from 377 million to 414 million, though some very poor countries such as Ghana and Malawi have bucked the trend. What has taken place over the last fifteen years in sub-Saharan Africa reflects a global pattern: a falling rate in most countries in the proportion of poor people and poor households, but an increase in the absolute number of poor people, the poorest of whom were over-whelmingly peasants. Globally, that number rose from 790 million in 2005 to close to 1.2 billion in extreme poverty (as of September 2013). Why, given these data, the MDGs were almost universally considered by those in attendance at the UN General Assembly meeting in September 2013 in New York to have been a triumph is anything but clear, given that for most, though certainly not all, of these hungry people, the best that can be said is that things have gotten no worse.[6]

Meanwhile, income inequality has skyrocketed across the continent, though this is a global phenomenon and not a purely African one. And counterintuitive though it may seem, economic growth does not automatically correlate with poverty reduction. Again, the key statistic that needs always to be kept in mind is that four out of every five poor persons in the world are to be found in middle-income countries like India. Those involved both with the MDGs and in the negotiations over what further goals need to be agreed to after 2015 know this, of course. That is why their supporters are right to insist that the assumptions underlying the MDGs represent a radical improvement in the understanding of the relationship between the economic growth of poor countries and poverty reduction in those countries—and herald new and better development practices worldwide. But at least some of this progress does not stand up very well to closer examination. For example, Ugandan growth rates rose throughout the 1990s and the 2000s, but as British development expert Steve Wiggins has pointed out, while poverty rates did fall in the 1990s, not only did the absolute number of poor Ugandans increase in the 2000s, but "the poor also [got] poorer."[7] It is clearly the assumption of the development mainstream that supports the MDGs that these indicators can and will be turned around, and, given that they are forecasting the end of extreme poverty by 2030, turned around very, very quickly. On past historical form, this does not seem at all likely, but then, those who believe the end of poverty and hunger to be attainable in their own generation sincerely believe themselves to be living in an era of unprecedented technological and, by implication at least (and this is where the antipoverty movement overlaps with the contemporary human rights movement), moral opportunities.

The stark fact is that though much development rhetoric has changed and new concepts have surfaced (most importantly, the idea of resilience, particularly on the part of farmers trying to cope with climate change), sustainability has been at the heart of pro-poor development for several decades at least. But it is not clear why the optimists are so convinced that assuming they are indeed successful in bringing an end to absolute poverty by 2030 (or whatever date they choose to aim for), this implies such gains will endure, that is, will actually be sustainable. For unlike famine, there does not need to be some apocalyptic exogenous event like the nightmare scenario of 4- to 6-degree-Celsius increases in aggregate global temperatures for the problem of chronic malnutrition to deteriorate rapidly. Indeed, a study by the distinguished MIT economist Ben Olken showed, by correlating half a century's worth of weather data, that every 1-degree-Celsius increase in the climate of a poor country over any given year lowered its economic growth by 1.3 percent. In contrast, Olken and his colleagues found that variations in temperature had no significant effect on the economic fortunes of rich countries. If anything, global warming might very well turn out to be a plus in at least some areas of the Global North, assuming, that is, that sea levels do not rise too dramatically.

Even the most sanguine climate change experts agree that a 2-degree-Celsius rise is inevitable, and the pioneering climatologist James Hansen, who heads NASA's Goddard Institute for Space Studies, has concluded that the best outcome the world can now reasonably hope for is a 3-degree-Celsius rise. Of course it is true that growth rates of themselves are in fact a rather inaccurate barometer of a reduction in poverty; food insecurity in poor countries as a general rule is made worse by lowered growth rates, particularly since even with high growth rates, countries that are seeing tremendous population increases must create enormous numbers of new jobs just so as not to regress economically. And for all the triumphalist claims the World Bank made in the first decade of the twenty-first century—not just, as the heading on its website states, "Working for a world free of poverty," but claiming that this goal was in sight—by 2013 even so determinedly optimistic a figure as the bank's president, Dr. Jim Yong Kim, was raising the alarm. "I'm very concerned about the impact of a 2-degree-Celsius-warmer world on Africa," he told an interviewer, "You know, by the 2030s we could see a situation where extreme heat and drought could leave 40 percent of land that's currently used in growing maize incapable of growing maize. Furthermore, the extreme heat is going to destroy the savannah grasslands that are supporting pastoral livelihoods. If we are to have any hope of ending poverty we have to make progress in Africa. If we don't do something about climate change mitigation, we are going to have a very difficult time ending poverty in the world and ending poverty in Africa."[8]

The realization since the middle of the first decade of the new century that what for convenience's sake has come to be called the global food crisis is in reality a crisis of the entire world food system that is inextricably linked in myriad ways to the seeming paradoxes of economic growth in the Global South has certainly not been "poor friendly" in the past in many parts of the developing world and may not become so in the foreseeable future. And looming behind all this stands the unfolding story of global climate change. The environmental movement is often accused of crying wolf. But in the case of climate change, the World Bank itself has all but conceded that the wolf is not so much at the door as padding his way, salivating, toward the master bedroom. The problem is that these admissions seem not to be reflected in the bank's other, far more sanguine pronouncements about the end of poverty. In one speech, Dr. Jim Yong Kim can warn that "we don't have enough food to feed our population, in which cities are inundated with water, and the window is narrow: we've got to take action now."[9] And yet in another speech,[10] Kim could insist that "there is a real opportunity to end extreme poverty within a generation," and then go on to say, as if the end of poverty would almost certainly occur, that "we know that this is not enough," and the bank was also committed to boosting the incomes of the poorest 40 percent of the world's people.

Obviously, the role of Cassandra makes a very bad fit with the job of being president of the World Bank. But given the apocalyptic quality of Kim's rhetoric about climate change, the irenic, sanguine character of his speeches about the end of poverty seem tone-deaf at the very least, no matter how much such confidence was what his audiences may have expected of him. The reality is that it would have been challenge enough to reduce radically the number of very poor people in an economic, political, and now climatic context where their situations were stable. But this is precisely the point: what climate change has done is to make the future conditions that will confront the nations of the world, rich, middle-income, and poor alike, very difficult to determine. And as Kim (in apocalyptic mode) has pointed out, the window is narrow and closing fast. Since no one yet knows just how bad global warming is going to be, the ideas of sustainability and resilience on which so many of the prognostications about the future of development depend themselves acquire a dimension of unreliability, not to say an unreality, that turns near-certainties into contingencies. However good the intentions, forecasting at one moment that humanity is within sight of the "broad, sunlit uplands," the future that Churchill had imagined once Nazism was defeated, and in the next that the boat is about to hit the iceberg if it does not change course immediately, is a mark of confusion, of the failure to grasp the nettle, not of resolve. The insistence that everything is going to be all right is not always as commendable as the early-twenty-first-century consensus makes it out to be.

The sudden onset of the food crisis of 2007–2008 was a stern reminder of this, as it demonstrated just how quickly and how badly wrong things could get for the world's poorest people. It also seemed to give justification to the anxiety, among some activists at least, that despite all the hubristic talk, even if the least likely (and to date, least successful) of the MDGs, that if ensuring environmental sustainability both by maintaining or increasing biodiversity across the world and by actually reversing the loss of global environmental resources, were to be miraculously realized, such hopes were still likely to be wildly overoptimistic. What the global food crisis had done was to drive home the point that the lives of "the bottom billion" are at least as likely to grow very much worse as to improve if nothing serious is done not just about global food supply but also about access to affordable food on the part of the global poor, and global action on climate change that already threatens both availability and access. In a world in which people were less besotted by progress narratives—which is to say in any era before the one that began in the aftermath of World War II—and in which they had not fetishized their hopes, blindly and willfully worshipping at the shrine of their own good intentions, this probably would have seemed obvious. Instead, the global food crisis came as an unalloyed shock, even though, long before the huge price rises of 2007–2008 and their political and economic aftershocks, the decline of famine itself provided strong support for the view that chronic malnutrition and undernutrition had already taken its place as the shame of nations.

How this could have been the case is difficult to fathom. Chronic malnutrition is anything but a stealth phenomenon, at least for anyone who knows what poor people in the Global South actually get to eat every day or, indeed, just pauses to think about what it must mean to try to get enough to eat when your income is two dollars a day or less, which is the norm for the bottom billion. But when most people in the rich world think of hunger specifically, rather than draw a mental picture of poverty more generally, they continue to tend to focus on famine rather than chronic malnutrition.

That is where the needs and priorities of the major international relief agencies have unintentionally played an unhelpful role. For in order to raise quickly the large amounts of money these NGOs require for their work in emergencies, the strategy these groups generally use is to saturate the media in their home countries both to get private and corporate donations and to mobilize public pressure on the leaders of powerful countries to act. This has further occluded the problem of chronic malnutrition, however understandable and well-intended the NGOs' actions generally are, and despite the fact that as, overwhelmingly, people of conscience, they themselves would wish it otherwise.

Even were NGOs to cease emphasizing famine, there are good reasons to doubt that they would have the same success mobilizing public concern about chronic malnutrition. Famine is instantly recognizable even to the most untutored eye. But not only do those suffering from chronic malnutrition rarely die from its effects, at first glance they are often hard to distinguish from those who are properly nourished. The Canadian nutrition expert John Hoddinott, who has focused much of his work on chronic malnutrition in children, has pointed that a child who may be as little as four centimeters shorter than his properly nourished comrades can be tremendously damaged neurophysiologically. And yet, again, unlike famine, this damage is tremendously hard if not impossible to portray visually or describe in a sound bite. Build a school, and you have an instantly understandable story to tell. Make sure a child grows that extra four centimeters, and you have a subject for satisfaction among experts, but not something whose importance can be easily or quickly communicated. Taken together, all of these factors made it easy for chronic malnutrition never to become the priority that it should have been all along, both in the poor countries of the Global South where it mostly occurred and in the donor countries in the Global North.

Throughout history, food has always comprised a far greater share of the family budget of the poor than it has of the rich, and today, in most parts of the world, the gap is greater than ever. The bottom billion spend an average of between 60 and 80 percent of their income on food.[11] In contrast, people in developed countries spend only a fraction of that. In the United States, the proportion actually declined from 19.2 percent in 1945 to a historic low of 10.5 percent in 1997, before beginning to rise at the beginning of the twenty-first century to somewhere between 13 percent and 15 percent,[12] even if it remained the case that the poor in Western Europe and North America still spent a larger proportion of their incomes on food than their prosperous fellow citizens. Starkly put, the rise in food prices in 2007 was somewhere between an annoyance and a problem that was in no way critical for the majority of people in the rich world. In contrast, it was an unalloyed human disaster in many parts of the Global South. Literally hundreds of millions of poor people suddenly found themselves fearing, often with good reason, that not only would they continue to have difficulty getting enough of the right foods, that is, with acceptable levels of calories and nutrients—for most of them, that situation had always marred their lives, and if many were unreconciled to this (realism, not passivity, is the curse of the poorest of the poor), it seems safe to say that few were surprised by it—but also that they would not be able to afford the food they needed to stay alive. For all that distinguishes chronic from acute malnutrition, the line between the two is one that is easily crossed. And in 2007 and 2008 it seemed like a real possibility that people who had already been born into suffering now faced the very real prospect of actually losing their lives. As always, children were the most vulnerable.

Before the crisis, the line taken in mainstream circles had been that while, to be sure, there were some problems in agriculture, no full-blown crisis was in the offing. A 2010 report by Derek Headey and Shenggen Fan, written for the widely respected International Food Policy Research Institute (IFPRI), stated candidly that, "with the benefit of hindsight, the causes of [crisis] are increasingly clear."[13] And that was precisely the point: as Headey and Fan conceded, it was *only* with hindsight that such admirable clarity had become available, since, as they put it, the crisis "took most observers by surprise, even most experts." If not false, this was true only if by "most observers," the authors meant most mainstream observers and experts. It is a measure of the distance between the mainstream food establishment, even in its most enlightened iterations such as IFPRI, and critics of the global food system, such as the Filipino sociologist Walden Bello, who had been warning of the possibility of just such an outcome for almost two decades. But until the 2007–2008 crisis, there had been little if any dialogue between the critics and the mainstream. The gap was simply too wide to be bridged. Despite protestations of the food establishment to the contrary, it is anything but clear that anything has changed since then.

In the aftermath of the crisis, both sides claim to understand now why prices shot up so suddenly. The problem is that for the most part, their accounts are largely incompatible, even including the date that the crisis started, which many activists believe was in 2006, a year earlier than the date that is commonly given in the media. For the activists, food is quite simply a right, and they categorically reject the idea that global market forces should determine how, in what quantities, of what type, and for what market farmers should produce their food. Instead, they usually insist that these market forces and mechanisms caused the crisis in the first place. In contrast, while those who accept the mainstream view are eager to find ways to guarantee food security for the world's rural poor, they insist that in an age of globalization, states and international institutions, working in tandem not just with "traditional" relief and development NGOs but also with multinational corporations, can fulfill this goal. Without the commitment of the private sector, they insist, progress will certainly come much more slowly, and the risk even exists that it will not come at all. And without new technology, there could be no enduring end to hunger. At a 2008 conference on Global Food Systems sponsored by the institution he leads, Jeffrey Sachs insisted that historically throughout the world this had been the only way to bring the poor out of poverty. The position was summed up in a speech that UN secretary general Ban Ki-moon delivered to a group of international business executives at the Rio+20 summit on the environment in late June of 2012, when he said that there could be no sustainable economic development without their "resources, technology, innovation, and engagement."

· 5 ·

The Global Food System and Its Critics

The existing food system has never been without its critics, above all critics of the central role of big business. To their credit, whether or not the solutions they offered were as effective as they believed them to be, the activists who opposed the status quo, many though not all of whom were aligned at least to some extent with either the environmental or the antiglobalization movement (or both), had been sounding the alarm about hunger long before 2007. It was they and not their mainstream intellectual and political adversaries who had tried to persuade anyone who would listen that the system was broken. But despite some desultory efforts at dialogue by mainstream figures, notably James Wolfensohn when he was head of the World Bank and Rajiv Shah when, in pre-USAID days, he was in charge of the Gates Foundation's agriculture programs, these anxieties were met largely with either indifference or outright hostility from the major global financial institutions that fund development in the poor world, above all the World Bank and the International

72

Monetary Fund (IMF), and among policy makers in Western Europe, North America, and Japan, which in 2007 together still accounted for 90 percent of official government development aid. To the establishment, the critics were not being "constructive," which in a sense was true, since the critics were not interested in contributing their brains, expertise, and experience to strengthening a system they believed bore responsibility for the crisis in the first place. For them, this was what in the business world is known as "brainstorming," not criticism.

What the mainstream wanted was for the critics to collaborate with them in engineering reforms that would prevent the crisis from recurring or at least find ways of protecting poor farmers and poor consumers alike from the worst effects of sharp price rises and of price volatility. For the most part, the establishment view was that there was no need for further debate about ethical and political first principles because consensus on those had already been reached. As Jeffrey Sachs put it in the concluding section of *The End of Poverty*, "[The present generation's] breathtaking opportunity [is] to be able to advance the Enlightenment vision of Jefferson, [Adam] Smith, Kant, and Condorcet."[1] Given the sweeping, quasi-religious nature of these claims—at another point in his book, Sachs speaks of the duty of the present generation being "to heal the world"[2]—the observation by Gilbert Rist, Swiss historian of development, that "[St. Augustine's] philosophy of history [took the form of] a history of salvation"[3] would seem appropriately applied to Sachs as well.

Sachs's view, though expressed in his characteristically florid terms, largely reflected the mainstream consensus: these Enlightenment ideals were morality enough; the system needed to be reformed, sometimes radically, and governments needed to play a far more active role in setting the rules that would allow a humane globalization to flourish, but there was absolutely no reason to try to dream up alternatives to it. And Sachs was curtly dismissive of the critics' opposition to globalization, which he called "passé."[4] Sachs did, albeit somewhat condescendingly, laud the antiglobalization campaigners for having the "right moral fervor and ethical viewpoint," but he reproached them for their "knee-jerk antipathy to capitalism."[5] They were quite simply wrong to see Microsoft as part of the problem rather than what he believed it was: part of the solution. The reason for this was quite simple: they were "too pessimistic about the possibilities of capitalism with a human face, in which the remarkable power of trade and investment can be harnessed while acknowledging and addressing limitations through compensatory collective actions."[6] Unsurprisingly, Marx's name does not even appear in the index of *The End of Poverty*.

It is ironic that Sachs uses the term "capitalism with a human face" since the expression, whether employed with regard to capitalism or any other ideology, is meant to convey the idea of a mask behind which exists the deeper and more odious essential reality. Far from believing there was much common ground to be found, most critics of the mainstream food establishment believed that collaboration was pointless. Instead, beginning in the 1980s and gathering force in the 1990s, they had joined with peasant and small farmers' groups determined to resist the encroachment of global agribusiness. The most notable of these was Via Campesina, an international association of peasant organizations that was founded in 1993. Rejecting what Sachs called "enlightened globalization," the only kind of global food system that these groups believed to be acceptable was one that was utterly incompatible with the mainstream view. For even assuming that all the reforms being discussed by groups like the Consultative Group on International Agricultural Research (CGIAR) and IFPRI at USAID, and the British government's Department for International Development (DFID), and within the UN system were actually implemented, the critics, for whom the end state had always been a postcapitalist global system, would have at most conceded this to have been a positive beginning to what needed to be eventually transformed into something far more radical. What was needed, they insisted, was not only a revolution in the mechanics of the global food system but a transformation of its political and ethical underpinnings as well. And they rejected the mainstream's engineering model, insisting instead, in Walden Bello's words, on "the inseparability of economic organization, technology, equity and sustainability."[7]

This mutual incomprehension on first principles was inseparable from the disagreement between the mainstream and its critics on the practical keys to curbing hunger among the world's poor, especially its rural poor. The establishment was focused on what came to be called food security. It was hardly a new idea. For as Olivier de Schutter, the Belgian lawyer who had succeeded the Swiss writer and activist Jean Ziegler as the UN's special rapporteur for food in May 2008, had noted in a 2011 report, "Since the 1960s, food has been linked largely to production," and he pointed to an overemphasis in the development world on "increasing agricultural outputs and lowering food prices, while scant attention was paid to ensuring the availability and accessibility of a wide range of diverse foods"[8] that children needed to thrive and that adults needed to be able to lead healthy, productive lives. As de Schutter readily acknowledged, the mainstream of the global food system was increasingly aware of this problem and trying to reconfigure programs accordingly. But as de Schutter also pointed out, the productivist model had only been modified, it had not been abandoned. "Increasing future food production to meet future needs," he wrote, "while necessary, is not sufficient."[9] Instead he proposed what had come to be known as "agroecology," which focused on the diversification of agriculture rather than the productivist model of its intensification, moving away from focusing on individual plant species to concentrate instead on "interactions and productivity across the agricultural system."[10]

De Schutter was correct in discerning a measure of progress in the development establishment's increasing focus on initiatives that would ensure decent incomes for farmers, above all for smallholders, even if the concept of food security itself could be challenged as being far too binary (food security as the solution to food insecurity). In contrast, the issue of *where* the food would be produced, whether it would be imported, and whether poor countries would be able to exercise any form of substantive sovereignty within the context of the global food system remained not just unanswered but, from the establishment's point of view, also not really worth being asked. Perhaps sovereignty, too, was passé. Jeffrey Sachs gave every evidence of thinking so when he called on the antiglobalization movement to become a "pro-globalization movement," advocates, as he put it, for "the kind of globalization championed by the Enlightenment—a globalization of democracies, multilateralism, science and technology, and an economic system designed to meet human needs."[11] The problem, of course, was that for the antiglobalization movement, the one thing that capitalism was not and could never be was a global system that could adequately meet human needs.

But neither side doubted that these needs could be met, assuming, that is, that their respective prescriptions were adapted—the mainstream's "let's try everything, and see what works and what doesn't approach," and the critics' mix of agroecology and political transformation. If they were heeded, each side claimed, then it should be possible to feed adequately not just a global population of nine billion but probably as many as one or two billion more people, whom a minority of demographers believed would be added before a demographic leveling off in the late twenty-first or, worst case, the early twenty-second century. To be sure, there were advocates on both sides who warned that there needed to be significant changes in the human diet, above all a radical diminution in the amount of meat people consumed, in order for the response to the enormous surge in global population to be successful. But in the words of David Cleveland, an environmental expert whose book *Balancing on a Planet: The Future of Food and Agriculture* is one of the most reasoned and thoughtful analyses from the viewpoint of a critic of the system, reducing consumption and changing what is consumed will likely be successful "only as part of a larger revolution in the way the world thinks about and moves toward sustainability, recognizing the limits to human carrying capacity [of the earth] and rejecting the double oxymoron of sustainable green growth."[12]

But while Jeffrey Sachs might tax antiglobalization activists for failing sufficiently to understand and appreciate the humanism of Adam Smith, the idea that any version of capitalism, no matter how enlightened itself and intelligently and effectively regulated by governments to force even the most recalcitrant among them to conduct their business in a way that would benefit humanity, could ever be so transformed as to be made compatible with a world system that was no longer dedicated to growth seems like quite the oxymoron in its own right. But before any of this came the question of where this food for the seven, the nine, and perhaps the eleven or twelve billion was to come from. Advocates of food security were agnostic on the subject: the food could come from imports anywhere in the world rather than being produced locally; it could be the product of corporate agriculture or of traditional peasant smallholders; and the foodstuffs being sold or distributed could contain GMOs. The criterion for success or failure was simple and straightforward: was adequate nutrition being provided and were farmers, especially smallholder farmers, earning enough to live with dignity? There was talk about good governance, anticorruption efforts, and the like, but these were clearly still subordinate (but important) questions in the minds of those who had developed the idea of food security.

For the critics, though, the mainstream position that it was possible to meet the needs of the poor and the hungry adequately without calling into question the social, political, and economic status quo was at best the purest wishful thinking and more likely needed to be understood as providing a form of "humanitarian" cover for the multinationals to dominate completely those areas of the global food system over which they did not already exercise control. The critics' analysis of the reforms being proposed by mainstream institutions was caustic and unbending. In its 2013 annual report, the Food First Information and Action Network (FIAN), which was one of the most knowledgeable and sophisticated activist groups, took on the mainstream's push for food security directly, observing that "several schemes related to food, agriculture and nutrition, led by the most powerful countries in the world in close cooperation with corporations, have gained unprecedented influence in recent years."[13] The current system was irredeemable, they insisted, continuing to remain true to the vision first articulated at a forum of food sovereignty groups held in Selingue, Mali, in early 2007, where these activists declared that their movement "offers a strategy to resist and dismantle the current corporate trade and food regime, and directions for food, farming, pastoral and fisheries systems determined by local producers."[14]

But this only presented in harshly negative terms what the mainstream food establishment saw as an essential new innovation that would almost certainly better the lives of the poor and hungry. The way forward, in the food establishment's view, had to involve more and more close collaboration between governments and UN agencies and NGOs on one side and multinational corporations, including fertilizer and seed companies such as Monsanto, Syngenta, and Yara International, on the other. And the more entrenched this view became, the harder it was to draw clear distinctions between the public and private sectors' involvement in the development project. If anything, the fear inside the food establishment was not that what came to be referred to as these public-private partnerships would distort the development project, but rather that in the twenty-first century success was only really likely to come through such cooperation.

Obviously, the food security paradigm advocates had a very different conception of what a new global food system should look like. For them, the food security paradigm that was being proposed only served to buttress what they called "the corporate food regime," which for them was based on large-scale farming in the context of what the mainstream called trade liberalization but which food rights campaigners viewed as a way of perpetuating the fundamental injustices of the current global food system while buttressing its political legitimacy. The real problem, they argued, largely stemmed from the sins of either omission or commission of an unholy trinity of global agribusiness, unchecked speculation on food prices in the world commodities markets, and diversion of food grains in the US to the production of biofuels. On the other side, the international food establishment tends to agree with its critics on biofuels while rather limply talking about the need for some form of regulation of commodity speculation in terms at once so tame and vague, both temporally and in terms of what concretely will be done, that one does not have to be a radical food rights activist to question if not the sincerity then certainly the seriousness of this commitment (as if the rejection of any systematic critique of the past actions of the global agriculture multinationals had not been indication enough).

One cannot credibly claim, as Ban Ki-moon did in Rio, and as did USAID, DFID, the Gates Foundation, and most if not all of the major institutions that make up the global food establishment do with regularity, that without global business there will be no real development and by extension no sustainable further reduction in world poverty, while at the same time insisting that the participation of these multinationals would be alright because these companies would in good faith accept codes of conduct including limitations on their business practices. The reason for this is simple: these companies have a long track record of fighting every regulation that parliaments and governments attempted to impose on them, while relying on highly paid lobbyists to prevent such measures from ever being proposed in the first place. But suddenly, with regard to the poor world, these same corporations were going to comport themselves in a wildly different, hyperresponsible manner? It hardly seemed likely.

To resurrect the old line of the onetime Black Panther militant Eldridge Cleaver, by and large the agricultural multinationals are now hailed, as Jeffrey Sachs did with regard to Microsoft in *The End of Poverty*, as being an essential part of the solution rather than as part of the problem, as the activists believe they are. As the FIAN report put it tartly, "The new precept in international affairs appears to be that no major development project can be carried out without the active participation of major corporations and their front foundations/agencies, often in the form of Private-Public Partnerships (PPP). There is an urgent need to question this trend as it should be clear to everyone that the interests of corporations do not always align with public interests.[15] Of course, that "everyone" includes virtually no one in the mainstream of the food system nor anyone who sees food security as the best answer to chronic malnutrition and undernutrition. Those holding such views tend to take as a matter of fact the good intentions of most international corporations, up to and including the seed and fertilizer giants such as Monsanto and Syngenta, whom the food sovereignty activists revile. It is an argument on which there is virtually no prospect of finding common ground. But for the sake of argument, put the case that groups such as Via Campesina and FIAN are largely correct and that the multinational corporations are the core of the problem. Then posit further that radical social change that breaks corporate monopolies (in so doing, ushering in a global system where profit is not the first priority) is the only viable long-term solution. And finally, go yet one step further and accept that Walden Bello was correct when he wrote that "even as the old [food] system unravels, alternative modes of agricultural production are alive, and offer the prospect of sufficient food for people along with equity and ecological sustainability."[16] The fact remains that in the second decade of the twenty-first century, these alternatives have not taken root widely enough, as even most activists would concede, or at least not so widely as to constitute a sufficient response to the current crisis of the global food system. In other words, even assuming Bello is right, and the agricultural status quo really is unraveling, it is not doing so fast enough to manumit the activists from the messy business of striking compromises with the food establishment, even if those critics view such negotiations as stopgap measures and, even while engaging in them, continue to struggle to bring the current global food system crashing down for good. And whatever one's sympathies, the reality is that at least as far as the general public is concerned, neither side has succeeded in definitively winning the argument (except in their own minds, of course). In contrast, what each side has been quite adept at has been pointing out the limitations and blind spots of their adversaries' explanations. The establishment is surely on firm ground when it points out that the activists' diagnosis, while long on broad criticisms of the capitalist system, pays insufficient attention to a range of more proximate causes. These include the long-term underinvestment in agricultural development in the poor world finally exacting its toll on food security, and the rise in global oil prices, followed by volatile price swings, that have had the effect of upping the price of petroleum-based fertilizers and which most agricultural production in the Global North and a rising percentage—this itself had always been the subject of acrimonious debate between the two sides—of the agriculture of the Global South as well. For their part, food rights campaigners have successfully challenged the assumption that the mainstream takes as its point of departure, which is that there is a broad-based global political consensus about what to do and how to do it. To put it another way, the activists have exposed both the extent to which the mainstream view is technocratic—an engineer's view of the world rather than a moralist's—and the degree to which this technocratic mind-set is inseparable from the belief that the world has entered a postpolitical age.

In fairness, Jeffrey Sachs is an exception to this. At the same 2008 Earth Institute conference where he used (or abused) his privilege as a convener to give a closing speech heaping scorn on those participants who view capitalism as being to blame for the crisis of the global food system, he also insisted that the "markets could care less about the [poorest of the poor], because these are people who have nothing. It doesn't mean capitalism is their enemy, it means it couldn't care less."[17]

The gap between the two viewpoints could hardly be wider. The food security template rests on the assumption, sometimes made explicitly, sometimes not, that liberal capitalism is really the only morally and practically licit ideological stance: in other words, the view that treats the public-private partnerships that FIAN warned against as an immense enhancement of the world's collective ability to reduce poverty and hunger. The food sovereignty template rests on a countervailing position that holds the present time has ushered in neither the end of history nor the end of ideology. For those hold this view, food security does nothing to mitigate what the FIAN report calls the perpetuation of "social exclusion [and] discrimination" that in fact "generate hunger, particularly in rural communities."[18]

Such "meta-questions" are hugely significant, and it is one of the most important intellectual weaknesses of the mainstream view that it only very rarely and grudgingly even acknowledges that these are issues worth considering. In the words of the authors of an important 2014 Australian study, "Taking Complexity in Food Systems Seriously"—a paper that unlike most work taken seriously in mainstream circles, treated the critics' views seriously and with respect— "Even when accessible and credible, [the critics' political/ecological] analysis and findings diverge too radically from mainstream development thought and practice, and thus its knowledge cannot usefully guide food security development interventions." They added that "as a counter narrative that contains zero-sum game thinking," these critiques would "always struggle for salience."[19] In fact, what adherents of the mainstream view have generally attempted to do is to contrast the critics, whom they dismiss as mere ideologues, with those like themselves who want to roll up their sleeves and start coming up with solutions to poverty and hunger. As Jeffrey Sachs put it, the critics had "a certain tendency to view issues as blame issues and also a tremendous, really profound simplification of what a market economy is, that leads to a great deal of rhetoric." And he added, "There are many, many tools that exist to combine a market economy with life, equity, environmental sustainability that we're talking about. . . . We could do with a little less of the rhetoric and more with the problem solving and the incentive structures."[20]

In the context of such unyielding disagreement, there is at least the consolation that there is no debate over the results of the crisis:

there, at least, hindsight has indeed been 20/20. In a very short span of time, the radical rise in the price of food staples led to a dramatic rise in the number of hungry people in the world. By most estimates, rising prices and, even after they had reached their acme, continuing price volatility, swelled the ranks of the truly hungry by between 130 and 150 million. Perhaps the symbolism can be overstated; nonetheless it is surely worth noting that at the height of the crisis in 2008, for the first time in human history, the numbers of chronically undernourished surpassed the billion mark. Unsurprisingly, most of them lived in countries with the highest number of what development economists have dubbed "the ultra poor," by which they mean the 160 million human beings—the overwhelming majority of whom live in sub-Saharan Africa—trying to survive on less than fifty cents a day. This certainly did not mean that "the medial poor" (those earning fifty to seventy-five cents) and "the poor" (those living on somewhere between seventy-five cents and one US dollar) were not also in grave danger, with pregnant and lactating women and their children in the most dangerous and urgent situation of all.

Like the feminization of poverty generally, this feminization of hunger had long been understood by relief and development workers, and for that matter, was regularly paid lip service at UN conferences and by senior officials from the major donor governments of the Global North. But the global food crisis exacerbated a malign trend that largely predated it. And, at least at the height of the crisis, it seemed as if the need to address it quickly and in a systematic way was finally beginning to be treated with at least some of the urgency that it of course had always deserved but up to that point had rarely been granted. Ministerial meetings followed one after the other, notably the Rome Food Summit of September 2008 and the so-called High Level Ministerial Meeting on Food Security for All, held in Madrid in January 2009. There was even some discussion, much of it animated by Olivier de Schutter, over whether food was best thought of as a basic human right and therefore the only enduring way to reform the food system was to view hunger in human-rights terms. Given the track record of most international conferences, even the fact that some concrete measures were enacted in the aftermath of these meetings was testimony to how seriously the food crisis was finally being taken. The Food and Agriculture Organization's Global Information and Early Warning System (GIEWS), established during the food crisis of the 1970s, was given an increased mandate and gained a measure of institutional visibility that had been so long denied it. But these are comparatively minor reforms if one considers how grave the threats really are that are posed by the global food crisis. And whether or not the powerful actors follow through on their promises to act coherently and seriously to address the crisis (as they failed to do in the aftermath of the 1970s crisis) or, as food activists predicted at the time, they prove to be no more prepared to follow through on their promises this time than they were previously (something recent international meetings like the Rio+20 conference, not to mention meetings of the G20 in the aftermath of the euro crisis, which effectively marginalized development issues, would seem to confirm), two things are clear: the fears the global food crisis engendered at the time were more than warranted, and the existential threat it continues to pose to the fate of literally hundreds of millions of people has not abated. To the contrary, there was a strong surge upward in food prices in 2010–2011, although fortunately it did not turn into the perfect storm of factors that made the 2007–2008 crisis so disastrous for the global poor, with damaging effects of the price rises of food staples compounded by export bans and other measures that the British food and development researcher, Alex Evans, has rightly described as a zero-sum game between nations.

Despite this new, sharper focus on the global food system, however, it is difficult to envisage, absent a vast catastrophe such as the reemergence of famine in Asia or the unexpected success of political and social revolution that is the core of the prescription of many activists, what might impel the mainstream institutions with the power to shape events to undertake a truly radical reconstruction of the global food system. But it is a catch-22. For unless the system is comprehensively reformed, it is virtually certain that price spikes in agricultural staples will become regular occurrences. Indeed, the question that remains to be answered is not whether these price spikes will occur but rather how severe they will be and how effectively the global food system will cope with them. After the 2008 financial crisis, Mohammed El-Erian, then the co-chairman of the enormous Pimco investment company, predicted that investors would have to get used to what he called "a new normal" of little economic growth, comparatively high levels of unemployment, and far lower rates of return on their money than those to which investors had become accustomed over the previous several decades. By analogy, the new normal of the global food system is likely to be one in which sharp and at times sudden price rises become the global norm, while at a more basic level, the general trend of food prices will be upward. These grim realities and the risk of even grimmer future possibilities comprise one side of the ledger. Again, while the situation is serious, it is not without at least some hopeful signs. Many of the more radical food activists, committed as they are not to reforming but, in the words of Annie Shattuck and Eric Holt-Giménez, "transforming" the global food system, would doubtless dismiss this as a case of rearranging the deck chairs on the *Titanic*. But for those more sympathetic to the idea of reform rather than revolution, the fact that agriculture had once again become a central element in all reputable thinking about development represented a crucial first step, even though obviously this did not guarantee that the right solutions could be agreed upon or, even if they were, that sufficient political will existed to put them into practice.

Still, for the first time since the Green Revolution in Asia of the 1960s and 1970s, when food security for the hungry of the world was not just an ethical but a strategic priority for the American and Soviet empires—development officials serving in President Dwight Eisenhower's administration believed "where hunger goes, Communism follows"—agricultural questions in general and the problem of chronic malnutrition specifically engage both the great powers that provide the bulk of development assistance to the poor world and the international financial institutions, above all the World Bank, which have had such an outsized role in the politics of development since their establishment in the aftermath of the Second World War. Researchers at mainstream institutions such as the International Food Policy Research Institute (IFPRI) and the Consultative Group on International Agricultural Research (CGIAR) are being listened to—perhaps still not sufficiently, but to an unprecedented degree. To be sure, the record is mixed. In a report written for the UK's Overseas Development Institute (ODI), Steve Wiggins has praised the international response to the 2007–2008 crisis as "remarkable and admirable for its size and urgency,"[21] but at the same time insisted that the effectiveness of the response had been mixed. But this does not detract from how important it is that the global food system has once again become a "first-rank" issue in world affairs.

Anyone watching the seeming incapacity of American and European governments and the international financial institutions to follow through on the measures they adopted during and in the immediate aftermath of the systemic crisis in finance capital that began with the events that led to the collapse of Lehman Brothers in 2008 would probably have dismissed the suggestion that the food crisis would continue to be addressed in a serious way once the prices of staples began to decline in 2009. After all, the financial crisis, if not checked, posed an existential threat to the economic prosperity of the Global North, whereas despite its knock-on effect, the global food crisis had largely left the rich world unscathed, even as it devastated the Global South. But while food activists are on solid ground when they complain that not enough is being done, the focus on global agriculture by major Western donors, the World Bank and the IMF, and major philanthropies since the events of 2007–2008 has not followed the earlier pattern of the raising of the global alarm, followed by relief that the crisis seemed to have passed, followed by neglect. To point to this welcome break from past practices is not the same thing as claiming that there is no cause for continued skepticism. Much of the explanation for the continued attention paid to the food crisis and to the possibility of its recurring regularly in the decades to come is that there is a consensus among policy makers across the world that such an eventuality is politically dangerous. One does not have to be terribly prescient to understand that people tend to grow restive when confronted by the real possibility that they will soon no longer be able to afford to feed themselves and their children.

The mass protests that erupted in sixty-three countries where the effects of price rises were particularly severe and that led to riots in twenty-one of them (and not only in destitute countries such as Haiti and Yemen but also in middle-income countries like Mexico) were proof of this and were rightly perceived as having the potential for being hugely destabilizing. And although in most of the major food exporting countries there were far fewer episodes of civil unrest (though there were some), nonetheless there was near-panic politically. The most common response in these countries was to try to reverse the (potentially socially explosive) rise in domestic food prices by curbing exports, while food-importing countries desperately tried to build their dwindling stocks by reducing tariffs on imported food staples. Although this was obviously not what policy makers in either exporting or importing countries had intended, these actions only made the problem worse. As Alex Evans put it in the authoritative paper that he did for Chatham House called "The Feeding of the Nine Billion," "The net effect of both sets of actions, however, was to increase world prices still further as increased demand met reduced supply."[22] The leaders of several Asian countries considered going further and gave serious consideration to an idea that had floated around for years among policy makers in the region about forming a rice cartel on the model of OPEC in order to ensure national food security. That same priority led to either the imposition of outright export bans or the raising of punitively high tariffs on essential foodstuffs by many of the main food-exporting countries, whether the staple in question was rice (Indonesia, China, Brazil, and Vietnam) or wheat (Argentina, Ukraine, and Russia). The crisis may not have been the beginning of the "imminent disaster scenario" that the food rights activists Eric Holt-Giménez and Raj Patel warned of in their book, *Food Rebellion: Crisis and the Hunger for Justice.* But one does not need to endorse all of Holt-Giménez's and Patel's views to be convinced that the crisis sowed real fear about how high prices would get before they eased and even more about what the political effects were likely to be.

As a result, however unwelcome it must have been, the realization began to dawn in the rich world that perhaps the more alarmist claims of the antiglobalization movement had not, in fact, been so alarmist after all. For example, the movement had been correct in warning that diverting corn produced in the American Midwest from its traditional uses as a foodstuff for both human beings and livestock to make ethanol for fuel would lead to a diminution of the global food supply and that this in turn would inevitably lead to a dramatic rise in food prices all along the length of the food chain in those parts of the world dependent on corn, which in practical terms meant any country where meat was an important part of daily diets. Perhaps this should have been obvious, and in fairness, as Hilary Benn, the former British government minister for international development, pointed out somewhat bitterly, some of the same NGOs that began to decry biofuels in the early 2000s had demanded in the 1990s that what was then widely seen as a clean-energy alternative to continued reliance on the use of fossil fuels be rapidly adopted.

But by the same token, surely it should have been obvious to European policy makers during the Maastricht Treaty negotiations that led to the adoption of the euro that a common currency without some form of financial union was doomed to failure. And it is surely not too extreme to insist that European and, for that matter, American policy makers certainly cared more about the euro, had thought more about it, and had more riding on its success than they did about the nutritional needs of the poor of the Global South. At least with the euro, many who had been part of its creation understood from the start that to be viable, at some point or another it had to lead to further economic union on the continent. But the food crisis had not been predicted and, in systemic terms, it seemed to raise the specter of starvation in more than a few developing countries even in Asia, where the supposed rising tide of globalization that was going to "lift all boats" has been most successful. Most menacingly of all, an increasing consensus among development experts, agronomists, economists, UN officials, and on Wall Street, in the Chicago commodities pits, and in the City of London that the century-long era of not just comparatively cheap food but steadily declining food prices as a percentage of family budgets was ending for the foreseeable future meant that, in a sense, the crisis was primordial—the return of hunger to center stage in a globalized world in which it had been assumed, and by no means in a Pollyana-ish or thoughtless way, that it had become or at least was becoming a bit player. Of course, informed people understood perfectly well that the prospect of starvation would for some time still be present in some places, above all in sub-Saharan Africa in the Sahel region, where the expansion of the desert continued steadily to consume vast swathes of agricultural land (a process that there is no evidence to suggest will abate in the foreseeable future). To that extent, at least, it was generally agreed that finding a way of at least mitigating the effects of what was taking place would be very difficult. But the conventional thinking was that globally the problem was likely to diminish over time in much the way polio has become more and more confined to a few poor countries and is slowly being eradicated even there. Whether such confidence was warranted or not was a different matter entirely. But in an age where the prospect of infinite progress, above all technological progress, was widely understood to be a certainty, not just a possibility, that was a thought so unwelcome that in both mainstream and food rights circles alike, it was almost always rejected out of hand.

· 6 ·

Promises to the Poor

The expression "crisis breeds opportunity" has become such a cliché that on those rare occasions when it has some basis in fact, there is something almost unlikely about it. But by any measure, the global food crisis of 2007–2008 was just such an occasion. The price of food staples had begun to fall again at the end of 2008. In the past, that would have been the end of it. The attention that the crisis had commanded would have been redirected elsewhere, and once more the vulnerabilities of the world's food system would have been left unaddressed. But what had happened in 2007 had been so alarming, and the consensus that similar price spikes in the future were probably unavoidable was so general that this time the international response had staying power. The crisis had finally exposed the fragility of the global food system in ways that simply could no longer be denied or avoided. It seemed that at long last the days of relegating agricultural questions to the status of something between the anachronism and the afterthought that they had been in the official development policies of the World Bank and the IMF, the UNDP, and the major Western donor governments since at least the late 1970s had gone for good. But how this system was to be reformed, assuming, that is, it could be reformed at all, was nowhere near as clear.

One difficulty was that despite the assurances made by advocates of "innovation," in Bill Gates's sense of the word, and by those in the development world who were convinced that with enough money, brain power, and international commitment, no problem existed that could not be solved, in reality finally understanding the gravity of the threat did not necessarily imply that there was actually a solution, at least, as food activists kept trying to point out, one that was compatible with the world system as it was currently constituted. That said, there can be no doubt that for international institutions like the World Bank and the development agencies of the major Western donors even to forge a new analytic consensus that it had been a mistake on the part of international institutions and the major Western donors to shrink development aid to agriculture from 17 percent in 1980 to 3.8 percent in 2006 was a major step in the right direction.

It would be inaccurate to say that there had been no critical thinking in mainstream circles before the 2007–2008 crisis. And by 2004, some influential people within the food establishment were increasingly distancing themselves from the view accurately summed up in the Gates Foundation's Agricultural Development Strategy Document that the "problem of inadequate food supply had been tackled," and that donors could safely shift their attention to other concerns. That same year, for the first time in more than two decades, there was a small rise in the proportion of official development aid allocated to agriculture—a shift, it should be pointed out, that not just food rights activists but also mainline development NGOs such as Oxfam and World Vision had been demanding for years. Still, it was the events of 2007–2008 that put agriculture back at the heart of the international development agenda. In 2008 and 2009, there were four global summits at which the subject of food security was central and after which $40 billion was pledged both for emergency relief in countries very hard hit by price rises and also price volatility in food staples, but also to "relaunch" investment in the agriculture of the Global South. The question, though, was whether, to paraphrase the title of an authoritative 2009 Oxfam research report, these promises and pledges would be turned into realities on the ground, or whether, as had happened so many times in the past, interest in doing so would eventually evaporate.

In any case, changing donors' attitudes was only part of the battle, since, in fairness, it is not as if between 1980 and 2004 the leaders of many countries in the poor world who were being urged by the bank, the IMF, and the major Western donors to reallocate development monies away from agriculture had taken much persuading. Over the last two decades of the twentieth century, many of these nations had faced severe economic crises. In many cases, this had meant going as supplicants to the bank and the donors. Even had the leaders of these countries objected to the economic policies that were being imposed on them as a condition for further aid, it is unlikely that their voices would have been heeded then, any more than the European Union (EU) and the IMF have heeded the views of the Greeks since the beginning of the government debt crisis in 2010. But what is missing from the narrative of what happened to agricultural development in the poor world in the twenty-five years after 1980 is a recognition that the leaders of poor nations were anything but pure victims of the international system who, left to their own devices, would not have ignored farming as they did. To imagine this would mean ignoring the extent to which the recommendations from the international donors fit comfortably with the viewpoints of local elites that had come to power in the aftermath of decolonization of the 1950s and 1960s. Despite a few notable exceptions, these elites were urban rather than rural. And when these same urban elites took power after their countries won their independence, not only did almost nothing change for the better in this regard, there was much that changed for the worse, with the result that income disparities between peasants and city dwellers grew wider and wider over the course of the first four decades after decolonization.

Could it have been different? The Australian economist D. A. Low has argued in a brilliant small book called *The Egalitarian Moment* that while decolonization in many parts of the world put an end to formal landlordism, what followed was not more egalitarian rural regimes but rather new economic forms that perpetuated the injustices of the colonial and, indeed, in many cases of the precolonial era. Low does not make this claim explicitly, but the logic of his argument strongly suggests that the failure of the new ruling elites to seize a historic opportunity to commit themselves to land reform was a huge factor in the subsequent economic failure of a great many developing countries. Instead, following independence, the political elite reinforced the unequal distribution of resources and of political power that had been the hallmark of colonial times. If anything, "homegrown" attacks on smallholder agriculture in many countries, notably in parts of Nigeria, Ghana, parts of Sudan, and Kenya, had been the norm long before the World Bank and the IMF imposed their draconian economic and social remedies on the Global South. As another Australian critic of development, Colin Leys, has put it, this process has been characterized by "the use of state power by emerging native capitalist classes to acquire land for capitalist [that is to say, large-scale] farming." Combine the international donors' economic theories with urban African elites' economic interests, and one begins to see why so-called "pro-poor growth"[1] policies have been so difficult to attain.

To mobilize another cliché, hindsight is indeed 20/20. But if anything should have been obvious at the time, it should have been that national growth and pro-poor growth are not the same thing. And yet it took until the 1990s, that is, forty years after the

European colonial empires had begun to crumble and the so-called development ideology first emerged, largely in response to this imperial collapse, for it to finally sink in that, counterintuitive though it may have been, increasing the economic growth rates of poor countries did not in fact correlate very well with reducing poverty in those countries. In fairness, the rapid pace of industrialization of many parts of the developing world and the mass migration of rural people to the mega-cities of the Global South has continued to accelerate relentlessly. For the first time in human history, more people now live in cities than in the countryside, thus recapitulating on a global scale what occurred in Europe in the nineteenth and twentieth centuries. And since urbanization—crudely put, the move from premodern agricultural society to a modern urban and industrial one—has historically been considered to be a sine qua non of progress out of poverty, this favoring of the urban over the rural seemed to make moral as well as economic sense and made agriculture—especially labor-intensive, smallholder agriculture, which is conventionally defined as farmers who work pieces of land measuring a maximum of ten hectares but far more often consisting of plots of one or two hectares and sometimes even less—a stepping stone for most people to a better life off the land.

This belief that pro-poor policies would also have to be in large measure pro-urban policies helps to explain why, for so long, development specialists managed to underestimate the critical importance of smallholder farming. And even today, many of those who have been most concerned with agriculture in the poorest parts of the world are adamant that the traditional smallholder farming methods are grossly insufficient to cope with the needs of a world of seven billion, let alone of ten or eleven billion. Only technology, they argue, can do this, a view that is now the conventional wisdom of government development agencies like USAID and DFID, of philanthropies like Gates and Rockefeller, of the global network of food research institutes, and of much, though not all, of the UN system.

As Jeffrey Sachs put it, "The way we got out of poverty generally in the world has been through new science and new technology."[2]

But despite the huge jump in the proportion of city dwellers in the countries of the Global South since the era of decolonization, agriculture remains at the heart of both the economies and the cultures of a great many countries in the poor world. In sub-Saharan Africa, well over half the total population—almost five hundred million people out of nearly nine hundred million—live in rural areas, and agriculture employs 65 percent of the total labor force. Globally, smallholder agriculture—in addition to the pastoralists who tend herds of no more than ten cattle or sheep—today supports almost two billion people globally, that is, two out of every seven human beings alive today, and in particular remains the "backbone" of African agriculture.

But the conventional wisdom in the aid and development world through the 1980s seems to have been that there was not much that either national governments or international donors could do to reform smallholder agriculture. In particular, the state was emphatically not viewed as having a central role in finding a solution. Indeed, the reigning consensus was that one of the root causes of the economic difficulties in which so many nations in the poor world found themselves was that historically states had intervened too much. Examples of this included setting exchange rates too high for agriculture, particularly agricultural exports, to be profitable, and competing with the private sector through marketing boards, high tariffs on imports, and other forms of excessive regulation. The argument was that had African governments in particular not insulated their economies from the working of global markets, they would already have become much more prosperous. And much was made at the World Bank and the IMF of the comparison with Asian countries, whose prosperity was identified as being due in large measure to the trade liberalization regimes they had adopted. In one influential 1996 paper, Jeffrey Sachs and Andrew Warner claimed that "Africa could have achieved per capita growth of 4.3 percent per annum if it had followed fast-growth policies," growth, they argued, that if sustained would have led to real incomes doubling every sixteen years. But instead, in the words of the economist Judith Dean, whom Sachs and Warner quote approvingly in their paper, "Only in Africa do we find little progress toward a liberalized trade regime. Here there have been important cases of reversal of policy, no liberalization, or increased export impediments." But Sachs and Warner insisted that there was no cause for pessimism about African economies because where what they called such "serious pro-growth reforms" had been undertaken, African countries had "achieved impressive growth rates."[3]

Not everyone was so sanguine, and one certainly did not have to be an "Afropessimist" to disagree. Instead, critics of the reigning consensus in the development world in the 1980s and early 1990s argued passionately that sub-Saharan Africa's weak position in the global trading system meant that the adoption of such wide-ranging free-trade policies could only lead to disaster. Far from setting the stage for more prosperity, the more these markets were opened, they predicted, the more unfavorable Africa's position was likely to become and the more damage would be done to African economies. For these critics, it was utopian footling to suggest that African farmers could soon match the rich world in financial resources, technology, or infrastructure, whether on the national level (roads, ports, bridges, etc.) or in the context of individual farms. Given these realities, a far likelier outcome was the further immiseration and marginalization of Africa's rural smallholders, while the most important enduring effect of trade liberalization was the creation of new markets for the agricultural producers of the Global North.

In a report published in 2010 in the *Proceedings of the National Academy of Sciences*, the Oregon State geoscientist Laurence Becker summed up this line of argument. At the root of reforms, he suggested, was the demand by the international donors that poor farmers view the removal of state-sponsored support systems as an opportunity "to compete with some of the most efficient agricultural systems in the world." And about that possibility, "A truly free market does not exist in this world," Becker said. "We don't have one, but we tell hungry people in Africa that they are supposed to."[4] On this, he was on solid historical ground. As the Cambridge University development economist Ha-Joon Chang has put it: "Country after successful country, from the 18th century Britain to the late 20th century South Korea and Taiwan, have first used various policy measures (trade protection included in most, although not all, cases) to create the space in which their producers can build up their productive capabilities before they can compete with better producers from abroad, either in the domestic market or in the export market."

Chang has focused much of his research on the South Korean case. In 1961, South Korea's per capita income was $82, half that of Ghana. Given South Korea's subsequent success, Chang asks, why has there been such "intolerance for those 'nationalistic' policies used by Korea in the past, on the part of the rich countries and multilateral institutions," particularly given the fact that while the United States became what Chang calls the "standard bearer of free trade in the recent past," America was one of if not the most protectionist global economy between the US Civil War and 1945?[5] Chang's most perceptive intellectual adversaries, notably Martin Wolf, a former World Bank official who is now the chief economics commentator for the *Financial Times*, have argued that overthrowing the neoliberal consensus and replacing it with South Korean (or, indeed, nineteenth- and early twentieth-century American) protectionism is no more likely to be a surefire recipe for economic development and poverty reduction than pure free-market-based policies have been, an argument that Chang accepts to a considerable extent. But even with this caveat, and no matter how well intended such a prescription may have been (activists too often mistakenly conflate malign intentions with malign effects), it would be difficult to make the case that the results have been other than disastrous.

The brute statistics speak for themselves. As a 2012 FAO report pointed out, "In 1980, Africa had an almost balanced agricultural trade when both agricultural exports and imports were at about USD 14 billion, but by 2007 its agricultural imports exceeded agricultural exports by USD 22 billion."[6] This increase in food imports had been disproportionately concentrated in basic foodstuffs, which was another way of saying that it disproportionately affected the food security of the poorest people across the continent and caused particular economic strains on the poorest countries. "Only about one-third (19 out of 53) of African countries," the authors of the report concluded, "had enough agricultural export revenue to pay for their food import bills, and the rest had to draw money from other resources or wait for food donations to ensure a stable food supply."[7] This pattern persisted even in relatively prosperous African countries. In Cote d'Ivoire, for example, which is both a rice-eating and a rice-producing country, 64 percent of consumption is of imported rice, mostly from Asia.

And yet despite the damning data that it offers, the FAO report, like so many issued by international institutions during the period, nonetheless offers a qualified defense of the untrammeled policy of free markets that the international donors, the World Bank, and the IMF, which depending on one's point of view, began urging or imposing on poor African countries in the early 1980s (in the case of the World Bank, by making loans to countries in desperate financial shape that were in no position to resist any conditions that accompanied them contingent on the adoption of such measures). "The long term objective of a more liberal agricultural trade policy regime is not questioned," the authors insist. And yet, at least where smallholder agriculture is concerned, the evidence of the report itself belies such confidence. "Under the fiscal reforms," it states, "subsidies (mainly of inputs) to farmers were abruptly canceled with dire consequences for poor food producers." It is chaste language to describe a period in the relations between the rich and poor worlds that again, no matter how good the donors' intentions, caused in reality an entirely man-made and unnecessary twentieth-century human tragedy.[8]

While it is obviously impossible to answer definitively, it is at least worth posing the question of what would have happened had the emphasis in the thinking of the development world during this period been on helping smallholder farmers remain on the land—in other words, strengthening and improving rural life as it actually existed—rather than on demanding profound structural changes to the agricultural sector. Whatever the answer, it seems hard to imagine how the record of poverty reduction for poor rural people in the Global South could have been much worse. But this was not what the mainstream of the development world was focused on for most of the second half of the twentieth century, and it is by no means clear that the current emphasis on food security, which, at least theoretically, is entirely compatible with countries remaining largely dependent on imports, represents much of a change.

In this context it is important to remember that, however counterintuitively, historically the development world has not always taken as its principal priority alleviating poverty in the near and medium term. Indeed, as Roger Riddell, by far the most judicious and evenhanded mainstream historian of post–World War II foreign aid, has written, it was only at the beginning of the 1970s that "official donors suddenly 'discovered' poverty."[9] The fact that this change took place in the wake of another global food crisis that started in 1972 and culminated in the oil shock of 1974 following the so-called Yom Kippur War in the Middle East (when the prices of agricultural staples rose to levels not seen since the end of World War II) hardly seems likely to have been a coincidence. Development specialists tend to emphasize technical problems and technical solutions, but like other central elements of the global system, food has always been first and foremost a political question. The prophet Ezekiel certainly understood this, even if the World Bank chose for decades to operate as if the institution was somehow "above" politics.

As it happened, the new focus of the mid-1970s would prove to be fleeting, and serious pro-poor growth policies would have to wait for nearly another two decades. This is not to say that there were no important changes in the governance of the global food system during this period, some of which predated the 1973–1974 food crisis and some of which were implemented in reaction to it. To the contrary, there were a number of highly significant ones. The salient question must be whether these new arrangements actually served the interests of smallholder farmers, especially of those living in sub-Saharan Africa, or whether, instead, they were devised principally to satisfy the concerns of the donors. There, the picture is a mixed one. There was certainly no new "master plan" for agriculture, much less a reconsideration of the fundamental ideological presuppositions of the Bretton Woods and UN systems. To the contrary, each of these changes had its own particular institutional and ideological logic and did not necessarily build on or complement earlier reforms. But with the benefit of hindsight, a pattern emerges. All of these measures now appear to have had one common effect: the progressive weakening of the UN's Food and Agriculture Organization (FAO).

Even the greatest partisan of the FAO would be hard pressed to claim that the organization has ever lived up to its promise. But then, neither has the UN system itself. And however one assigns the blame, again, like the UN, the promise of the FAO was far greater than what it became or, more properly, was allowed to become. Yet for all its faults and weaknesses, from the late 1940s to the beginning of the 1970s, the FAO exercised as the UN's "Ministry of Agriculture."[10] Had the organization's first director-general, Lord Boyd Orr, who in 1949 was awarded the Nobel Peace Prize for his work, had his way, the FAO would have tried to move global food policy a great deal further away from the national interest of individual states and toward one of collective action (much along the same lines as the original UN concept of a permanent Military Staff Committee was meant to guarantee global security, with, if necessary, troops from the permanent members of the Security Council put at the UN's disposal). As Nora McKeon has rightly emphasized in her own eloquent writing on the food crisis and the structures of global governance needed to prevent its recurrence, Boyd Orr had pressed his UN colleagues hard for the creation of a World Food Board, arguing that food was unlike other commodities and that this alone justified his belief that the world required "a food policy based on human needs," not one subordinate to the imperatives of the global market. In this, Boyd Orr, who was a convinced World Federalist, was putting forward views that in important ways reflected the idealism of the founders of the UN and prefigured the arguments that food rights activists and members of the antiglobalization organizations would begin to make three decades later and that still lie at the heart of their arguments today.

The crisis of 2007–2008 obliged the global food establishment to revisit the question of how free a hand markets (the euphemism for this was market *forces*; the invisible hand and all that) should be given in determining the prices of food staples. And in 2011, the G20 nations created a group they called the Rapid Response Forum that was to be made up of senior officials from both the major exporting countries and those largely dependent on the import of food staples, which was exactly the sort of supervision Boyd Orr had called for. According to the G20's founding communiqué, the forum was "meant to allow countries to communicate with one another so as to avoid that any one of them take individual decisions that would be irrational from a collective point of view."[11] Given the way in which the international donors had whittled down the role of the FAO over the decades, there was a bitter irony to the fact that these discussions were mandated as having to be based on the technical information provided by the new Agricultural Market Information System (AMIS) that the G20 had created at the same time and had housed within the FAO, using FAO personnel. Whether the organization was up to the task was unclear after decades of comparative marginalization and in the immediate aftermath of the departure of its longtime director general, Jacques Diouf, who had been detested by a significant number of his own subordinates. AMIS's purpose, as its secretary Abdolreza Abbassian explained in an interview in *Le Monde*, was to improve "transparency and the information about [what is going on] in the markets for the four principal staples (wheat, rice, maize, and soya) needed for global food security."[12] The problem was that although, once it was up and running, there was little doubt that AMIS could provide the necessary data, there was and remains justified skepticism over the extent to which powerful governments were willing to establish controls over markets and rein in speculation.

When AMIS was established, the FAO took the view that it had been given important new responsibilities by the G20. If so, this was the first step back from the systematic narrowing of the FAO's mandate that had begun in 1963, that is, less than two decades after the institution's founding, when the task of providing food aid to the hungry poor was hived off from the FAO and transferred to the newly created World Food Programme (WFP). This institutional loss for the FAO was compounded in 1971 with the establishment of the Consultative Group for International Agricultural Research (CGIAR). The idea behind CGIAR was to join together in one administrative context all of the most important agriculture research centers in the world. CGIAR had been the brainchild of the Rockefeller Foundation, which, beginning in 1943 as part of its funding for the researcher that provided the scientific basis for the Green Revolution, had funded one research institute devoted to studying rice and a second, in collaboration with the Mexican government, to improve strains of wheat and maize. In 1966, these institutions became independent of the Mexican government and instead wholly dependent on the Rockefeller Foundation, and were renamed CYMMIT, the Spanish-language acronym for what in English was called the International Maize and Wheat Improvement Center. In 1969, a commission on international development chaired by the former Canadian prime minister Lester Pearson called for a renewed global effort to underwrite "research specializing in food supplies and tropical agriculture."[13] A year later, Rockefeller proposed just such an institution, and the year after that, CYMMIT and the International Rice Research Institute (IRRI), which had been jointly funded by the Ford and Rockefeller foundations, formed the nucleus of CGIAR.

The FAO was a stakeholder in the new body, and its role was formalized in the decision to house CGIAR's technical secretariat in the FAO's headquarters in Rome. But the dominant sponsoring organization behind CGIAR was unquestionably the World Bank, whose president in the early 1970s, Robert McNamara, was the key figure in its creation. As McNamara puts it in a video that can be seen on the CGIAR website, "My establishment of the CGIAR is one of the things I'm most proud of."[14] Since then, the bank has continued to be first among equals of CGIAR's backers, housing CGIAR's secretariat, providing the consortium with all but one of its chairmen, and remaining either its first or second most important contributor, even though it no longer plays the role of being what one internal World Bank evaluation called CGIAR's "donor of last resort." Anyone writing a history not just of the global food system but of the foundations of capitalist globalization would do well to look at the interplay of American megaphilanthropies such as Rockefeller and Ford and the World Bank in the founding of CGIAR.

Narrowing the focus somewhat, whether or not this was the intention, the result of this privileged role for the bank in CGIAR's management and funding decisions meant that virtually all agricultural research done outside the communist world in effect took place under the tutelage of an institution whose presidency was understood always to have to go to an American put forward by the US government, which had very profound ideological commitments to an export-driven, free-market-based global food system and maintained close relations to global agribusiness. Only a few years after CGIAR's founding, an emergency world food conference was held in Rome that was meant to set the terms of reference for a global food system that the food crisis of 1973–1974 had shown to be dysfunctional in a number of crucial ways. It was at this point that the

FAO's mandate was narrowed drastically. For at the conference, the preparatory steps were taken for the founding of the International Fund for Agricultural Development (IFAD), which in 1977 became the UN's thirteenth specialized agency. IFAD's specific mandate was to finance projects that sought to alleviate and, where possible, end hunger and rural poverty. With its role in those activities so drastically reduced by the WFP on the one hand and now IFAD on the other, the FAO began to redirect its original focus away from rural poverty, which, when all is said and done, is an essentially political question, and instead focused on more narrowly technical subjects. In fairness, these new institutional arrangements and rearrangements at least demonstrated that some serious thinking was going on within the UN system about what agriculture's role in successful development needed to be.

The new institutions endured. Unlike the WFP, which over the decades has become the provider of food of last resort to hungry people in the poorest and most deprived parts of the world, IFAD has never quite lived up to its advance billing. Today it is now very much the junior partner in comparison with the FAO and the WFP. But if the UN's food institutions took their place in the global caritative bureaucracy, the renewed global focus on agriculture of the early 1970s did not turn out to have similar staying power. By 1976, food prices had dropped sharply, the beginning of a genuine secular decline. The problem was that too many people who should have known better mistook this long-term trend, which was to last until the early 2000s, for a permanent change. This belief that food prices would continue to drop added to the sense among donors that not only had the world weathered the 1973–1974 crisis, but that it was unlikely to recur. And for more than three decades, these expectations seemed warranted. There were voices warning that a global food crisis would recur, but they were almost completely ignored. Writing in 1980, the agricultural economists Alberto Valdés and Ammar Siamwalla wrote that while "world food security has ceased to be a major concern for the press and the general public . . . the underlying causes of food crises such as the one in 1972–74 have not disappeared."[15]

The consensus view, however, was that there was no reason to call into question even the rosiest scenarios involving future price expectations for food staples across the world. The fact that the problem of food security seemingly had been "solved" certainly contributed to the broader shift in the rich world in its thinking about development. The 1970s had seen a move toward putting direct poverty reduction at the center of the development enterprise. But by the early 1980s, major donor governments had followed the lead of the World Bank in repudiating this emphasis in favor of a basket of neoliberal strategies, including with respect to agriculture, where, again, the agendas of many of the most important institutions, notably CGIAR, increasingly reflected the bank's own thinking and priorities. This shift was probably inevitable, since after all, the early 1980s marked the ideological apogee of Reaganism and Thatcherism. It was hardly likely that the thinking of the World Bank, whose directorship, then as now, was an American monopoly, would not have reflected this new right-leaning consensus. And Alden W. "Tom" Clausen, who had been the chief executive of the Bank of America when President Reagan, shortly after coming into office, asked him to become the World Bank's sixth president, reshaped the institution's activities along just these lines. As the entry on the bank's own website rather euphemistically summarizes his presidency, "Clausen's fundamental commitment to free markets, private flows of capital and international cooperation, together with his commercial banker's knowledge of finance, inspired innovations concerning investment guarantees and co-financing with commercial banks. It also determined which of the Bank's ongoing programs should be emphasized."[16]

It was under Clausen that the bank began to institute what it rather euphemistically called its Structural Adjustment Program (SAP) for poor countries—a set of policies that involved, in the words of the bank's own website, shifting "the concern from the distribution of wealth back to economic growth," and taking "its cues from the financial markets rather than the demands of the developing countries." These policies would later come to be known as the Washington Consensus, even if John Williamson, the economist who coined the term in 1989, would later insist that he had never intended to be used "as a synonym for neoliberalism or market fundamentalism," which, as he put it in a 2004 paper, Williamson said he regarded as "a thoroughly objectionable perversion of its original meaning." However, that had been exactly how the World Bank under Clausen's stewardship had interpreted it. To quote the bank's website again, "As a commercial banker [Clausen] looked for solutions in market-oriented development strategies." This was because, as the entry explains, he simply "felt more comfortable with the private sector than with government bureaucracies."

The bank's new orthodoxy went much further than that, and started from the premise that the state was an important impediment to successful development, if not, indeed, the principal roadblock to it. The bank's short biography notes that the Reagan administration saw " 'poverty alleviation' as a 'welfare giveaway' program," and it was from that vantage point that Clausen ran the bank. What needed to happen, he thought—and in this, anyone who followed the arguments of bankers in the aftermath of the 2008 financial crisis will be struck by how consistent and unchanging the views of Wall Street and the City of London actually are—was that the state simply needed to get out of the way, thus freeing the invisible hand of the market, in Adam Smith's famous though much-understood phrase, to do it its prosperity-creating work. The fact that this was a gross misrepresentation of Smith was no more compelling to Clausen than it would be three decades later to the Congressional Republican Party of the Unites States. The state was public enemy number one. As a bank report of that period argued, "The main factors behind the stagnation and decline [of sub-Saharan Africa during the 1970s] were poor policies—both macroeconomic and sectoral—emanating from a development paradigm that gave the state a prominent role in production and in regulating economic activity."[17]

It was a view from which, despite the fact that it has now adopted as its slogan the phrase "Working for a World Free of Poverty," the bank has never entirely retreated. Indeed, it was only in the mid-1990s, after James Wolfensohn was nominated by President Bill Clinton and named the bank's ninth president, succeeding former J. P. Morgan CEO Lewis Preston, who had died in office, that the emphasis on structural adjustment would be modified significantly. The bank was already under pressure from activists who had marked the occasion of the bank's first half century with the campaign "Fifty Years Is Enough." Wolfensohn seems to have understood from the start that the status quo was no longer acceptable. While he never explicitly repudiated structural adjustment, he recast the bank's image, in no small measure thanks to Mark Malloch Brown, a public relations expert specializing in political campaigns who would go on to head the UN Development Programme (UNDP). The view of many activists, above all those associated with the "Fifty Years Is Enough" campaign, was, as Walden Bello put it, that with regard to the centerpiece of Wolfensohn's reform, the so-called Poverty Reduction Strategy Programs that were presented as a replacement for the SAP, "the rhetoric of change did not, however, match the reality of continuity."[18] Wolfensohn's defenders viewed such criticisms as unreasonable and emphasized the limits of how much change even the most well-intended president of the World Bank could effect. Wolfensohn would certainly never have been named president of the bank had he ever intended to undermine the capitalist system, which, when all was said and done, was the end state Bello and like-minded activists were campaigning for. To the contrary, the system had made Wolfensohn rich and he believed in it. But Wolfensohn was also genuinely interested in poverty alleviation in a way that none of his predecessors had been. More importantly, even if the shift was in many ways only rhetorical, the recasting of the bank's mission from one that was about helping poor nations grow economically to one that was focused on fighting poverty was a genuinely radical step. And to put in a word for rhetorical change, a radical change in rhetoric has historically often been the harbinger of a different reality. When, for example, the current president of the bank, Jim Yong Kim, writes in a blog post, "The biggest development question of all: How do we most effectively deliver on our promises to the poor?," he is making a claim for the bank that not just Tom Clausen but *all* of his predecessors before Wolfensohn would have rejected out of hand.

But whether one views Wolfensohn's tenure at the bank as representing a real break with the institution's past or as a period in which it succeeded in giving the SAP a politically correct makeover, the fact that the bank remained wedded to the SAP well into his tenure and has not entirely manumitted itself from today is difficult to understand, given what even the most charitable observer would be hard pressed to describe more positively than its mixed results. To be sure, there were success stories that the bank, at least, attributed to structural adjustment, both in terms of steep rises in growth rates in a handful of countries and a more widespread fall in food prices for urban consumers. But if officials at the bank and at the IMF did not see that these open markets Clausen and his colleagues had championed so inflexibly were progressively destroying the livelihoods of smallholder farmers who could not compete with cheaper imported food staples, it was either because they were stupid or because they were free-market ideologues. And they were anything but stupid. Instead, they were true believers in the dogma that prosperity over the longer term depended almost exclusively on currency devaluations, the primacy of the private sector, and export-driven free markets. For them, everything else was a sideshow. As Dambisa Moyo, who is one of the sternest critics of development from the perspective of unashamed free-market capitalism (no protectionist she!), has pointed out, these development policies, like Reaganism and Thatcherism more broadly, "bore all the hallmarks of an economic revolution, and there was little room for compromise."[19]

· 7 ·

Cassandra and Doctor Pangloss

In revolutionary moments, institutional thinking tends to be formulated in zero-sum terms. And even in nonrevolutionary moments, once a course of action is undertaken that its architects believe will be transformative, admitting failure or, worse still, error, or for that matter even changing course without any such admission, is not something that ever comes easily to large, powerful institutions such as the World Bank, the development agencies of major Western donors, or the major philanthropies and development NGOs. But the insistence that given time and done properly, the SAP would work was not due mainly to institutional pride or stubbornness. Instead, at the heart of the difficulty in changing course lay the reality that while in some important ways structural adjustment was a radical departure from previous development orthodoxies, in other ways, particularly where the role that was to be assigned to agriculture was concerned, it was only a comparatively modest recalibration of the set of assumptions that had been at the heart of development from its colonial beginnings, when it was used by British thinkers to justify the continuation of empire on the grounds that only in this context could necessary modernization be achieved.

For its part, the neoliberalism of the Reagan-Thatcher era, radical as it was in certain ways, where development was concerned was only a modest revision of that overarching dogma called modernization theory, whose importance in twentieth-century history would be hard to overstate, particularly once colonialism ended and the Cold War had begun. The Swiss historian of development, Gilbert Rist, has underscored the importance of the fact that the development paradigm, which is now taken for granted as both a central collective moral obligation of humanity and as one of the central organizing principles of the current world system, was not just first proclaimed by then–US president Harry Truman in a speech in 1949 that came to be known as "Point Four," and that was delivered at a moment when the Cold War was growing fiercer. It also reflected the American predilection for construing the world in postideological terms. As Rist put it, "Unlike in the colonial period, the action required is not a transfer of values or a pedagogical program in which people from the outside have the initiative but, rather, an 'international effort,' a 'collective enterprise' based upon an increase in production and better use of the world's natural and human resources."[1]

"Hegemony" is an overused word, but as Rist pointed out, the picture that Truman drew in his speech of how to address the world's problems once and for all was genuinely hegemonic "because it appeared to be not only the best [solution] but the only possible one."[2] If in his *History of Development* Rist could describe the progress of the development project as having evolved from "Western origins to global faith," what seems most striking from the vantage point of the early twenty-first century is how little has changed. If anything, it is more difficult to question development today than it was in the 1950s because of the addition of a new element—a techno-utopianism that insists that inventions, technological breakthroughs, and scientific discoveries *not yet in existence* are so certain to occur that they can be counted on to address the world's problems. On the moral and ideological plane, the same absolutism prevails. Rist finds this already in Truman's speech. The first part, he writes "recalls the desperate straits—the horror of hunger and want—in which more than half the world's population live. Then the good news is given that, 'for the first time in history,' something is at hand that will bring happiness and make it possible for their lives to be transformed. [But] this will not come unless energies are mobilized to produce more, to invest, to get down to work, to expand trade. But in the end, if the chance is seized and people agree to the efforts required, an era of happiness, peace and prosperity will dawn from which everyone stands to benefit."[3]

The early-twenty-first-century consensus, which is that it is somehow immoral to argue that there are limits on what can be accomplished, is already present in embryonic form in the Truman speech. As Rist notes, "One was quite free to debate [development's] forms, the way of accelerating growth or distributing its effects more equitably," but the development project itself was off limits. "You don't argue about the obvious," Rist writes, "the most you can do is try to improve it."[4] Now there's hegemony!

Then as now, this purportedly postideological doctrine was in fact intensely political, as can reasonably be inferred from the fact that many of the most important architects of American modernization theory were ardent Cold Warriors. This made it all the more ironic that for all that they viewed themselves as being in fundamental competition with each other, the views of these mid-twentieth-century modernization theorists, such as Edward Shils and the Rostow brothers, and those of Soviet and Maoist ideologues of development had a good deal in common. In both schemas, industrialization was viewed as the absolute priority if development was to succeed, and, as Colin Leys has pointed out, both sides spoke of development in terms of poor countries "catching up" with the rich world.[5] Writing in 1960,

Walt Whitman Rostow, who himself came from an immigrant Jewish socialist background (his brother was named after Eugene Debs), and whose thought, anticommunist though it had become, overlapped uncomfortably enough with Marxism to have titled his most important book, *The Stages of Growth: A Non-Communist Manifesto.* Rostow argued that what he called the "take-off point" for poor economies occurred when "industrialization increases, with workers switching from the agricultural sector to the manufacturing sector." The Soviet model was by no means identical but it relied too on large-scale labor and capital-intensive industrial projects to modernize the economy. Mao's China adopted the same approach, first during the massive technology transfer from the USSR to China that took place between the Communist victory in 1949 and the end of China's first (again, Soviet-style) Five-Year Plan in 1957. A year later, this reliance on industrialization would become one of the main contributing factors to the Chinese famine of 1958–1962. Mao believed if China was to develop, the role of agriculture needed to be subordinate to that of industry and, indeed, for the former to underwrite the latter so as to achieve the goal Mao set in 1958 of overtaking Britain in steel production within fifteen years.

The criminal folly of Mao's decision to set such priorities and then to insist that they be seen through no matter what the cost is self-evident. It cannot be legitimately compared to the decision by major Western donors and the Bretton Woods institutions to turn their collective backs on Third World agriculture. But while these latter policies were not criminal, they were radical. Indeed, it would be hard to overstate how transformative they were intended to be and how much change they succeeded in bringing about. The bank continues to insist that from its inception, agricultural reform "was high on the adjustment agenda."[6] But what this involved in practice was pressing African governments to curtail food price subsidies on both the producer and the consumer level, reorient agriculture toward exports, and remove currency controls to make these exports more competitive. In contrast, aiding farmers directly was sharply curtailed. As shown by figures contained in studies by DFID, the United Kingdom's overseas development ministry, although bilateral as well as multilateral assistance to agriculture continued to increase in the 1970s and early 1980s (though its proportion in relation to other aid sectors and also the question of whether it kept pace with rapidly rising population are separate matters), it cratered after that. Between 1980 and 2002, total aid went from $6.2 billion per year to $2.3 billion, a reduction of almost two-thirds. This was during the same period that overall aid flows to the poor world *increased* by two-thirds, rising from $37.1 billion to $61.4 billion.[7]

As if this had not been bad enough, while the biggest cuts in international assistance for agriculture—83 percent over a twenty-year period—were made in Asia, where the Green Revolution, whatever its drawbacks, had undeniably led to a huge increase in agricultural productivity (above all in the Indian subcontinent and in the Philippines), aid to Africa was cut in half. And yet Africa had had no Green Revolution and consequently no huge leap in per-hectare yields. If one believed that the Green Revolution had provided a lasting technological fix to the problem of hunger, then it did indeed make sense for the major donors from the rich world to conclude that they could dramatically reduce their aid to Asian agriculture. But to argue that the same strategy would be effective for Africa flew in the face of the facts on the ground there. The absence of a Green Revolution was only part of it. Sub-Saharan Africa had been 14.7 percent urban at the time of decolonization. By 2000, that number had risen to 37.2 percent. But despite the hectic pace of urbanization across most of the continent, and even with migration to the cities or emigration to Europe relieving some of the pressure on the countryside, two-thirds of the population still lived in rural areas. And rapid population increase meant that agricultural holdings of less than one hectare, on which even the most determined farm family could not hope to survive economically, were steadily increasing. Under these circumstances, the failure of the development world to make the strengthening of smallholder agriculture a central priority is surely a textbook case of grasping defeat from the jaws of victory.

To put the matter this strongly is not to claim that policy makers in Washington, New York, London, Paris, and Brussels had no rationale for the policies that they opted for, let alone that they acted out of pure malevolence or in the furtherance of some sinister capitalist plot to make the life of the poor of the world even more hellish than it already was. Such exercises in conspiratorial demonology, so self-flattering on the part of those who indulge in them, should be left to writers such as Jean Ziegler, the influential Swiss sociologist and politician who would later become the UN's first special rapporteur for the right to food. Extrapolating from a premise that while controversial is widely shared not only by other food activists but by many important figures in the mainstream food establishment as well—that there is more than enough food in the world for everyone and that the real problem is one of pricing, availability, and access—Ziegler came to the conclusion that if hunger still existed, it was the product of organized crime, which for him was a synonym for global capitalism. Ziegler does not shy away from the implications of this. If anything, he seems to revel in them, charging in his book *Mass Destruction: The Geopolitics of Hunger* that any child who dies of hunger has in fact been murdered.[8]

Claims in a similar vein have been made by the Indian physicist turned eco-feminist, organic farming advocate, and food rights activist, Vandana Shiva. She has blamed the entire food crisis on the capitalist market, insisting that "nature shrinks as capital grows,"[9] as if no other factor—not the explosive growth of the world population from a little more than two billion in 1950 to seven billion in 2011, nor the rise of the first truly global middle class, which in terms of consumption is now making very much larger demands on the global system than has ever been known before—needed to be taken into account. This does not mean that her indictment of the current system is not a powerful one, particularly her emphasis on the ever-increasing degree of corporate control over that system, and more recently, the increasing reliance on those in the mainstream who believe that these same multinational corporations can be trusted as partners in the effort to reduce hunger and absolute poverty and who seem to have no objection to these companies' increasing control over the seeds farmers use. For Shiva, this has meant agreeing to the idea that seeds should no longer be treated, as has been the case traditionally, as the common property of all but rather viewed as legitimately the intellectual property of agricultural multinationals, commodities that they have the right to control, even if of course farmers are not obliged to buy them and thus accept the conditions under which they are sold.

Shiva's critics insist that she is guilty of a kind of utopian nostalgia on the basis of which she claims that were farmers in poor countries to return to the principles of traditional agriculture, this would go a long way toward solving the crisis of the global food system. But on this she has not always been clear. If she really means traditional agriculture, then there is ample reason for skepticism, since that form of what is, after all, a variant of subsistence farming was helpless to prevent famine century in and century out since the beginning of recorded history. If, on the other hand, Shiva is talking about a new form of agriculture, one that combines traditional knowledge with the modern principles of agricultural and ecological science, that is of the agroecology Olivier de Schutter campaigned for throughout his term as UN special rapporteur for the right to food, then she is on much firmer ground, even if her rhetoric is too strident to resonate with anyone not already firmly in her camp.

Then again, Shiva is a campaigner, and what campaigner worth her salt does not make maximalist demands? The question, however, is whether, even assuming the increasingly corporate character of the global food system could be undone, this would lead inexorably to the restoration of a world where, in the specific case of agriculture, food security based on ecologically sound farming principles could be put into practice. Is this one possible outcome? Of course it is. But at least on historical form, there are others that are considerably more plausible. The activists are right to tax the food establishment with viewing things through a technical rather than a political lens. They would be well advised to pay more attention to a member in good standing of the mainstream. The Inter-American Bank's Eugenio Diaz-Bonilla has written that "poverty is a complex phenomenon in which inherent causes are compounded by human biases and discriminatory policies that are accentuated by the tyranny of the current global system."[10]

This does not mean that the utopian "Salvationist" politics of the global left, framed though they rightly are in political language, are politics worthy of the name. There are many reasons to doubt the food critics' ability to alter the trajectory of events on the ground, first and most obviously with regard to climate change but also concerning the rising middle class of Asia. In coastal China, parts of India, and increasingly in Sri Lanka, Vietnam, Indonesia, and Malaysia, there are now hundreds of millions of people who are living more comfortably and eating better than all the generations that came before them. Many believe that they will soon enjoy the standard of living of middle-class Americans and Western Europeans. Whether or not this is in fact feasible with regard to the availability of finite natural resources or longer-term environmental sustainability, it is not an ambition that people in Shanghai, Delhi, or Saigon are likely to be willing to abandon in favor of Vandana Shiva's rural arcadia. Those in the new middle class of Asia are just as persuaded as the antiglobalization movement that another world is possible. But the world they dream of is one closer to the way Americans, Japanese, and Western Europeans live today, and, as anyone who has spent time in these cities quickly discovers, unlike in the West, guilty consciences are as thin on the ground as vegetarians in China.

Regrettably, Ziegler's and Shiva's views about the global food system are strongly reminiscent of Noam Chomsky's theories about the United States as the fundamental source of all the world's evils. When all was said and done, all Chomsky accomplished by doing so was to take American exceptionalist self-absorption and turn it on its head. Yes, on his account, the United States was the villain rather than the hero of the global story, but his perspective was every bit as America-centric as the exceptionalists his work excoriates. A similar case can be made that the so-called dependency theory, originally formulated in papers by Hans Silber and Raul Prebisch in 1949— useful as it was in refuting the mainstream view of modernization, that the development process is similar for all societies—is to a large extent a Marxist inversion of the capitalist modernization theory that it was meant to refute. For dependency theorists, the rich core is the rich core and the poor periphery the poor periphery, and nothing short of the transformation of global society can change this. But having already acquired a momentum that seems unstoppable short of some apocalyptic event, what the extraordinary capitalist development that has already taken place in Asia reveals is the folly of hewing to such discrete, impermeable dualisms, demonstrating instead the penetrability of what was the core (Europe, North America) by the periphery and indeed the possibility, as indicated by the rise of China as the world's principal creditor and the United States as its principal debtor, of core and periphery trading places.

Ironically, it may even be the fact that there is no conscious, nefarious plan hatched by the OECD countries in collaboration with rapacious multinational corporations, who in turn are allied to local plutocrats and oligarchs, that has made the crisis of the global food system far worse than it would have been had the kind of grand, system-wide malign conspiracy that the Chomskys, Zieglers, and Shivas believe that they have identified had any large basis in fact. While it is certainly not the norm, there are no shortages in history of examples of successful resistance to tyranny. One has only to look at Cochabamba, Bolivia, in 2000, when peasant organizations successfully rebuffed the ambitions of foreign water companies, or the decade-long fight in Orissa, India, where tribal groups have been able to stymie the efforts of the Vedanta mining corporation to evict them to mine for bauxite, to see examples of how effectively resistance on a massive scale can be mobilized and struggles won when corporations backed by states act with undisguised rapacity, as companies involved in the extraction of natural resources still do so often. But outside the extractive industries, most twenty-first-century corporations present themselves, and, no doubt often conceive of themselves sincerely, as concerned global citizens, in business not only for their shareholders but, to use the contemporary term of art, for all their stakeholders. Peter Bakker, the chairman of TNT, the Dutch multinational delivery company, told the journalists Roger Thurow and Scott Kilman that after 9/11, instead of trying to decide whether his company should sponsor a Formula One race or a golf tournament, he instead began to ask himself, "How can we sponsor the world?"

For those who remain unconvinced that human betterment is best achieved via corporate sponsorship, however, the more salient question would be, "How does one fight Dr. Pangloss?" When business leaders in effect declare that what problems still exist are, for the first time in human history, on the cusp of being put to rest by the coalition into which they have entered with governments, scientists, and a broad public of concerned citizens and that today all these groups are working together in seamless, disinterested moral harmony to realize Dr. Pangloss's dream of the best of all possible worlds, can any alternate vision of how to achieve the same goal of reducing poverty and hunger ever hope to compete? So far at least these corporate "glad tidings," constantly heralded by the multinationals themselves but endorsed by political leaders, famous entertainers like Bono, George Clooney, and Bob Geldof, and most of the global media, have succeeded in marginalizing if not drowning out those dissident voices that still persist in asking if the world has really changed so much that it is reasonable to believe that multinational corporations are now truly as dedicated to the global public good as they are to the interests of their own shareholders. As the Delhi-based food rights activist Dr. Arun Gupta, who as the head of the Breastfeeding Promotion Network of India, wrote ruefully in an e-mail sounding the alarm over the Nestlé Corporation's attempt at what he called "greenwashing" itself, corporate promotional strategies "are becoming smarter every day," with companies using new-age smart communication strategies that include "cause-related marketing" and "association with celebrities."[11]

It is a commonplace that shameless self-promotion is all but inscribed on the DNA of contemporary culture. Go on Twitter and you'll find a huge number of the tweets go roughly, "A wonderful article/speech/intervention by John Smith," and then you note the heading reads, "Retweeted by John Smith." When Norman Mailer published a collection of essays in 1959 called *Advertisements for Myself,* such self-promotion was thought by many to be unworthy of the serious writer Mailer certainly was. Today, promoting oneself isn't viewed as shameful, it is actually viewed as part of doing one's job. And as we all seem so hell-bent on "branding," and advertising seems reasonable to people even though advertisements are manipulations at best and usually outright lies, what matters more and more are one's good intentions, not whether one is telling the truth. How else to explain the twenty-first-century fashion among philanthropies, UN agencies, and campaigning groups (including a number involved in food issues, notably Bono's ONE Campaign) to ask people to vote on what kind of world they want? Have people become so skilled at quelling their own common sense that they believe such appeals, which are essentially polls, and polls taken in a world increasingly run as a plutocracy, with inequalities of money and status not seen in Europe or North America since Balzac's time, can translate into political or social power? But as in the proverbial case of the emperor's new clothes, it is in no one's interest to say what a sham, what a simulacrum of democracy this particular fashion in self-flattery and the manufacturing of consent really is.

But even such shamelessness has its limits. Is it an exaggeration to assert that in the early twenty-first century, it can sometimes seem as if there are really only four categories of people who acknowledge no such limits and seem to believe that, basically, they are entitled to act as they please—children, psychopaths, victims, and philanthropists? Of course, it is. But that does not make it a total falsehood. And if even in this society, with its crippling sentimentality about childhood and its inability to distinguish reliably between celebrity and notoriety, there is no strong social pressure to admire the insouciance of the child, the compulsion of the psychopath, or the argument "from necessity" that individual victims and states that construe their history as one of victimization so often advance.

In contrast, the freedom of the do-gooder goes unchallenged. And the deepest reason for this is the respect accorded not to the do-gooder's or the philanthropist's actions but to his or her good intentions, which would seem to indicate that in this culture the understanding contained in the old saying that "the road to hell is paved with good intentions" is now well past its sell-by date. The consequences of this have been far more significant than is commonly supposed. For, once established, it is precisely those good intentions that lead most people to stipulate the inherent virtue of the philanthropic enterprise, whether carried out by UN specialized agencies, NGOs, or private foundations. Language matters. If poverty is "the bad guy," then everyone fighting poverty is "a good guy." Anyone questioning this must be a cynic, or so the argument goes, Panglossian to the core.

How could reality have become so simple? The short answer is that it didn't. For as soon as one takes one's distance, there is no reason to think any such thing. What is presented, preeningly, as idealism is in reality a "feel-good" prophylactic against thought. The tragic nature of human existence is to be denied at all costs, replaced by hubristic suggestions that to say that one wants something is any indication of whether it is possible to secure it. Business is still business, politics is still politics, and these are not the End of Days. And yet that is precisely what the rhetoric of the Millennium Development Goals, of the end of poverty and the end of hunger, is actually asserting. We will *get* the future we want! As if it were the norm in this world to get want you want.

It would be interesting to know when this great cognitive shift, from "the road to hell is paved with good intentions" to "good intentions will inexorably lead to good realities" up to and including the end of extreme poverty and hunger, came to be so unquestioningly accepted as an accurate depiction of global reality within the UN system, aid departments of rich nations, NGOs, and philanthropies. Why did officials of these bodies treat as irrelevant artifacts of the past the myriad historical examples of peoples and movements, European imperialism being a representative case in point, that were persuaded they were contributing to the greater good of humanity but we now understand to have acted with incredible cruelty and perpetrated unspeakable crimes? The American officer in Vietnam who famously declared that he and his men had to burn the Vietcong-occupied village "in order to save it" was being perfectly sincere. His was cruelty that did not even know itself to be cruelty. The fact that he sincerely believed himself to be on the side of the angels does not alter the facts of what he and his comrades did. For almost twenty years bank officials and development experts had insisted passionately and with the best intentions that smallholder agriculture in Africa had to be starved and African governments (among others) forced to open up their markets to agricultural imports priced so low that local farmers could no longer compete, in order to modernize agriculture. This was because, in their view, only modernization along free-market lines could ever bring prosperity on any sustainable basis. But while this helps explain what they did; it does not excuse it. To the contrary, it offers one more illustration of Pascal's great intuition that "man is neither angel nor beast; and the misfortune is that he who would act the angel acts the beast."

So while there is little empirical basis for sustaining the charges made by Ziegler, Shiva, and other like-minded activists that the architects of structural adjustment did not sincerely believe that the key to development, above all but by no means only in sub-Saharan Africa, was the integration of these countries' national economies into the global economy, this does not mean what these architects did was right; it only means that they thought what they were doing was right—a different matter altogether. Faced with the indisputable fact that Africa had stagnated and that many countries on the continent seemed to be in increasingly dire economic shape, even as other regions, above all Asia, were growing, many economists who did not share Tom Clausen's free-market biases concluded that growth had to be the overarching priority, taking precedence over all other goals and requiring that existing programs be recast accordingly. In the words of one World Bank report, "a broad-based pattern of rapid economic growth is vital to reducing poverty in sub-Saharan Africa."[12]

Even in the 1990s, that is to say, long after the human costs of the SAP had become apparent even to many officials within the bank, there was still a consensus that Africa had "to adjust."[13] Instead, Africa stagnated. South Korea's success has been so stunning that the comparison between its GNP and that of Ghana or Kenya is the best-known example. But the comparison of Asia with Africa that is so much to Africa's detriment is far more widespread. Indonesia's GNP was lower than Nigeria's, and Thailand's was lower than Ghana's. Fifty years later, South Korea had become a member of the OECD, and Indonesia and Thailand were well along on the same route toward membership in this "club" of developed countries, while Kenya, Nigeria, and even Ghana, though doing far better than many of its neighbors, remained mired in poverty. The problem, then, was not with the World Bank's analysis of the basic facts, but rather that its solutions were based on a highly debatable understanding of why Africa remained mired in poverty. The result was everything the critics had feared: a lost decade for Africa generally, and a catastrophe for smallholder farmers.

But for the World Bank, the explanation seemed self-evident. What was needed was not new medicine but more of the medicine of structural adjustment, though as the years went on, the feeling grew that perhaps it did need to be more skillfully applied. Where officials at the bank were unyielding was in their conviction that poor countries would never become prosperous without, as so many of its reports during the period emphasized forcefully, "putting exporters first." What this meant in practice was not only the radical reconfiguration of the national economies of many African countries so that export was favored over domestic consumption; the sources of domestic consumption were transformed as well. This process went under the title of "liberalizing" import regimes, which in plain English meant countries affording virtually free access to their domestic markets for foreign companies. And all of these changes were understood to take place in a framework of fierce economic austerity and budgetary retrenchment, although the bank preferred to put this in terms of nations "reestablish[ing] a balance between income and spending."[14] Where agriculture was concerned, this "exports first" model meant favoring agricultural production destined for sale internationally while permitting agricultural staples from the rich world, no matter at what price they were set, to compete with locally produced foodstuffs. Essential to that outcome was replacing the state's control over marketing and pricing of agricultural staples through government-run national marketing boards with prices based on what these commodities were worth on the global market or would fetch in the domestic one and more generally favoring the production of tradable goods over that of domestic goods.

Proponents of structural adjustment believed that the more such integration progressed—"unleashing a formal market," as one report put it, though whether this was a direct reference to John Maynard Keynes's image of unleashing the animal spirits in the economy is unclear—the more efficiently the economies of poor countries would function. It was to be a virtuous circle: the more such efficiencies were achieved, the more poverty would be reduced, at least over the longer term. There were many problems with this theory, no matter what sector of the economy they were to be applied in. But nowhere was the virtuous circle less virtuous than with regard to agriculture. Idealizing the market as the proponents did, it seems never to have occurred to them that, as subsequent studies would show, markets could actually work against the poor. Instead, the architects of the SAP somehow persuaded themselves that increases in the prices of agricultural commodities, which were often based on changing what was being cultivated to satisfy external rather than domestic demand, was bound to make small farmers richer. Such programs went under a number of different names. In Kenya in the 1990s, they were called "commercialization projects" and were jointly funded by the Kenyan authorities and the World Bank. There were profits. The problem was that these rarely made it into the hands of smallholder farmers. For them, unlike, for example, newly prosperous grain traders, who prospered thanks to these schemes, or multinational corporations that now had access to markets in Africa previously closed to them, the end of the marketing boards was anything but good news. In at least some countries, and for many small producers across the subcontinent, it was an unalloyed disaster. Eventually, farmers become so impoverished that they began to migrate in steadily increasing numbers from the rural areas to the cities. One enormously important effect of this on the continent as a whole was that Africa went from being a net exporter of food at the beginning of the 1970s to importing almost a quarter of what it required at the end of the century.

The proselytizers for globalization believed that by making exports the motor for jump-starting domestic development in poor countries, if accompanied by good governance, the reduction of fiscal deficits, and what in World Bank–speak was rather chastely called "policy distortions," led to a payoff in development terms almost certain to be enormous. What they do not seem to have been able to do was take in the full implications of the fact that smallholder farmers did not produce only for the market, whether foreign or domestic, but also for themselves. What were poor farmers supposed to do while the infrastructure and relatively efficient market structures without which the utopian hopes of these programs had no chance of being successful were being created? The question was never really addressed. Instead, World Bank study after World Bank study insisted that structural adjustment had been "pro-poor in the aggregate,"[15] to quote one report that perhaps revealed rather different truths from those it had intended. But at the time neither the urban bias of such a transformation of development policy (a bias fully shared by most African governing elites) nor the fact that stimulating the overall economic growth of a poor country might not lead to an improvement in the lives of the poor (and ran the risk of in fact making things worse for them) were things the proponents of the SAP were ever willing to consider seriously. The great physicist Max Planck once criticized his colleague James Jeans for refusing to relinquish one of his theories even in the face of facts that should have caused him to do so. Jeans, Planck wrote to a mutual colleague, "is the very model of a theorist as he should *not* be, just as Hegel was in philosophy: so much the worse for the facts if they don't fit."[16] The same could be said of the bank as it clung to the SAP, no matter what devastation it caused.

Despite the claim that for all its weaknesses, the SAP had helped the poor, what actually took place in the 1980s and 1990s in sub-Saharan Africa and in other parts of the poor world was that the situation of smallholder farmers continued to deteriorate. What African farmers in particular experienced was the elimination of already fragile support systems (above all, the marketing boards) without any significant countervailing benefit. It would have been one thing had the institutions and Western donor governments opening markets, removing government price supports on which so many small farmers depended, and calling for export-driven agricultural policies been willing to acknowledge fully the human toll that their vision of how to make poor countries richer was exacting, especially on people in the countryside; some palliative measures could have then been taken. But instead, they insisted—in the teeth of much of the empirical evidence readily available at the time—that everything was going according to plan. And where the World Bank blazed the trail, the major donor governments followed, apparently feeling no anxiety about radically altering their development aid policies in a way that changed the agriculture sector from being a principle focus to almost an afterthought.

We now know that what underwrote the confidence of so many development officials, economists, and agricultural experts at the time was what was then viewed as the triumphant success of the Green Revolution in transforming agricultural productivity in Asia in the 1960s and 1970s. Who needs marketing boards when you have technology that can work miracles? The view seems to have been: first get African countries' macroeconomic house in order and then bring the lessons learned from the Green Revolution in Asia and apply them to Africa, thus marrying the new agricultural technologies to the newly opened free markets. In fairness, this enthusiasm was not without basis.

According to the canonical narrative, the Green Revolution combined transformative developments in crop science, above all the development of new hybrid seed varieties of wheat and rice that matured more quickly and offered higher yields, while more broadly instituting the structural changes that led in many countries to much traditional agriculture being replaced with modern technologies, above all inorganic fertilizers and mechanization. This made food security possible for hundreds of millions of people in Asia for whom it had always been out of reach. There are many problems with this account, the least controversial being that it is centered too much on the technology and not enough on the politics of the Green Revolution, which were inextricably connected to the prosecution of the Cold War. As the American academic specialist Nick Cullather shows in his brilliant book, *The Hungry World: America's Cold War*

Battle against Poverty in Asia, American policy makers believed that as a State Department white paper stated unambiguously, Mao's victory was in no small due to America's "failure to provide China with enough to eat."[17]

Obviously, such concerns are no longer of anything but historical interest. Today, the Green Revolution's most enduring legacy appears to be the extent to which mainstream views about coping with the global food crisis continue to be informed by the reliance on technological innovation in agriculture and more broadly by a faith in all-conquering science, both of which were the intellectual hallmarks of the Green Revolution. Whether its critics will eventually succeed in challenging this narrative remains an open question, though the effort is one that is at the heart of the efforts of food rights campaigners and supporters of ecological agriculture throughout the world. The problem for them is that the experience of modernity is Promethean, that is to say, once something has been discovered or even held out as a possibility, there is almost no way of unlearning or of forgetting it. Given the undeniable success that the Green Revolution had in significantly altering not just the farming practices but the deep cultural structures of rural life in the poor world, from attitudes about self-sufficiency to the role of technology, it seems highly unlikely, in the absence of the deus ex machina of some catastrophe, that small farmers could return to the agriculture their ancestors practiced.

One of the great slogans of the antiglobalization movement has been: "Another world is possible." But to rest the effort to redress the injustices of the current global food system on such millenarian hopes in this, an era when the half-life of hope has been so drastically reduced (think of global expectations in the aftermath of the fall of the Soviet Union compared with those for the Arab Spring, and even those have not exactly been borne out by events), seems not just sentimental but morally reckless. The old adage is wrong: one can indeed live on bread alone. As Brecht put it, harshly but accurately: First grub, then ethics. What one cannot do is live exclusively on hope.

· 8 ·

Is Reforming the System Enough?

The architects of the Structural Adjustment Program (SAP) had a far more consciously radical and systematic modernization project than did the architects of the Green Revolution, who, after all, were mostly agronomists, not macroeconomists. Recalling his early work in Mexico in the 1940s, Norman Borlaug described his colleagues and himself as "neither consultants nor advisors, but working scientists getting our hands and boots dirty, and demonstrating by our own field results what could be done."[1] It is true, of course, that once it had taken place, Borlaug and his colleagues took part in debates about the food system in its totality. Borlaug, for example, worried a great deal about the population explosion, though never in an explicitly Malthusian or fatalistic way (like Bill Gates, his faith in technological innovation and scientific discovery remained unswerving). Indeed, in his acceptance speech after winning the Nobel Peace Prize in 1970, Borlaug was categorical that "there can be no permanent progress in the battle against hunger until the agencies that fight for increased food production and those that fight for population control unite in a common effort."[2]

But for the most part, the architects of the Green Revolution stuck to their science and, whether or not this was their intention, as a result were largely able to preserve their innocence, even if this involved turning a blind eye to a great deal, above all to the political context of the Green Revolution. They must all have known that the Green Revolution's principal funder, the Ford Foundation, like most other major US philanthropies in the 1950s and 1960s, had, in the words of the writer, Jason Epstein, "to a certain extent always acted as [an extension] of government."[3] In the case of the SAP, however, any such willful blindness or genuine naïvety was impossible from the start. For it had been based almost entirely on an explicit macroeconomic understanding of development and poverty reduction and an implicit geostrategic one. That proponents of the SAP could have started from the presumption that their prescriptions would be beneficial on this macro level is perfectly understandable. Why the reasonable supposition that any set of policies that would have such a transformative effect was bound to create not only profound economic dislocations but social, political, and cultural conflicts as well seem to have weighed so little in their deliberations is not.

It was one thing to dismiss what the World Bank under Tom Clausen would have dismissed as "statist" approaches that went with the ideological territory. But the experience of the Green Revolution itself suggested that it was not enough to set in motion a kind of agricultural Big Bang. To put the matter starkly, only a utopian could believe that you can make people richer by investing less in them and waiting for the invisible hand of the market to work. In the pre–Ronald Reagan/Margaret Thatcher days of the Green Revolution, this was understood in Washington and by the international financial institutions. But by the time the SAP was conceived and then imposed on those poor countries seeking the bank's assistance, this lesson had apparently been forgotten.

To this day, the official line at the bank is that, on balance and despite their drawbacks and failings, the programs that constituted the core of the SAP helped significantly in restoring Africa to economic health and in doing so began to reduce poverty significantly on the continent. For example, in May 2013, Shantayanan Devarajan, the outgoing chief economist of the World Bank's Africa division, conceded that these programs had not worked when they were first applied in the 1980s and 1990s but that over the course of the next fifteen years they had worked very well indeed. What accounted for the different result was not the policy prescriptions themselves—these, he said, had been "exactly the same" during both the earlier and the later periods—but rather that where such policies had not worked when imposed by the Global North, when these identical policies were "home grown and owned" by African governments, it was "beyond dispute" that they had worked brilliantly and delivered both economic growth and poverty reduction." Whether speaking glowingly, as Devarajan did, of an African "political consensus"[4] made either intellectual or moral sense—given the lack of democratic accountability (or worse) in most sub-Saharan African countries and the pro-urban, antirural biases of most African elites—or deserved to be taken uncritically is another question entirely. Anyone doubting the persistence of these urban biases and their effects on agricultural development had only to read the 2012 edition of the FAO flagship publication, "The State of Food and Agriculture," to see that while agriculture was not being ignored to the degree it had been in the 1980s and 1990s, "[the] trends in government spending for countries in Sub-Saharan Africa are discouraging in that they indicate a failure of government budgets to prioritize agriculture."[5]

The World Bank in its reformed twenty-first-century iteration has been presided over first by James Wolfensohn, then by Robert Zoellick, and finally by Jim Yong Kim (who in his youth belonged to "Fifty Years Is Enough," the movement calling for the bank's abolition), all of whom laid heavy emphasis on the extent to which its thinking had evolved since the high-water mark of an intellectual and economic consensus within the bank in favor of the SAP. But Devarajan's comments suggested that at least in some sectors of the institution there had been little or no rethinking of any substantive kind, except related to the need that such programs should be perceived in the poor world as homegrown rather than having been imposed by Washington or Brussels. Devarajan was adamant that "most of the constraints to Africa's transformation [were] government failures, not market failures," which was the old orthodoxy in virtually undiluted form. He even denied that the cutbacks in social spending that had been one of the most bitterly criticized of the SAP's effects had actually had any especially negative results, insisting that in light of the pervasive failure of governments across Africa, "it is not clear that an increase in public spending in education and health will lead to better human development outcomes."[6] Devarajan went so far as to claim that the work of Joseph Stiglitz, one of the SAP's severest critics, actually supported his claim that state-led economic policies had neither worked in the past nor were likely to work in the present or future because of political corruption.

It is true that Stiglitz's views have changed considerably since his World Bank days. Still, there is little justification for Devarajan's claim. To the contrary, the results would seem to confirm the insights of the policy's most severe critics. As Anup Shah, author of *Structural Adjustment—A Major Cause of Poverty*, has put it, the SAP's emphasis on debt reduction, privatization, and a focus on exports in effect amounts to a demand "that poor nations lower the standard of living of their people."[7] Some antiglobalization activists insist that this approach was a conscious effort by the rich world to keep the poor world in a state of permanent dependency. If true, like colonialism itself, this would make it a kind of criminal conspiracy. But even if one rejects such claims and ascribes benign intentions to its architects, the SAP does seem to have been based on not just an ahistorical but an antihistorical perspective. Even one of Devarajan's

most distinguished former colleagues, the World Bank's chief economist Justin Yifu Lin, has argued vehemently for governments in
the Global South to identify and support industries that can foster
growth, rather than simply provide the infrastructure and legal regimes that even those who believe markets should be allowed to operate with minimal interference from the state concede are necessary.
In Lin's view, poor countries simply cannot ignore market failures
only because they are afraid of government failures.

This last point is especially relevant in the agricultural sphere.
The architects of the SAP were well aware of the importance—some
might say the centrality, though whether for better or worse is of
course another question—of international development assistance to
the countries of the Global South. In retrospect, the fact that they
hewed for so long to the position that they could struggle to secure
this while for all intents and purposes starving agriculture of government investment and somehow expect the invisible hand of the
market to take up the slack seems absurd. And yet, while there is no
way to prove or disprove this, it seems to have been exactly what they
did think was going to happen, assuming, that is, that they thought
about the subject at all. Was this a matter of institutional blindness?
To some degree, perhaps it was, but a far greater influence was the
example of the Green Revolution itself, which seems to have been
so compelling that trying to find a way to alleviate rural poverty
without a "modernizing" technological transformation appears not
to have ever been seriously considered. As Olivier de Schutter has
pointed out, making agricultural productivity the sole measurement
of success made it easy to ignore the need not just to provide an adequate diet to very poor people but to do so in the context of "social
equity and environmental sustainability."[8] And yet, given the way the
development project has been yoked from the start to a productivist
model, what is surprising is less what has been retained but rather the
extent to which the new model has diverged from it.

Pure productivism is simply not a viewpoint that even those who defend the broad outlines of the SAP continue to try to justify in the second decade of the twenty-first century. Nor do those who (intelligently) celebrate the achievements of the Green Revolution deny that, as Bill Gates put it, "there were also some serious unintended consequences."[9] Just as the social injustices committed in the name of the SAP are usually glossed over by the World Bank, an institution that is an elephant with regard to poverty reduction but a flea with regard to democracy, so the negative and harmful consequences of the Green Revolution loom rather larger than Gates seems to understand. One can argue whether or not the massive number of farmer suicides that Vandana Shiva and many other Right to Food activists view as a consequence (direct in Shiva's view, indirect in the view of some of her fellow campaigners), or whether, as many pro-GMO scientists and journalists as well as the public-relations arms of many of the most important agricultural multinationals believe, there may be correlation but the statistics actually show that there is no demonstrable causation. One can argue about the safety or danger of GMOs. And one can debate how important to bringing masses of people out of poverty it actually is that traditional agriculture is one of the most important aspects of rural culture in the deepest sense of the term.[10] But the Green Revolution's emphasis on mechanization created enormous unemployment among the rural poor, who, with fewer resources to buy food, have often found themselves more rather than less food-insecure, this despite the very considerable leap in crop yields that the Green Revolution undeniably made possible.

Coming on the heels of the Green Revolution, the SAP struck smallholder farmers with a second body blow in the form of the withdrawal of state subsidies for farming and at least partly protected markets for agricultural products, while the United States and European Union were permitted to subsidize their farmers. The global context of this was that capitalism as it had been understood in the era of Dwight Eisenhower, with its confidence that government could and, more importantly, needed to play a key role, had been replaced by the extreme version of laissez-faire capitalism that had come to dominate the thinking of Western elites during the Thatcher and Reagan years, and in which the radiant future would be brought about through the invisible hand of capitalist market. The main thing that was needed, the argument went, was to remove the dead hand of the state. If that was done, prosperity might not be assured, but at least poor countries would be headed in the right direction. Even assuming this had been right—and despite the continued rearguard actions at the bank, reminiscent of nothing so much as people who defend communism but say that its every manifestation has been a distortion of its ideals, it seems hard to believe that something with such disastrous effects on the poor of the Global South could be "right"— the immiseration of the rural poor in particular was a calamity in practice. As Joseph Stiglitz once quipped, "The reason the invisible hand is invisible is partly because it's simply not there."[11] The effect in the real world, far from the bloodless fantasies of Milton Friedman and the other "Chicago boys," was that development policies largely dictated by the World Bank to countries where, in many cases, half or more of the population was made up of smallholder farmers, was to starve agriculture of the monies it so desperately needed—again, this at a time when both bilateral and multilateral development aid was being vastly increased for other priorities more congruent with the presuppositions inherent in the SAP.

In effect, the SAP undermined not just traditional agriculture in the poor world but also the traditional coping mechanisms of smallholder farmers. Today, we are supposedly wiser. They may still be fighting a rearguard action to justify the program, but almost no one at the World Bank seems to want to talk about structural adjustment anymore. Instead, catchphrases like "poverty reduction" are all the rage. Go to the World Bank website, and you find myriad references to "innovation, transparency and accountability." It is an interesting choice of words, more for what it leaves out than for what it puts in. "Innovation," of course, is a technocrat's word, utterly value neutral (you can innovate in weapons development or, more to the point, derivatives trading, just as easily as in sustainable agriculture). "Transparency" is of great concern to the citizens of donor countries, and something of a mantra within those NGOs particularly involved in campaigns to further global "good governance." Whether that project, however laudable, is of any great relevance in the near term to a smallholder farmer in Guinea or Bangladesh is very much open to question. And as to "accountability," since when are the powerful ever accountable to the poor? There is no question that words help shape reality. But to deploy them while turning one's back on, if not flatly denying, inconvenient, unpalatable truths about the way so many of the poor live *now* has a quality of magical thinking to it, as if describing the world often enough in this positive way would sooner or later cause the reality to become more positive as well.

We are back to Gilbert Rist and his argument that development is much more than a program, but rather a global faith. After all, if one believes that the solution to hunger and extreme poverty is not just possible but virtually guaranteed, assuming everyone does their part, and that the only question is how fast this (historically utterly unprecedented) better world can be achieved, then everything now standing in its way must also be destined to disappear. Rist has pointed out the undertones of Christian Salvationism in this. In fairness, the role of the prophetic in radical social movements is a long and distinguished one. And it is simply a fact that such millenarian expectations have been inscribed on the DNA of the development project from its beginnings. Perhaps it could not cohere without them. But meanwhile, even though the bank's website is full of images of smiling poor people from the developing world, it is difficult to find much serious engagement with what these people might want in those documents in which the institution presents its macroeconomic analysis and the policy prescriptions that flow from it.

Lip service is not the same thing as service. But what is most remarkable about the World Bank's politically correct slogan is the words that it leaves out. There is no mention of democracy and no mention of rights. Instead, as William Easterly pointed out in *The Tyranny of Experts*, his passionate critique of the development project, since the bank could obviously not avoid some discussion of the nature of government in development, it has always restricted itself to the term "governance," which can mean almost anything, and which, according to a a study done by Franco Moretti and Dominique Pestre, appears in bank publications and other public documents as often as "food," ten times more often than "law," and a hundred times more often than "politics."[12] As I noted earlier, according to Easterly, a World Bank press official told him the World Bank was legally forbidden under the terms of its own charter to use the word *democracy*. And what Easterly rightly describes as "linguistic evasions" are not mere artifacts of the "bad old days" of the SAP, before the bank had its James Wolfensohn–era makeover and stopped speaking of making poor countries rich but rather of ending poverty. To the contrary, they very much reflect the bank's current practice as well.

And democracy does indeed pose a challenge to institutions such as the World Bank. The reasons for this are simple: for all the ways in which their meanings have been misused and at times abused, *democracy* and *rights* are words that at least can have profound moral, legal, and political consequences. This is not merely a debater's point. The SAP was a diktat on the part of the international financial institutions and the principal Western donor governments. Undemocratically arrived at and undemocratically administered, whatever its intentions, its effect on smallholder agriculture throughout the poor world was devastating. The current global food crisis has arisen in the context of that devastation, and if it is understood as simply a technical problem, as too many people in the Global North continue to believe it to be, susceptible to a largely technical solution along the lines of a more ecologically sensitive Green Revolution, then the result this time around will be more devastating still. That is what the activists fear, and in this they are almost certainly right, though whether, in an era when technology is almost universally viewed as the ultimate deus ex machina, it is possible to think in the radically different way needed is, to say the least, an open question. Nor is it clear, for all the talk of listening to the world's poor that has become pervasive at the bank and at major donor institutions like USAID and DFID, whether the development is any more democratic today than it was during the heyday of the SAP. The current diktat may well be far more sensible than the bank's previous prescriptions, but it is anything but clear that the tyranny of experts and the "authoritarian development" that William Easterly denounced in his book has lessened to any significant degree.

Can the crisis of the global food system be addressed successfully through expert knowledge and technological innovation? The stakes could scarcely be higher. It is not hyperbole to say that the global food crisis—not just the events of 2007–2008 themselves but, even if one takes a largely positive view of the Green Revolution, almost half a century of failed agricultural policies in rich and poor countries alike—has already been a tragedy of world-historical dimensions. The poor of our world, above all, poor farmers, have paid dearly for the SAP,[13] and if the global food crisis is not seriously addressed, they will pay more dearly still. Olivier de Schutter, one of the most important voices of reason in the current debate over how to forge an effective and decent global food system (they are not necessarily the same thing, as any utilitarian knows), has held out the hope that there is indeed at least the possibility of turning the crisis into an opportunity. But for his (cautious) optimism to be warranted, many of the trends of the past thirty years would have to be reversed. In 1979, aid focused on agricultural development comprised 18 percent of all international assistance to poor countries, both directly from rich countries and through the United Nations system; by 2006—that is, a year before the food crisis erupted—it had fallen to 2.9 percent.[14] For all intents and purposes, it had disappeared from the global development agenda. Because of the food crisis, it is back. But it is one thing to want to put things right and quite another to know how to do so. Certainly, de Schutter never claimed the massive changes needed in the global governance of agriculture would be easy, and there too he was correct. Sometimes a crisis is just a crisis.

What is now clear to practically everyone is that the price spikes of 2007–2008 were not a historical anomaly but rather are almost certain to be repeated time and again (as they were in 2011–2012), and that what we are living through is not some transitory crisis that after dominating the headlines for a season or two, will then be replaced by another apocalyptic anxiety—global *cooling* perhaps, as the El Niño effect takes at least temporary hold, or the possibility that there is less oil in the world than had been previously assumed, or, alternatively, that the world will not be weaned from its dependence on fossil fuels before, from an environmental standpoint, it is too late. To the contrary, in a world in which food is a great deal more expensive and in which the world's population continues to grow, above all in its poorest regions, one of two things is going to happen: we will find a way of growing more food with less environmental cost, or tens of millions if not hundreds of millions of people are going to go hungry. Even if that proves too alarmist a prediction, at the very least, there is an increasing consensus among all the relevant players—development experts, agronomists, economists, United Nations officials, and on Wall Street, in the Chicago commodities pits, and in the City of London—that the nearly century-long era was coming to the end not just of comparatively cheap food but of steadily declining food prices as a percentage of family budgets in both the rich and in the poor worlds, and that even if the prices of foodstuffs eventually came down—as, by the fall of 2008, they in fact did—it was virtually certain that food was going to be costlier in first half of the twenty-first century than it had been in the second half of the twentieth.

This, though, is as far as the consensus goes. That people are finally paying attention to global agriculture indisputably marks a sea change in attitudes. But whether the upshot of this renewed focus will turn out to be fewer hungry people is another matter entirely. Even assuming that the claims for what had been accomplished were justified, and the new agricultural technologies, including GMOs, turned out to deliver stunning results in terms of crop yields and drought and pest resistance, all at seed prices that smallholder farmers in the poor world could afford, the very real possibility exists that climate change would first halt and then undo much if not all of that progress. In development circles, talk of resilience and adaptation to climate change are the order of the day, with some even marrying a favored buzzword of the past with a current favorite, so as to speak of "sustainable resilience." But even assuming that rich countries make good on their pledges to provide the UN's Green Climate Fund $100 billion (and the fact is that historically, rich countries have rarely fulfilled such promises in their entirety), and assuming as well that successful adaptation practices are widely instituted in the poor world, the fact remains that success will still depend on holding global rises in temperature to 2 degrees Celsius. And as Saleemul Huq, the director of the International Centre for Climate Change and Development at the Independent University, Bangladesh, has put it, "If temperature rises to over 4 degrees—the trajectory the world is on now—then even rich countries will reach the limits of their ability to adapt."[15]

Is it likely that serious efforts will be initiated in time? On past performance, certainly not: governments, and NGOs have been focused on anthropogenic climate change since 1990 with virtually nothing practical to show for it, despite the abundance of study groups, scientific reports, expert commissions, and conferences that have come and gone without making the slightest difference in the only way that really counts: limiting the extent of the rise of global warming. To the contrary, hundreds of new coal plants are already on the drawing board, the devastation of the Brazilian and Ecuadorean

Amazon only gathers speed, and hydraulic fracturing ("fracking") to obtain natural gas seems poised to become a reality on a mass scale in much of the United States and Canada. Meanwhile, the emerging powers such as China, India, and Brazil, on one side, and the United States, Canada, and the European Union, on the other, remain at loggerheads on everything from the amount of permissible emissions to which each country will be entitled to how curbing emissions and financing mitigation efforts in poor countries will be paid for and by whom. This was presumably not what UN secretary general Ban Ki-moon had in mind when in 2013 he called on climate negotiators meeting in Warsaw to rise to the challenge of climate change with "wisdom, urgency and resolve,"[16] or World Bank President Jim Yong Kim meant in 2014 when he called for a comprehensive plan "equal to the challenge," and mourned the fact that to date none existed or even seemed in the offing.[17] Small wonder, then, that public interest has remained fleeting even when an extreme and ominous event occurs, as when, in May 2014, it was determined that the glaciers of the western part of the Antarctic had begun to collapse and that it was quite simply too late to halt the process, which also meant that it was too late to halt a considerable rise in sea levels, the only question being how big a rise and how quickly it would take place.

Starkly put, even comparatively cautious projections about the effects of global warming are incompatible with the triumphalist rhetoric about ending hunger that has become the norm in the early twenty-first century. Jim Yong Kim, who seemed particularly drawn to this rosy scenario early in his tenure at the bank, has grown far less sanguine, warning on the eve of the bank's 2014 annual meeting that "fights over water and food are going to be the most significant direct impacts of climate change in the next 5 to 10 years."[18] What Kim did not say, though it was implicit in his statement, was that not only would these conflicts halt progress toward ending hunger and extreme poverty in significant parts of the poor world, but that it called into question the reigning assumption in the development world that the progress already achieved was irreversible. To be clear the *proportion* of hungry people in the world has indeed diminished (although setting climate change to one side, it is less clear that there will actually be a sustainable decrease in their absolute numbers). But the places where progress has been most striking—Bangladesh and Brazil, to cite two of the most important examples—are the same countries and regions where global warming is likely to exact a particularly severe toll. In *The End of Poverty*, Jeffrey Sachs rousingly summed up the emerging mainstream view, writing that "the time to end poverty [had] arrived."[19] But as Sachs himself seems to have begun to realize in the years since he wrote those lines, the sending out of what he called "mighty currents of hope" could not possibly achieve the millenarian outcome that he claimed to be within humanity's grasp if global temperatures rose more than 2 degrees Celsius.

Just as good nutrition is not simply a question of sufficient calories and proper nutrients but rather of a reasonable standard of health care, decent sanitation, and, at least arguably, most importantly of all, the emancipation of women, so any lasting progress in reforming the global food system will depend on climate change not becoming virtually uncontrollable. If it does, then Sachs's mighty currents of hope will prove to be less visionary than delusional. Just as, in medicine, the fact that something is not incurable does not mean that it will be cured, so, too, the facts that the hungry are no longer all but invisible to those who make global food policy and that there are things that can be done at least to alleviate their suffering does not mean that those things will be done. In an era in which good intentions are too often conflated with good deeds and good deeds with effective ones, this is a very inconvenient truth indeed. And yet, however unpalatable, the fact remains that the window of opportunity to fend off what the Chinese climate specialist Changhua Wu has called "the coming heat age"[20] of 3 or even of 4 degrees Celsius is closing fast. And if it closes, posterity is likely to view with bitter derision not only the global food establishment's reliance on the *deus ex machina* of scientific innovation sufficient to meet virtually any challenge posed by the world of nine billion people, but also the system's critics who seemed to believe that once food was recognized as a human right, the eradication of hunger and malnutrition would be acknowledged as an achievable goal.

In his final report before stepping down from his post as UN special rapporteur for the right to food, Olivier de Schutter made this case with great aplomb. But his confidence that what he was recommending was practicable rested on the highly debatable implicit assumption that democratizing the global food system was a realistic and achievable goal. The late twentieth and early twenty-first centuries had indisputably been an era in which absolute poverty had indeed generally decreased. But it had also been a time where income inequality had radically increased in almost every part of the world, rich and poor alike. This alone made the democratization of the global food system a far less straightforward matter than de Schutter's official reports made it appear to be. Around the same time that de Schutter was issuing his last list of policy recommendations as special rapporteur, the French economist Thomas Piketty published his magisterial *Capital in the Twenty-First Century*, in which he showed that inequality was growing ever more entrenched and thus more defining of global capitalism as a system. If Piketty was even half right, then de Schutter's mapping out of what he presented as a viable path toward the democratization of the global food system was doomed from the start because of the stark fact that the wider global system of which it was only one element had demonstrably been growing less democratic for years. Insisting, as Jim Yong Kim did in a 2015 interview he gave to the Spanish newspaper *El País*, that because "the world now knew how the [global] rich live, and because of that it [*sic*] will demand more equality" was neither helpful nor convincing.

Piketty's view that income inequality would remain inscribed on the DNA of capitalism unless redressed by high, globally applied wealth taxes at least offered a way out, but it was hardly without its detractors. But one did not have to be a fierce critic of the current world system, let alone agree with Piketty's solutions, to see income inequality as a pressing threat to the current global order. To the contrary, if anything, "enlightened" defenders of that order took an even more alarmist view. For example, the Davos World Economic Forum's 2014 Global Risks report named "severe income disparity,"[21] even in countries and regions where the incomes of the very poor were growing, as one of the highest risks of global concern and first in terms of its likelihood of occurring, overshadowed only by "fiscal crises in key economies, structurally high unemployment/underemployment, [and] water crises," and placed above the possible "failure of climate change mitigation and adaptation."[22]

Obviously, not all analysts were as troubled by the implications of rising inequality for democracy as were either Piketty and his followers or the World Economic Forum. To some, inequality posed little societal hazard so long as the incomes of the poor continued to rise and incomes for most people in the rich world did not continue to stagnate, as they had done since the 1980s. But the case that the world was becoming less democratic does not depend on what is fundamentally a moral intuition rather than an indisputable fact about the social consequences of income inequality. Instead, there is ample evidence in reports from groups such as Freedom House that in the early twenty-first century, democracy has been in retreat in many parts of the world, if not formally then certainly substantively in the sense that Fareed Zakaria intended when he anatomized the phenomenon of "illiberal democracy." They also seemed to refute the widespread assumption of the immediate post–Cold War era that, in the words of Joshua Kurlantzick in *Democracy in Retreat*, which he wrote for the Council on Foreign Relations, that, "as countries develop economically, they will also become more democratic." Instead, a constellation of factors, as Zakaria argued, "from the rise of China to the lack of economic growth in new democracies to the West's financial crisis, has come together to hinder democracy throughout the developing world." And Kurlantzick was anything but optimistic that this would change in the foreseeable future. "Absent radical and unlikely changes in the international system," he wrote, "that combination of anti-democratic forces will have serious staying power."[23]

As their unstinting praise for undemocratic and (at best) authoritarian regimes such as Ethiopia and Rwanda illustrates, for those institutions in the development world that have placed their faith and, in the case of official development agencies like USAID and DFID and philanthropies such as Gates and Rockefeller, their vast resources and pools of expertise in largely technocratic and arguably post- if not antipolitical responses to extreme poverty and hunger, the issue of democracy never loomed very large in the first place. Assuming it was indeed taking place, there was no reason for the de-democratization of the world to dampen their optimism about ending extreme poverty and chronic hunger. But the same could not be said for those who viewed *sustainable* progress in this struggle as being inseparable from securing basic human rights for the poor and reducing income inequality globally. In light of this, Bill Gates's optimism was entirely understandable. But when Olivier de Schutter insisted that food systems had to be "with a view to ensuring social equity," and gave every indication of believing that this could be done without a radical transformation of the entire global political system, not just food and agriculture, his was not.

· 9 ·

The Case for Optimism

There are slightly over seven billion people alive today on the planet as I write this in the spring of 2015. A year from now, by the time this book is published, the world's population will have increased by more than seventy million people, that is to say by the equivalent of the current population of France plus five million. In theory, it is of course possible that before the nine billion threshold is reached, a catastrophe will occur that will be so lethal, so widely distributed geographically, and so long-lasting in its effects that the increase will not be nearly that high. But it would have to be on a scale unknown in modern times, one that would be far, far greater than the 20 million Russians who died in the Second World War, or those who perished in the Chinese famine of 1959–1962 or in the AIDS pandemic that began in the 1980s, none of which curbed population growth in the affected regions for long.[1] In fact, there are no modern precedents for such a demographic reversal caused by a disaster, though, as Juvenal said, luxury is more ruthless than war, an adage whose truth is demonstrated by the current fall in birth rates in the Global North to the point that in most rich countries they are below replacement level. Instead one would need to go back to the plague of the fourteenth century, the so-called "Black Death," which is thought to have wiped out 30 percent of the population of China (where it is believed to have originated) and up to 40 percent of the population of medieval Europe. But whereas it took Europe almost a century and a half to reach again the population level of the early fourteenth century, even with the terrible losses of World War II, Russia's population of over 214 million in 1960 was almost twenty-five million higher than its prewar population of approximately 180 million.

Population tends to be a maddening subject in both senses of the term. Add the question of whether the food supply can keep pace with demographic increase, and one can get the impression that for many, no scenario is too apocalyptic, above all, among those contemporary heirs of Malthus who are to be found at the fear-soaked fringes of the environmental movement. Writing in 2012, more than thirty years after the first publication of Paul and Anne Ehrlich's *The Population Bomb*, the widely read British writer and environmental campaigner George Monbiot could present as if it were a simple statement of fact the claim that "as the population rises, structural global famine will be avoided only if the rich start to eat less meat."[2]

Like the Ehrlichs before him, Monbiot's arguments are hardly baseless. But they are not nearly as ironclad as his unqualified words suggest. Even leaving aside the question on what, if anything, a *structural* global famine actually means, Monbiot's certainty that death by starvation for hundreds of millions of people is assured unless people stop eating so much meat is at best—and in my view even this concedes too much to his argument—an extrapolation from present trends. In this, Monbiot is proceeding along the same lines Malthus did, which, given that unfortunate precedent, at the very least means that he could be mistaken. Monbiot is obviously right to emphasize the strain on the environment that the privileging of meat production has caused. But his dystopic determinism is simply the mirror image of the utopian determinism of those within the global food establishment who believe that a second Green Revolution not only will play a central role in continuing to ensure that famines remain things of the past but will sooner rather than later make chronic malnutrition and undernutrition history as well.

But however dire the future may turn out to be, where chronic hunger is concerned, the world of the present—that is, of the seven billion—is quite bad enough. Despite all the undeniable progress that has been made in reducing global poverty, at the present time, depending on the year (the figures tend to fluctuate), somewhere between nine hundred million and over a billion—that is, nearly one in seven—people will at least intermittently have the experience of going hungry at various points during their lives. And even when they are able to get enough to eat, the chronically hungry live in that perhaps rather too antiseptically christened state of food insecurity.

This deficit can be seasonal, for the most part linked to those periods of the year when there is less food available, at least at an affordable price. Or it can be directly related to shortfalls in income, as is the case, for example, with poor people in the developed world whose salaries or social assistance payments are exhausted by the beginning of the last week of the month and from then to the first of the following month simply don't have enough money to buy all the food they need. These are some of the variants of what, for simplicity's sake, nonspecialists think of as chronic malnutrition, though many are undernourished as well. Scientifically, malnutrition and undernutrition are not the same thing, though of course many poor people suffer from both. Undernutrition is largely a question of quantity, and for the most part those whom it affects are simply not getting the minimum number of calories human beings need in order to flourish. In contrast, malnutrition occurs when a person is not getting enough vitamins, salts, minerals, or protein, even if the calorie count of what he or she is consuming is more than sufficient.

We associate both malnutrition and undernutrition with the citizens of the poor world, and rightly so. But there are a surprisingly large number of malnourished and undernourished people in the richest countries of the world, notably in the United States and in the United Kingdom, though to a lesser extent in other EU countries as well. In both countries, steep rises in poverty rates since the turn of this century have led to startling increases in the incidence of both malnutrition and undernutrition, with a disproportionate impact on children and the elderly. In 2013, a group of senior researchers at the British Medical Research Council issued a public letter claiming that hunger in the UK had come to constitute a "public health emergency."[3] There are estimated to be three million malnourished people in Britain, a disproportionate number among the old. If one were to include the obese in this statistical profile, the number would be considerably higher. According to Bread for the World, 14.5 percent of US households struggle to put enough food on the table. More than forty-nine million Americans—including 15.9 million children—live in these households.[4] Almost nine million people get some form of food assistance, largely through the so-called WIC program (Women, Infants, Children), which was instituted in 1972, and was the brainchild of Sen. Hubert Humphrey, the last great champion of American New Deal liberalism.[5]

In the fall of 2013, conservative Republicans in the US Congress were able substantially to reduce the amount of money granted under the Supplemental Nutrition Assistance Program (SNAP), which used to be called the Food Stamp Program, to food-insecure American families. For example, in New York City the reduction cost 160,000 people an average of $90 a month in food stamps. In doing so, these legislators made it clear that their desired end state was eventually to get rid of most federal food aid programs entirely. Should they succeed at some point, which, given the political realities in early-twenty-first-century Washington, is entirely possible, it is a foregone conclusion that the number of undernourished, malnourished, and food-insecure Americans would increase still further. At least in part, they were able to cut SNAP because the last period when the ongoing food crisis of the poor in the United States received even a small fraction of the attention it deserved was at the time of President Lyndon Johnson's Great Society initiatives in the mid-1960s. And while part of this is due to a lack of political leadership on the part of even those leaders who favor the SNAP program, the fact that the preponderance of those who go hungry in early-twenty-first-century America are malnourished rather than undernourished makes the task of communicating the crisis far more difficult. As for those millions of Americans who are food-insecure, they owe the dubious blessing of this unhealthy form of satiety to salty and sugary snacks and sugared soft drinks, whose calories are largely empty of nutritive value. It is not called junk food for nothing.

Such dependence on junk food to stave off hunger continues to grow. Sugary soda is the greatest single source of the calories in Americans' average daily diet, accounting for 7 percent of the total.[6] The US statistics are considerably worse than those in Western Europe, where the figure is 3 percent, but on both continents the trends are going in the same unfortunate direction, with malnutrition often manifesting itself as obesity—overnutrition as opposed to undernutrition—whose rates globally have doubled since 1980. People who should know better too often think of obesity as yet another manifestation of the privilege of the rich. This was true in the nineteenth and early twentieth centuries, but if anything, the reverse is the case today. Still, above all when it is contrasted with the stereotypical media images of the starving famine victims from Ethiopia or Somalia, it is understandable that the old Christian reflex of seeing obesity as exemplifying the sin of gluttony, that is, as a moral flaw, manifests. In fact, just as with AIDS, obesity is now overwhelmingly a disease of the poorest quartile, not an affliction of the prosperous.

In the last three decades, obesity has spread at a steadily expanding rate throughout the world, beginning with many so-called middle-income countries like Brazil, Mexico, and Egypt—where obesity rates, starting in childhood, have increased at a vertiginous rate—and more recently to poor countries. In sub-Saharan Africa, for example, obesity rates among urban women have skyrocketed since 2000. This has served further to complicate efforts to mitigate food insecurity and address the problems of malnutrition and undernutrition. It should come as no surprise to anyone that in every part of the world, malnutrition and undernutrition are far more likely to affect women, children, and racial and tribal minorities. Indeed, this has always been the commonsense departure point for all development efforts, no matter how radically these approaches otherwise differed one from the other.

In contrast, what had been considerably less clear before the global food crisis of 2007–2008, at least to nonspecialists, was the extent to which it had been a mistake to imagine that poverty reduction could be effective on a sustainable and enduring basis while the problem of chronic malnutrition remained unaddressed. And yet this is precisely what the consensus had been in the development world, at least through the 1980s. Alan Berg, a World Bank official who was an early champion for making nutrition a central element in poverty reduction programs, once wrote, "For years, nutritionists have challenged the broader development community to take nutrition seriously." But even in the 1990s, when, as Berg put it, "much of [the international development community took] seriously the need for better nutrition,"[7] and nutritionists no longer had the sense that they were "walking up the down escalator,"[8] this refocusing remained too narrowly concerned with calories and micronutrients, fortified foods and the role of proteins; that is, as a set of specific technical problems that, to be sure, the development world now conceded needed to be addressed rather than lying at the heart of the kind of development that would succeed in benefitting the poorest of the poor.

In retrospect, it is all but incomprehensible how long it took for nutrition to stop being treated as a freestanding problem, largely divorced from health and sanitation. But then, the same was true of the broader problem concerning what ailed smallholder agriculture in the Global South and where agriculture in the poor world fit in the global food system, and also about whether nutritional redress efforts at a country level could ever be sustainable as long as these macro-level questions regarding agriculture continued to go largely unasked and, even when such questions were raised, almost wholly unanswered.

That in itself was a prescription for failure. For without such political and social analyses of the two ends of the agricultural barbell in the poor world, smallholder agriculture on one side and large-scale tenant farming (what in Latin America are known as *latifundias*) on the other—that is, the agricultural systems in most of those countries where nutrition problems were at their most acute—it is difficult to understand how nutrition experts, even once they began to be properly funded again in the 1990s, could imagine their efforts would be sustainable. In part, this was the product of the nutrition world's own unexamined assumptions about the role of politics and ideology. For in nutrition, as with development more generally, the talk was of sound policies about which it seemed to be assumed that everyone was largely in agreement, rather than of competing ideologies, that is to say, of fundamental differences in both identifying what was really keeping people in poverty and, of course, doing what needed to be done to change that. And while the mainstream development world paid a great deal of attention to what institutional underpinnings in poor countries were needed for programs to have a good chance of succeeding, the political and, above all, the moral legitimacy of these institutions, not to mention that of the aid givers themselves and more generally of the Global North's aid programs, were all but invariably taken as a given.

These unexamined ideological assumptions were far more

important than the mainstream of the development world has ever been willing to concede.[9] Was it an overreliance on the supposedly apolitical "natural disaster" model of public health interventions of the sorts nutritionist were trained to engage in that helps explain why politics and ideology got such short shrift after nutrition once again became a priority in the development world? After all, in the 1950s and 1960s, Western development efforts had been intensely political, indeed had been inseparable though not indistinguishable from the prosecution of the Cold War. But in 1993, at the time Berg was writing, the Cold War had been won, and the United States and its allies were convinced that what might be called the NATO version of liberal capitalism was the only politics left standing, not just at the time but in the future. It was a utopian claim every bit as doctrinaire as those made by Soviet leaders in the USSR's heyday. For all practical purposes, the development agencies of Western governments, the Bretton Woods institutions, the UN, and the major philanthropies were basing their development and antipoverty strategies on the assumption that ideology no longer mattered or, more precisely, that liberal capitalism had won and that its version of what in the USSR had been called "the radiant future" had arrived. In fairness, if this was what one believed, then it was perfectly reasonable to view all development issues as technical problems that were simply awaiting their eventual solutions, whether the solution in question was salt infused with iron and iodine, or good governance, or targeted food subsidies, or all of the above.

By the end of the 1990s, though, even those who reveled in the prospect of what Jeffrey Sachs called "Enlightened Globalization," in which, as he put it, "technological progress enables us to meet basic human needs on a global scale,"[10] had come to recognize the degree to which the problem of chronic hunger had been neglected. As Berg put it, "Over the decades in which famine was being tamed across the globe "the nutrition arithmetic has barely changed."[11] This is not to accuse malnutrition experts of some kind of "famine envy" or to imply that any serious person concerned with chronic malnutrition and undernutrition ever believed that successful strategies for coping with famine could simply be transferred. For example, what would it mean to set up the kind of early warning systems for malnutrition, which is a long-term crisis whose beginning and whose end are alike nowhere in sight, that were meant to predict famine? Even so, it is difficult to see how the comparison with famine could not have been made.

Nonetheless, this kind of rhetoric has been extremely counterproductive. For counterintuitive though it may appear to be at first, although no one but the most nihilistic East Asian social Darwinist or American Tea Party Republican would even consider denying that combating famine is unquestionably a moral imperative, there is little or no evidence that even the greatest of successes in that arena will much alleviate endemic poverty any more than emergency relief during a cholera epidemic can be expected to improve the medical infrastructure of an affected area in any enduring way. To cite the most obvious and in many ways the most seemingly intractable case, there has not been a wide-scale famine in India since 1943, but at the same time, as the UN's own reports on the MDGs document, this has had little effect on improving the nutritional status of the poorest Indians, which, decade in and decade out, has remained among the worst in the world.

Viewed from this perspective, the relationship between chronic malnutrition and famine has some striking similarities with that between emergency relief and development. Indeed, it has become a commonplace for humanitarian NGOs to think in terms of a relief-to-development continuum, to use what has long been the accepted term of art, on the principle that without engaging in an expansive notion of development work that includes human-rights work and conflict-resolution efforts, then even if the aid workers are successful in stopping an epidemic or taming a refugee crisis, they will, in the words of the Australian relief official, Fiona Terry, be "condemned to repeat" their emergency interventions ad infinitum. Just how successful these NGOs have been in shifting gears in so fundamental a way is another question, and there are sharply differing opinions on the question within the mainline relief agencies. Oxfam is an emblematic case of a relief-and-development agency that in institutional terms has been comfortable with this comprehensive approach. Others, notably Médecins Sans Frontières (MSF), have been reluctant to accept the commensurability of the humanitarian and development imperatives. Given the fact that there is always the danger that chronic hunger will morph into acute malnutrition, which is famine's immediate precursor, it would be reasonable to expect that there would be fewer divergences among groups concerned with food aid. But somewhat counterintuitively, the link has proved to be more rather than less tenuous. Famine is correctly understood as an immediate, existential emergency; chronic hunger is not, which has meant, and not wrongly, that combating and preventing famine has always taken both moral and operational priority over chronic hunger.

When famines were both far more common and far more intractable, this made sense. But today, when chronic malnutrition and undernutrition are far more likely to persist than famine (with a few specific geographical exceptions, above all the Horn of Africa) and to affect exponentially more human beings, the moral imperative is far less clear. Famines kill, while chronic malnutrition and undernutrition do not. But in terms of their long-term effects on the societies in which they are endemic, the moral calculus is nothing like as clear, since the widespread incidence of chronic malnutrition and undernutrition almost invariably condemns whole societies to abiding poverty.

In case after case, famine has actually proven more tractable than chronic hunger, in the narrow sense that it is a good deal easier to get people enough food to keep them alive than to get them the minimum of calories and micronutrients they need to consume in order to flourish over the course of a lifetime. In part, this is because of what Simon Maxwell, the former head of the UK's Overseas Development Institute, has called the "emotional weight" that the term *famine* has always rightly carried. For all the continuing controversies about why famines occur and why they do not, the centrality of famine has never been challenged. And innovations such as early warning systems to sound the alarm about incipient famines have been put in place even though their effectiveness has often been found wanting, which was what occurred in Somalia in 2012, when the UN declared a famine to have occurred for which the international system had not been prepared. In reality, it is a distortion to think of famine as a single "explosive" event.

Somalia in 2012 was a case in point. A measles epidemic broke out that was very largely due to the refusal of the Al Shabaab insurgents to permit vaccination programs, and the forced displacement caused by the ongoing conflict of tens of thousands of pastoralists and farmers played at least as important a role as the drought. But however inaccurate such thinking may be, it is in an important sense a "useful" mistake in that it has engendered a wide range of responses and initiatives. In contrast, though chronic malnutrition can also be usefully described as a crisis, constructs such as early warning systems do not make the same kind of intuitive sense, not least because chronic malnutrition and undernutrition have never acquired the kind of emotional resonance Maxwell rightly identified as underpinning global responses to famine.

It would be a grave moral solecism to deprecate the significance of these symbolic and subjective factors that give famine a special status very similar to the one the crime of genocide occupies in international humanitarian law. But acknowledging that famine and genocide alike are in some essential sense *sui generis* should not serve to obscure, as it too often has done, that the global response to chronic malnutrition and undernutrition, above all the link between proper nutrition and poverty reduction, was not a principal focus of mainstream thinking about development until the early to mid-1990s. Two decades earlier, in 1973, Berg was already warning that "malnutrition adversely affects mental development, physical development, productivity, the span of working years—all of which significantly influence the economic potential of man."[12] But until quite recently, there were insufficient scientific data to back up his claim. The neurobiological effect of poor diet on the life chances, above all the educational and by extension the economic expectations of children, had simply not been sufficiently well understood scientifically to hypothesize about possible causal links.

Much still remains to be understood about the exact contribution of dietary deficiencies to this process. But what is no longer in dispute is that the physiological effect of poor diet plays a key role in retarding intellectual development in early childhood, resulting, in many cases, in the inability ever to resolve significant cognitive difficulties. Most scientists working on these questions readily concede that there are other factors at play and that they are not yet able to describe with sufficient rigor the interaction of the nutritional deficits with the lack of access to education that is one of the great scourges of the poor and more broadly with the social effects of extreme poverty itself. Nonetheless, it is possible to claim with great confidence that the failure to provide mothers with nutritious food starting in the period between the tenth and eighteenth week of gestation—the time when the brain of a human fetus begins to grow rapidly—poses a direct risk to the proper development of the nervous system, the development of the glial cells that provide physical support for the neurons, and growth. Such damage is not necessarily permanent, but it is often enough so that as the German neuroscientist C. Forster has shown, across broad populations in which malnutrition and undernutrition are common, there is a plethora of evidence showing the correlation between nutritional deficits in early childhood and intellectual deficits in later life.

The markers for this appear very early. As a general rule, people who are chronically malnourished from gestation through their third birthdays are at least somewhat undersized—what public health doctors call "stunting"—and also somewhat underweight—which they call "wasting." Increasingly, scientists and physicians have been coming around to the view that the life chances of a human being are determined to a very large extent by the nourishment he or she receives and the environment in which he or she experiences the first one thousand days of life. After those first one thousand days, damage is thought to be irreversible. The tragic blighting of individual lives is more than tragedy enough. But it would also be difficult to overstate the dangers posed to any society when there exists a significant proportion of nutritionally injured children in a particular region or among a particular group. It is important to be clear: not everyone who is malnourished or undernourished as a child will grow up with cognitive or other neurological deficits or physical challenges, any more than everyone who smokes will get lung cancer. But the proportion of those who will suffer such effects is high enough that no amount of inspiring personal stories of survival and success can make up for it; indeed, the enthusiasm with which such stories are heralded (too often, unfortunately, by well-intentioned NGOs acting sometimes out of decency, sometimes out of self-promotion, and of course sometimes out of a bit of both) can have the perverse consequence of making a crisis seem less dire than it actually is.

Worse still, the stark reality is that since the damage occurs so early in life, traditional development strategies such as building schools, no matter how committed the authorities are to building and sustaining them and how able and committed the teachers are, come too late for many children. Indeed, many specialists in the early development of poor children are convinced that while the development model that has held sway for decades and puts great emphasis on primary schooling has done a great deal of good (they are emphatically not suggesting that fewer schools be built in the Global South), where the bottom billion are concerned, its success depends to a large extent on whether the children coming to these schools have been properly nourished from two months after conception. If they are even partly right about this, it means that trying to do development without emphasizing early child nutrition is like trying to put together a puzzle from which several important pieces are missing. This may not be welcome news everywhere, above all to officials of development ministries in donor countries, who, for understandable reasons, seek visual images to show to the general public that their tax money is being well spent, nor to officials in countries in the Global South who score political points both at home and abroad by being pictured at the opening of new schools or clinics. In contrast, because it is a process and as such cannot be posed in front of as one does in front of a building, declaring your support for early child nutrition programs is far less likely to attract media attention, even if over the longer term the benefits may be at least as significant if not more so.

But however difficult rethinking development to emphasize early childhood health and nutrition may prove to be, and despite the gaps in knowledge that remain, the broader effects of poor early childhood nutrition are now generally agreed upon, thanks in large measure to the two series of papers published in the British medical journal *The Lancet*, the first in 2007, and the second in 2011, on the general theme of child development in the Global South. For the authors, the question of whether development strategies were too often biased toward older (e.g., school-aged) children rather than toward children between one and four years of age was critical and confirmed the contentions (and the fears, were nothing to change) of the early childhood development specialists. As the authors of one of the 2007 series of papers reported, "We have made a conservative estimate that more than 200 million children under 5 years fail to reach their potential in cognitive development because of poverty, poor health and nutrition, and deficient care."[13]

It was a vicious circle. The risks these children faced—the most important of which were poor cognitive stimulation, stunting, iron deficiency, iodine deficiency, and iron-deficiency anemia—hobbled their future life chances. And the worse these life chances were, the more likely it became that the cycle of poverty in their communities and their countries would be perpetuated. As the authors put it, "These disadvantaged children are likely to do poorly in school and subsequently have low incomes, high fertility, and provide poor care for their children, thus contributing to the intergenerational transmission of poverty."[14]

Broadly speaking, what the *Lancet* studies showed was that the inevitable consequence of these injured lives was and would continue to be injured societies. And even were one to take at face value the claims of success that have been made for the MDGs and, regardless of who deserves the credit, acknowledging the vast numbers of people who no longer live in abject poverty, the fact remains that taken together, the undernourished and the chronically malnourished now comprise fully one in five of everyone now alive. But it was really only in the aftermath of the global food crisis of 2007–2008 that the principal global institutions—governments, NGOs, and philanthropies, with power to reform the world's food system—began to emphasize that proper nutrition both for mothers and for their children during the first one thousand days of life was more than simply one development priority among many others, but rather that without this, many other development goals, including education, were not likely to be successfully attained. In this sense, at least, without proper nutrition it is extremely difficult to envision any set of programs and interventions that can legitimately be called pro-poor development.

This was the lesson that the mainstream development world finally fully took on board in the aftermath of the crisis of 2007–2008. In 2010, a consortium of UN specialized agencies, USAID, and the Irish government—which for obvious historical reasons had long made alleviating hunger the focus of its development efforts in much the way Norway has carved a niche for itself on the international scene by focusing on the diplomacy of peacemaking—and a number of mainline international NGOs, notably Save the Children, World Vision, Bread for the World, and Concern Worldwide, launched the

Thousand Days Initiative, meant to vastly increase nutrition efforts throughout the developing world. As Concern's then-CEO, Tom Arnold, who has played a key role in both the Thousand Days Initiative and the so-called Scaling Up Nutrition movement (SUN), summed up the reality these efforts hoped to transform: "We have never had as much knowledge, evidence, political will and grassroots engagement as we do today to make malnutrition history. Despite this, almost one billion people face food insecurity and 171 million children are stunted, physically, mentally or both, because they did not have enough nutritious food to eat in their early childhood."[15]

Not having the luxury of removal and the license to say whatever one thinks, unconstrained by obligations practical and moral first to judge what the consequences will be for an institution of which one is a part and in whose work one passionately believes (as critics such as myself enjoy), Arnold was making the case for optimism. It was no less than any committed campaigner must do if he or she is to galvanize public support and try to catalyze action. Arnold was every bit as aware as any critic of the global food system of the mortality of past certitudes about humanity standing at the threshold of the end of extreme poverty and hunger. But nonetheless, he seemed persuaded that there was a serious possibility that it really was "going to be different" this time. Of course Arnold knew full well that this raised one of the deepest dilemmas of campaigning groups: the question of whether an NGO has to devise strategies designed to reassure donors, whether governments, philanthropies, or individuals, that with a bit more effort, success would be at hand, so that people who were not development professionals (or even professional altruists, as some campaigners can appear to be at times) could keep supporting your efforts. And how far should NGOs be willing to go? For example, how much should NGOs rely on celebrities to serve as spokespersons for their causes, "to sugarcoat the substance with celebrity,"[16] in the words of Jamie Drummond, one of the directors of the ONE Campaign that Bono cofounded in 2002?

But promoting one's organization or one's cause, extolling its accomplishments, downplaying its failures, and painting as optimistic a portrait of the future as one defensibly can, have become so commonplace that objecting to such strategies is almost as pointless as complaining that it is hot in winter or cold in summer. Can the same be said about the millenarian expectations that are now the default position of much if not most of the development world? Why does Jamie Drummond feel it necessary to claim that "our one human family faces an imminent choice," one in which the world's political leaders "either . . . will seize the opportunity to build on great progress and virtually eradicate extreme poverty, hunger, and preventable treatable disease—or . . . will falter and fall back, risking rampant pandemics, corruption, and instability"?[17]

What would have been wrong with simply saying, "We've made and are making great progress and hope to do better still in reducing poverty and hunger in the years to come"? The infection of NGO discourse (as of practically everything else) by the language of advertising doubtless provides part of the answer. More baffling, and in my view at least, far more troubling is that the millenarian talk of many of those who foresee the imminent end of hunger and extreme poverty often comes twinned with the threat that if humanity refuses to make the correct choices, then instead of living in a world that literally all past generations would have viewed as heaven on earth (no hunger, no poverty, the end of all treatable diseases), we will get the apocalypse. And there is certainly that possibility, but here again, in my view, what for lack of a better term might be called the "vanity of the living" intrudes here. Everything must happen in this generation. Mere progress is not enough. And if it doesn't happen, then its antithesis must occur. In the development world of the early twenty-first century, "mere" progress is no longer enough.

· 10 ·

Science to the Rescue?

The forceful but calm vision of the future of nutrition and the global effort to end hunger that Tom Arnold advanced could scarcely have been rhetorically further away from Jeffrey Sachs's soaring claims that the generation alive in the early twenty-first century had a chance to "sen[d] forth mighty currents of hope," and to "work together to heal the world."[1] And yet Arnold's claims for what could now be done were hardly less ambitious or categorical. "We believe," he would say, "that we have reached a turning point in the fight to end child hunger."[2] He did not believe the system to be broken but rather that it had been on the wrong track for many years in crucial areas but was now firmly back on the right one. For Arnold, it was essential to link the science with the politics, and he extolled the "collaboration between civil society, donors, multilaterals and the private sector."[3] And he was entirely correct in saying that these post-2007–2008 collaborations had both widened and deepened. Indeed, it can be argued that by 2014, the

162

consensus view in the development world was that ending extreme poverty and hunger would only become a reality if the private sector became an even closer partner than it already was.[4]

Before going any further, I want to invite those reading this to keep in mind that the consensus view in the development world that both Jeffrey Sachs and Tom Arnold in their very different ways reflected—which is that history will record that in the first third of the twenty-first century humanity put an end for good to extreme poverty and hunger—may yet be proved right, and my skepticism largely misplaced. But I would hope that even they would concede that such success has been predicted many times before, only to end in disappointment and dashed hopes. For example, if one looks at nutrition, which everyone agrees is one of the keys to success, its history reveals a pattern in which certainty is followed by doubt, which in turn is then followed by a letting-go of the previous orthodoxy in favor of another one. As Nick Cullather pointed out in 2007 in a brilliant essay in the *American Historical Review*,[5] even the calorie is as much a political fact as a scientific datum that measures the energy content of food. To say this is emphatically not to argue that it is inaccurate or that malnutrition is in any way a cultural construct or some figment of the Western imperial imagination. The data in the *Lancet* studies demonstrate the catastrophic effects of chronic malnutrition and undernutrition on small children far beyond any reasonable doubt. But this does not mean the data can be properly applied without thinking through the politics as well as the science. Here again, though, the ideology of the End of History reigns, in the sense that the Western nutrition world acts as if it assumes all the political questions have already been settled and that therefore everyone should get on with the (very) hard work of trying to find ways at least to mitigate or, preferably put an end to chronic malnutrition and undernutrition.

But as Cullather put it, "The calorie has never been a neutral, objective measure of the contents of a dinner plate. From the first, its purpose was to render food, and the eating habits of populations,

163

politically legible."[6] What he calls this "rendering [of] food into hard figures" dates from 1896 and was overwhelmingly the work of the American chemist Wilbur Atwater at Wesleyan University, who invented a device he called the "respiration calorimeter," which allowed him to develop a system that would measure in units the energy created by food. But the fact that this metric is now accepted everywhere in the world should not be confused with its having no politics. As Cullather points out, Gandhi associated it with the industrial civilization he abhorred and once summed up as "gauging progress in terms of calories and comforts."[7]

And even within the broad framework that the adoption of Atwater's measurement system gave rise to, the particular emphases on what the nutritional priority should be have shifted over time almost as decisively as phases in development thinking. The sciences may not be as susceptible to intellectual fashions as the humanities, but they are scarcely immune to them. In the 1950s and 1960s, for example, protein was the focus. But as Professor Ted Greiner of South Korea's Hanyang University pointed out in a paper published in 2012, "Companies and entrepreneurs in the rich countries began to show their concern (all the way to the bank) by developing fish protein, single cell protein, and even protein from microorganisms grown on petroleum. But this agenda came to a screeching halt after 1974 when Don McLaren published 'The Great Protein Fiasco' in *The Lancet*. He pointed out that in nearly all cases traditional diets, when adequate in quantity, provided enough protein. From being at the top of the nutrition policy agenda, protein deficiency has since been relegated to a position of minor importance."[8]

By the late 1970s, as Greiner documents, "micronutrients (certain vitamins and minerals) began to take center stage."[9] Greiner is not persuaded. Instead, he has argued that just as had been the case with protein, the scientific evidence with regard at least to vitamin A, one of the most highly touted of these vitamins, making an essential difference in children's lives is clearly excessive claims.

The paradigmatic contemporary example of such overreach was the development in 2000 of so-called golden rice, a genetically modified rice variety high in vitamin A's precursor, beta carotene. When it was launched, golden rice was hailed as a milestone in improving child nutrition in the poor world—a view that, generally speaking, still prevails at the UN and almost all other mainstream institutions. Greiner ascribes the development of this consensus, which if anything has only grown stronger, in large measure to the excessive influence of Western donor countries and the interests of multinational corporations, about whose motives he remains decidedly skeptical.

But one does not have to accept his account of the political and economic interests behind the push for vitamin A supplementation to be troubled by the evidence he presents about its ineffectiveness, above all in reducing child mortality—one of the principal MDG goals—for which it has been claimed to be particularly valuable.[10] Greiner has been wholly unwilling to take at face value the claims of its boosters that the success of anti-GMO campaigners in denying golden rice to the poor has been a historic injustice. An emblematic expression of this view can be found in a 2014 University of California report in which three distinguished agricultural researchers wrote that, "Golden Rice could have saved millions of lives and avoided blindness, vulnerability to childhood infections, anemia and poor growth in millions"[11] of people since the engineering process for adding vitamin A to rice was identified in 1999. And more recent research would seem at the very least to buttress the case for caution. Most notably, a 2014 update by the International Rice Research Institute (IRRI), which oversees the golden rice project and has been resolute in insisting on the project's great promise, conceded that the average yield of golden rice have been "unfortunately lower than from comparable [non-GMO] varieties already preferred by farmers" in the Philippines, where most of the testing had been taking place.[12]

But assume for the sake of argument that the disappointing results for golden rice represented only a temporary setback and that more broadly the confidence with which Tom Arnold claimed that we knew more than we ever had about what needed to be done to end malnutrition, including scientifically and technologically, was warranted. This still begs the question of whether he and his colleagues were right to insist, as Concern had already done in its 2008 report, that the G8 countries had an opportunity to make undernutrition history. In reality, the answer to that question was less clear than perhaps he and his organization might—again, out of the best of intentions—have wished it to be. The first problem was that such confidence required one to believe that, this time, the G8 was truly in earnest. But given the history, there was ample room for skepticism, at least assuming skepticism was still considered morally licit in the development world, which at least some of SUN's reactions, public and private, to sharp critical challenge, was by no means certain. The second problem was the assumption that the countries of the Global South that had committed themselves publicly to the SUN process were in earnest about seeing through this revolution in nutrition that SUN was heralding, despite the fact that in many cases the regimes in question were extremely undemocratic and in some cases brutally repressive. If one combines these facts with the failures of the past, at the very least—though the architects of SUN would almost certainly not agree—it gave rise to the question of whether such claims *once again* represented the proverbial triumph of hope over experience.

Gilbert Rist has called development a "global faith," in much the way Nadine Gordimer once referred to human rights as a kind of "secular religion," so perhaps instead it was the triumph of faith over experience. But faith alone cannot account for the complacency of the SUN movement's architects about what it was on the threshold of accomplishing that was evident in the draft strategy document released in August 2008. It is only in the last page and a half of a twenty-six-page report, after mission statements, declarations of its principles, detailed descriptions of its stakeholders, its barometers of progress, its systems of accountability, and endless charts and graphs, that almost as an afterthought, there appears a section called "Constraints, Risks, Mitigation." Compared with the effusion of the previous sections, it is terse. And most of the risks that are listed concern such questions as the failure to obtain sufficient resources and the "value add of SUN not understood or clearly articulated." Only in bullet point two of a seven-bullet list, sandwiched between "SUN countries fail to prioritize nutrition effectively" and "In-country SUN focal points are not resourced sufficiently or lack skills," does one find the sentence, "Sufficient high-level political commitment is lacking."[13]

As with the MDGs, the blithe expectations of success that this reveals can seem reasonable only if one has unquestioningly accepted the fundamentally postpolitical order that Francis Fukuyama has posited. If it is in fact true that there is one set of global goals to which all responsible actors subscribe, even if certain "spoilers"—warlords, terrorists, profiteers, and the like—remain outside the warm embrace of the End of History, then the expectations for the Thousand Days Initiative and for SUN are far more likely to seem plausible, even if some of the more fantastic utopian pronouncements of officials involved in these programs are not. It is hard to know whether UN secretary general Ban Ki-moon was serious when, at a meeting on SUN held at the UN in the fall of 2012, he went from the perfectly defensible statement that "in our world of plenty, no one should be malnourished" to the utopian fantasy not simply of a world with no hunger but of one in which "all food and agriculture would be sustainable, and no food would be lost or wasted."[14] In reality, for such a world to come into being there would have to be the most radical *political* reordering, one in which inequality would be lessened rather than widening dramatically, as was happening when Ban gave his speech and shows every sign of continuing to do.

To put the matter starkly, if agriculture is not sustainable, this is not by some oversight; rather, it reflects profound social assumptions, entrenched political arrangements, and above all, immensely powerful financial interests. Ban surely did not suppose that these dominant social classes, ruling political elites, and multinational corporations whose profits from the current system of industrial agriculture are, to put it chastely, considerable, were miraculously going to have a mass conversion, à la St. Paul on the road to Damascus. But assuming his speech was not completely pro forma and that he actually thought the vision he was outlining was a credible one (to be fair a UN secretary general is obliged to say all sorts of things he cannot possibly believe), what else could Ban have meant?

The answer once again was that with the End of History at hand, it was assumed that there was no need to debate what kind of just society was needed if there was to be any hope of achieving this goal and, more broadly, those outlined both in the MDGs and the other goals that were being devised to follow onto them after 2015. Didn't we all agree that it was liberal capitalism, buttressed by the rule of law, a proper social safety, etc.—in other words, the current system, though admittedly with a few major changes and lots of minor touch-ups? Those who were outside this consensus were often referred to as spoilers, a term with its echoes of "those who spoil the party," that probably conveys more than it was meant to. These spoilers included some dictators from the Global South, though not, to be sure, those such as the "presidents" of Ethiopia and Rwanda whose determined commitment to making development work was thought to justify ignoring or glossing over their equally determined commitment to making repression work at least as well. And of course, they included warlords and corporations that intentionally despoiled the environment, even if by the second decade of the twenty-first century practically every publicly traded corporation denied this.[15] Finally, they included those in the antiglobalization movement who denied the system could be reformed, as well as those who simply questioned this optimistic vision of the future.

Like Ban's antipolitical pronouncement, even most of the more levelheaded descriptions of what SUN has promised to accomplish have contained at least the implicit claim that with the social and political problem transcended and the technical solutions either at hand or in the process of being developed, the focus could be on the task of implementing with dedication and intelligence the will of the international community.

But what if this consensus, this mustering of collective will, that the SUN project takes as a given is actually more appearance than reality? Even if it were real, what if it proved to be as evanescent as so many other enthusiastic commitments by the development world had proved to be over the decades? Even some of the most eager participants in the SUN and Thousand Days Initiative processes have warned of just this possibility. At the African Nutrition Summit held in Bloemfontein, South Africa, in September 2012, the incoming president of the International Union of Nutrition Sciences, Professor Anna Lartey of the University of Ghana warned that while the international focus on nutrition was intense at the present time, it would not last forever. Because she was so certain of this, Lartey urged her colleagues to "lock in" the engagements that had been made as soon as possible. And Tom Arnold himself, in a blog post he wrote soon after returning to Ireland from the 2012 G8 and NATO summits in Washington and Chicago, could report that he had felt "a critical mass beginning to form in the fight to end global hunger," and that what was needed was to "seize the moment." But even as he allowed himself to hope, Arnold was careful to add the necessary caveat born of long and unhappy experience. "It's a feeling I've had before," he cautioned, "perhaps not this strong, [but] only to be disappointed when promises went unfulfilled. We must keep calling our leaders to persevere, especially those in the G-8, to ensure that does not happen this time."[16]

It was hardly that Arnold was only then coming to grips with the political impediments to the effort to end chronic undernutrition. Quite the contrary: he was far too experienced and his organization had far too long a history of emphasizing them to make such a mistake. In Concern's 2008 report, which had been published in the aftermath of the G8 meeting in L'Aquila at which the donors had committed $22 billion over three years in financing for agriculture and food security—the so-called L'Aquila Food Security Initiative (AFSI), it said, "While broadening the scale of [the] specific interventions that would address the immediate causes of child undernutrition, a longer-term solution is required to tackle the underlying socio-economic and health determinants that drive it." And it concluded, "Concern's experience in low-income countries suggests that tackling inequality and strengthening health systems and services is one way to achieve this aim."

It is a campaigner's duty not to just hope but also to speak and act as if the cause one is championing will not succeed. And certainly Arnold would have been derelict had he not steadfastly maintained that malnutrition and undernutrition among the world's poor children would finally be effectively addressed. But there is simply too much that is conflated in Concern's action plan. To begin with, there is simply no comparison between the project of strengthening health systems—which is in large measure a technical problem for which technical solutions exist, provided sufficient financial and human resources are made available—and tackling inequality—which, in much of the poor world, is a revolutionary idea that would involve overturning political arrangements and, in the case of gender relations, without which no assault on social inequality can succeed, turning social and cultural reality on its head. Nor is it clear that a national development ministry from a country in the Global North, let alone a development NGO, even one as capable and, more importantly perhaps, as reflective as Concern, has any expertise, not to mention legitimacy, in seeking to transform political, social, and gender relations in a country in the Global South. Most mainline NGOs, including Concern, are perfectly aware of this. (The one exception to the rule might be Oxfam, which for all its accomplishments often behaves more like a political movement than an NGO.) And yet when it comes time to offer policy recommendations, it can often seem as if they have forgotten not just other people's politics but their own.

And viewed from other perspectives, notably from that of the parts of the world where traditional societies are still the rule rather than the exception, this political project is extremely radical. For example, it posits gender equality when, especially in much of the poor world, patriarchy remains the norm. And yet gender equality is put forward as if its ethical and social presuppositions are as obvious as day and thus require only the caritative, apolitical language of public health. This is one of the reasons, I think, that there is so much discomfort in the development world when questions are raised about the human rights abuses of governments that are doing well in terms of their development goals and whether donor governments and development agencies are right to believe that if the unhappy choice has to be made, human rights, while obviously very important, have to take a back seat.

Like every secretary general before him, Ban has exemplified this will to ignore politics, not just that of his own organization and that of the world system that it services but also of those who believe that system has to be overturned. When Ban declared that, "SUN is rallying governments, civil society, the private sector and international donors. It is breaking down barriers separating different disciplines, and galvanizing experts in agriculture, health, social protection and finance,"[17] the blandness of his words was forgivable—a professional deformation, as the French say. What was culpable, though, was Ban's misrepresentation of the world as a place in which all relations, once embarked upon, were essentially complimentary. In this antidialectical world in which, assuming that one marshaled the needed expertise (as SUN was unquestionably doing), then all would be well, it was indeed possible to maintain the belief that almost any problem that arose in the future was likely to be one of communication and mobilization rather than contested first principles. But however understandable in the short run, it was a view that over the longer term is almost certain to undermine global development efforts, including those concerned with nutrition, unless, to restate the obvious, one indeed believes the early twenty-first century marks the end of history. One cannot misrepresent the world and also expect to be able to heal it with tools and methodologies derived from that misrepresentation.

To be clear, this does not mean that nothing will come of these efforts to reduce global hunger, or, lest my criticism be misunderstood, that it would be better that these efforts not be undertaken (even if I remain convinced that the chances of success would be enhanced if less utopian promises were being made about what can be achieved). As of this writing, it is far too soon to tell what the outcomes will be. But for now, despite this renewed international focus on nutrition from the major donor countries, above all from the United States, where, during her term as secretary of state between 2009 and 2013, Hillary Clinton made the issue one of her particular causes, the number of chronically malnourished people has not diminished significantly. The UN's own 2012 progress report on the MDGs concedes that in both sub-Saharan Africa and South Asia—the two regions where chronic malnutrition and undernutrition are most widespread—the goal of halving extreme hunger by 2015 will not be met "if prevailing trends persist."[18] And even at his most enthusiastic, as he was in *The End of Poverty*, Jeffrey Sachs was careful to make the point that while he believed his generation could "choose to end . . . extreme poverty by the year 2025," he was "not predicting what will happen, only explaining what can happen."[19]

Those who share Sachs's view are absolutely right to insist that there is much good news. But there is contraflow as well—failure or at the very least lack of progress that it is by no means clear will be overcome. In the case of the MDGs, for example, Lawrence Haddad, who strongly supports them, has emphasized repeatedly (and his candor is wholly admirable as it is very much an argument against interest), "If stunting were an MDG indicator, based on current rates of progress—about 1 percentage point a decade—Africa would meet its 2015 target in the 22nd Century."[20] South Asia and sub-Saharan Africa are not the only regions of the globe where the news about hunger is bleak. In West Asia and Oceania, the report concludes, either there has been no progress at all in reducing hunger or the situation is deteriorating. There are several explanations for this. The situation in West Asia, for example, includes Afghanistan, torn apart by war. But it is hardly coincidental that all the regions where the goal of halving hunger, with the exception of West Asia, also have very high poverty and very rapid population growth.

It is a correlation that should come as no surprise. For the problem of population is central, and the failure to address it is a catastrophe, even if motivated by the understandable reluctance of Western donor governments to advocate policies that can easily be interpreted, given these countries' imperial and racist pasts, as one more expression of Western racism. This historical subtext was an important contributing factor to population control having fallen off the development agenda in the mid-1970s, when, previously, it had been seen as an essential component of any development policy with the slightest hope of enduring success. However, it would be wrong to imply that the de facto dismissal of population control from the rota of development priorities was due to some sort of premature political correctness run amok. What really made this radical shift in priorities possible was the apparent success of the Green Revolution. By drastically boosting crop yields, the Green Revolution was believed to have permanently laid to rest Malthus's argument that in the race between food production and population growth, population would always outstrip the earth's capacity to yield enough food to sustain life for everyone. Instead, the lesson the mainstream of the development world had drawn from the Green Revolution was that food production had now become (and was likely to remain) in the ascendant, and that as a result, dramatic population increases in the poor world might remain a complicating factor but not a determinative one.

For the sake of argument, put aside the claims of food rights activists and other responsible serious and well-informed critics of the Green Revolution that the rises in agricultural productivity it had fostered were based on an environmentally and financially unsustainable model of industrial agriculture that was far too dependent on expensive inputs such as chemical pesticides and herbicides and synthetic nitrogen fertilizer. Put aside as well all the Green Revolution's human costs, above all putting hundreds of thousands of farm laborers out of work as combine harvesters replaced human muscle in the wheat fields of Punjab and the pesticides sprayed on the paddy fields of the Philippines killed off the fish and wild vegetables on which poor Filipino farmers had always relied. Instead, take as a given the mainstream view that all these problems (and many others) can now be rectified, thanks to both deeper understanding of social costs and more sophisticated, less environmentally damaging technology. After all, even Norman Borlaug never claimed the Green Revolution had left no problems unsolved. To the contrary, he had insisted that while it had represented "a change in the right direction, [it had not] transformed the world into a Utopia." And that "change in the right direction" had been epic, with grain production increasing by 250 percent between 1950 and 1984.[21]

This helps explain why the claim of the development establishment is the diametrical opposite of the legally required warning contained in the fine print of most reputable mutual fund investment offerings: past performance is no guarantee of future success. When Bill Gates makes the claim that there will be almost no poor countries by 2035, he is in effect saying that past performance is indeed a guarantee of future success, and even when it isn't, extreme poverty and hunger will still be eliminated, because new and as-yet-unforeseen technologies will be developed, as they have again and again over the past two hundred years, that will solve those problems that even Gates would presumably concede at the present moment have no obvious solution.[22]

In their book *Science and Innovation for Development*, Sir Gordon Conway, the former head of the Rockefeller Foundation (which provided the early funding for the first Green Revolution), and

Professor Jeffrey Waage write that their confidence is based on agricultural science's "long history of success and the clear indication that problems encountered in the past when applying science to development are being addressed."[23] Apparently, they believe that this record, as well as the promising developments in crop science, animal husbandry, biology, nanotechnology, and even, as Conway and Waage emphasize, information and communications technology, should quell all serious doubts, and they criticize what they refer to as the prejudice of those who entertain any serious doubts about the promise of science. Reading them, one would never know that if one is thinking seriously about the history of science, the reality is rather less heroic. Some innovations have been tremendously useful, while others have proven to be a poisoned chalice. Anyone doubting this need only think back to the creation of the atomic bomb, which, well before Hiroshima and Nagasaki, Albert Einstein, Leo Szilard, and Neils Bohr all begged Washington to abandon. Or else one can leap forward to the very real possibility that corporations will quite literally be able to patent life.

In making their assessment, though, those who believe that technology is perpetually improving have in mind medicine, above all public health medicine, not physics. But even where medicine is concerned, great promises have led to great disappointments as well as great triumphs. The continuing lethality of so many cancers despite all the research and money and brain power that have been committed to curing them is an object lesson in this regard. By the same token, surely the onus is on those who believe that in the past the Green Revolution was on balance a great success to explain why they are so categorical in their assertions that it will be similarly successful in the future. It is all rather like generals developing a battle plan that has no fallback position, no set of tactical alternatives should things go wrong, and that is only configured for victory. If one stops thinking of technology as a magic wand (the image is a coinage of the fine critic of technoutopianism, Evgeny Morozov), there is simply no way for them to know, and as a consequence no justification for them to assert, that technological innovation will *always* provide the necessary solutions.

To point this out is not to claim, as some twenty-first-century Luddites certainly do (Conway and Waage are right about this), that science holds *no* promise. But limitless promise? Saul Bellow once observed that given that our own times are the ones in which we were born and will die, we always accord them a special privilege. But simply as a matter of probability, it hardly seems objectively (as opposed to sentimentally) reasonable to posit that whereas we made mistakes that could not be rectified and ran up against insuperable obstacles in the past, today there is no problem that can't and won't eventually be solved. One does not have to share the food activists' skepticism about technology in general and their specific opposition to GMOs and industrial agriculture to doubt the maximalist claims of a Gordon Conway. For example, one could accept that great progress has been made but that this progress is neither limitless nor irreversible. And one can certainly imagine a second Green Revolution that would not be anywhere near as environmentally damaging as the original and that increases crop yields considerably, above all in regions where the first Green Revolution never took hold.

So far, so good, but then the difficult questions come fast and furious. The most obvious and pressing of these is simply: What if, because of the rapid growth of the world's population and the simultaneous worsening of global warming, while we will be able to produce a great deal more food than we do now, we fail to produce quite enough to feed nine or ten billion people? And almost as urgently, will producing more food lead to the poor having access to it? After all, more than enough food is being produced today to feed the seven billion people currently alive on the planet. And yet two billion people suffer from chronic malnutrition or undernutrition. Conway and Waage themselves write of the need to learn whether "science and technology [have] improved the capacity of poorer countries to deal with the successive agricultural, health and environmental shocks"[24] that they quite rightly point out are certain to come. But they make this point only at the conclusion of their book, whereas one might have thought they would want to establish with a reasonable degree of certainty the answer to that question before making the kinds of claims they do for science and technological innovation.

And yet, in *The Doubly Green Revolution*, Conway writes categorically of satisfying the aspirations of the poor and hungry "by bringing the power of modern technology to bear on the problem of providing food security for all in the twenty-first century."[25] But in the same spirit that the SUN movement proceeds as if a global consensus had already been reached on the political and social order needed to end hunger, so Conway writes as if the global food crisis is fundamentally a problem of supply, even though the present crisis shows clearly that this is not the case. Like practically every other serious person concerned with the global food system, Conway writes admiringly of Amartya Sen. And yet Sen's greatest contribution has been precisely to show that the deep problem of food is not supply but access, not production per se, but justice. The implications of this are stark: Conway and Waage may well be proven to have been absolutely right in their predictions of how much food can be produced, assuming that both rich and poor countries adopt the right policies and that the promise of the new technologies is fulfilled, while being proven completely wrong about whether such production will make the predicament of the poorest people in the world any less awful when there are nine billion people alive on the planet than it is now with seven billion.

More immediately, what is so striking in the mainstream view is the degree to which it oscillates between steely optimism, whether the object of that optimism is Jeffrey Sachs's MDGs, David Nabarro's SUN, or Gordon Conway's green productivism, and a panic very much in the same register as that expressed in the 1970s and 1980s by Paul and Anne Ehrlich and other like-minded demographic catastrophists. For example, the Wesleyan University political scientist

Robert Paarlberg, who has been a tireless campaigner for GMOs, insisting that GM crops must play a central role if hunger in Africa is ever to be mastered, has flatly accused those who continue to oppose GMOs of setting the stage for new famines across the subcontinent. It is a view shared by Professor Nina Fedoroff, a distinguished plant scientist who served for a time as science advisor to Hillary Clinton between 2007 and 2010, both during the period when Mrs. Clinton was in the Senate and after she became Barack Obama's secretary of state and, after leaving government, became the president of the American Association for the Advancement of Science. In her book, *Mendel in the Kitchen*, Fedoroff compared present-day resistance to genetically modified foods (GMOs) to the opposition to smallpox vaccinations when these were first developed. Fedoroff's argument was not simply for technology-based solutions in general but for the centrality of GMOs, arguing that most increases in global food production had and would continue to be dependent on their use.

The extreme quality of this sort of rhetoric should not be allowed to obscure the fact that those who dismiss the problem of population, as so many food activists and antiglobalization campaigners too often do, are indulging in their own form of magical thinking, while in the development world, where discussions of population are no longer taboo, as they became in the 1980s, the subject remains an unwelcome one, and understandably so. Population is such a difficult and, even more importantly, such a politically, religiously, racially, and ethically loaded subject that of course it makes human sense not to want to confront it. But the facts plead for a different choice. Having already cited these statistics at several points in this book, they are nonetheless worth repeating: the population in sub-Saharan Africa, that is generally thought to have risen from 100 million in 1900 to 770 million in 2005, will grow to somewhere between 1.5 and 2 billion people by 2050. And there are simply too many variables and too many unknowns to make much more than an informed guess as to when the demographic transition will begin in many sub-Saharan African countries, and a majority of the so-called Sahelian countries (Chad, Niger, Central African Republic, etc.) south of the Maghreb. The central question is: Will this demographic transition occur before it is too late?[26]

Gordon Conway would doubtless reject the comparison, but in his confidence that everyone can be fed, no matter how many there are of us, there is a distant echo of Gandhi's celebrated observation that "the world has enough for everyone's needs, but not for everyone's greed." This is certainly one of the mantras of the food rights movement, whose activists insist that in a decent world system liberated from the capitalist market, there is no technical reason that twelve billion people cannot be fed properly—in other words, that the global food crisis fundamentally is one of justice and not of production. So in this sense, at least, there is a measure of agreement, but one of such a sterile nature that it does little or nothing to narrow the gap between the two positions. And the debate has been so bitter precisely because both sides are convinced that the solution they believe to be the right one is no temporary fix but rather the ultimate solution to the global food crisis. If you were a technoproductivist and you were certain that food production could be increased sufficiently to feed even a much more crowded planet, you would probably be furious that the food activists continue to ignore the scientific evidence and not only refuse to get off their Luddite plinths but continue to have some success in opposing technological innovations in agriculture, both those that involve genetically modified plants and those that do not.

And yet, however understandable, given their belief that if only it is allowed to go forward, the twenty-first-century iteration of the Green Revolution will have all the benefits of the twentieth-century original (but this time with none of its environmental or social problems), the demands of the technoproductivists that the food activists abandon their anxieties about GMOs are quite simply a misreading—whether out of arrogance or ignorance, it is not for me to say—of the passion and seriousness of their adversaries. For some pro-GMO scientists, even the suggestion that politics should enter into a discussion of whether GMOs should be allowed is of itself somehow outrageous.

As the German agricultural economist Alexander Stein put it in an e-mail response to a series of questions I had asked him, "If the debate is about 'powerful industry players and philanthrocapitalists,'[27] then the issue of GMOs is simply a pawn in an ideological discussion at a much higher level, namely which type of society we want."

As Stein saw it, if the problem was political, then that needed to be addressed by "changing the politico-legal framework, if the current framework does not achieve socially optimal outcomes, not by opposing a technology." But there are several difficulties with this view. First, as the British physicist Jon Butterworth has pointed out in an article in the *Guardian* in 2012, "Politics at all levels influence the science we do."[28] The validity of a scientific conclusion may be a matter for science alone, but the practical application of that science in the form of technology cannot reasonably be accorded similar protection. As Butterworth put it succinctly, "Science will not tell you what your policy should be." Making an analogy between the opposition of food activists to the deployment of Golden Rice to the anguish of many of the scientists who split the atom over their discoveries being used to fashion bombs that killed hundreds of thousands of people in Hiroshima and Nagasaki may seem far-fetched. But if you believe that the continuation of the current productivist/technological model is a disastrous mistake, then on reflection it may not be that far-fetched after all.

Moreover, the separation into two distinct realms, each with its own discrete areas of concern, that Stein seemed to be trying to erect—though, to his credit with little of the uncontrolled anger that so marks (and mars) the writings of Fedoroff, Paarlberg, and some of their other, like-minded colleagues—between science and politics is an unsustainable one. To begin with, proponents of GMOs have based a great deal of their case for them on the basis of their being a "pro-poor" technology. Not only is this of itself a political statement in any context other than that of the End of History, it is a justification for GMOs on moral rather than exclusively scientific grounds.

And in any case, one does not have to share the anti-GMO campaigners' apocalyptic anxieties about the dangers of this technology; indeed, one can agree that GMOs had to be part of the mix if there were going to be enough food for the world of nine billion, without accepting the (increasingly routine) claims by experts such as Paarlberg or Federoff and, less stridently, by Gordon Conway, Sir David Baulcombe (a distinguished specialist on plant disease resistance at Cambridge University), and others that there was no compelling need for further debate on what consequences this emphasis on GMOs would have on other possible solutions. As Ian Scoones, the codirector of the STEPS Centre of Sussex University's Institute for Developmental Studies, has put it, "The near obsession with GM solutions can act to crowd out alternatives."[29] Unlike many anti-GMO campaigners, Scoones did not see the funding linkages and movement of personnel between agribusiness firms such as Monsanto and Syngenta and the international public food research institutes such as CGIAR, IRRI, IITA, and CIMMYT as part of some dark conspiracy. Nonetheless, he was adamant that "some companies, most notably . . . Monsanto, have hooked their fortunes on GM technologies." The result, Scoones argued, was that "as funders of much so-called public research," the big companies reinforced a dynamic in which the search for "pro-poor" agricultural innovations became "locked into a particular trajectory."[30]

Nor did he appear to share their conviction—a view, it should be emphasized, shared by many of the world's leading researchers in crop science, including Sir David Baulcombe—that GMOs were not just one element among many but a central part of any solution to the global food crisis and to extreme poverty. But with that important exception, Stein's essential argument was largely congruent with theirs. "In opposing GMOs," he wrote me, "[activists] don't do anything to change the system [they] dislike, but damage those who suffer under this system." It is a view that is shared by many of Stein's colleagues at IFPRI, IRRI, CGIAR, the Gates Foundation, USAID, Cornell, and so on. For them, the only licit position, given the needs of hungry people, is for those sincerely concerned with malnutrition and undernutrition to use, as the cliché goes, every tool in the toolbox, including GMOs, though in no way limited to them. What was puzzling about this argument was not that it is pro-GMO but rather that those advancing it viewed it as a compromise between those who believe only in GMOs and the "antis" who are trying to prevent research from going forward. What Stein did not seem to see was that from the point of view of someone for whom GMOs are a great danger, what he was proposing was no real compromise at all, since it basically involved that they drop their opposition and rely instead on scientific ethics, safeguards, and government regulatory oversight. His side was giving up nothing, since he and his colleagues never thought GMOs were the *only* answer or solution, just one of them.

Stein may have been dismissive of their arguments, but it seems clear that as Scoones's STEPS colleague Dominic Glover put it in a 2009 paper, "Undying Promise Biotechnology's Pro-Poor Narrative Ten Years On," although anti-GM campaigners in places like India and South Africa "have been vigorously criticized for the lack of academic rigor in their reports, [they] have undoubtedly done a great service in compelling the advocates of crop biotechnology for the developing world to sharpen their focus on the real, situated impacts of GM crops."[31] And while writing about the specific case of Bt cotton, Glover makes a point that goes to the heart of what is mistaken in the pro-GMO argument of people such as Stein that technology should not be held hostage to politics. "It has only been by scrupulously isolating Bt cotton from its socio-economic, agronomic, and institutional context," Glover writes, "that it has been possible to keep the technology pristine."[32] (Bt cotton is a genetically modified variety of cotton that produces an insecticide.)

Toward the end of his paper, Glover calls for "the heroic simplification of the 'GM crops are good for the poor' storyline [to be] finally laid to rest."[33] But the simplifications of the radical critics of the current global food system are, if anything, at least as heroic, and their demands more heroic still. To accede to them would for the corporate establishment equate to committing some form of collective class suicide, and there is hardly any more chance of that happening than there is of food activists becoming enthusiastic proponents of genetically modified food staples or conceding that cultivation techniques that are heavily dependent on petroleum-based fertilizers may be an important element in resolving the food crisis. Not only is there little evidence of either side moving toward the middle, but all one has to do is to go on Twitter and look at the feeds of campaigners on both sides to see that if anything, the divisions are only becoming sharper, the debate fiercer and more rancorous, and finding solutions to the crisis of global agriculture remains a zero-sum game pitting against each other two diametrically opposing visions of what lies at the root of the global food crisis and how it can be first mitigated and eventually resolved. The conviction on both sides of the ideological divide that one's political and scientific adversaries are either devils or cretins (or both) has left the argument completely frozen, with each side holding out for the unconditional intellectual and policy surrender of the other. It is a stalemate that can only harm the poor and the hungry. And they deserve better than that. The problem is that they always have; and in an important sense, where one stands on whether and, if so, how—depending on one's politics and moral understanding—to reform, transform, or revolutionize the global food system largely determines whether one thinks that these times really are different or whether instead harboring such hopes contains more hubris than it does analysis.

· 11 ·

Falling in Love with the Private Sector

In his introduction to his organization's *2013 Global Food Policy Report*, Shenggen Fan, the director general of the International Food Policy Research Institute (IFPRI), wrote that reaching the goal of "eliminating hunger and under nutrition sustainably by 2025" required "a more inclusive global partnership, one that includes regional and country levels and spans government, civil society and the private sector."[1] Coming from the head of IFPRI, which is viewed even by many critics of the global food system as the preeminent research institution working on agriculture, hunger, and nutrition, such an opinion carried a great deal of weight, and rightly so, even though in the instance Fan was using his personal authority and IFPRI's to repeat what had become the conventional mainstream view. But whether intentionally or unintentionally, his words also served, to an outsider at least, a more original purpose, that of clarifying what had changed. For all the actors Fan described as necessary to success—governments, NGOs, local groups—had all, in one iteration or another, been part of the mix of groups working on hunger and on malnutrition and under-nutrition since the post–World War II beginnings of the development project—all that is, save for one: the private sector.

During the entire period between the early 1950s and the mid-1990s, the separation between NGOs and private business was well-nigh absolute. Given that many development NGOs, particularly those such as Oxfam that have profound historical affiliations and affinities with the political left—a worldview that in principle might have been expected to preclude viewing their understanding of development for a more just and equitable future as being compatible with the agenda of the corporate world—there was what seemed at the time like an all-but-unbridgeable political gap as well. Indeed, even relationships with official government development agencies were more often at arm's length than they were collaborative, both in policy terms and in terms of funding.[2] The statistics on where the NGOs got their funding reflected this. According to a 2005 paper issued by the International Committee of the Red Cross (ICRC), public funding accounted for only 1.5 percent of NGOs' budgets in 1970—powerful evidence of the independence of the private voluntary sector. But by the mid-1990s, contributions from states either directly or through the UN system had soared to 40 percent. Independence had mor-phed into deep dependence. As the ICRC report put it laconically, "This increasing reliance on government aid raises questions about the extent to which NGOs really are *non* governmental."[3] And the percentages have only risen since then. To cite only one example, in 2008 USAID made grants of $3 billion to US NGOs alone.[4]

If it was only in the 1970s that Western donors began to view NGOs as significant actors, if not yet as partners, in the development project (and at first that recognition was quite tentative), it was only in the post–Cold War era, as the development specialists Michael Edwards and David Hulme have emphasized, that the num-ber of NGOs dramatically increased, with many going from being relatively small organizations to expanding into the vast institutions that they had become by the early twenty-first century. Before that, as Edwards wrote, as a sector the NGOs were "a backwater in international affairs."[5] And it was not just that governments started taking NGOs more seriously in the aftermath of the Cold War. It was also a period when, recognizing the opportunity, many NGOs were themselves trying to determine how to transform, which is to say "upgrade," their role—a goal that was first formalized at a conference Edwards and Hulme organized in Manchester in 1994, whose theme was "Scaling Up NGO Impact on Development."

In an important sense, though, these development NGOs were knocking on an open door. By the early 1990s, Western donor governments had reached the conclusion that the government-to-government development model on which they had relied since the 1950s not only had proved largely incapable of delivering the promised results in terms of either economic development or significant poverty reduction in the poor world, but also was unsalvageable in its present form. Their response took the form of what came to be known as the New Policy Agenda, though there is no single document in which the approach is laid out. But its main thrust was clear enough. In the words of David Lewis, the director of the Centre for Voluntary Organization at the London School of Economics, the New Policy Agenda was a combination of "neo-liberal economic policy prescriptions with a stated commitment to 'good governance.'"[6]

In retrospect, it seems clear that Western donor governments had actually been moving in that direction since the mid-1980s. Governments in the Global South were perceived as being unwilling, unable, or just too slow and inefficient to follow through effectively on the commitments they had made to donors, even after they had been made to understand that aid was partly contingent on a vastly reduced role in the economy for state structures in conformance with the World Bank's Structural Adjustment Program. The donors had also come to believe that the problem of corruption in poor countries was both so endemic and so deep-rooted that a significant amount of their development aid was simply never reaching the intended beneficiaries. To break what they viewed as this vicious cycle, the donors searched for other institutions, conduits, and mechanisms to deliver their development aid. And that was where Western NGOs came in. As David Lewis has put it, the donors had come to see Western development NGOs as "efficient and responsive alternatives to the state and as organizational actors with the potential to strengthen democratic processes" in the nations of the Global South in which they worked.[7]

The donors' thinking in the 1980s was informed by the radical economic changes taking place in their own countries. During Ronald Reagan's presidency in the United States and Margaret Thatcher's premiership in the United Kingdom, a wide range of regulatory regimes were loosened dramatically and in some cases done away with altogether. And this went forward in tandem with the systematic derogation to the private sector of many enterprises and social functions that had previously been considered legitimate state monopolies. To name only the most obvious examples, the railways, the electricity sector, and, in the United States at least, the prison system were privatized either in whole or in part. In that policy environment, it should have come as no surprise that Western donor governments would choose to apply the same methodology to relief and development.

Reagan and Thatcher are long gone, but the belief that government-led solutions—even in the rare instances where they were judged to be efficient—were simply never going to be as effective as nongovernmental ones is if anything even more entrenched in the early twenty-first century than it was when they left office, deepened by the policy decisions of both Democratic and Republican administrations in the United States and Tory and Labour governments in the United Kingdom. Nevertheless, the idea that these NGOs, which the World Bank had specifically defined in a policy paper in 1991 as being "characterized primarily by humanitarian or cooperative, rather than commercial objectives,"[8] should work in tandem with major international for-profit corporations does not seem to have much of a role in the thinking of these governments nor officials concerned with aid issues at the bank—who were then at the height of their confidence in the Structural Adjustment policy—nor even of the NGOs themselves. Instead, donors and NGOs alike were working on how they should best structure their relations with each other rather than on how both would collaborate with the private sector. And if collaboration with business was absent from that agenda, the idea does not yet seem that it would be an expanding universe of new philanthropies, the Gates Foundation first and foremost, that were based on the related idea that what Bill Gates called "creative capitalism" and what journalists Matthew Bishop and Michael Green had dubbed "philanthrocapitalism" would come to be seen as almost as important a driving force in ending extreme poverty and hunger.

It would be absurd to reproach the NGOs for failing to be clairvoyant. And in fact, from the beginning of their rise in the mid-1990s, they were quite farsighted about the role many donors had in mind for them in the new script for international development that the major Western governments were crafting. As Edwards and Hulme themselves have written, only a year after that first World Bank report on NGOs was issued, Western donors and the Bretton Woods institutions saw NGO expansion as "complementing the counter-revolution in development theory that underpins the policies of liberalization, state withdrawal and structural adjustment. . . . NGOs are viewed as the 'private non-profit' sector, the performance of which advances the 'public-bad,' and 'private good' ideology of the new orthodoxy."[9] Indeed, the key question for the 1994 Manchester conference was "Will NGOs be co-opted into the New Policy Agenda as the favored child, or magic bullet for development?" In the language that was common at the time, would they become "too close to the powerful, and too far from the powerless?"[10]

To Edwards, who was a participant in these debates and who

has remained since then one of the most discerning analysts on the interrelations between NGOs, governments, business, and philanthropy, the answer to those questions is complicated. He absolutely rejects the contention of their harshest critics that "the world would be a better place without the rise of development NGOs, however patchy their impact may have been." But he is also adamant that the NGOs were mistaken in their belief that foreign aid would in time "be replaced by a different, healthier and more effective system of international cooperation in which the drivers of development and change would no longer be based around North-South transfers and foreign intervention." Instead, as he puts it, "From Jeffrey Sachs to Bob Geldof, the new orthodoxy asserts that more money *will* solve Africa's problems, and, if we add in an American twist, make the world safe from terrorism too."[11]

In the second decade of the twenty-first century, this is not the only thing that has turned out very differently from how the conventional wisdom indicated that it would. In a 2013 blog post provocatively titled "Aid and the Private Sector: A Love Story," Erinch Sahan, Oxfam's "private sector advisor" (that Oxfam had such a senior staff member itself speaks volumes about how much had changed in the NGO world during the previous twenty years), could write of "the rise and rise of private-sector-focused aid," and characterize the new consensus among the major donors that business, not NGOs, "will end poverty"[12] as if it were the most normal thing in the world. And in a sense it was, or, at least, it was the logical next step of a process in which the move away from government was generally considered to be pragmatism, not ideology. In the left-liberal precincts of the development world, quoting Ronald Reagan is almost unheard of, but the consensus over business's limitless potential for doing good and government's limitless potential for making a mess of things was very much of a piece with Reagan's famous wisecrack that "the nine most terrifying words in the English language are, 'I'm from the government and I'm here to help.'"

It is safe to say that from the time they assumed the leadership of their respective countries, neither Ronald Reagan nor Margaret Thatcher had many admirers among those who staff development NGOs, who, sentimentally at least, are overwhelmingly of the left. The reality, though, is far less straightforward. In "development speak," and certainly in terms of the "elective affinities" of members of staff, NGOs are conventionally regarded, and tend to regard themselves, not without reason, as part of civil society, or as it is sometimes called, "the third sector." But while NGOs are indeed not-for-profit entities, in fact they, too, are part of the private sector, which explains why another commonly used term for many (though not all) NGOs is "private voluntary organizations" (PVOs). That is why, although it was by no means obvious at the time, the real Rubicon for donor governments was the decision effectively to privatize much of their development aid. By comparison, to move from believing that this was best accomplished by turning to nonprofit businesses as the key development actors and transferring it instead to for-profit business seems far less radical and more like a further step along a trajectory that to a large degree had already been determined.

Unsurprisingly, this is not the way the NGOs saw things, not at first, anyway, dazzled as they were by the prospect of a new and more central role. In his influential book, *Out of Poverty*, Paul Polak, himself an entrepreneur who has described himself as someone who designs "market-based solutions to global poverty" through his organization International Development Enterprises (IDE), wrote that when he first started IDE, development NGOs viewed multinational corporations as "evil oppressors of the poor, and business as the enemy. Now many of them see them as white knights ready to slay the poverty dragon."[13] What is less clear is whether most of them gravitated voluntarily to this new perspective or instead did so only because they had so little choice in the matter. Whichever is the case, though, the notion that the NGOs were the victims of, to use the Wall Street expression, some sort of hostile takeover by multinational corporations is unsustainable. Instead, as Michael Edwards has argued, rightly in my view, it was a classic case of cooptation, in which movements for social transformation that were founded and operated for decades as solidarity-based alternatives to the most powerful elements of society were "being turned into an integral component of the social capitalist economy," in which a very "different ethos of competition and technocracy"[14] is assumed to be the only viable way to effect social transformation.

There is no evidence that many NGOs—whether, as was the case with Greenpeace or Oxfam, their history of antiestablishment militancy or, like the World Wildlife Federation, they were always much more mainstream—attempted to do anything else but energetically accommodate and try to benefit as much as possible from the changed reality of a business-dominated development world. In the second decade of the twenty-first century, examples of collaborations between the two sectors abound. An emblematic example was a report issued jointly by the Coca-Cola Company, the brewer SABMiller, and Oxfam America, "Exploring the Links between International Business and Poverty Reduction." According to the report, "Small enterprises and large multinationals alike are creating innovative new products and services that simultaneously satisfy the needs of people at the base of the [economic] pyramid, achieve a development impact and create new consumer markets."[15] And as collaborations have deepened, a more corporatized self-conception has taken root among many mainline NGOs. In their book *Protest, Inc.: The Corporatization of Activism*, the Canadian writers Genevieve LeBaron and Peter Dauvergne report that Amnesty International hired GlobeScan, the marketing firm whose other clients included Barrack Gold, Chevron, and Goldman Sachs, "to build a revitalized brand identity."[16]

To insist on the point that the partnerships between NGOs and multinational corporations reflected more their ideological convergence in the early twenty-first century than anything else does not mean that, even had they wanted to, they could have resisted the pressures that would have been brought to bear on most of them by their donors—by USAID, DFID, the UN specialized agencies, and of course the Gates Foundation. Bill Gates has had a key role in the increasing erasure of boundaries between government donors, development NGOs, multinational corporations, and philanthropies. In the fields of global health and particularly agriculture, Gates now does far more than underwrite programs: he drives international policy. In fact, there are few places or institutions concerned with shaping this policy that Gates does not have a hand in, from something as major as CGIAR, the vastly influential consortium of international agricultural research institutes, to the section of the *Guardian* newspaper's website devoted to development issues. Alumni of the Gates Foundation, most notably Rajiv Shah, who ran the agricultural side of the foundation before going to USAID, are now in government in many donor countries, while many development ministries in the poor world have close partnerships with Gates. And by now, such a high percentage of the experts on agriculture, nutrition, and global health throughout the world either are directly employed by the Gates Foundation, have served as consultants to it, or work for institutions that receive some of their funding from Gates that in 2008 a World Health Organization (WHO) official was moved to complain that the WHO was having difficulty finding evaluators for research proposals who did not have such conflicts of interest. To insist on the centrality of this is emphatically not to imply that there is any conspiracy or subterfuge involved. To the contrary, the Gates Foundation is quite transparent about what it does (if anything, it boasts of, rather than tries to, conceal its influence), while donors and NGOs tend to emphasize rather than downplay their relations with Gates.

If this shift toward including philanthropy in what some development experts had taken to calling "the golden quadrangle" of principal development actors might well never have occurred had Bill Gates not decided to leave Microsoft and throw his energy and (literally) unparalleled resources into his philanthropy, the donors' turn toward business was almost certainly inevitable. For already by the turn of the century, it was becoming clear that they had come to feel that the not-for-profit model had failed and that it was time to replace it with an entrepreneurial model. C. K. Prahalad's influential 2004 book, *The Fortune at the Bottom of the Pyramid*, which, years before he coined the term "creative capitalism," Gates himself described as "an intriguing blueprint for how to fight poverty with profitability,"[17] was an emblem of this new approach. Prahalad's premise was one of a virtuous circle in which business would provide the poor the products they needed, the poor would buy them, and as a result business would profit and the poor would be empowered. Another was the plethora of organizations that have been started since 2000 based on the idea of social entrepreneurship and inspired by the conviction that companies and individual entrepreneurs alike are every bit as interested in ending poverty as any NGO but, because of their vastly superior competence, the vast resources at their disposal, their (supposedly) greater openness to new ideas, and their culture of efficiency, are far more likely to do so successfully and sustainably.

Google is certainly not a perfect indicator of where consensus lies, but it is a suggestive one. And if you Google the words "only business can end poverty," you will get 28,300,000 results. But Google the word "inequality" and you get 9,180,000, less than a third of that figure. And Michael Edwards points out that between 2004 and 2012 the number of Google searches for "civil society" fell by 70 percent, while searches for "social entrepreneurs" rose by 90 percent. These numbers reflect a sea change in the corporate world's self-image and in the role that many of the world's biggest companies assign to their giving. It also reflects the immense growth of the philanthropic sector, particularly in the United States, where, in constant dollar terms, the total amount of money given by foundations has gone from $16 billion in 1997 to $39 billion in 2006,[18] and $46.9 billion in 2011.[19] In 2012, philanthropies contributed almost half of this—$19.1 billion—to what the Lilly Family School of Philanthropy at Indiana University, which tracks these things, calls "international affairs," out of which development constitutes the most important recipient.[20]

It is not only a matter of charitable giving. To the contrary, by the 1980s some corporations had already begun redefining themselves. This invariably involved not just boasting of their charitable giving but rather making very large and almost wholly unprecedented moral claims for what they did as businesses. Instead of highlighting their role as upstanding corporate citizens (though of course, they did that too), they attributed moral worth to the products they were manufacturing and selling. Unsurprisingly, this movement began in Silicon Valley,[21] where, as Thomas Frank has pointed out, the capitalist ju-jitsu of "commodifying your dissent"[22] originated. Google was a pathfinder in this. In the documents accompanying its initial public offering in 2004, the company produced a mission statement titled "'An Owner's Manual' for Google's Shareholders." It spoke of developing "services that significantly improve the lives of as many people as possible." Google, wrote the company's founders, Sergey Brin and Larry Page, would operate on the principle, "Don't be evil." Whether the implication was that other companies were in fact evil was left unclear, even if the self-love was not. But the sentences that followed certainly seemed to apply to more than just Google, to encapsulate that vision of an enlightened capitalism committed to human betterment on a global basis that has since become the moral default position of the corporate world. "We believe strongly," Brin and Page declared, "that in the long term, we will be better served—as shareholders and in all other ways—by a company that does good things for the world even if we forgo some short term gains. This is an important aspect of our culture and is broadly shared within the company."[23]

Such statements were radical in their day. But within the decade they had become so commonplace that it was businesses that did not claim to be making the world a better place that were becoming the exception. To cite only two of a plethora of examples, in 2010, in the aftermath of the earthquake that destroyed much of Port-au-Prince, Coca-Cola announced the "Haiti Hope Project." As the press release put it, "We believe the Coca-Cola system is uniquely positioned to contribute to the economic recovery of this island nation." Or take Unilever, which is often put forward as exemplifying everything the socially responsible twenty-first-century multination corporation should aspire to be: in 2013, the company announced that along with Ashoka Changemakers, an organization founded by the former McKinsey management consultant Bill Drayton, which has become one of largest international groups promoting social entrepreneurship, it was initiating the "Young Entrepreneurs Sustainable Living Awards" under the sponsorship of the Prince of Wales. Unilever's chairman, Paul Polman, declared that the award would be "a focal point for the power and creativity of young entrepreneurs who want to help find solutions for some of the world's most urgent issues." And he added, "There is no better way to use our energy, innovation and resourcefulness than spending it trying to create a better future for all in a world we want."[24]

Polman has been a particularly ardent proselytizer for "creative capitalism" à la Bill Gates. In an essay published on the McKinsey and Company website, Polman wrote that it was imperative to "face up to the realities of a world where 9.5 billion people will put enormous strains on biophysical resources." The rapidly growing populations of India, China, and Indonesia "will all aspire to the lifestyles and living standards enjoyed by the Germans and the Californians."[25]

People unfamiliar with the ideology of the new poverty-fighting, environmentally friendly, collaborative capitalism might have assumed that this was bad news. They would have been wrong. For in the very next sentence of his piece, Polman declared evenly that "there is nothing that we can, or should do to stop that." As far as he was concerned, the dawning demographic and environmental challenges were nothing to fear, provided, of course, that capitalism became more "collaborative, innovative, and inclusive than it had been in the past."[26]

Eloquent as Polman is, unsurprisingly it is Bill Gates himself who has remained what in any other era or context would be called the chief ideologue for this new revolutionary capitalist project. "The genius of capitalism," he has written, "lies in its ability to make self-interest serve the wider interest."[27] And it had proven itself time and time again. As Gates put it, capitalism "is responsible for the great innovations that have improved the lives of billions."[28] These claims have been fleshed out by former senior officials of the Gates Foundation such as Rajiv Shah, as well as by economists whom Gates admires, notably Charles Kenny. It was Kenny who wrote in *Foreign Policy* magazine in 2013 that although there was "much to dislike" about Walmart, "for all its manifold offenses, [it] may have done more for poor consumers in the United States, and around the world, than any other business in American history." Shah was more circumspect. But when he assumed the leadership of USAID, he insisted time and time again that as he put it in one interview, "One of the big failings in food security in particular has been a lack of working with the private sector effectively." In that same interview, Shah was very candid about the fact that his approach to his role as USAID's administrator was grounded in business practices, which not so very long before had been anathema in the (largely left-leaning) development world. Recalling his experiences working with Bill and Melinda Gates, he said, "I've tried to bring that business-like rigor and the tendency to ask questions . . . to make sure that when [USAID is] spending taxpayer resources, we're doing it with the absolute focus that we are making an investment."[29]

Bishop and Green are absolutely correct when they claim in *Philanthrocapitalism* that "today's philanthrocapitalists see a world of big problems that they, and perhaps only they, can and must put right."[30] And while neither most NGOs nor indeed the development agencies of the major donor governments would be prepared to go quite that far, there is broad consensus that these problems will never be solved *without* corporations playing a central role. With regard to food and agriculture, Britain's minister for international development at DFID, Justine Greening, was quoted by Marc van Ameringen of the Global Alliance for Improved Nutrition (GAIN) as having said at a meeting in Davos in January 2014 that "in the case of hunger and malnutrition, it will primarily be the private sector that delivers the solutions." The reason for this was simple: "to reaching billions who are malnourished, and do it in a few decades, will require the technology and marketing skills of business to be harnessed for the public good." Ending hunger and malnutrition in the next several decades was a "realistic goal," Greening insisted. But she warned: "We will not get there if we do not bring the private sector with us."[31]

The business world could not have gotten a better encomium had some multinational corporation commissioned the speech itself. But then, since the beginning of the new century the question of where the donors' role ends and where the corporate role begins has grown steadily harder to answer. The advent of the integration of corporations into the development project has been reified in the form of a radical transformation of development language. Bishop and Green are very good on this, writing that as philanthrocapitalists "apply their business methods to philanthropy, [they] are developing a new (if familiar-sounding) language to describe their businesslike approach. Their philanthropy is 'strategic,' 'market conscious,' 'impact oriented,' 'knowledge based,' often 'high engagement,' and always driven by the goal of maximizing the 'leverage' of the donor's money.' Seeing themselves as social investors, not traditional donors, some of them engage in 'venture philanthropy.' "[32]

If at the beginning of the 1990s the NGOs seeking to become indispensable to the donors were pushing on an open door, the donors have flung the door wide open for the corporate world. Crucially, while the donors never relinquished the whip hand in their relations with the NGOs, they apparently believe doing so with regard to the multinationals is entirely appropriate. One illustration of this was the speech DFID's Justine Greening delivered at, appropriately enough, the London Stock Exchange. In it, she hailed "the strategic partnership" between DFID and the exchange. It was, she said, the beginning of a "transformational," "radical" journey. For Greening, the reality was simple. Only economic development could ultimately "defeat" poverty. And while she emphasized that DFID would continue what she called "traditional aid—helping more children into school, beating killer diseases like polio and malaria, supporting countries like the Philippines when disaster hits"—her department was going to provide as much of what she called "smart aid" as possible. And what was this smart aid to consist of? Greening's description of it sounded like nothing so much as the wish list of a lobbyist for a multinational corporation. "Smart aid," she said, "can take the form of building a better tax regime, helping to reduce trade barriers, or giving entrepreneurs and small businesses an economic launch pad." And, she continued, Britain's development aid would help "build the institutions, the values by which individual rights to liberty and property are safeguarded . . . elements that represent a green light to companies thinking about investing in a frontier market."[33]

Greening was candid about the self-interest involved. In her London Stock Exchange speech, she said that, "as a former treasury minister, I'm acutely aware that Britain's future economic strength depends on us increasing our global exports." Development aid, she argued, was a way of making that happen. "Many of the countries my department works in," she said, "have high levels of growth, young and growing populations, and a wealth of natural resources. . . . We could wait until these markets have grown, until they are less risky and the opportunities are more obvious. But how much better to start our relationships with these countries sooner rather than later."[34]

Rajiv Shah had already outlined a similar view when, at the 2011 World Economic Forum in Davos, he unveiled what the subsequent USAID press release described as the agency's "leadership in creating synergies between the public and private sectors to meet the global food security challenge."[35] On his blog, Shah would later be even more explicit. In a post entitled "Embracing Enlightened Capitalism," Shah wrote somewhat reproachfully that the "development community" had not always been prepared to "embrace the encouragement of private sector activity as part of [USAID's] core mission." This had been a mistake, he argued, for it was the working of markets that "can deliver profits and create jobs *and* deliver economic opportunity for women, minorities and the poor."[36]

In reality, statements like Greening's and Shah's were elaborations of commitments the donors had begun to make some years earlier and that had already been formalized in 2010 in a "Bilateral Donors' Statement in Support of Private Sector Partnerships for Development," signed by almost all the major donor agencies, including USAID, DFID, SIDA (the Swedish government's development arm), and Danida (SIDA's Danish equivalent), that is to say not only by the neoliberal United States and United Kingdom but by the ostensibly social-democratic Scandinavians as well. The statement all but attributed the success to date of the MDGs, and indeed, as the statement accurately noted, one of the MDGs' ten goals had been, "Develop a Global Partnership for Development," and in the statement, the donors declared solemnly, to the point of using quasi-religious language, that "in the ten years since the MDGs were established, the international community has made great progress in developing partnerships with business and we come here today to renew and give greater meaning to our commitment." Henceforth, the private sector would be regarded not "merely as resource providers, we choose to recognize the private sector as equal partners."[37]

Given that in their statement, the donors had affirmed without reservation that the private sector was "the engine of economic growth and development," an equal partnership was arguably the least they could do. Unsurprisingly, public-private partnerships had no greater champion than the US government. Under the Obama administration, even though it emphasized the role of food security for development to an extent none of its predecessors had come close to, at least since the era of the Green Revolution, USAID not only continued the partnerships between governments and multinational corporations that were the order of the day during George W. Bush's presidency but also deepened and broadened those links to an unprecedented degree. The occasion for all of this was the public launch of a World Economic Forum project called "Realizing a New Vision for Agriculture," undertaken in collaboration with the management consultants McKinsey and Company, which prepared the report that launched the project, and, to employ the report's flagrantly imprecise linguistic formulation, "championed" by seventeen global corporations. The firms in question, with whom Shah was promising that USAID would collaborate and by doing so was providing not only his agency's ethical stamp of approval but by extension that of the US government, were a virtual Who's Who of the longtime players in global agribusiness (both in seeds and in the manufacturing of petrochemical fertilizers, food processing, and food and drinks retailing): Archer Daniels Midland, BASF, Bunge, Cargill, the Coca-Cola Company, DuPont, General Mills, Kraft Foods, Metro, Monsanto, Nestlé, Pepsico, SABMiller, Syngenta, Unilever, Walmart, and Yara International.

But while this outraged the many critics of the global food system who believed, with the antiglobalization movement, that another world was possible, in almost every other quarter these changes were greeted with enthusiasm or, failing that, resignation. And even some development experts who remain agnostic in principle as to what the appropriate role for the private sector should be insist that their inclusion is simply an irreversible fact of the contemporary struggle to tame hunger.[38] Lawrence Haddad, who at the time was the director of the Institute of Development Studies at Sussex University, struck this same note of realpolitik when he wrote that, "if the private sector is to be involved in shaping nutrition outcomes then the feeling from much (I think) of civil society is 'they are only out for profit.' Well, guess what, they are already involved in shaping nutrition outcomes for profit."[39] Under the circumstances, Haddad insisted, the important question to ask was not how to limit private-sector involvement (that was a nonstarter), but rather, "how can we begin talking to them to find and increase the overlaps between good profit outcomes and good nutrition outcomes?"[40]

The premise is that "doing good things for the world" transcends ideology. Indeed, ideology itself is seen as a distraction for hardworking members of what some people within the UN system have now taken to calling the "Golden Quadrant" of "private companies, civil society, knowledge institutions, and government."[41] As Raj Shah put it while still at the Gates Foundation, "This big debate about who is making the world safe for whom is the wrong debate. The right debate is how to help people. We simply don't take an ideological position. Instead, we're results oriented . . . open to working with anyone who will work with us, and even more open to learning from all sorts of groups, very much including our critics." In another interview, Shah remarked that, "We don't have a specific point of view except to help people move out of poverty."[42]

There is no reason to doubt that Shah was being entirely sincere when he said this. But development is not simply a set of practices, it is an ideology, and Shah's own statement was dependent in its intellectual force and coherence on the (very ideological) idea that ideology no longer mattered. As LeBaron and Dauvergne point out in *Protest, Inc.*, the consequence of what Shah and like-minded officials described as an entirely pragmatic approach to ending extreme poverty and hunger was to marginalize, if not delegitimize, "advocacy for far-reaching change in world politics."[43] And they quote the Italian Marxist Antonio Gramsci to the effect that the corporatization of activism in general and of the development project in particular is narrowing "the limits of the possible," to which one might add "the limits of the imaginable" as well.[44]

One cannot say at once that one is willing to "learn from one's critics" and at the same time that only business and the market can end extreme poverty and hunger, unless all one means by this learning is the openness to exchanging ideas about what works best within an *unalterable* broader framework of liberal capitalism, albeit that modern version of the creed that in Bill Gates's words, is a "hybrid engine of self-interest with a concern for others."[45] What Shah either genuinely does not understand, which, given his intelligence, seems highly unlikely, or else prefers not to confront is that for anti-establishment groups like Via Campesina or the organizations loosely aligned with the Food First Information and Action Network (FIAN) to accept his premise, they would first have to accept that the only durable solution to hunger and extreme poverty is inseparable from increasing poor people's access to markets in such a way that will bring them into the system—in other words, that there is no viable alternative road to freedom from want other than through capitalism. And given their own beliefs, this is of course the one thing they cannot do.

That Shah, despite his formidable intellectual qualities and political sophistication, does not see this, and instead hews to a view that is entirely of a piece with the conventional wisdom of the age, perfectly illustrates the observation by Gilbert Rist that I quoted in another context earlier in this book: "You don't argue about the obvious; the most you can do is try to improve it." In fairness to Shah and to Justine Greening, such ideological conformity predates considerably their becoming heads of USAID and DFID, respectively. During Robert Zoellick's tenure between 2007 and 2011 as president of the World Bank, he spoke a good deal about a "human right to food" and declared that investment in export-driven agriculture alone without other investments in the agriculture that "feeds local communities" cannot lead to prosperity.[46] At the time, this seemed surprising given that it is a position generally associated with critics of the current global agricultural system. But from the point of view of serious critics of the global food system, Zoellick's démarche was far less radical that it seemed, since he also insisted that any reform of the system would be best implemented not by "prosecut[ing] or block[ing] markets, but [by using] them better."[47]

In effect, Zoellick was positing a world system in which it would be possible to retain the essence of the neoliberal policies whose avatar the bank had long been. But in this revised framework—call it neoliberalism 2.0—the expectation among more "enlightened" policy makers was apparently that it would be possible to combine the technoproductivist vision of agricultural reform with annealing doses of equity and justice. The appeal of such a vision is obvious, for it posits the same vision of the world that Shah and Greening have upheld—a world in which no hard choices need to be made. The idea that there could be fundamental disagreements about what constitutes a just society or even a somewhat more equitable one, which cannot be reconciled by people of goodwill, is categorically excluded. If we all agree on first principles, that is, if we are all committed to human betterment, if all the stakeholders, as they are referred to in the jargon of development, except for a few spoilers (Islamists, warlords, and in the left-liberal version, a few—but only a few—"bad apple" corporations), want the same good things, and we all believe that there are few problems that the *deus ex machina* of technology cannot solve, then we don't really need to worry about such pesky subjects as economic justice or the possibility that the only way to make food security for hungry people a reality is to rein in the power of corporations rather than corporatizing development by putting public-private partnerships at its center.

But even when such dissenting views are given a hearing by the development establishment, while they may on occasion be treated with forebearance, they are almost never taken seriously. Again, this is not a matter of malign intentions but of an excessive faith in the modern liberal progress narrative, with its serene confidence that history, for all its fits and starts, is always going in a positive direction. To speak in terms of faith is not a metaphor, for historically, the view that history is a progress derives originally from Christianity and in the twentieth century was taken up by what are, when all is said and done, the secular successor faiths of Marxism or latterly neoliberalism and what might be termed "human rightism." But what if history were a cycle, as it was understood to be in both classical Greek and classical Indian culture? The short answer is that in the positivist vision of the world, in which there is no room for incommensurability, the view that it is possible to see the world in multiple ways and that there is not one single, fair method of seeing which is right, a cognitive nonstarter for the contemporary positivist.

The technological worldview insists that even the hardest problems can be solved if there is enough money, brainpower, and will to do so. In contrast, critics of the mainstream view insist that the more the global food crisis is seen as a technical problem, the less likely it is to be addressed effectively. On this account, there is less than meets the eye to the renewed attention that has been paid to agriculture by donor governments, the World Bank and the IMF, philanthropies like the Gates Foundation, and relief NGOs since 2007. And some activists go much further, arguing that the reforms now being supported by Western governments through their development agencies or ministries and elaborated by the Bretton Woods institutions are more refurbishing of the SAP than genuine reconsiderations of it. For example, the agrarian economist and activist Haroon Akram-Lodhi has dubbed this approach "the modernization of subordination,"[48] while Michael Edwards has spoken of the current system "[turning] helping others into another form of domination."[49]

Are Akram-Lodhi, Edwards, LeBaron, Dauvergne, and, as no one who has read this far will be surprised to learn, as right in believing that, as LeBaron and Dauvergne put it in their book, the stronger the consensus becomes "that voluntary action by business [to] decrease inequality, advance human rights, and slow environmental destruction," the more "campaigns for system-wide change [will be marginalized]"?[50] As Shah's remarks illustrate, the mainstream development world is determined to dismiss all systematic criticisms of the policies they are implementing as artifacts of now largely irrelevant ideological quarrels or as the sour grapes of those who Bishop and Green refer to disdainfully in *Philanthrocapitalism* as "charity traditionalists."[51] Perhaps they will be proven right. But if they are wrong, the fallout from their refusal even to consider that possibility will leave the development project once again in shambles, in all probability even worse off than it was after the failure of Keynesianism in the 1940s, of modernization theory in the 1950s, and of structural adjustment in the 1980s. *Caveat emptor*.

And lest anyone forget, we have seen the end of ideology predicted before, always wrongly. As Mark Twain once quipped, "History doesn't repeat itself, but it often rhymes." The global food crisis looked on course to illustrate that observation to the letter. More prosaically, given the very real prospect that if nothing transformative can be done, and a techno fix accompanied by pious bromides about good government, transparency, and accountability, which, when applied to the cruel societies—let us at least call them by their right name—in which hunger is endemic, seems like a fantasy that borders on obscenity, is all that is on offer, decades from now and perhaps much sooner, the 2007–2008 crisis will come to appear in retrospect like only the overture to a series of disastrous dislocations to the global food system that the world will experience in the twenty-first century. This is what makes it so urgent to explore any comprehensive solution that might have a chance of staving off such a future. The question, though, is whether that is really best done through initiatives that too often seem like "new and improved" versions of past development approaches to food and agriculture. It is an approach whose Achilles' heel lies in assuming that the problems with what was done previously were more with faulty execution or even lack of execution than with the fundamental assumptions behind those policies.

A controversy that erupted in 2013 between the SUN movement and critics of the global food system over SUN's activities in India illustrates the gulf between the two positions. Like the Gates Foundation, or USAID during Shah's tenure (he left in February 2015), the SUN movement has from the beginning presented itself as a "broad church." To the critics, though, what this actually meant in practice was a refusal to take seriously the possibility that antagonistic power relationships and competing interest between small-scale food producers and private interests and powerful governments, which SUN itself did not deny had existed in the past, could not be reconciled; that is to say, the possibility that the mainstream view was mistaken and that there was no win-win but rather that hardy perennial, the zero-sum game. Wherever SUN worked, it always emphasized the centrality of civil society's participation and of local "ownership" of its initiatives. But to the activists, such commitments were belied by putting efforts to combat child malnutrition and undernutrition largely in the hands of a few powerful actors. And the emphasis that SUN has put on close collaboration with large corporations involved in the agricultural, pharmaceutical, and food manufacturing and merchandizing sectors has deepened the activists' anxieties still further.

In the Indian case, the activists' dismay crystalized when David Nabarro, the UN special representative for food security and nutrition, and the chairman and also very much the "animating spirit" of the SUN movement, named Vinita Bali, the managing director of Britannia Foods (one of the largest Indian food conglomerates), to the leadership group of SUN. Many in the mainstream of the global food establishment as well as in academia considered Bali a philanthropist, pointing to her founding of the Britannia Nutrition Foundation in 2009, whose goal was expressly to fight child malnutrition and which has been active in distributing fortified biscuits to Indian schoolchildren as well as organizing regular conferences and seminars on nutrition and food security issues. Many others were aghast, believing that this only confirmed the views of the significant section of civil society activists in India who had always viewed SUN as a vehicle for enabling business interests, and allowed that subset to exercise an inappropriate influence on national food policies and global nutritional norms. As the food rights monitoring group FIAN warned in the section on SUN in "Alternatives and Resistance to Policies that Generate Hunger," its 2013 annual report, "While businesses can play a role in development, their fiduciary duty lies first with shareholders, not with public health. SUN's promotion of partnerships with businesses thus provides corporations with unprecedented opportunities to influence, national, regional and global policies."[52]

SUN's leadership indignantly denied any intention of showing some special favoritism toward business. Indeed, in private correspondence with food rights activists, important figures in SUN pointed out that business leaders felt they had more than proved their commitment to ending hunger and were aggrieved that their motives could be questioned in this way—a stance that mirrors the attitude often encountered with officials of agricultural multinationals such as Monsanto and Syngenta and their supporters in the scientific world, NGOs, and the media, who in 2012 and 2013 began to routinely "rebrand" themselves as the victims of the irrational fanaticism of anti-GMO activists.[53] SUN's leaders tended to behave in an equally aggrieved manner when questioned about their active solicitation of partnerships not just with agricultural conglomerates such as Cargill, Monsanto, and Archer Daniels Midland but also with major food manufacturing firms such as PepsiCo, Kraft, and Danone. The argument that in doing so they were facilitating what amounted to a partial takeover by corporations of nutrition policies in the poor world cut little ice with them. Activists might be convinced that it was either naivety or bad faith to suggest that it was possible to redress the causes of hunger successfully so long as existing power relations within the global system were left unchanged, but SUN seemed to see nothing but stakeholders, whether from government, the UN system, the NGOs, activist groups, or business, none of whom should be excluded as long as they adhered to the principles of the movement, the right checks and balances, and an appropriate degree of transparency. The problem was that such a view made sense only if the inequities of power (in terms of both influence and resources) were ignored.

For Indian food activists, SUN's embrace of Vinita Bali and Britannia Foods was a perfect illustration of the organization's fundamental blind spot, just as Bali's participation was emblematic of the destructively self-interested motives of the business world as a whole. The specific complaint was that several years earlier, when she had been serving as chair of the Indian Biscuit Manufacturers Association, Bali had lobbied the Indian government to replace the hot, cooked, midday meal of rice, lentils, and vegetables served in Indian schools with packets of fortified biscuits. At first it seemed that Bali's lobbying effort would be successful, but eventually the plan was shelved, largely through pressure from the Indian Right to Food movement, which in this case was backed by both Amartya Sen and Montek Singh Ahluwalia, then still serving as the powerful deputy chairman of the Planning Commission of India, who was also a confidante of then–Prime Minister Manmohan Singh. But for SUN, the opposition to Bali playing such a large role was a major impediment to ending malnutrition and undernutrition in India, which, given the acuteness of the problem there, was especially urgent. As far as SUN's leadership was concerned, instead of win-win it was lose-lose.

In the Hollywood film *The Usual Suspects*, Kevin Spacey's character says, "The greatest trick the Devil ever pulled was convincing the world he didn't exist."[54] Perhaps twenty-first-century liberal capitalism's greatest trick has been convincing so much of the world that it is not an ideology, and as it did so, convincing itself as well. In their own collective imagination, liberals are the antithesis of ideologues and, in Franklin Delano Roosevelt's great phrase, reject all dogmatic approaches in favor of "bold, persistent experimentation." But Roosevelt's project was nothing less than to save liberal capitalism, in an important sense to save it from itself. As the historian William E.

Leuchtenberg put it in his authoritative *Franklin D. Roosevelt and the New Deal*, Roosevelt's programs "rested on the assumption that a just society could be secured by imposing a welfare state on a capitalist foundation."[55]

Bill Gates's project is dissimilar to Roosevelt's in the obvious sense that he neither holds nor seeks political office and as a philanthropist conceives of his role as that of a technocrat, not a political leader. But when he talks about "market-based social change," in which "governments, businesses, and nonprofits work together to stretch the reach of market forces . . . doing work that eases the world's inequalities,"[56] one begins to see a family resemblance not just to Andrew Carnegie's *Gospel of Wealth*, on which Gates is said to have modeled his philanthropic ethos, but to the New Deal, albeit a globalized and privatized version of it. For both Roosevelt and Gates, the essential project calls for a redesign of capitalism to serve better those excluded from its benefits. The alternative, as in Roosevelt's time, would be the far more radical political and social changes many peasant activist groups and food rights campaigners have called for. Gates is far too intelligent not to see this, but there is no evidence that he takes these opposing views seriously. And it must be admitted that so far he hasn't had to. Still, one hardly has to be the reincarnation of Antonio Gramsci to see the essentially political character of Gates's philanthropic project in particular and that of the global food establishment in general, even if he and they do not or will not.

· 12 ·

Philanthrocapitalism: A [Self-]Love Story

There is an old Hawaiian joke about the first American missionary families to arrive on the islands in the 1820s: "They came to do good and they did very well indeed." Neither Rajiv Shah nor Justine Greening were alone in thinking that the United States and the United Kingdom could profit materially from the good they believed their new vision of business-focused development was already doing, not to mention the far greater good they were confident it would do in the decades to come. Historically, both in peace and war, development aid, however much good the donors hoped it would do, was understood as simultaneously serving these donors' geostrategic and geoeconomic interests. The Marshall Plan and the Green Revolution were classic successful examples of this; a classic unsuccessful one was USAID's effort throughout the Vietnam War to win the "hearts and minds" of ordinary South Vietnamese. So a skeptic listening to Shah or to Greening would have been within his or her rights to inquire why anyone should have imagined that these officials would frame development issues in any other way than free-market capitalist terms.

Earlier versions of the arguments from (national) interest that Western development officials had presented had been as informed by geostrategic imperatives as by charitable ones, even if, as Nick Cullather has shown in his work on the Green Revolution and the Cold War, "the terminology of alliances, iron curtains, and armaments [often] gave way to a language of takeoffs, five-year plans, and [economic] growth rates."[1] Western aid was an integral part of the Cold War contest with the Soviet Union. In contrast, the development project Shah and Greening evoked was presented as being devoid of any competitive spirit except, that is, the healthy competition for recognition that Gates described in his Davos speech on creative capitalism as being the reward corporations would get for "good behavior" in situations where profits are not to be had. What was being described was frictionless development, "a hybrid engine of self-interest and concern for others,"[2] as Gates put it, that was completely of a piece with the world of "frictionless capitalism" he had so often spoken of. And if politics in the normal sense of the word had gone by the wayside, this was all to the good. As Sylvia Mathews Burwell, who was the chief executive of the Gates Foundation before she went on to become secretary of health and human services in the Obama administration, described to me when I met with her in Seattle some years ago, the foundation's "focus [was] on the individual rather than on the macro [economic and political]." This was by far the best approach, she said. As if by way of illustration, she then pointed to a photo on the wall of her office of a small African child holding a blue plastic pail. "We refer to this person as 'the boss,'" she said, "and I give a copy of this picture to every new person who comes to work here at the foundation."[3]

In the 1960s, the German Marxist political theorist Herbert Marcuse coined the term "repressive tolerance," by which he meant that in capitalist societies, the "marketplace"—the expression itself is revelatory—while appearing to be open, was in reality monopolized by a limited number of views. Marcuse, writing in 1965 (i.e., half a century before the US Supreme Court's Citizens United decision put an end to virtually all limits on corporate contributions to political causes), had already discerned that in the United States "the ideology of democracy hides its lack of substance," and that this went "hand in hand with the monopolistic or oligopolistic concentration of capital in the formation of public opinion."[4] Even assuming that the Gates Foundation's support for virtually every important food research institution anywhere in the world—its major contributions to key programs of both the World Food Programme (WFP) and the World Health Organization (WHO), even its sponsorship of the *Guardian*'s Global Development site, now the most important mainstream global website on these questions in English—is not intentionally monopolistic in the way his business strategy at Microsoft unquestionably was,[5] it fits Marcuse's template to a T. It operates on two levels. First it denies that there can be real ideological disagreement, at least of the kind that would preclude everyone eventually reaching a consensus. And second, because there is no (legitimate) disagreement of this kind, anyone who does disagree is, to use a term often used by UN negotiators to describe warlords who will not come to peace talks, a "spoiler," whose *actions* may damage efforts to make progress toward ending poverty, or disease, or hunger but whose *views* no decent person is under any more obligation to take seriously than they would those of a Holocaust denier or a 9/11 "truther."

In 1961, two and a half years after taking power, Fidel Castro gave a celebrated speech to the Cuban artistic and cultural elite that came to be known as "Words to the Intellectuals." "What are the rights of revolutionary or non-revolutionary writers and artists?" he demanded. Then, answering his own question, with particular focus on nonrevolutionary writers, he declared that "intellectuals who are not genuinely revolutionary [must be allowed to] find a place to work and to create within the Revolution." But Castro was quick to add that this freedom had its limits. "Within the Revolution," he thundered, "everything goes; against the Revolution, nothing . . . no rights at all."[6] Bill Gates couldn't be more different temperamentally nor further away politically from Fidel Castro, so far, in fact, that he once characterized everyone who challenged the current intellectual property laws, specifically those guaranteeing software patents, as a "new modern-day sort of communist."[7] But there is the same steely moralistic dualism that Castro was famous for in Gates's responses to critics of his foundation's philosophy of aid and development, the same insistence that those who do not agree with him do not deserve to be listened to. One example of this was Gates's attack on Dambisa Moyo, the Zambian economist whose book *Dead Aid* is a prosecutor's brief for development aid to Africa having done more harm than good.[8] Asked about the book during a Q&A he did in May 2013 at the University of New South Wales, Gates not only dismissed Moyo as "not knowing much about aid and what it was doing in Africa," which was a harsh judgment but one Gates had every right to express, but went on to say that "books like that are promoting evil,"[9] a judgment that in its own context was every bit as totalitarian as Castro's.

Within the revolution, everything goes; against the revolution, nothing. Gates was talking of a different revolution, of course, but his reaction to a leading figure who had challenged his philanthropic revolution was every bit as totalitarian in spirit as Castro's response had been more than half a century earlier to those Cuban intellectuals who might dare challenge his political and social revolution. And Gates most definitely does see himself as a revolutionary. In the 2014 commencement address that he delivered jointly with Melinda Gates at Stanford University, Gates reminisced that when he and his partner Paul Allen started Microsoft, one of the "pioneering books in the field had a raised fist on the cover, and it was called *Computer Lib*." At the time, he said, "Only big businesses could buy computers. We wanted to offer the same power to regular [*sic*] people—and democratize computing."[10] Short of repeating the far-left slogan of the time, "Power to the People!," it's difficult to imagine how Gates could have been clearer that Microsoft was a revolutionary movement. And if others saw it as a monopoly, well, that was presumably their problem.

In his speech, Castro said that the revolution "signifies the interests of the entire nation," and dismissed those who "renounced" it as having allowed themselves to be "perplexed by falsehood."[11] Gates's attempt to dismiss Moyo has something of the same quality to it. "She is an aid critic," he said, "[and] there's not many because it's moralistically a tough position to take given what aid has been able to do." And he continued: "If you look objectively at what aid has been able to do, you would never accuse it of creating dependency. Having children not die is not creating a dependency, having children not be so sick they can't go to school, not having enough nutrition so that their brains don't develop, that's not a dependency, [and saying] that's an evil thing."[12]

There is a breathtaking vainglory in Gates's attempt to exclude anyone who questions the basic premises of his philanthropy from the aid debate on the basis of their supposed moral turpitude. But in fairness, while such an anathematization, coming from the richest man in the world, who runs the richest foundation in the *history* of the world, was bound to receive exponentially more attention than similar or related comments from anyone else in the development world, no matter how distinguished, Gates's view cannot be dismissed as a billionaire's pique at being harshly criticized rather than flattered, applauded, and courted. Jim Yong Kim has no vast fortune to his name, and yet he took just as hard a line in his 2014 speech that I quoted early in this book, when he declared that "optimism is your moral duty when working with the poor," a statement that implicitly levels the charge that being pessimistic, for any reason whatsoever, is an immoral act. For his part, Jeffrey Sachs has taken a similar line, though in his case there has been nothing implicit about it. In an opinion piece he wrote for the *Los Angeles Times* in 2006,

Sachs charged that "foreign aid skeptics thrive on pessimism."[13] And in a tweet he posted in the spring of 2014, he wrote that, "Cynicism is biggest obstacle to challenges such as ending poverty and fighting climate change. Cynics aim to stop positive action."[14]

Leaving aside the not-unimportant fact that by taxing both cynics and pessimists with the same moral solecisms, even if, for him, cynicism is worse, Sachs writes as if the distinction between pessimism and cynicism were inconsequential, which it is not, any more than the difference in meaning between optimism and hope is insignificant; the fact that Sachs can seriously propose that cynicism is the *biggest* obstacle to ending hunger and extreme poverty or limiting the extent of global warming is baffling. Does he really imagine the threat to be greater than the environmental damage done by industrial agriculture? Or greater than the deforestation caused by agricultural expansion and demographic increase? Or greater than the return of war in the early twenty-first century and the public health calamities (the return of polio to the Middle East, for example, in the wake of the Syrian Civil War) and mass migrations that have become war's predictable aftereffects? To be sure, Sachs has a history of making histrionic and hyperbolic statements, including the last sentence of *The End of Poverty* in which he enjoins his audience to "[send] forth mighty currents of hope," and to "[work] together to heal the world."[15] So were he alone in making such a claim, one might attach no great significance to it. But Jim Yong Kim, who is not given to hyperbole at all, has leveled a similar charge, if not, indeed, a graver one, since where Sachs only accuses the naysayers of being a huge obstacle to progress, Kim has accused them of being guilty of the worst imaginable forms of immorality.

Still, while one may reject Kim's anathematization of anyone who does not share his view that optimism is the only licit moral stance for anyone involved in development, the act of moral reasoning that led him to take this position cannot be challenged on factual grounds. In contrast, Bill Gates was factually completely wrong when he informed his Australian audience in the course of leveling his own modern-day version of a charge of heresy against Dambisa Moyo that there were "not many" aid critics like her. As they say in the military, in war the enemy gets a vote. And the reality is that there are a great many aid critics and they come from across the political spectrum, ranging from such figures as Walden Bello, Susan George, and Jonathan Glennie on the antiglobalization left to Moyo herself and William Easterly on the Hayekian free-market side. And whether Gates would acknowledge the point or not, a pressing problem for those who believe, with him, that development aid as presently constituted has already delivered a great deal and stands poised to deliver a great deal more is that as was implicit in Jeffrey Sachs's warning that cynicism posed a major obstacle to current efforts to end poverty and hunger, there are too many such critics who too often are able to secure too much of a hearing.

We've all taken our wishes for realities at some point in our lives. And for an activist multibillionaire, be it Gates, or George Soros, or Charles and David Koch, the temptation must be far greater than for those who will never be in a position to found, virtually at will, powerful institutions dedicated to making these wishes come true. In *Philanthrocapitalism*, Bishop and Green describe these people as "hyperagents," and approvingly quote a definition of that role as being that of "individuals who can do what it would otherwise take a social movement to do." "Richesse oblige," they conclude, "and a belief in hyperagency are the driving spirit of philanthrocapitalism."[16]

But "richesse" doesn't just expect to oblige, it expects to be obliged as well. One of the more cringe-inducing experiences with regard to Bill Gates is to go online and read the encomia to him being produced by organizations whose institutional survival depends in large measure to his financial grace and favor. The ONE Campaign is a group cofounded by Bono and originally made up of eleven NGOs, including Oxfam America and Bread for the World, which describes itself as "an international campaigning and advocacy organization of nearly 6 million people taking action to end extreme poverty and preventable disease, particularly in Africa." In its financial statement, ONE declares itself "especially grateful to our friends at the Bill and Melinda Gates Foundation for their long-time partnership and major support for our 501(c)3 operations." One form that gratitude has taken is ONE posting "Fascinating Facts about Bill Gates," which include that Gates has "saved over five million lives by bringing vaccines and improved healthcare to children internationally."[17]

This is the kind of treatment traditionally accorded to kings and dictators. While Gates and his fellow philanthrocapitalists are neither, the philanthrocapitalist project is irreducably undemocratic, if not, indeed, antidemocratic. Even its most fervent boosters concede this, even if they often do so in terms that usually skirt the essential issues of accountability in the name of efficiency. Bishop and Green's version of this is emblematic. "As hyperagents," they write, "the superrich can do things to help solve the world's problems that the traditional power elites in and around government cannot. They are free from the usual pressures that bear down on politicians and activists and company bosses with shareholders to please."[18] Later in the book, they put it even more bluntly, observing that "philanthropists have no one to answer to but themselves," a state of affairs they categorize as one of "all assets and no liabilities."[19] It is something Bill Gates has himself pointed out on many occasions, though his remedy for, as he puts it, not having "to worry about being voted out at the next election or board meeting," is to "work hard to get lots of feedback."[20] Nowhere in any of this, though, is even the slightest recognition that there could be a moral problem with this search for feedback being entirely at Melinda and Bill Gates's own discretion, or that accountability that is entirely self-imposed and unenforceable by anyone else is not accountability at all in any serious sense of the term.

In response, one needs to be equally blunt: a world in which democracy is counted, chartered accountant–style, as a liability rather than an asset is a world in which the most powerful are already looking in the rearview mirror, seeing democracy receding, and not minding it a bit. This democracy deficit is the ghost at the banquet of philanthrocapitalism. If the Gates Foundation decides, say, to "double down" on a commitment, as it has in the case of the second Green Revolution, not just through funding but through actively lobbying both African governments and the major Western donors, it is difficult to see what can stop it. In fairness, as the food rights activist Raj Patel has pointed out, the reason that the Gates Foundation could "play God" in the way it has, particularly with regard to global food policy in general and African agriculture in particular, is that until relatively recently, "almost no one else was trying to help." Still, he said, "there has to be something problematic about a few big brains in Washington State, making decisions about an entire continent. At the very least, shouldn't this make any small 'd' democrat queasy?"[21]

To be clear, this question is not particular to Gates but rather applies to all major private philanthropies that are committed to using their money to effect social, economic, or political change. For example, one could fairly describe the activities of the Soros Foundation in at least some countries in which it operates as trying to engineer democratic outcomes through the undemocratic means of George Soros's money, his influence and, above all, his access to policy makers in the major Western capitals and his ability to enlist many of the best and the brightest in the countries in which he chooses to be active to run his national foundations. Some of Soros's more florid critics, like the Columbia University free-market economist Jagdish Bhagwati, have tried to draw a line between Soros's supposed intrusion into the politics of the nations in which his foundations work and Gates's supposed lack of a political agenda, but this is as specious as the Fox News Channel's claim to be "fair and balanced." To accept it would require one to believe that free-market capitalism was not a politics—something that might even give pause to Bill Gates himself.

Then again, perhaps it wouldn't. When I visited the offices of the Bill and Melinda Gates Foundation's Seattle headquarters in 2009, I noticed that the default screen saver on the staff computers is a slide show of the organization's fifteen guiding principles. Some of these make refreshingly modest claims about what even the Gates Foundation can accomplish. "Philanthropy," reads one, "plays a vital but limited role." Others are almost admonitory, both on the internal, workplace level—"We treat each other as valued colleagues" and "We demand ethical behavior of ourselves"—and in terms of how the foundation must pursue its goals—"We advocate vigorously but responsibly in our areas of focus." But one is steelier and more revealing. It reads simply, "This is a family foundation driven by the interests and passions of the Gates family."

When I inquired about this, several senior officials of the Gates Foundation pointed out that the foundation was rarely, if ever, the majority funder of any of the efforts it supported, from education in the United States, to global health, to a second Green Revolution for Africa. But this response occludes the fact that just as with a minority shareholding in a company that gives the person or institution holding it a disproportionate say in its governance, the Gates Foundation's involvement has been decisive time and time again. For example, the foundation's role with regard to vaccine research has often been dispositive. It would be unjust to blame Gates for underwriting programs and research initiatives that looked promising but in the end did not pan out. The question, and it was one that was raised about what many regarded as Gates's predatory and monopolistic practices when he was still running Microsoft, is whether monopolizing the research agenda in the way that the Gates Foundation does, at least to some extent, in whatever field in which it involves itself, risks a situation in which there is a possibility that Gresham's Law (the economic theory that bad money drives out good) is going to apply. For all the hype about scientific nonconformity, researchers go where the money is, just as they have since the days of Oppenheimer and his team at Los Alamos working on the atomic bomb. And by now Gates's influence is so pervasive that it would probably be an act of personal or institutional suicide not to sign on.

Again, the essential point is that unlike in democratically accountable institutions, when the foundation does make a mistake, there is really no recourse for anyone on the outside. Melinda Gates has said that she and her husband "learn from their mistakes." But even if this is what the Gateses make every effort to do, and I see no reason to suppose that this is not the case, the problem is that this "learning" takes place wholly on their own terms—to put the matter politely, according to their passions and interests, or less politely, according to whether or not they choose to learn from them. Unlike government development aid, there is literally no check on what they can do except their own resources and desires, and no way of making this learning process, when and if it happens, anything more than a voluntary act on their part.

Nor is their own self-criticism likely to be systematic, for, again, this would require the foundation to be open to the idea that their fundamental assumptions on a given issue—most obviously, that sustainable growth is feasible and is not a contradiction in terms for the obvious environmental reasons—something Bill and Melinda Gates and their senior staff have never shown the slightest evidence of taking seriously, even as a fairly remote possibility. But then, even to advance this as a legitimate expectation assumes that the spirit of the age that advocates of the philanthrocapitalist model say it exemplifies is still a democratic one in any real sense. But as the Canadian philosopher John Ralston Saul once observed, "You can usually tell when the concepts of democracy and citizenship are weakening. There is an increase in the role of charity and in the worship of volunteerism."[22]

The privileging of public-private partnerships in the effort to end hunger and extreme poverty confirms Shah's diagnosis. Shortly after becoming administrator of USAID, Shah proclaimed a "new model of development" for combatting extreme poverty, and declared that "increasingly, the best ideas aren't just coming from development professionals who have been in the field for three decades. They are also coming from scientists, inventors, and entrepreneurs around the world."[23] As fascinating as where Shah thought the best places were to look for the ideas that would lead to greater and greater successes for development—that is, among technologists, innovators, and capitalists—was what he left out. Democracy went unmentioned, at least democracy in any other sense than democracy *à l'américaine*—liberal capitalist democracy in which the freedom of private business to invest without hindrance was thought inseparable from freedom itself.

Shah elaborated these ideas in an important speech he delivered in June 2011 in Arlington, Virginia, to a USAID-sponsored conference on "promoting democracy, human rights, and governance." In it, Shah acknowledged that there was "some merit" to the criticisms of USAID that reproached the agency for having "worked too closely with governments that refuse to respect the rights of their people . . . pulled our punches, [and been] complicit in unbalanced relations between autocrats and their people." But Shah assured his audience that President Obama understood that "we are living in a new world, with a new paradigm of national interest," and that henceforth USAID would no longer, as it had done so often in the past, "act as though democracy and development are two different objectives." There would be no more "equating a country with its government." Instead of limiting its assistance to "groups that have been endorsed by [these] governments," USAID would "partner much more closely with an entire range of stakeholders: parliaments, opposition parties, civil society, and most crucially, the citizens themselves."[24]

To his credit, Shah conceded that the examples of China and Vietnam demonstrated that democracy was not "a *sine qua non* of economic growth." But he insisted that "for every country that manages to grow quickly without embracing democracy, there are five dictators who consign their countries to economic and political despair." The example of the Arab Spring, he told his audience, should remind everyone that "economic prosperity and political freedom must go hand in hand." If not, USAID's development work would not "achieve the sustainable results we seek."

But what did this political freedom consist of? Shah's short list consisted of the following: "capable, transparent, and accountable public institutions, . . . political stability [and] property rights, . . . [and lowering] the investment risk that private-sector partners face." This might have been jarring to anyone not already familiar with what the early-twenty-first-century consensus in the development world had become. To anyone familiar with it, however, Shah's emphasis was simply the conventional wisdom stated a bit more bluntly. As a March 2014 European Commission report put it, since a job (what kind of job was left unspecified) was the best way out of poverty and the private sector provided some 90 percent of jobs in developing countries, the private sector was thus "an essential partner in the fight against poverty," was needed "as an investor in sustainable agricultural production if the world is to meet the challenge of feeding 9 billion people by 2050," and "through innovation and investment in low-carbon and resource-efficient solutions," had "a major role to play in the transformation towards an inclusive green economy."[25]

The view was an ideological one that not only was liberal capitalism the best, if indeed not the only, way to organize international society humanely, but that despite the Chinese and Vietnamese "exceptions" that Shah had conceded, it was still the best if not the only way to end extreme poverty and global hunger in the world. That is to say, it could be disputed on ideological grounds, but there was no factual inconsistency on Shah's part in maintaining it, even if there was great disagreement among its advocates on what the respective roles of business, states, and civil society should be, and at least some groups—notably, the UK watchdog, the Independent Commission for Aid Impact—had warned that "the private sector is not a development panacea."[26] In contrast, Shah's claim—which, to be clear, was virtually identical to ones made routinely by his opposite numbers at institutions such as the development arm of the European Union, DFID, and the World Bank—that USAID was committed to linking its development and democracy programs simply does not bear up to scrutiny. For Shah has gone out of his way during his tenure as USAID administrator to heap praise on Ethiopia, Rwanda, and other tyrannical regimes in Africa that have shown success in poverty reduction, diminution in the rates of malnutrition, and improved health care, above all in maternal and infant health. He has also spoken in tremendously upbeat terms about his agency's programs in Central America at a time when, as the unprecedented wave of unaccompanied child migrants to the United States from El Salvador, Guatemala, and Honduras demonstrated so painfully, virtually every social indicator, including the fact that in 2013 Honduras became the country with the highest murder rate in the world, shows that these three nations are in free fall politically and socially.

But if Shah's promise in his Arlington speech, couched in the management consultant's language that had become his rhetorical signature, that USAID would undertake "democratic credit check[s]" that would determine whether USAID's "investment could empower a government at the expense of its people" was an empty one, it also reflected the enthusiasm for regimes such as Ethiopia's and Rwanda's that Shah shared with Bill and Melinda Gates, Jim Yong Kim and his colleagues at the World Bank, Tony Blair's Africa Governance Initiative, Jeffrey Sachs, and leading celebrity philanthropists—or "celanthropists," as Bishop and Green dub them in *Philanthrocapitalism*—such as Bono and Bob Geldof. An emblematic expression of this was that of Kanayo F. Nwanze, the president of the International Fund for Agricultural Development (IFAD), one of three UN agencies specializing in food issues along with the WFP and the FAO, who told an interviewer in 2014 that Ethiopia, Ghana, Rwanda, and Togo were already "showing the way" to making economic growth on the African continent "inclusive."[27]

Nwanze seemed unconcerned by the fact that Ghana is a democracy but that Togo is now run by the son of Gnassingbé Eyadéma, the general who ruled the country from 1967 to his death in 2005, and that Ethiopia and Rwanda are de facto one-party tyrannies.

Ethiopia has been a particular favorite of the international development world; indeed, it is often put forward as the poster child for development success. And yet, according to Human Rights Watch's 2014 country report, "Ethiopia's ambitious development schemes, funded from domestic revenue sources and foreign assistance, sometimes displace indigenous communities without appropriate consultation or any compensation."[28] And after describing in detail the Ethiopian government's imprisonment on a wide scale of nonviolent opposition leaders and journalists and denial of the right to assembly, among many other violations of human rights, the report notes that while Ethiopia receives donor assistance of almost $4 billion a year,[29] "as partners in Ethiopia's development, donor nations remain muted in their criticism of Ethiopia's appalling human rights record and are taking little meaningful action to investigate allegations of abuses associated with development programs."[30]

Was all this self-deception on Shah's part? A cynical view would be that given the US government's rhetorical commitment to human rights, any administrator of USAID would have to make the claims Shah did in his Arlington speech, whatever the realities of US policy actually were. To go a step further, as King's College London legal scholar John Tasioulas has observed, in recent times the "discourse of human rights has acquired the status of an ethical *lingua franca*."[31] Give Shah the benefit of the doubt and say that his claims were entirely well intended and that if they were misleading, this was not due to hypocrisy, but, at worst, to self-deception or wishful thinking. As Tasioulas's Oxford colleague Joseph Raz observed, "The self-deceived pay homage to the standards they distort by acknowledging . . . these are the appropriate standards" by which to judge the importance of human rights in international affairs.[32]

In contrast to his former protégé Shah, while Bill Gates is passionately interested in human welfare, human rights has not been an important subject for him. To illustrate this, beginning in 2009 Bill and Melinda Gates have written an annual Gates Foundation letter, whose purpose Bill Gates has described as an effort to "share in a frank way what our goals are and where progress is being made and where it is not." The term *human rights* did not appear in that first letter nor, as of this writing in 2015, has it appeared in any of the subsequent ones. Matthew Bishop and Michael Green have followed up on their work on philanthrocapitalism (where human rights is mentioned only twice, and then very much in passing) and, in collaboration with Harvard Business School professor Michael Porter, who is generally viewed as the leading authority in the world on competitive business strategy, have developed what they call a "Social Progress Index," intended to be independent of economic indicators and based partly on the ideas of Amartya Sen. But as the development commentator Tom Paulson noted, "Rwanda—which is often considered the development community's big African success story—ranked near the bottom of the list. Mozambique, Uganda, Nigeria and Ethiopia were the only nations with lower scores."[33]

To Gates's critics, this comes as no surprise. Whether Gates is personally indifferent to human rights, or whether it is simply that the political character of the regimes he supports is of secondary importance to him when compared with the degree of progress they have made in tackling poverty, disease, and hunger and in attaining various quantifiable development goals, is impossible for anyone not in his confidence to know for certain. But it is unimaginable that the graphic in the 2013 annual foundation letter titled "Bringing Health Care to the People: Ethiopia's Success Story" would have been accompanied by another that would read (just as accurately) "Taking Human Rights Away from the People: Ethiopia's Shame," or anything of the sort. And Gates's own response to Dambisa Moyo and that of Geoff Lamb, Bill and Melinda Gates's chief economic and policy advisor, in his review of William Easterly's attack on Gates's "technocratic illusion" in *The Tyranny of Experts*, suggest neither Gates nor the senior staff at the foundation take such criticisms seriously. Lamb's breezy dismissal of Easterly on Gates's "Impatient Optimists" blog was particularly revealing. In it, he referred to USAID's "support for democratic movements" as if it were an undeniable fact, one that obviated any need on his part to address a core element in Easterly's argument, which was that this was precisely what USAID was *not* doing in Ethiopia.

Could Gates have been serious after all when he insisted that Moyo was one of only a handful of critics ignorant or foolish enough to suggest that aid might be doing more harm than good? It is of course theoretically possible that he really does not know the depth and extent of the opposition to the aid paradigm that he has done so much develop. But it hardly seems likely. If nothing else, even if Moyo's and Easterly's critique from the perspective of their particular fusion of Hayekian individualism and human rights commitment came as a surprise, Gates must surely have been aware of the huge antiglobalization demonstrations during the 1999 ministerial meeting of the World Trade Organization that briefly brought his home city of Seattle to a standstill. In *The End of Poverty*, Jeffrey Sachs even talks of walking with Gates's father through the demonstrations: "I whispered to my walking companion, Bill Gates Sr., that it was probably just as well that he was not recognized by the crowds!"[34] And Bill Gates Jr. is a voracious reader who regularly posts detailed book reviews on his personal website, The Gates Notes. In a September 2013 *New York Times* op-ed piece, "The End of Poverty, Soon," Sachs observed that the idea that extreme poverty could be ended by 2030 was "[taking] hold at the highest levels."[35] He was absolutely right, and since very few critics of aid hold such positions, and given the exalted circles in which Gates generally moves except when visiting beneficiaries of his foundation's work, this may help explain why Gates thinks critics are as thin on the ground, just as he does that they are evil.

It would be impossible to overstate the importance of Gates's views in the current orientation of the development project. And yet, if allowances are made for the differences in sensibility and rhetorical style between the Seattle of 2014 and the Washington of 1949, very little separates Gates's confidence that his approach to development is the only correct one[36] and that to systematically oppose it is to stand in the way of all decent human hope for ending the scourges of poverty, disease, and hunger, from those expressed by development experts going as far back as President Truman's elaboration of Point Four in his second inaugural address in 1949, that is, at the dawning of the modern development era. In *The History of Development*, Gilbert Rist broke down that speech into four parts: The first recalls the desperate straits—the horror of hunger and want—in which more than half the world's population live. Then the good news is given that, 'for the first time in history,' something is at hand that will bring happiness and make it possible for their lives to be transformed. [But] this will not come unless energies are mobilized to produce more, to invest, to get down to work, to expand trade. But in the end, if the chance is seized and people agree to the efforts required, an era of happiness, peace and prosperity will dawn from which everyone stands to benefit."[37]

As Rist goes on to point out, from the beginning, implicit in this was the message that the solutions being offered by development were quite literally "the only solution to the problems of humanity."[38] If one accepted this, one was a friend of humanity or, in Jim Yong Kim's terms, established oneself as a moral person. In contrast, to reject the claims made for what development had accomplished and could go on to achieve was to do nothing less than stand athwart the path to progress for the poor and the hungry, delaying, as Jeffrey Sachs has insisted cynical naysayers have the power to do, this generation's chance to "heal the world." Viewed from this perspective, for Gates to denounce Dambisa Moyo as evil was simple common sense. If what needed to be done was both obvious and feasible, then to oppose doing it was surely the act of a lunatic, a nihilist, or, as Gates strongly implied when he called Dambisa Moyo's book evil, quite simply an enemy of the human race.

But if the Manichaean moral vision of the development world, in which, to borrow the historian Peter Gay's description of the European Enlightenment, the "party of humanity" tries to persuade a cynical world that as Jeffrey Sachs has put it, "the sweetest fruits [of the Enlightenment agenda] are just within our reach,"[39] has remained unchanged since the mid-twentieth century, the remedies put forward as best suited to achieving this have not. Instead, the history of the development world is one in which theory after theory, paradigm after paradigm, has risen to become the consensus, only to fall out of favor and be replaced with some very different set of analyses and prescriptions. As Paul Krugman recalled in a speech he delivered on the work of Albert Hirschman, high development theory in the West was deeply influential among economists and policy makers from the early 1940s to the mid-1950s, at which time it "rapidly unraveled." By the time he started to study economics in the 1970s, Krugman recalled, "it seemed not so much wrong as incomprehensible."[40]

This should hardly be surprising. In *The Rise and Fall of Development Theory*, Colin Leys narrates the historical trajectory of development thinking, in which the initial "positive orthodoxy" of 1940s, based in large measure on Keynesianism and the lessons drawn from the Marshall Plan, gave way in the 1950s to Rostow's modernization theory, which in turn gave way in the 1970s to left-leaning "dependency theory" on one side and on the other, early forms of neoliberalism in Washington and the major European donor countries, with its gradual abandonment of Keynesianism, which is to say of virtually the entire international trading system as it had been envisaged at the Bretton Woods conference in 1944. In the 1980s Dr. Gro Harlem Bruntland put forward the idea of "sustainable development," but while that became a key term, the ideas behind it were largely shunted aside by the architects of the Washington Consensus and its brainchild, the World Bank's Structural Adjustment Program. It was only after the SAP failed to live up to expectations that the development establishment turned to what came to be known as "pro-poor growth." These commitments, though, have coexisted, however immiscible these ideas seem to some us, with the belief that the state should no longer play the main dispositive role in the development project, the (relative) subordination and political neutering of the NGOs, and the ascendancy of the role of private business that constitutes the development consensus in the early twenty-first century.

LeBaron and Dauvergne have argued that this latest development paradigm threatens no one in power. But one can go much further. As Garry W. Jenkins, a professor of law at Ohio State University, has put it, "With its emphasis on superrich hyperagents solving social problems, philanthrocapitalism [has amplified] the voice of those who already wield substantial influence, access, and power." And Smith argues that "an explicit strategy of philanthrocapitalists is to seek the ultimate leverage of philanthropic giving by influencing government to *follow their lead* in choosing what social initiatives (both problems and preferred solutions) are worthy of support."[41] What this means is that for the first time in modern history, it has become the conventional wisdom that private business—the most politically influential, the most undertaxed and least regulated, and, most importantly, the least democratically accountable sector among those groups that dispose of real power and wealth in the world—is best suited to be entrusted with the welfare and the fate of the powerless and the hungry. No revolution could be more radical, no expectation, no matter how much this was the product of the ceaseless promotion of this view in both old and new media, could be more counterintuitive, more antihistorical, or require a greater leap of faith.

· 13 ·

The End of Hunger?

B ill Gates would surely reject the suggestion that it was a leap of faith for him to have predicted in his 2014 foundation letter that "by 2035, there will be almost no poor countries left in the world," and that almost all countries "will learn from their most productive neighbors and benefit from innovations like new vaccines, better seeds, and the digital revolution." On the contrary, like Jeffrey Sachs and Jim Yong Kim, Gates has never wavered in his insistence that if he was an (impatient) optimist about the future, it was because, as he put it, "a realistic appraisal of the human condition compels an optimistic worldview." Much as Sachs had done in *The End of Poverty*, Gates has often qualified this claim with the warning that while such progress was likely, it was not inevitable. But this did not make optimism any less of both a moral and an operational guiding principle in his work, and for Gates this was virtually a distinction without a difference. As he said to Stanford's 2014 graduating class in his commencement speech, "Even in dire situations, optimism can fuel innovation and lead to new tools to eliminate suffering."

To a development skeptic, Gates's vision of the future was Pollyannism on steroids. But there was absolutely nothing Pollyannaish in his evaluation of present trends. There, somewhat surprisingly, Cassandraish was closer to the mark. "If we project," Gates had written in his 2010 annual foundation letter, "what the world will be like 10 years from now without innovation in health, education, energy, or food, the picture is quite bleak. Health costs for the rich will escalate, forcing tough trade-offs and keeping the poor stuck in the bad situation they are in today. . . . We will have to increase the price of energy to reduce consumption, and the poor will suffer from both this higher cost and the effect of climate change. In food we will have big shortages because we won't have enough land to feed the world's growing population and support its richer diet."[1]

Why then, was he so convinced that these outcomes would not occur? Gates's answer was simple and direct: it was the power and hence the promise of innovation that had convinced him that humanity's future was bright rather than bleak. In a video clip he made for USAID, Gates declared flatly that "all the progress in the past, and the source of all progress in the future, will be innovation."[2] And for Gates, innovation and optimism were two sides of the same future-welcoming, past-dismissing coin. As he said in his 2014 commencement speech, "If Melinda and I had to put in one word what we love most about Stanford, it's the *optimism*. There's an infectious feeling here that innovation can solve almost every problem." And Gates made it clear that he believed this just as applicable to poverty, or disease, or hunger as it had been when he and Paul Allen had started Microsoft "[believing] that the magic of computers and software would empower people everywhere, and make the world much, much better."[3]

In much the same way that what Warren Buffett says—and more importantly what his company, Berkshire Hathaway, is buying—can often move the financial markets, so what Bill Gates says—and more importantly, what his foundation is focusing on—can often shift the development debate. But in this case, Gates's point of departure, which is that innovation has become the crucial element in business success, has been the consensus view in corporate America and, increasingly even if still to a somewhat lesser extent, among the business elite in most other developed countries for some years. It dates back to the publication in 1997 of *The Innovator's Dilemma* by Clayton Christensen of the Harvard Business School, one of the most influential business books ever published. A decade later, in 2007, a survey done by the *Economist*, a journal that for decades has incarnated whatever the enlightened conventional wisdom of the business establishment happens to be, "long-run economic growth depends on the creation and fostering of an environment that encourages innovation."[4] And a *Business Week* study of corporate performance found that between 1995 and 2005, the median profit margin at the top "innovative" firms was 3.4 percent, whereas the average of other firms in the S&P Global Index was 0.4 percent. Small wonder, then, that by 2012 survey data showed that four out of ten CEOs of major US corporations had appointed a so-called chief innovation officer.

In the early twenty-first century, this analysis of how businesses succeed—which, lest it be forgotten, was what Christensen had actually been writing about in *The Innovator's Dilemma*, even though subsequently he published books applying his theories to health care and to university education—had become a general theory that what was needed by society as a whole to succeed was first and foremost innovation. The corollary to this was what Sussex University economist Mariana Mazzucato, one the increasingly rare dissenters of the reigning consensus, described as the constant depiction of government "as a heavy-handed impediment to innovation and entrepreneurship." The distinguished Northwestern economist Robert Gordon was representative of this when he said that he was "extremely skeptical of government" as a source of innovation. "This," he added, "is the role of individual entrepreneurs. Government had nothing to do with Bill Gates, Steve Jobs, [or Mark] Zuckerberg."[5]

Mazzucato had tried to counter this view in a 2011 book, *The Entrepreneurial State*, arguing that it was based on ideology, not evidence, and that in reality, the state had played a central role in producing the world-transforming breakthroughs usually associated only with corporations. A prime example of this is Apple. As Mazzucato points out, "nearly every state-of-the-art technology found in the iPod, iPhone and iPad is an often overlooked and ignored achievement of the research efforts and funding support of the government and military."[6] But such dissents have carried little weight, above all, I think, because governments themselves had signed on to the view that innovation was best left to business, with government largely restricting itself to providing an enabling environment.

This held true not only with regard to what the best route was to economic progress at home, but with regard to international development as well. During the Obama administration in the United States, for example, it became commonplace to claim that the president, in the words of Under Secretary of Commerce Patrick Gallagher, had made innovation "the centerpiece of our economic agenda." The reason was quite simple, Gallagher said: it had become "the key driver to our economy."[7] ECOSOC, the Economic and Social Council, is generally viewed as one of the few UN bodies in which the views of the Global South are adequately represented and for that reason often incarnates a very different view of the world from that of Washington, Brussels, or indeed, Davos. And yet if anything, ECOSOC's former president, Néstor Osorio, was even more categorical, declaring at a 2013 meeting in Dar es Salaam, Tanzania, that "innovation is the essence of our modern societies. Without harnessing its power, we will not be able to create a healthy, educated or inclusive society."[8] Any realistic hopes for sustainable development, Osorio insisted, depended on it.

This was unquestionably the consensus view among those concerned with agriculture and nutrition. A representative example was a briefing note by the Farmer First organization for a conference to be held in 2008 at Sussex University's Institute for Development Studies. It stated matter-of-factly that "over the past 20 years, the contexts for agricultural research and development have changed significantly. Farmers must engage as entrepreneurs in complex, sometimes global, marketing systems, often without state support."[9] The conference succeeded in assembling a great many of the most distinguished and influential academic specialists and practitioners in the field of agricultural development. And as the final report put it, "Everyone [sic] agrees that engagement with the private sector is critical."[10] This was not just a fact of life but rather was, it seemed, most welcome. In an echo of entrepreneurial business rhetoric about the superiority of business of government in terms of efficiency and expertise, the report spoke of the "large, lumbering research and development organizations" that had been the focus of Farmer First "reformers." Today, though, they "were only part of the picture," and in many places a decreasing one at that. And the report approvingly quoted Shambu Prasad, an influential academic specialist in rural management, who had asked, "How do we transform the rich (cacophony of) organizational diversity into (a symphony of) innovation?"[11]

The Farmer First workshop did raise a warning flag, cautioning that to have the hoped-for effect, these innovative technologies would have to be applied in ways that were "pro-poor," an echo of the James Wolfensohn–era World Bank slogan "pro-poor growth," though, given the line being taken by USAID, DFID, and the other major Western development agencies, it hardly seemed likely that leaving things to the private sector was anything other than welcome to the major Western donors. For its part, in the first decade and a half of the twenty-first century, the World Bank seems to have grown ever more convinced that innovation was the prerequisite for making food security an enduring reality in the poor world. In 2013 the bank embraced what it heralded in 2012 as "the emerging principles of Agricultural Innovation System (AIS) analysis and action" designed to help "identify, design, and implement the investments, approaches, and complementary interventions that appear most likely to strengthen innovation systems and promote agricultural innovation and equitable growth." This, the bank stated, was essential "if farmers, agribusiness, and even nations are to cope, compete, and thrive"[12] in the changing agricultural conditions of the twenty-first century. The fact that agribusiness was mentioned as an equal partner, or in the jargon of development, as a "stakeholder," on a par with farmers and with the state, was particularly clarifying. So was the assumption that an ethos of competition should inform not just what agribusiness did but what farmers and states did as well.

For his part, Jeffrey Sachs, whose views, both through his own work and as the head of the UN's Millennium Project, which had provided the MDGs with their intellectual armature, were immensely important in framing the development debate, had always been a firm believer in innovation. Indeed, in 2002, in a conference paper he called "The Global Innovation Divide," he had argued that "the divide in the world between [the countries that are] the technology innovators [and those that are] non-innovators" is "considerably starker than the global divisions of income."[13] Given this view, it came as no surprise that one of the key conclusions of one of the UN Millennium Project's task forces was that without innovation, which one of its task force reports defined as "applying knowledge in development," none of the MDGs were likely to be achieved. The report declared that "science, technology, and innovation underpin every one of the Goals," and that without them, it was "inconceivable that gains can be made in health and environmental concerns."[14] And its preface ended with a quote from Spinoza: "I do not know how to teach philosophy without being a disturber of established religion"—a resonant way of underlining the task force's call to developing countries "to have the courage to break with traditional approaches and explore the role of science, technology, and innovation in their development strategies."[15]

All these claims, including Christensen's original formulation, to one extent or another had been foreshadowed by decades of work done by the distinguished New York University economist William J. Baumol, one of the great world authorities on the role of entrepreneurship in the economy. Baumol had long argued that capitalism's success was due to its being an extraordinarily effective "innovation machine." If poor nations in Africa and Latin America were failing to converge economically with the rich societies of North America, Western Europe, and Japan, Baumol said in a 2002 interview, it was because government interference in the market in these countries had proved to be "the surest way to prevent innovation,"[16] and that innovation is essential for economic growth in any capitalist economy. But unlike Gates, Sachs, or Kim, Baumol has said repeatedly that he does not expect progress to be quick in the poor world. Nor did he dismiss those who worried about the effects of globalization. "The economists who have denied that really have not looked at reality," he told his interviewer.[17] On the contrary, for Baumol, while the eventual benefits of globalization for the world's poor were real, and indeed were, as he put it, "the one hope we have for the long run,"[18] it will make life "harder and worse for a substantial period unless government intervenes in reasonable ways."[19]

In fairness, this was just what Gates, Sachs, and Kim seemed convinced many governments, including profoundly undemocratic ones such as Ethiopia and Rwanda, had already begun to do responsibly and successfully, even if, obviously, more nations needed to act in the same way and a great deal more needed to be done even by those nations that had made these commitments.[20] In theory, this was certainly possible, especially if governments in the poor world would, in Sachs's words, "do their jobs in setting up the right rules"[21] for the private sector's involvement in development. But how likely was this? Virtually everyone across the political spectrum, whether they welcome or bemoan it, agrees that a principal effect of globalization has been the weakening of the authority of the national governments. And yet the development optimists have continued to insist that there is nothing unrealistic about expecting the (on average) much weaker governments in the Global South to set and enforce stringent rules on multinational corporations and to accomplish this feat in an era when, as the aftermath of the 2007–2008 financial crisis has shown, even most governments in the rich world have proven largely incapable of imposing effectively at home in the matters that really counted, above all with regard to taxation.

This is where the antipolitical or at least postpolitical bias of the twenty-first-century development consensus came to affect what otherwise might have seemed like a fruitless quest to square the proverbial circle. As Sachs's preface to the Millennium Project's task force report on innovation put it, "Responding to challenges in areas such as economic productivity, agriculture, education, gender inequity, health, water, sanitation, environment, and participation in the global economy will require increased use of scientific and technical knowledge. Technological innovation and the associated institutional adjustments underpin long-term growth and must be at the center of any strategy to strengthen the private sector."[22] That the private sector needed to be strengthened was apparently so obvious that it did not even have to be argued. And the fact that all the political questions about what kind of society could be subsumed in the category of "institutional adjustments" testified eloquently to the extent to which the best and the brightest in the development world believed that to speak of politics in such an old-fashioned way need no longer be an intellectual priority, let alone that there might actually be a moral obligation for them to do so. It was not only those who opposed (capitalist) globalization who retained their doubts. There were even probusiness economists who also remained unconvinced. In the late 1990s, for example, the distinguished British development economist Deepak Lal argued that "the globalization of the economy is by no means inevitable. First it has to survive the politicization of society."[23]

For Bill Gates, politics of any stripe was at best of secondary importance. As he put it in a long interview he gave to *Rolling Stone* magazine in 2014, "Our modern lifestyle is not a political creation. Before 1700, everybody was poor as hell. Life was short and brutish. It wasn't because we didn't have good politicians; we had some really good politicians. But then we started inventing—electricity, steam engines, microprocessors, understanding genetics and medicine and things like that.[24] Yes, stability and education are important—I'm not taking anything away from that—but innovation is the real driver of progress."[25]

But however quick Gates has always been to dismiss his pessimistic critics as being guilty of what in his Stanford commencement address he called "false hopelessness . . . the attitude that says we can't defeat poverty and disease," and no matter how convinced he was that "innovation will create new possibilities and make the world better,"[26] however unacknowledged by him or remarked upon by those who shared his views, there was a pessimistic or, perhaps more accurately, an apprehensive subtext to his claims. Gates made this clear in a public conversation he had with Warren Buffett, after Buffett's announcement of his intention to bequeath almost his entire fortune, estimated to be somewhere around $30 billion, to the Gates Foundation. During their talk, Gates approvingly quoted a passage in the memoirs of the American nuclear physicist, Edward Teller, conventionally regarded as the father of the hydrogen bomb. In Gates's retelling of it, Teller had confessed that "if he didn't believe in innovation, he would have been a communist" Gates added, with an ideological flourish, that "if the economy is a zero-sum situation, then you ought to try some crazy sharing thing. It's only the innovation and pie-growing activity that made Teller feel comfortable with the capitalist approach."[27]

That there was a similar "last-ditch" character to the role Gates assigned to innovation was clear from his insistence that if one extrapolated from the present, things looked very bleak indeed. For "communist," read "pessimist." For implicit in what Gates was saying was the fear that if innovation ever failed, then the pessimists might be right after all. This is not to say that either Gates or anyone who shared his expectations about the future believed this ever actually would or, given their susceptibility to deterministic thinking, perhaps even ever could happen. But the Achilles' heel of this analysis is that it allows for no fallback position, no "Plan B," were it to turn out that the as-yet-not-even-thought-of innovations in whose limitless potential to solve any problem Gates believed so profoundly ended up falling short. In a fierce critique of Clayton Christensen's ideas that Harvard historian Jill Lepore wrote for the *New Yorker* in 2014, she described innovation as the idea of progress "scrubbed clean of the horrors of the twentieth century, and relieved of its critics."[28] Even assuming she was right, an optimist might have matched sarcasm for sarcasm and replied that as long as the future cooperated, there was still no problem. But what if the future failed to cooperate?

Gates's view on climate change illustrates this. Virtually every reputable study concurs that if current policies are not changed radically and change doesn't come fairly quickly, a median global temperature increase of between 3.6 to 5.3 degrees Celsius is all but certain. Everyone in the development world knows this, even if, much like many scientists, many prefer not to acknowledge it publicly, which is why climate change is the one area where even the most die-hard optimists will generally concede that if much more is not done soon to limit the rise in global temperatures and mitigate its worst effects, the scenarios of continued global improvement may not play out as they anticipate. And Gates was no exception. In his *Rolling Stone* interview, Gates was, by his standards at least, quite downbeat about the problem, pointing out that what made its challenge "so hard" was that "by the time we see that [climate change] is really bad, [our] ability to fix it is extremely limited." He even conceded the possibility that, as he put it, "even when you turn virtuous, things are actually going to get worse for quite a while." And he added a warning, saying that "you can't take the progress we've made and linearize it—if you do, you really are going to find out how bad climate change can be."[29] He was right, of course. In the words of one of the placards one frequently sees at environmentalist rallies, "There is no Planet B."

This is not to say that Gates's anxieties about climate change had shaken his confidence that the future would be far better for the poor and the hungry than the present. They hadn't. As he assured his *Rolling Stone* interviewer, "I think we will get our act together on climate change." The significance of this was that apart from a pandemic or nuclear disaster or bioterrorism, and in global terms, the more parochial question of whether the US political system would "ever right itself," global warming has been the only major contemporary problem that Gates has conceded might actually be worse in the future, at least for a while. In a 2010 TED talk on energy and climate, Gates even used the word "miracle" to describe what was needed, though he was quick to add that by miraculous, he emphatically did not mean impossible, and that as far as he was concerned, the microprocessor, the personal computer, and the Internet had also been miracles. But he was equally quick to point out that what was required was unprecedented, even by those standards. "Usually," he said, "we don't have a deadline, where you have to get the miracle by a certain date. Usually, you just kind of stand by, and some come along, some don't." But climate change, he warned, was a case "where we actually have to drive at full speed and get a miracle in a pretty tight timeline."[30] And Gates has clearly become sufficiently alarmed that in his 2015 foundation letter, he commits himself to become a great deal more involved in trying to cope with climate change. But he makes it clear that this will be in a private capacity and not in the context of the foundation.

Whatever the extent of Gates's commitments, the idea that a miracle can be on a timeline would have seemed like a moral contradiction in terms at any era in human history until the latter part of the twentieth century. But in the context of what the writer Rob Cox has called "the moral exceptionalism"[31] of Silicon Valley and Jaron Lanier, the computer scientist (and current Microsoft research fellow) turned critic of the Internet, has characterized as its "missionary reductivism,"[32] such hubristic statements of entitlement have become so commonplace as to no longer feel hubristic. And despite the materialist and science- and technology-based grounding of Gates's perception of the world, in his work both as a capitalist and as a philanthropist, the idea that one can hasten miracles certainly sounds more like faith than it does "impatient optimism." Presumably this was what Jaron Lanier was trying to convey when he wrote that "a self-proclaimed materialist movement that attempts to base itself on science starts to look like a religion rather quickly."[33] If he is right, then it is a religion in which the equivalent of the heretic or the apostate is the pessimistic naysayer, and in which, as Jill Lepore put it, the business media's fascination with innovators has been the modern equivalent "of what, a century ago, were known as 'sketches of men of progress.'" For Lepore, "innovation is the idea of progress jammed into a criticism-proof jack-in-the-box."[34]

One might add, inside a politics-proof jack-in-the-box as well, or at least one in which politics is viewed as some kind of mystifying impediment to the Golden Age of zero hunger and the end of poverty that philanthrocapitalism stands on the threshold of ushering in, if only the politicians would get out of the way. For example, in a 2014 public conversation that the cofounder of Sun Microsystems, Vinod Khosla, held with the cofounders of Google, Larry Page and Sergey Brin, Page said that when he looked at government, its way of operating seemed "pretty illogical" to him.[35] For all his optimism, Bill Gates seemed more mystified still. Convinced that it was technological innovation and not politics that was responsible for virtually all the progress of the past three centuries, he was honest enough to admit in his *Rolling Stone* interview that the intractability of events such as the war in Syria "raises questions for somebody who thinks they can fix Africa overnight." "I understand," he said, "how every healthy child, every new road, puts a country on a better path, but instability and war will arise from time to time, and I'm not an expert on how you get out of those things." And he concluded somewhat wistfully, "I wish there was an invention or [scientific or technological] advance to fix that."[36]

Given how rarely this has been a major focus of the development debate, especially with regard to what needed to be done to make the global food system serve the needs of the poor and the malnourished, that Gates was willing to acknowledge this was to his great credit. For the most part, though, even the best and most sophisticated reports about what needed to be done to produce more food for a population of nine billion while at the same time improving the lives and livelihoods of smallholder farmers, whether they came from respected institutions within the food establishment such as IFPRI and CGIAR, think tanks such as the Chicago Council on Foreign Relations, or major NGOs and philanthropies including Gates's own foundation, were written as if one could make serious suggestions about how to reform agriculture without matching them with equally serious ones about how to maintain peace in fragile societies that were soon to be made even more fragile by climate change. Thus the CEO of CGIAR, Frank Rijsberman, told the SciDev.Net website in a 2014 interview that "in the coming years, investment in innovation in agriculture will be key to addressing issues facing sub-Saharan Africa and other developing areas of the world."[37] In a similar vein, a 2014 FAO working paper entitled "The Challenges of Managing Agricultural Price and Production Risks in Sub-Saharan Africa" mentioned every challenge that sector is likely to face (the report is particularly good on the possible effects of climate change, though that is not its main focus) *except* war and migration.[38] And the conclusion to the Alliance for a Green Revolution in Africa (AGRA) annual report acknowledges "the persistence of low levels of food production increased food insecurity, unstable agricultural prices, and increasing costs of inputs,"[39] but proceeds as if food security has any chance of being secured in a period of growing, continent-wide political insecurity—a trend that barely gets a mention in the report.

Even reports exclusively concerned with the effects of climate change on food security almost invariably deal only cursorily with the issues of peace and war, political instability, and intercommunal strife that one did not have to be an expert to see would be of central importance. For example, the Chicago Council on Global Affairs' extensive and extremely well-researched and -presented 2014 report, "Advancing Global Food Security in the Face of a Changing Climate," which was underwritten by Pepsico and the Gates Foundation, opens with the commonsense observation that "in the decades to come, our global food system will face unprecedented strains."[40] But as was the case with the council's 2013 report, "Advancing Global Food Security: The Power of Science, Trade, and Business," virtually every strain the current system faced was examined *except* that of political security and stability. Street protests, some violent, occurred in roughly thirty countries in 2008 after food prices shot up, and the US Department of Defense warned that "climate change could have wide-ranging implications for US national security due to social unrest spurred by reduced water availability, degraded agricultural production, higher food prices, damage to infrastructure, and changes in disease patterns."[41]

But the measures that the report recommended in order for the world to avoid such outcomes were almost entirely technocratic—a recapitulation of the post-2008 crisis consensus calling for "developing the necessary scientific breakthroughs and broadly disseminating them," "reducing barriers to the global food trade," and, in the specific case of the United States, "[rallying] international resources and [deploying] its agricultural research enterprise—its universities, research institutes, and agrifood businesses to gather more information about how climate change will affect the global food system and develop the innovations to manage its impacts."

The FAO's comprehensive 2013 publication, *Climate-Smart Agriculture Sourcebook*, was another instance of an authoritative study in which the question being asked—"how and to what extent can agriculture and food systems can contribute to climate change mitigation without compromising food and nutritional security?"—was an urgent one.[42] But the report's sophistication about every aspect of how agricultural practices needed to be overhauled and, more broadly, what restructuring needed to be done within societies as a whole if they were to reap the benefits of climate-smart agriculture was accompanied by a level of political ignorance that was hard to credit and, more problematically from a practical standpoint, a level of political expectation that seemed almost divorced from reality. Thus, the report insisted that "to create an enabling environment for the development and mainstreaming of [Climate-Smart Agriculture] in the overarching national plan, appropriate institutions with effective and transparent governance structures are needed."[43] This would have been fine had the report made a serious effort to develop recommendations about how these institutions could be created in the many countries in which they did not exist or given some real authority in nations where they did but had always been powerless.

The sole major exception to the welter of reports in which the political context received such short shrift was "The Feeding of the Nine Billion: Global Food Security for the 21st Century," the brilliant report that Alex Evans, the New York University development specialist, prepared for Chatham House in 2009. Written in the immediate aftermath of the 2007–2008 food price crisis, Evans, while critical of the mainstream food establishment view, was far from that of their radical critics in the food rights, agroecology, and antiglobalization movements. He, too, called for a twenty-first-century Green Revolution, but only, he emphasized, if certain conditions were satisfied. In other words, there were fundamental issues of fairness at stake. Evans quoted Gandhi's celebrated observation that there was enough for everyone's need, but not for everyone's greed, remarking that it was "becoming truer all the time." And he offered a stark warning. "Perhaps the most fundamental requirement," he wrote, "is for policy-makers to remember that innovation alone is not enough. . . . This time around, innovation will need to be married with commitment to social justice and political sophistication."[44] The problem is that in the early twenty-first century, with climate change bearing down, political sophistication and, for that matter, a complex view of political institutions were just what the food establishment in the age of public-private partnerships had divested itself of.[45]

That the establishment is full of extremely intelligent and sophisticated people should go without saying. So the question is: Why have they undertaken this reckless act of renunciation? As I have made clear in this book, their views are very far from my own, but it should be obvious that one can agree with every last recommendation made by the Chicago Council, or the FAO, or AGRA about what technologies and what transformations in market structures would be needed to permit farmers to thrive even in areas, such as the Sahelian countries, where climate change was likely to be most extreme; and one can support GMOs and market-based solutions and believe that development cannot succeed unless the private sector plays a central role in it; but what one cannot do, if one is looking at the world as it really is rather than as one wants it to be, is to discuss these things without discussing *in equal detail* the social and political pressures that have already led to insurgencies or civil wars from northern Nigeria all the way across to Somalia, and unprecedented and ever-increasing mass migration to Europe from across Africa.

To be clear, the mainstream view has always emphasized that hunger is a huge political and social problem. A good example of this is the entry on world hunger in the "Hunger" section of the WFP's website, which states that "solving hunger is also a contribution to peace and stability. When governments can no longer guarantee adequate food supplies, states are prone to fall. Volatility on food markets can quickly translate into volatility on the streets."[46]

The problem is that this gets the political and social sequence backward. As the FAO's first director, Lord Boyd-Orr, put it, "You can't build peace on empty stomachs and human misery."[47] That is why, to "solve" hunger—and the use of that verb, as if hunger were a puzzle or, worse, a software problem, illustrates the degree to which a technologist's mind-set now dominates much of the global food establishment—there needs to be peace, and yet for all the talk of Africa rising, peace is unraveling across that continent at a terrible rate of speed. Moreover, since malnutrition and undernutrition are now found more in middle-income countries than in very poor ones, the central issue is almost never the availability of resources but rather of their allocation, and of what Amartya Sen calls "entitlements." And since decisions about allocation and entitlement are ultimately in the hands of governments, we are back at where we started, with ethics and politics and, to some degree at least, basic questions of distributive justice.

Sen understood this. In his book *Development as Freedom*, he argued that for all that otherwise differentiates them, whether they have identified development "with the growth of gross national product, or with the rise in personal incomes, or with industrialization, or with technological advance, or with social modernization," all of these development paradigms have suffered from the same defect of simply being too narrow. Sen was convinced that "development requires the removal of the major sources of unfreedom: poverty as well as tyranny, poor economic opportunities as well as systematic social deprivation, neglect of public facilities as well as intolerance of overactivity or repressive states."[48] And so he proposed that it was the expansion of freedom, in the context not just of economic opportunities but of political liberty, that was "both the primary end and the principal means of development."[49]

At least some voices in the mainstream food establishment have emphasized the need to think politically. One of the most eloquent of these, Dr. Stuart Gillespie, who is a senior research fellow at IFPRI, has argued that to make serious progress in reducing chronic hunger, campaigners and specialists need first to "disabuse [them]selves of the notion that under nutrition is an apolitical issue, which is how it is often framed."[50] But while Gillespie decried this approach as "myopic and self-defeating," the framing of most reports either is entirely apolitical or else takes the idea that the political consensus on food issues is now so general that ticking the relevant boxes—the need for political will on the part of the donors and for good governance, transparency, accountability, and so on—is statement enough. But it should be obvious, even if one is sympathetic to this approach, that these choices rest on the assumption that the contemporary international order, at least where development is concerned, is both coherent and cohesive. What may be less obvious is the degree to which they also rest on Francis Fukuyama's contention that what justified his speaking of the End of History was that "all societies, regardless of cultural starting points, must [sooner or later] accept [the] basic terms of reference" of economic modernization. And if history "leads ultimately to liberal democracy and capitalism," what gives it this "fundamental direction and progressive character is modern natural science."[51]

The problem with this line of argument, as John Gray has pointed out, is "that it assumes that the sort of advance that has been achieved in science can be reproduced in ethics and politics."[52] He might have added "in culture" as well. Gray was not exaggerating. Nor was the editor of Buzzfeed, Ben Smith, when he said that the massive economic and cultural transformation driven by Silicon Valley had meant that for many, "technology isn't a section in the newspaper any more, it's the culture."[53] And when Bill Gates defines technology as the "unlocking [of] the innate compassion we have for our fellow human beings,"[54] one can only assume that for him, the distinction between technology and ethics no longer makes sense. And in a sense, it shouldn't. After all, in Gates's form of (updated) utilitarianism[55] mixed with scientism, human betterment *is* material betterment, a series of problems that human ingenuity could and would solve—"the smartest, most creative people working on the most important problems," as he said at Stanford, and always with results that could be measured, quantified, and studied.

Assuming that one believes, on the one hand, that innovation bears limitless promise, and thus societies that commit to innovation either are or at least at some point will become successful societies, and on the other, that the great ideological battles have been fought and that liberal capitalism—the right and deserving side—has won, then Gates's utilitarianism is going to seem like nothing more than simple common sense. But there are historical reasons to doubt this. The Sorbonne economist Thomas Piketty has tried to show that the era of equality in capitalism was in fact a historical anomaly and that for structural reasons it is inequality that is the capitalist norm, Northwestern economist Robert Gordon, whom I mentioned earlier as one of staunchest defenders of the proposition that innovation is best left to the private sector rather than to the government, has nonetheless argued that "the rapid progress made over the past 250 years could well turn out to be a unique episode in human history."[56] But assume for the sake of argument that Gordon is wrong and that Gates's view, which in the twenty-first century is the majority view in the world of the global elite, is correct. No matter how extraordinary its accomplishments to date and its promises for the future—and is there anything that would be more extraordinary than the end of hunger?—can a technological order endure for long in the absence of a moral order of equal power and seriousness?

To be clear, to ask this question is emphatically not to say that Bill Gates doesn't have a moral vision, for he clearly does. But it is to claim that a moral vision based on solving problems and, by doing so, reducing inequities is thin at best. One does not have to be a person of faith to understand that Andrew Carnegie's *The Gospel of Wealth*, or rather, Bill Gates's twenty-first-century version of it, which seems to have fulfilled Carnegie's prediction that in the future "the most talented business men shall find their most cherished work in carrying on immense concerns, not primarily for their own personal aggrandizement, but for the good of the masses of workers,"[57] is never going to be a sustainable substitute for the biblical Gospels. Does Gates's sincere conviction that the times will just get better and better help account for the thinness of his project's moral dimension? Whatever the explanation, what word other than "thinness" is appropriate for a man who accounts for his extraordinary philanthropy by saying, "I've been very lucky, and therefore I owe it to try and reduce the inequity in the world"? Gates has said that he now "participates" in the Catholic Church that his wife and children attend, and thinks that "the moral systems of religion . . . are superimportant."[58] But pressed by his interviewer from *Rolling Stone* to say more about what that importance consisted of, Gates could only reply, "I think it makes sense to believe in God, but exactly what decision in your life you make differently because of it, I don't know."[59]

· 14 ·

"Fertilizing the Land with Money"

The Indian plant geneticist M. S. Swaminathan was arguably Norman Borlaug's most important collaborator in the practical application of the Green Revolution during the 1960s. He subsequently became the director-general first of the Indian Council of Agricultural and later of the International Rice Research Institute (IRRI). And although, more recently, Swaminathan has emphasized agroecology and placed more of a premium on crop diversity and less on commercial crops than some of his colleagues, in most respects his views remain very much within the mainstream. Throughout his very long career, he has remained an unswerving defender of Green Revolution, including to some degree on ecological grounds, arguing that were India compelled to return to pre-1965 crop yield levels, it would need to bring another thirty-five million hectares of land under cultivation, which would entail the leveling of most of the nation's remaining forests. And if, like all sensible supporters of the first Green Revolution, Swaminathan has acknowledged that for all its accomplishments it also did significant "ecological and social harm," he has also argued that the "Evergreen Revolution"[1] he has campaigned for (he dislikes the term "Second Green Revolution") will be able to avoid these thanks to "a paradigm shift in production technology."[2] Here too, Swaminathan's view, which emphasizes, as he has put it, "harnessing the best in frontier technologies and blending them with . . . ecological prudence,"[3] does not diverge all that much from the mainstream consensus. Where he is very much the dissenter, though, is in the firmness of his conviction that Gandhi was right when he insisted that the ending of what he has called "unacceptable poverty" will not and indeed cannot take place without the ending of "unsustainable lifestyles" as well.[4]

Throughout his career, Swaminathan has strongly identified himself with this Gandhian worldview, especially with the concept of *sarvodaya*, a Gujarati term Gandhi invented using two Sanskrit roots that can be translated as "universal uplift" or "progress for all." For Swaminathan, *sarvodaya* is also a call for "a society in which there are no winners and losers."[5] Where the Right to Food and antiglobalization movements' critique of the global food system is largely materialist and communitarian, Swaminathan's is largely based on claims that have their deep basis in ethics rather than in economics. Because of the far greater overlap between his views and the reigning ones within the mainstream food establishment in the current age of capitalist triumphalism—and what other word is there for an era in which the claim that philanthrocapitalism will "save the world" is considered by many to be an entirely reasonable one?—Swaminathan is rarely thought of as a radical. But this is a mistake. Development in all its forms has, to put it crudely, been focused on coming up with appropriate policies so that the poor, that is to say, the economic and social losers in the world as it now exists, will become winners instead. But Swaminathan's point is that this won't solve the problem, because celebrating winners is just as morally unacceptable.

There is simply no way of squaring even the most modest definition of creative or "philanthro"-capitalism—such as that of writer and former Microsoft employee Michael Kinsley, who summed it up as trying to expand capitalism "into new areas and using it to solve problems that were previously assigned to charity or to government"[6]—with the claim that a decent society has no winners either. The early twenty-first century may indeed be, as the business establishment and the development world claim, the era of corporate social responsibility, but to use a term of art associated with this trend, even responsible global citizenship has its limits. What capitalist would accept the demand that there be limits on how much money it is morally licit to make and, having amassed it, that there be limits on what he or she could buy, consume, or otherwise spend it on? The response of the chairman of Google, Eric Schmidt, to an interviewer's question about whether successful start-ups actually foster inequality was emblematic of just how alien such thinking remains in the business world. "Let us celebrate capitalism," Schmidt declared. And referring to the specific example of Croesus-like enrichment of a few that had provoked the question, Facebook's acquisition of the fifty-employee firm WhatsApp, Schmidt was categorical. "$19 billion for 50 people?" he repeated. "Good for them."[7]

Most philanthrocapitalists would share Schmidt's response, though in fairness, many would not go along with the related idea that what the rich do with their money is no one's affair but their own. Bill Gates, Warren Buffett, and a number of other philanthropically inclined billionaires have emphasized both the idea of "giving back" and that of the rich leaving their money to charitable trusts rather than to their children. But contra Swaminathan, they would also make two additional points. The first is that had they not been big winners in their businesses, they would not have had the money to apply to making progress in curbing or, better still, eliminating whatever social ill they wish to help eliminate. And however one judges either the morality or the efficacy of private philanthropy, assuming one starts with the fact that these great fortunes exist and that one does not enter into a debate about the social and institutional context in which they were amassed, this claim is irrefutable. But the second point is at once more interesting and more open to question. It is the deeper philanthrocapitalist assumption, which increasingly has become the global consensus as well, that while, indeed, many of the gravest problems that beset the world in the early twenty-first century are the direct result of masses of people having too little, they do not derive in any significant way from a far, far smaller number of people having too much, let alone lead to the conclusion that a truly moral society would not allow such imbalances to occur.

Given the commitment of so many philanthrocapitalists to spend most if not all of their money in efforts to improve the human condition, it should hardly be surprising that most of them either do not wish to accept or in some cases seem not even to understand the idea that it might be morally wrong to have too much money. If anything, it was the reverse that was the case, just as it had been in the age of Andrew Carnegie (all that is missing is a twenty-first-century author to recapitulate the "rags to riches" novels of Horatio Alger). This is not, or at least not mainly, because of some tropism toward delusions of grandeur, even if, in his excellent 2008 book *Small Change: Why Business Won't Save the World*, Michael Edwards reminds us of the salience of John Quincy Adams's remark that "power always thinks it has a great soul and vast views beyond the comprehension of the weak."[8] From everything Bill Gates has said, it is clear that to the contrary, he believes his foundation to be working on behalf of the weak. And he has consistently emphasized the point that as he put it in the commencement speech he gave at Harvard in 2007, "reducing inequity is the highest human achievement."[9]

The question, though, is whether, when Gates speaks about "inequality," a term he uses interchangeably with "inequity," he is employing it in a way that would be intelligible to those who view widening economic disparities, even in rich societies whose poorest citizens are comparatively well-off, especially when compared with the bottom billion, as an affront to justice, a threat to social peace, and, as such, a politically unsustainable as well as an immoral state of affairs. On balance, it would appear that the answer to this is no. Gates has made it very clear that he supports the idea that even if the poor never become rich, at a minimum society must be reformed to the point where those who are now worst off are able to earn decent livings, get proper and affordable health care when they require it, and have access to decent educations. But a commitment to meeting more of the needs of the world's poor, even on the scale of the one that underpins the immensely ambitious work of the Gates Foundation, is not the same thing as an acceptance of any urgent need to reduce global inequality for its own sake. For although the two terms are frequently used interchangeably, they are not identical. As the great Indian sociologist Andre Beteille pointed out in a 2003 article on the subject, "Poverty and inequality vary independently of each other, and it is misleading beyond a point to treat the one as the marker of the other. . . . [They] do not change at the same pace, and they may even change in opposite directions."[10]

The statistics bear this out: Seven hundred million fewer people lived on under $1.25 a day in 2010 than had done so in 1990, which translates as almost a 50 percent reduction of the rate of extreme poverty in two decades. During those same twenty years, the proportion of undernourished people in the Global South decreased from 23.2 percent to 14.9 percent. To be sure, these figures, which provide the statistical basis for supporters of the Millennium Development Goals to dub them, as UN secretary general Ban Ki-moon put it, "the most successful global anti-poverty push in history," are somewhat misleading. For as William Easterly, Dambisa Moyo, and other free-market critics of development have rightly pointed out, three-quarters of the global decline in extreme poverty since 1981 occurred in China. Without that extraordinary accomplishment, the goal set out in the MDGs of halving extreme poverty by 2015 would not have been met. And yet the MDGs played no significant role either in China's successful strategy for reducing poverty at home nor in the way it has structured its overseas development assistance programs. In contrast, in Africa, where the MDGs have been and remain the dominant development paradigm, extreme poverty fell only 8 percent between 1990 and 2010. And according to the 2013 edition of the authoritative Global Hunger Index produced by IFPRI and the Irish NGO Concern, while some progress had been made, both undernutrition and stunting rates remained stubbornly high in every country in sub-Saharan Africa, the only exceptions being Ghana, Gabon, and South Africa. This should have put a damper on some of the triumphalist rhetoric in development circles concerning the MDGs (though of course it hasn't).

This is not to deny that significant reductions in poverty outside of China and in other rapidly growing East Asian countries have occurred over the past twenty years, including in Africa. But even taking this progress into account, and further assuming that Bill Gates's and Jeffrey Sachs's broader claims that the unprecedented material progress made over the last 250 years will continue far into the future and benefit humanity in as-yet-unforeseen ways, the lack of improvement during the past three centuries in the rates of global inequality and, in some cases at least, the widening of those rates make it hard to avoid the conclusion that if anything, Beteille was understating the case when he insisted on the need to distinguish between progress in reducing poverty and progress in curbing inequality. Of course there have been exceptions, the most notable of which, as Thomas Piketty has pointed out, occurred during the three decades after the Second World War, when middle-class incomes and those of the rich in the developed world largely rose in tandem. In the early twenty-first century, however, income inequality has again risen sharply in the rich world, most dramatically in the United States, where in 2014 it reached levels not seen since the late

1920s. And since, as most economists recognize, income inequality frequently (though not always) rises when economies grow quickly,[11] inequality has also increased in the developing world.

This is the ghost at the banquet when the business world argues that the only way to lastingly reduce poverty and hunger, including that suffered by smallholder farmers in the Global South, is through the liberal capitalist understanding of economic growth as coming through market-based solutions. These are generally thought to include more openness in the developing world to foreign direct investment and the curtailing of protectionist import regimes and, as one World Bank report euphemistically put it, "loosening" labor market regulations, even those "designed to protect the interests of workers, and, particularly with regard to agriculture, the use of new seed, harvesting, and storage technologies,"[12] as well as helping farmers become more "resilient" to shocks and new difficulties, up to and including those due to climate change—resilience being a term of art that by the second decade of the twenty-first century had become as central a framing device in the development world as "sustainability" or "pro-poor growth" had been in previous decades. These were also the essential features of the reorientation of the development project toward an approach in which the private sector will take the lead, *even* when, as is the case with the poorest of the poor, the lack of purchasing power means that needs do not translate into the demands on whose fulfillment the capitalist model has always been based—development assistance being viewed as helping speed up the rate at which people's incomes increase and substituting for the demand they lack.

Assuming that Bill Gates was right when he said that the early twenty-first century was "a fantastic time to be entering the business world," and his friend Warren Buffett equally so when, in 2014, he predicted "substantial" gains in the stock market in the decades to come, then even if the most optimistic global development scenarios prove correct and extreme poverty and hunger really are done away with by 2030, not only will there still be inequality, but it will almost certainly have worsened rather than improved. Of course if, like Jagdish Bhagwati and other important free-market economists, one thinks inequality is of no consequence because economic growth translates into everyone, rich and poor alike, becoming better off, then there is little or no problem with this. But Bhagwati's is hardly the majority view, even within the establishment. One of the bases of the so-called "pro-poor" growth model adopted by the World Bank during James Wolfensohn's presidency (1995–2005) was that income distribution matters as much as growth in any successful effort to reduce poverty. And there are strong, if less easily quantifiable, links between income inequality and political instability, social cohesion, health, and education. In any case, while even many of its critics, though of course not those from anticapitalist peasant groups such as Via Campesina or from the antiglobalization movement, would accept that the development project can address issues of poverty and hunger, there is absolutely no reason to suppose it can do the same with regard to inequality, again, assuming that doing so remains a priority, which is anything but clear.

For even assuming that the global system, both in the United States and internationally, can be transformed—as Gates, Jeffrey Sachs, Jim Yong Kim, and others assume it can be, to the point where virtually everyone in the world will have access to proper education, health care, etc.—will this, as Gates has insisted, "really change the inequality balance"? Surely the answer to this depends on what time frame one is envisaging. It is certainly arguable that this might be true in the *very* long run in much the same way that it is possible that once emerging economies have grown past a certain point, income inequality may start to decline. But in the near and medium term it will do little or nothing to rectify the current severe income disparities between the global rich and everyone else nor bring to a halt the ever-increasing concentration of economic resources among fewer and fewer people, which, as I write, has reached the point that the wealth of the richest 1 percent of the world is $110 trillion, sixty-five times that of the bottom 50 percent of the seven billion people now alive on the planet. Again, while access to basic services, improved livelihoods, and the better health, nutrition, and educational outcomes that go with them can certainly reduce poverty, they will not necessarily do anything to make the world any less unequal.

The reasons for this should be apparent. As a thought experiment, let us imagine that most of the preconditions for agricultural development and global food security that Sir Gordon Conway lays out in *One Billion Hungry: Can We Feed the World?* are met to a significant extent.[13] Donor nations honor their aid commitments; trade liberalization policies are put in place that work in favor of poor farmers rather than, as food rights campaigners fear, to their detriment; fair and efficient markets are brought into being; what Conway calls the "Doubly Green" and Swaminathan the "Evergreen" Revolution is implemented; biotechnology, including GMOs, lives up to its promise; and agriculture adaptation to climate change is speeded up, both through methods such as improved mixed livestock, integrated pest management systems, and saltwater harvesting, and through programs to foster resilience. If all these things are done, then whether or not the poverty reduction really proves to be on the scale predicted by Bill Gates, described as perfectly feasible by Jeffrey Sachs, and called for in the MDGs, there will certainly be some significant reduction in extreme poverty and hunger, even if a skeptic, particularly one who believes it is simply too late to prevent an average global temperature rise of 3 or more degrees Celsius, might legitimately ask how sustainable this reduction will actually prove to be. But while it is reasonable (though in my view, far less likely than the mainstream food establishment view holds it to be) that such a mix of technocratic innovation and economic reform can improve the life chances of the masses of the poor, it will do nothing to put a brake on the ever-increasing concentration of wealth among a tiny minority of very rich people.

To do that would require a very different development debate, one focused less on the metrics of what new agricultural techniques or market reform work best and should be developed and more on what kind of society we want and what has to be done in order to attain it—in short, a political debate focused around justice rather than a debate about technical means, of which the MDGs in their florid depoliticization have been an emblem, that somehow are assumed to lead to just society without the need to think through what a decent society consists of beyond the easing of extreme poverty and hunger.

What is breathtaking about the mainstream food establishment's view is how often its leading figures treat politics as something important but nonetheless no weightier than, say, getting microcredit right. The conclusions of Conway's *One Billion Hungry* are a perfect illustration of this. In his concluding chapter, "Can We Feed the World?," he lists twenty-four prerequisites to answering his question in the affirmative, ranging from #1, "We recognize food security affects us all and the time to act is near," to #24, "We recognize that public-private-community partnerships are crucial to successful scale-up." But politics is only addressed in earnest in #6, "The appropriate governance for food security and agricultural development is in place," and is sandwiched between #5, "There is explicit attention to the creation of enabling environments" (mostly about how macroeconomic policies need to favor markets and trade), and #7, "Fair, efficient output and input markets are created on a countrywide basis." And yet in #6, Conway concedes that "seventeen of forty-one countries in Sub-Saharan Africa are, or recently have been, categorized by the World Bank as 'chronically politically unstable,' "[14] and concludes, "Without good governance there can be no food security."[15]

Writing of the ongoing debates over the so-called Sustainable Development Goals that are supposed to be the global development blueprint that will succeed the MDGs from 2015 on, the editor of the *Lancet*, Richard Horton, bitterly attacked their definition of sustainability, which, he said, were doomed to fail because they ignored the fact that the final determinant of sustainability was "the strength of our civilizations—their solidarity and wealth, their degrees of inequality and corruption, their susceptibility to conflict, and the quality of their deliberative institutions."[16] Instead, he pointed to the argument Amartya Sen and Sudhir Anand made in a 2000 paper in which, as Horton paraphrased it, they attacked "the prevailing idea that, if poverty is our target, wealth maximization should be our weapon," and that "the exclusive concentration only on incomes . . . ignores the plurality of influences that differentiate the real opportunities of people."[17]

If the abolition of poverty is for many a moral duty, equality is something somewhat different: a moral ideal. This is why Beteille has been so insistent on the difficulty of making "any meaningful statement about the relationship between the two without specifying which conception of poverty and which aspect of inequality one has in mind."[18] But if the conception really is to reduce inequality, again, as opposed to helping the poor become more prosperous, healthier, better educated, etc., one certainly would have to start from the top down as well as from the bottom up. And philanthrocapitalists are hardly likely to be the initiators of that process, for obvious reasons of self-interest, of course, but not only for those reasons. As Michael Edwards has written, "No great social cause was [ever] mobilized through the market in the twentieth century."[19] Contrasting it with creative capitalism, Edwards points out that the American civil rights movement "didn't fit any of the criteria that are at the top of the philanthrocapitalists' agenda: It wasn't data driven, it didn't operate through competition, it couldn't generate much revenue, and it didn't measure its impact in terms of the number of people who were served each day."[20]

In any case, there is no consensus as to how widening inequality might be halted and lessened. Is Thomas Piketty right to suggest that the antidote to the rise of patrimonial capitalism in the twenty-first century would lie in imposing step inheritance taxes so as to set an upper limit on the amassing of capital and making other changes in nations' tax codes that are unfavorable to the rich? Or in contrast to Piketty's prescription, which would leave the basic structures of capitalism in place à la Franklin Roosevelt in the 1930s, is the only way to accomplish such a goal the more far-reaching, radical reordering of society that the antiglobalization movement has been calling for? But if one believes that redressing that "severe income disparity" is a matter of urgency, which is what not just anticapitalist campaigners but also the übercapitalist World Economic Forum at Davos asserted in its 2014 "Global Risk Report," then poverty reduction will not secure it.

It would be irrational to expect Bill Gates to have much to contribute much to the answer. To begin with, his perspective has always been scientific. This is key because, in contrast to the humanities, in the physical sciences, as in Gates's own field of computers, how things unfolded in the past does not provide the same degree of guidance about how one judges the present and what one can expect to happen in the future. In proper context, Gates's scientism is unexceptionable, given that in some scientific disciplines, and in medicine as well, more has been learned and applied in recent decades than in all previous centuries. But when combined with the mind-set derived from the European Enlightenment, in which it was an article of faith that a new and unprecedented moral and physical dispensation for humanity was inevitable, and modified by the conviction that American-style (and perhaps even Silicon Valley–style) liberal capitalism is the apotheosis of these inexorable, progressive trends, a perfectly defensible claim morphs into something at once far more ambitious and far more debatable. It is difficult to imagine Gates replying to Michael Edwards's strictures on the history of social movements with some twenty-first-century reworking of Henry Ford's brutish axiom that "history is more or less bunk." He is far too intelligent for that. But having said that politics played a comparatively minor role when, in the eighteenth century, the course of human history was fundamentally altered for the better by scientific discoveries and their technological applications, and that humanity's progress since had the same source, it is easy to imagine Gates replying that "politics is bunk," even though, of course, that is itself an inherently and irreducibly political statement.

But assume for the sake of argument that Gates is right and the human past, before the European Enlightenment and the Machine Age, really is irrelevant to the development project's present and future (not to say that of humanity itself). And, focusing in on the global food system, take that a step further and stipulate that the anxieties about development based on public-private partnership in general and about Gates's philanthropy and that of his fellow plutocrats are wholly misplaced. Accept that the G8's "for Food Security and Nutrition in Africa" really represents, in the words of a 2012 USAID press release, "a shared commitment to achieve sustained and inclusive agricultural growth and raise fifty million people out of poverty over the next ten years,"[21] rather than, as many activists believe, a new form of colonialism in which African governments in consultation with donor governments and global agribusiness agree to rewrite their laws concerning seed patents, land ownership, and taxes on multinationals in favor of private investors and to the detriment of smallholder farmers. Conclude that the history of Bill Gates's intermittent personal financial involvement and that of his foundation's charitable trust with substantial share positions in Monsanto and Cargill and the appointment of former senior employees of these companies to important positions at the Gates Foundation have had no influence on his advocacy for GMOs. And despite the rhetoric in a 2013 FIAN document that described Africa as being "'the last frontier' in global food and agricultural markets,"[22] reject the claims of a World Development Movement document asserting that market-driven development aid to African farmers has not been at its core yet another neocolonial scramble for market share for multinational corporations but is rather just what the British government has declared it to be—an important step toward curbing hunger, poverty, and malnutrition on the continent.

Even conceding all this and more, there is still much in the global food system's reigning paradigm that should give pause to anyone who is in principle willing to accept the mainstream's own account of its motivations and of its actions. Indeed, the more one looks at the paradigm of the public-private partnership and endeavors to parse the assumptions, the reasoning, and the hope and optimism of the establishment that now subscribes to it, even if one accepts that it operates with the best of intentions as, unlike many of the system's critics, I largely do,[23] the more one begins to wonder whether those who hold the private sector up as the key to development's future have actually looked at how the system works and what it actually does. To repeat, in order to try to understand this, I am assuming for the sake of argument that the critics are wrong and that the possibilities that the mainstream of the development movement, both governmental, nongovernmental, and philanthropic, discern in new agricultural technologies and better governance truly exist and offer at least a significant part of solution to the crisis of global agriculture. But even putting the case that this is indeed right and that claims on the order of the one made by the African Centre for Biosafety that AGRA should be understood as "a political project, a 'proof of concept' to show private owners of capital that there are profitable opportunities for investment in African agriculture,"[24] there are other impediments to realizing these goals that seem far more constraining than what Michael Edwards has called the "business-is-best" philosophy would lead one to believe.

This is not because of political opposition from the antiglobalization left, Right to Food activists, and peasant movements. The critique that they have offered of the capitalist model of agriculture and its call to private investors to "fertilize this land with money," as the FAO's president, Jose Graziano da Silva, put it in a 2012 report,[25] has been powerful and sustained. And peasant groups have achieved some impressive successes, particularly on issues of land and water rights, while for their part, Right to Food activists have scored important victories in the courts, most notably in India. But the fact remains that, so far at least, these movements have largely failed in halting either the throwing open of markets or the spread of the use of GMOs through much of the developing world, including Latin America. This is not to say that this will not change in the future, but the "food rebellions" that Eric Holt-Giménez, Raj Patel, and Annie Shattuck heralded in their book of that title have not turned into revolutions.

A far more powerful constraint is the nature of twenty-first-century capitalism itself, the dark side of whose reality one would never know existed if one depended on the sunny talk at USAID, DFID, Gates, the Clinton Global Initiative, the Millennium Development Project, and the ONE campaign about how sustainable agricultural development was only really possible if effective, lasting partnerships could be forged between government and the private sector. In fairness, this endless lavishing of praise on multinationals such as Walmart, Pepsico, Unilever, Nestlé, Syngenta, and Monsanto only mirrors the grandiloquence with which, in the age of "corporate social responsibility," these companies regularly trumpet their own resolve to do good while doing well and extoll how successfully they are realizing their social, environmental, and developmental commitments. Examples of this abound. Indeed, today what is rare is to find a multinational that does not make such claims, including mining, mineral, and oil companies whose activities might have been supposed to make a mockery of them. For example, on its website, British Petroleum said that despite significant corporate changes, it had kept the name BP because "the name stood for the new company's aspirations: 'better people, better products, big picture, beyond petroleum.'"[26] The fact that it had acknowledged its responsibility for the largest spill in US history, paid a $4.5 billion fine to the US

Justice Department and safety regulators to settle criminal charges, paid out a further $13 billion in claims, advances, and settlements to people and businesses in the affected areas of the Gulf Coast, still faced important class action suits for damages, and might yet have to pay up to an additional $13.7 billion for violations of the US Clean Water Act somehow was not supposed to make such self-flattering claims ring hollow.

Such is the way of the world in the era of "branding" and "re-branding," terms taken from advertising, which is to say, taken from an industry whose main currencies are spin, lies, and illusion. Lest this seem like hyperbole, here is Starbucks' chairman How-ard Schultz: "A great brand raises the bar—it adds a greater sense of purpose to the experience, whether it's the challenge to do your best in sports and fitness, or the affirmation that the cup of coffee you're drinking really matters."[27] Aldous Huxley, call your office. As the management consultant Douglas Holt put it in his widely read how-to book about successful branding, *How Brands Become Icons: The Principles of Cultural Branding*, "Iconic brands create 'identity myths' that, through powerful symbolism, soothe collective anxieties resulting from acute social change."[28]

Of course, branding is no longer for corporations only. There is now "nation branding," two examples of which are the Blair govern-ment's "Cool Britannia" campaign in the United Kingdom in the 1990s and the BJP's less effective "India Shining" campaign in its losing bid in the national elections of 2004, which was successfully resurrected in 2014 when the party's candidate resoundingly won the premiership. In an age when the private sector is held to be the most innovative, able, etc., political parties and politicians, hospitals, universities, philanthropies, and human rights, humanitarian, and development NGOs all engage enthusiastically in what Holt calls "the cultural brand management process" in which institutions ac-tively engage "in the myth-making process making sure the brand maintains its position as an icon."[29]

And where rebranding is concerned, the major agricultural multinationals have shown themselves to be second to none. For example, on its website Syngenta describes its central challenge as a company not as making money and increasing shareholder value but as "sustainably feed[ing] a growing population" through its "Good Growth Plan," whose principal commitments are "more food, less waste," "more biodiversity, less [soil] degradation," and "more health, less poverty."[30] For its part, Monsanto now describes itself as "a sustainable agriculture company" focused on "empowering farmers—large and small—to produce more from their land while conserving more of our world's natural resources."[31] To express doubt that this is anywhere near the whole story, let alone to suggest that today's Monsanto Corporation is not far removed from yesterday's Monsanto—the one that made the defoliant Agent Orange[32] that the US military used to such murderous effect during the Vietnam War, to the point that even US soldiers fell victim to the cancers that are widely claimed to be its lasting aftereffect—is simply not something that the mainstream food establishment seems to consider a legitimate subject for debate.

There are a number of possible explanations for this. The first and most obvious is that the philanthrocapitalist view is as indifferent to corporate history as it is to every other kind of history except, of course, the history of science and technology. If all that really needs to be taken into account is the present and the future, then even the murkiest past should be no cause for skepticism, let alone cynicism. The past is, well, the past, which is another way of saying that it is irrelevant.

To be sure, reality sometimes breaks through anyway. Take the case of Walmart. In January 2013 the company's CEO, Doug McMillon, announced that it would join twenty-seven other multinational corporations, including all the major agribusiness firms, in the World Economic Forum's New Vision for Agriculture (NVA) initiative, and launched the NVA's "New Models for Action." The project would be aided by the McKinsey and Company consultancy group, which the report characterized as having contributed "expert input to the initiative's strategy."[33] The hope was that, "with global food systems at risk,"[34] the NVA's new approach would "[transform] whole value chains and systems, harnessing the power of market-based solutions, and engaging local and global stakeholders in an unprecedented joint effort."[35] Nine months later, in September 2013, Raj Shah traveled to the company's home state of Arkansas to sign a memorandum of understanding between USAID, Walmart, and the Walmart Foundation. As administrator of USAID, Shah had repeatedly expressed his determination to work more closely with Walmart. That moment seemed to be at hand. In the words of USAID's press release announcing the agreement, they would all join together to "improve livelihoods around the world by promoting women's economic empowerment, sustainable agriculture, environmental sustainability and vocational and life skills training for youth."[36] And in a statement after meeting with senior executives from the company, Shah said that USAID was "excited about this latest landmark in our relationship with Walmart," and described their "global partnership" as "emblematic of USAID's new model of development and our commitment to work with private sector companies to end extreme poverty around the world."[37]

This picture of Walmart is completely at odds with the one painted by labor unions and antiglobalization and environmental campaigners, which have repeatedly accused the company of unfair labor practices and have pointed out that its employees in many US states are either at or near the top of the list of private-sector workers on food stamps and other assistance programs for the poor (the company's announcement in February 2015 that it was raising salaries for five hundred thousand of its employees, while welcome, is unlikely to change this picture all that much, since for many workers, the raise amounts to approximately one dollar per hour). But in the global food establishment, indeed, in the mainstream development world generally, the consensus is that Walmart is one of the paradigmatic socially responsible corporations. To his credit, in his *Foreign Policy* piece on Walmart, the influential economist Charles Kenny, whose optimism about the global future I discussed earlier in this book, readily acknowledged the company's "union-busting employee rules, putting mom-and-pop grocery stores out of business, all that plastic garbage that it sells, [and] the shady business scandals."[38] But at the same time, Kenny heaped lavish praise on the company, beginning with his piece's title, "Give [Walmart founder] Sam Walton the Nobel Prize." For Kenny, there are really only "two ways to help poor people buy more of what they need. One is to help them make more money. The other is to make the money they have go further." Walmart, Kenny argues, "has proved incredibly adept at that second approach," which leads him to conclude that, "if that's rapacious, Walmart-style capitalism, let's have more!"[39]

Unlike Kenny, Raj Shah has never publicly conceded the possibility that there might be anything to dislike about Walmart, let alone any reason to proceed with caution when partnering with the company. Indeed, he has often spoken as if he found any such suggestion not just wrongheaded but mystifying. As he put it on one occasion, "Over the last several decades, it's been controversial to have companies like Walmart in the development solution."[40] Assuming he is being sincere, one can suppose that he rejects the critics' attacks and instead finds persuasive what the company's senior executives say about it. An example of that is the statement Walmart CEO Lee Scott made in 2008 when he said that "I firmly believe that a company that cheats on overtime and on the age of its labor, that dumps its scraps and chemicals in our rivers, that does not pay its taxes or honor its contracts will ultimately cheat on the quality of its products. And cheating on the quality of products is the same as cheating on customers."[41]

Scott's words, particularly the reference to taxes, do indeed make it sound as if Walmart has been and plans to go on being an exemplary corporate citizen. And yet in April 2012, three and a half years after he made that statement, a *New York Times* investigation that eventually won the paper a Pulitzer Prize revealed that despite the anticorruption policy adopted by Walmart's board in 2004 forbidding all company employees from "offering anything of value to a government official on behalf of Walmart," from 2002 through 2006, the company and its Mexican subsidiary, Walmart de México, had systematically bribed Mexican officials in order to facilitate the rollout of its stores there and then tried to cover up the scandal. But this did not appear to have shaken Shah's or USAID's "excitement" about working with Walmart or even lead it to investigate the charges against the company, even though the prima facie case against Walmart was strong and, if borne out, made its actions of bribing Mexican officials a crime not only under that country's laws but US law as well, according to the US Foreign Corrupt Practices Act of 1977. To the contrary, a month *after* the *Times* series appeared, Shah gave an interview to *Foreign Policy* magazine in which he argued that one of the principle failings in USAID's work in food security had been its failure to act effectively with the private sector, and used USAID's collaboration with Walmart in a program targeting fifteen thousand farming families in Honduras and Guatemala as the "type of engagement" that had been especially successful.

Give Shah the benefit of the doubt and assume either that he was not aware of the bribery accusations against Walmart or else that he believed them to be false. The fact remains that when he went to Arkansas to sign the memorandum of understanding with the company, its ethical bona fides, which both USAID and, of course, Walmart itself had asserted, had been publicly called into question not by trade unionists, environmentalists, locavores, antiglobalization campaigners, or, for that matter, by the *New York Times*, but rather by two extraordinarily powerful mainstream institutions. In 2006, the Norway Sovereign Wealth Fund, which, with current estimated assets of $900 billion, is said to control more than 1 percent of global equity markets and is the largest single owner of European stocks, had sold its entire holding of Walmart because, it announced, it believed the company to be a persistent violator of human and labor rights. And in January 2012, the Netherlands' biggest pension fund, Algemeen Burgerlijk Pensioenfonds, with $300 billion in assets, announced that it was blacklisting Walmart because of the company's violation of UN Global Compact guidelines on corporate compliance with international human rights norms, labor and environmental standards, and anticorruption guidelines.

These abuses, and those of a significant number of other companies, are all too real. But if there is a basis, as I believe there is, for challenging the development world's embrace of the private sector as intrinsically vastly more innovative and creative than governments or NGOs and the business world's confidence that where poverty reduction is concerned, only capitalism is really fit for purpose, it must be grounded in the structure of the system as a whole. That is why it is actually misleading to focus on widely reviled companies such as Walmart or Monsanto. For that would imply that the problem would be resolved if these corporations would just reform themselves, taking such measures as paying their employees better or reinforcing internal corporate controls to put an end to the bribery of foreign officials, as, without of course admitting guilt, Walmart seems finally to have done after its Mexican bribery scandal was revealed. In reality, though, as welcome as these measures would be, they would not address those essential elements of twenty-first-century capitalism that make philanthrocapitalism not a dream but a mystification.

· 15 ·

Optimism as Moral Victory, Pessimism as Moral Affront

I n an era in which even raising the possibility that no matter how committed, intelligent, and determined the people addressing them are, extreme poverty and hunger are not "problems" that can be solved is regarded as a form of cynical defeatism and in which, conversely, almost no expression of optimism, no matter how extravagant, is deemed to be unwarranted, disparaging utopian capitalism as a mystification will appear to many like the intellectual equivalent of the cook spitting in the soup. When, for example, @GatesPoverty tweets, "Our friend Raya supports access to water and sanitation worldwide,"[1] presumably the expectation is that this will seem touching and perhaps even inspiring rather than as infantile and unserious, despite the fact that the Raya in question is not a human being but rather Raya the Sanitation Muppet, created by the television show *Sesame Street*, partly thanks to a Gates Foundation grant, for use in public service announcements in India, Bangladesh, and Nigeria. And when the tweet then goes on to ask,

"Do you?"—a question, to be clear, that is here being posed to the adults who follow @GatesPoverty on Twitter,[2] not children in Dhaka or Kano—one is presumably expected to respond affirmatively and in as enthusiastic a tone as the one in which the question has been posed, without spoiling the party by asking who and where these adults are who staunchly oppose universal access to water and sanitation.

The reader may object that all this is harmless and ask: What is so wrong about the deployment of a bit of feel-good rhetoric? The answer is that there is quite a lot wrong with it. In an essay called "Deconstructing Development Discourse: Buzzwords and Fuzzwords," Sussex University development specialists Andrea Cornwall and Karen Brock coined the term "consensual hurrah words"[3] to describe words such as *participation*, *empowerment*, and *poverty reduction*, words, they observed, "it becomes more difficult to disagree with."[4] "The nicer [words] sound," they write, "the more useful they are for those seeking to establish their moral authority."[5] @GatesPoverty's entirely rhetorical question belongs in that same manipulative and celebratory, not to say self-congratulatory, register, in which critical thinking is not just beside the point but at odds with it. Cornwall and Brock argue that what matters in such presentations is emotional identification, not rationality. This helps explain why such exercises so often seem like the development world's online secular version of an Evangelical church service during which the congregation is invited by the preacher to affirm and reaffirm that one does indeed love Jesus.

Equally impermeable to adult reasoning are the fanciful claims about what individuals can accomplish with little more effort than the click of a mouse. A representative expression of this was the ONE Campaign's 2015 Online Action Pledge exhorting young people to "build the world you want to live in."[6] While as an organization, the ONE Campaign seems more focused than other campaigning groups on what Cornwall and Brock, writing of the development world as a whole, describe as the "almost ceremonial" purpose of "bolstering a feeling of togetherness and purposefulness,"[7] the Internet is chock a block with such exhortations. For example, the UN has run a number of online campaigns along the same lines. The one in 2014 was called "Vote for the World You Want to See," and was billed as "allowing people for the first time to have a direct say in shaping a better world."[8] In both cases, the message seemed to be that were such a vote to be substantial enough, this would at least somewhat advance the possibility of this better world finally coming into being.

To be sure, this is lowest-common-denominator solidarity. Just as @GatesPoverty could in fact be certain there would be universal approbation for anything likely to improve the access of poor people to water and sanitation, so the ONE Campaign could be certain that, outside of South Africa anyway, very few people indeed could fail to bow their heads before the moral example of Nelson Mandela, in whose reflected glow ONE could thus safely bask. It has done something similar with Malala Yousafzai, the Pakistani schoolgirl who was badly wounded when the Taliban tried to murder her after she blogged about the horrors of living under their rule. One tweeted in celebration of the young woman's birthday, which a ONE Campaign staffer, Emily McKhann, declared to be "Malala Day."

Given how many detractors the UN has from across the political spectrum, it is always going to find itself on shakier rhetorical ground than a campaigning group. And as if in recognition of this, the various voting options the UN offered in its online questionnaire were accompanied by a pop-up box titled "Why Does My Vote Matter?" But the answer, which was that the vote would "inform" the work of defining the global agenda for the coming decades and would "be used by decision makers around the world,"[9] could make sense only to someone who either had not fully been seized of the profound democracy deficit that marks the international system even when it is working reasonably well or had not taken in just how rarely the UN, which at least arguably has had failure inscribed on its DNA from its inception and has demonstrably grown more dysfunctional with every passing decade, has ever been successful in influencing these global decision makers to do anything they had not already decided to do anyway.

On the ONE Campaign's website, Emily McKhann is identified as the founder of TheMotherhood.com, and as believing "deeply in the power of moms online to change the world."[10] And claims of this nature are commonplace among online activists. Indeed, where marketing begins and campaigning ends is by no means always clear. In this sense too, McKhann is quite representative. Her TheMotherhood.com organization is in fact a business, which she describes as "an award-winning digital PR and marketing firm that provides social media consulting, opinion research and marketing services to more than 150 blue chip companies and national non-profits, and includes a network of thousands of mom and dad bloggers."[11] For his part, British marketer Stuart Ralph, founder of MorallyMarketed.com, praised on his blog an Oxfam ad called "Lift lives for good," and others in a similar vein, for "painting hopeful futures instead of a painful past." The reason for this, he wrote, was that "everyone wants to be someone's hero, and by charities painting an optimistic future they are giving people the opportunity to be that hero."[12] The self-referential character of all this, the emphasis on narratives that as Cornwall and Brock put it, "compel people to listen because they themselves are the main protagonists of the story,"[13] is often caricatured by more radical campaigning groups that do not share Oxfam's view that, as their website puts it, "business has great potential for alleviating poverty."[14] A particularly trenchant visual rendering of this critique was created by Hannah Clifton, a young development student, on her blog Discovering Development: The Dreams and the Damage, and later used by the NGO Health Poverty Action in an analysis detailing the huge disparity between the aid that sub-Saharan African countries receive from outside the continent and the resources leaving Africa. It shows a helmeted and armor-wearing LEGO-like crusader knight, and underneath the caption: "Africa needs YOU! Text, 'I AM A HERO' to 3333 now and all their issues will be solved."[15]

But such bitter ironizing remains the exception. As a rule, such online campaigns are treated with respect and often with admiration. To be sure, there have been a few exceptions, most notably the so-called Kony 2012 video and the campaign that gave rise to it. Made by a small Evangelical group in California called Invisible Children, the video had been intended to make the murderous Ugandan warlord Joseph Kony "famous" on the theory that such global focus would push governments, above all the US government, to act and thus hasten his capture. Kony 2012 almost immediately became wildly popular on YouTube, Facebook, and Twitter (both Bill Gates and Rihanna retweeted it) but almost as quickly began to be fiercely excoriated, notably by many Ugandan and other African commentators, one of whom declared Kony 2012 to be a class example of the "White Savior Complex." But such controversies are rare.[16]

These campaigns have come to be referred to by the generic title "clicktivism," a term that was coined in 2010 by Micah White, a fierce critic of the practice, but that unlike the indigestibly derogatory "slactivism," has somewhat surprisingly also been adopted by those who see in it a very promising context for social action. For example, Gabrielle Fitzgerald, the former director of Program Advocacy for the Gates Foundation, has referred approvingly to the "clicktivist era" in which such online activism gives rise to "catalytic coalitions to help solve today's global challenges."[17] This could not have been further from White's view. He had defined clicktivism as a "model of activism [that] uncritically embraces the ideology of marketing, [accepting that] the tactics of advertising and market research used to sell toilet paper can also build social movements." But the reality, he argued, was that in "promoting the illusion that surfing the web can change the world, clicktivism is to activism as McDonald's is to a slow-cooked meal. It may look like food, but the life-giving nutrients are long gone."[18]

Obviously, no one who sees clicktivism as one (though, in fairness, by no means the only) useful way of adapting activism to the realities of new social media in an online age would accept White's damning judgment that by "exchanging the substance of activism for reformist platitudes that do well in market tests, clicktivists damage every genuine political movement they touch."[19] To the contrary, in the words of the mission statement of Change.org, a for-profit company now partly owned by the Omidyar Network that hosts sponsored campaigns for groups such as Amnesty International as well as acting as an online clearinghouse for tens of thousands of online petitions each year from its 35 million members, clicktivism offers the real possibility of "empowering people everywhere to create the change they want to see."[20] This power that individuals have to bring these changes about is somehow never assumed to apply with equal force to, say, ISIS in Iraq and Syria, which dreams of restoring the Caliphate, or the RSS in India, which wants to see Muslim citizens disenfranchised. This is reminiscent of the way in which the term "civil society" has been transformed from a descriptive to a prescriptive term encompassing only "enlightened" citizens' groups, such as an Amnesty International or a Human Rights Watch, but not "unenlightened" ones, such as the National Rifle Association in the American context or antiabortion campaigners in Western Europe.

But clicktivism is more than an important illustration of how entrenched the assumption has become that any change that groups of people want badly enough can sooner or later be made to come to pass.[21] It also typifies the belief that not only are advertising and data (big and otherwise) central in contemporary life, but that they have always been central. As Nate Prosser, who runs the website Clicktivist. org, has put it, "Advocating for a cause has always involved marketing . . . selling an idea."[22] Prosser's use of the term "selling" would seem to confirm an essential element of White's analysis. Historically, most social and political activists would have seen truth in advertising as an oxymoron and have believed that their task was to *argue* for their ideas or their causes, not package and try to sell them as one would any consumer product. In the early twenty-first century this is no longer the case, and many campaigners boast of using advertising techniques, including a reliance on celebrities, to sell the cause in question, no matter how broad or inchoate that cause might be. For example, at the US-Africa Summit held in Washington in August 2014, John Prendergast, a former American government official who founded the human rights NGO the Enough Project (the reference is to genocide and crimes against humanity), told an audience that "celebrities play a huge role. I mean, we have a culture that is very, very interested in what Akon is going to be eating for breakfast. So if he and some of the people you mentioned and many others become interested and engaged with what's going on in Africa, it will bring more and more people into at least contact with these issues."[23]

Far from wondering whether celebrity involvement was appropriate, if anything, the problem for NGOs is now more likely to be what one major British campaigning group described as "the growing competition among charities for celebrities' time," adding that, "even small charities [now have celebrity coordinators] and artists have to be really considered about who to support and that they don't support too many different charities."[24] But when a campaigning group does get celebrities to sign on, they play it for all it is worth. For example, on the Look to the Stars: The World of Celebrity Giving website, one finds dozens of these stars, Cruz, Jolie, Pitt, and Clooney among them, as their supporters.

It is emblematic, I think, of the moral and psychological distance we have traveled and the conflation of the wish to be informed with the wish to be enchanted that few people appear to be troubled by the fact that not only are many of these actors, fashion models, and musicians also paid spokespeople for major multinational corporations but their pitches for the social causes with which they align themselves use the same marketing techniques employed to sell commercial products. For example, Angelina Jolie is associated with the St. John clothing company, her partner Brad Pitt with Heineken Brewing, and Penelope Cruz with the Lancôme perfume house. And George Clooney, who, along with Jolie, a celebrity well known for championing many social causes, notably Save Darfur, is the main global pitchman internationally for the Nespresso coffee pods. According to the company's Australian marketing manager Nicole Parker, "His charm and his humor have been really essential to people's understanding of Nespresso as a brand."[25] Replace the word "Nespresso" with the word "Darfur" and the sentence could have come from a publicist for the Enough Project. But in the early twenty-first century, the majority view seems to be that there is no problem with this, any more than there is with using Raya the Sanitation Muppet, as even advertisers rely heavily on cartoon characters to sell to children, not just on television but increasingly on the new social media as well (Coca-Cola, for example, now has fifty-eight million Facebook fans). Researchers at Yale's Rudd Center for Food Policy and Obesity estimated that children and adolescents see an average of twelve to fourteen food ads each day on television, with the top four categories being fast food, sugared cereals, sugary drinks, and candy.

It seems safe to assume that many of the same campaigners who find nothing problematic about relying on celebrities to promote social causes would be harshly critical of the advertising practices directed at children of global food companies, on the grounds both that the products being sold are unhealthy and that children are not educated consumers. But as campaigners know perfectly well, even if one grants that the celebrities publicizing various causes are well informed about them, not just moved by them, the audience being targeted for the most part does not. By definition, people who already care about a cause don't need to be mobilized, which is, after all, why campaigning groups have felt they needed to turn to celebrities in the first place. Obviously, celebrities are ideal vehicles for this, since the public's identification with stars is by definition subjective and irrational, just as advertising, whatever its objective, is fundamentally based on seduction and the manipulation of people's emotions. And yet the campaigners seem to be assuming either that there is a bright line between the form of advertising and its content or that the erasing of that line is nothing to worry about. But this is anything but self-evident, as Marshall McLuhan, the Canadian social theorist who predicted the World Wide Web decades before it was invented, showed half a century ago in his pathbreaking book, *The Medium Is the Message.*

This is by no means the only difficulty with using the language of public relations to mobilize the public on a given issue. That is because the bar is higher, or, rather, *should* be higher, for causes than it is for products. Therein lies the relevance of McLuhan's work. For the idea that the language (in the broad sense that includes marketing) appropriate to talking about wants is not only applicable to but is indeed the most effective way of defending or mobilizing people on behalf of needs, mistakenly assumes that the form is irrelevant to the content or, more precisely, that some forms are ethically inappropriate vehicles for some content. Yes, one may rue the pride of place that boundlessly acquisitive consumerism enjoys in contemporary society, and by no means only in the Global North. But however manufactured such desires may be (though arguably no more than the fame of the celebrities themselves, which, lest it be forgotten, is itself the work of publicists, advertisers, movie or record studios, and the like) they involve mainly the things people want rather than the things people need. But whatever else they are, they are not needs. And the distinction is fundamental. It has a particular relevance to the global food system, a subject to which I will return. To put it starkly, one needs food, water, shelter, and a minimum of physical safety in order to survive.[26] But while one may desperately want (or be seduced into wanting) the Nespresso coffee pods, Gucci Italian suits, Bacardi liquors, and Fiat minivans George Clooney has been the pitchman for over the course of his career, one certainly does not need them.

Anyone inclined to take a more indulgent view of the unabashed use of stars to sell social causes, the usual grounds for this being that surely it is better their fame be put to good use, might want to consider the disastrous effect that advertising has had on politics. There, too, the use of celebrities can be justified on similar grounds. But such use does not occur in a vacuum. To the contrary, it exists in a context in which marketing has come to be seen as essential to almost every activity—noble, venal, and everything in between. In the case of politics in Western democracies, electoral success now depends to a large extent on which candidate's marketing strategy is superior, as is the case in a particularly extreme form in the United States today, but increasingly in Western Europe as well, and when slogans devised by the political marketing gurus also known as "spin doctors" replace debate, and causes become products, democracies are in trouble. And in an age where it is a fact and not an opinion that inequality is deepening across the world, that power and wealth are more and more concentrated in the hands of a tiny minority of the world's population, and that politics even in democratic countries is increasingly unresponsive and in many cases largely determined by money (the United States, again, being the prime example of this among developed countries), all this talk about individuals making a difference and everyone's opinion counting is at best a consoling farce.

But this is precisely what advocates of so-called social branding reject. On the "Social Impact Hub" of the *Guardian*'s Sustainable Business blog, which is funded by the giant mining multinational Anglo American, a firm once known for its close collaboration with the apartheid regime in South Africa but which has now rebranded itself as a paragon of the socially responsible corporation, a recent entry spoke of the new trend of "meaningful marketing." It did not go nearly as far as did Stuart Ralph of MorallyMarketed.com when he wrote on his blog that as "the corporation becomes the 'moral' teacher of society it's on us the marketer[s] to create the world we want to see."[27] But the author of the *Guardian* post, Oliver Burch, did explain that "advertisers are desperate for us to emote. More than that, they want us to know they care. So it's out with the obvious sales pitch and in with tear-jerking or heartwarming storytelling around an issue people feel passionate about."[28] And Burch quotes one well-placed digital media executive, Sam Barcroft, to the effect that "in a world awash with hype and hyperbole, substance sells."

That calling such appeals to the emotions "substance" and arguing that one should accept at face value the claims of a company to share its potential customers' values, even though self-evidently the ultimate rationale of the exercise is to cement brand loyalty and increase market share, no longer appears ludicrous to a great many people testifies to how profoundly the present era has confused consumership with citizenship, seduction with deliberation, good intentions with understanding, and public relations with news. The reality is that public relations and marketing, which, to restate the obvious, are about making the best possible case for what the client wants sold, regardless of whether it is a sports car or a humanitarian intervention in Darfur, now dwarf journalism, whose traditional role was precisely to refuse to take such claims at face value, in other words, to serve as naysayers, precisely what the optimists, impatient or otherwise, insist it is inappropriate to do. According to the Pew Research Center's 2014 Fact Tank, News in the Numbers, in "The Growing Pay Gap between Journalism and Public Relations"[29] by Alex T. Williams, between 2004 and 2014, the number of reporters in the United States declined by 17 percent, from 52,550 to 43,630, while the number of public relations specialists grew by 22 percent, from 166,210 to 202,530.

This has played out as a steadily increasing overlap in media new and old between public relations and news. This can take the form of a philanthropy or a multinational corporation sponsoring some subset of the media outlet it finds of particular interest. The *Guardian* has been a pioneer in this, as evidenced by the Gates Foundation sponsoring its development site and Anglo American underwriting the paper's Social Impact Hub. In these two cases, at least editorial autonomy could be preserved. Not so with "Guardian Labs," which was described by the paper's press office as "at its heart a collaborative and participative approach to developing brand stories that resonate amongst the highly engaged communities across all the Guardian platforms."[30] The venture's launch partner was Unilever, which made a multimillion-pound commitment to the project. But money, it seemed, was only part of the story. In the words of Guardian Labs' managing director, Anna Watkins, the partnership with Unilever "is a fantastic example of collaboration based on our shared values."

The *Guardian* is not alone. The Pew Research Center's report emphasized that in the US media, "one of the greatest areas of revenue experimentation now involves website content that is paid for by commercial advertisers—but often written by journalists on staff—and placed on a news publishers' page in a way that sometimes makes it indistinguishable from a news story." Most major American newspapers have such initiatives. At the *Wall Street Journal*, these ads are produced by the paper's "custom content division." The *Journal's* editor-in-chief, Gerard Baker, has insisted that he was confident that the paper's readers would "appreciate what is sponsor-generated content and what is content from our global news staff."[31] But this hardly seems likely, since surely, from an advertiser's perspective, confusing the two was the main purpose of the exercise.

This moral revaluation of marketing that such conflating of advertising and news has been so helpful in advancing is only one element of a larger project: the moral revaluation of capitalism, at the heart of which is the supposedly socially and morally transformative doctrine of corporate social responsibility. When, in the 1990s, Michael Ignatieff argued, and with considerable justification though overbroadly, that the post–World War II world had seen a "revolution of moral concern,"[32] one doubts he had the corporate sector in mind as being the point of the spear for that revolution. And yet the social marketers seem increasingly convinced that this is precisely the role business needs to play. In his *Guardian* piece, Oliver Burch quotes an executive at a firm called Inspire, a subsidiary of the advertising conglomerate Young & Rubicam, to the effect that "attitudes toward business are transforming," and millennial consumers expect "their favorite brands to make a difference in the world." The executive then proceeded to out-Ignatieff Ignatieff, telling Burch that, "at a more general level, the Western world is undergoing a values revolution."[33]

This is now the consensus view. It extends from Western governments and international institutions to NGOs and philanthropies, and holds that in the age of corporate social responsibility, the interests of business and the broader interests of society are not only not in conflict, but largely speaking, are one and the same. But this view did not arise on its own. To the contrary, long before the shift in the way advertisers sold companies' products, this new set of social and moral assumptions about not just the essential benignity of capitalism but its superior capacities to bring about social change was itself fiercely marketed. There are those in the antiglobalization movement who view the business community's narrative of a future in which not only will the rich go on getting richer and richer but while they are doing so, they will end poverty, hunger, and (most) disease as well, mainly as a moral flag of convenience for staving off demands for redistributive justice. As the executive director of War on Want, John Hilary, put it in his book, *The Poverty of Capitalism*, corporate social responsibility (CSR) is a way of "restricting the parameters of the possible and denying more radical visions of change." In this way, Hilary argues, quoting Gerard Hanlon of the University of London's School of Business and Management, CSR "ensures that subversive alternatives suffer the fate of utopias—they are dismissed as impossible however attractive we find them."[34]

I greatly admire both Hilary's and Hanlon's work, but at the risk of sounding like—well, like what I am—a person with just such a resigned view (even while hoping that I am wrong), an argument can be made that although this has been one of the major *effects* of the public-private partnership model of development, I don't believe this has been the conscious intent at all. To the contrary, in my experience at least, there is nothing cynical about the philanthrocapitalist project. In the specific case of Bill Gates, it seems far more humanly credible that he is being entirely sincere when he describes his work both at Microsoft and at his foundation in terms of their socially emancipatory character while dismissing the importance of the fact that he created two successive monopolies. Yet in both instances the facts are quite clear cut. In 2000, Microsoft was actually ruled an unlawful monopoly by a US federal court and narrowly escaped being broken up for using the stranglehold it had over the PC market—thanks to its Windows operating system—to exclude other companies' products.

The Gates Foundation's monopolistic tendencies have been expressed more subtly, of course. But whatever the goal, the effect has been to marginalize the most important competing worldviews. This happened when Gates threw his power, money, and influence into what proved to be the successful effort to put in place a global regime for the distribution of AIDS medicines that involved subsidizing their distribution but leaving drug companies' patents inviolate. Another example is the foundation's proselytizing for GMOs, and, as of this writing, its ongoing campaign to undo bans in various countries against their use in agriculture. A memo written in 2008 by the head of the World Health Organization's malaria programs, Dr. Arata Kochi, to the WHO's director-general provided a rare insider's view of this. In the memo, Dr. Arata observed that because the Gates Foundation was now funding almost every leading scientist studying malaria, one of the core principles governing biomedical research, independent peer review of proposals, was becoming all but unworkable.

Still, those doubting Gates's sincerity as a philanthropist need to ask themselves why, then, he has chosen to spend his money on malaria, AIDS, and agricultural research rather than on Manets, Maseratis, and private islands. I very much doubt it can be explained solely by the thirst for recognition, even though Gates once described that as a "proxy" for profits where these are not on offer and an added incentive where they are. And if I am right that the philanthrocapitalists and the much larger number of corporate CEOs who have embraced CSR are in earnest about their social commitments, then their stance actually seems to me to be far more puzzling than if the skeptics are in fact right, and the assurances from the business world about its determination to play a leading role in finding solutions to the great problems of the day were either rhetorical fluff or a mask for some more malign agenda. For even if one accepts the basic Enlightenment narrative of inexorable human progress, what is it that has convinced these business leaders that it is they, in their roles both as corporate titans and as philanthropists, and not members of social movements, scientific discoveries and the new technologies derived from them, and not politics, who will lead us to this promised land in which there are no poor countries and even the poorest people will at the very least be able to satisfy their basic needs? For if this is indeed what they think, then to me the conclusion becomes inescapable that a great many of the most important, talented, and successful figures of late-twentieth- and early-twenty-first-century capitalism, not to mention their myriad imitators and admirers, have fundamentally misdescribed *to themselves* the nature of the system in which they have made their immense fortunes and whose paladins they are rightly seen (and see themselves) as being.

To be sure, outside the mainstream such questions resonate, even if the preference tends to be for more malign interpretations than I believe are warranted. Within the development establishment, however, they rarely if ever even need to be dismissed, for the simple reason that they are barely if ever posed by anyone whom philanthrocapitalists and their admirers consider worth taking seriously. And it is an open question whether this would have ever changed had Peter Buffett, Warren Buffett's son and, like all of Buffett's children, thanks to a major bequest from his late mother, a philanthropist in his own right, not chosen to make the point that the development establishment seems either incapable or unwilling to confront. In a 2013 op-ed in the *New York Times* that he titled "The Charitable-Industrial Complex," Peter Buffett wrote that "because of who my father is, I've been able to occupy some seats I never expected to sit in. Inside any important philanthropy meeting, you witness heads of state meeting with investment managers and corporate leaders. All are searching for answers with their right hand to problems that others in the room have created with their left." And he added, "As more lives and communities are destroyed by the system that creates vast amounts of wealth for the few, the more heroic it sounds to "give back.""[35]

Peter Buffett knows many of the philanthrocapitalists in question and is entitled to his psychological speculations. I do not and therefore have no right to engage in anything of the sort. I certainly have no idea whether certain rich people need to feel "heroic" any more than I know whether the CEOs of multinationals that have subscribed to the doctrine of corporate social responsibility have done so out of some psychological need to feel virtuous. As I have repeated a number of times in this book, my preference has been to take the philanthrocapitalists' and CEOs' accounts of their motives at face value and the consensus within the development establishment that sees business as the point of the antipoverty spear, especially with regard to agricultural livelihoods and nutrition, as based on conviction rather than expediency. But where I think Peter Buffett is absolutely right is in his focus on all the ways in which the capitalist system that has created many if not most of the problems it now seeks to solve. Indeed, I think he could have gone further in his critique, given that in a number of crucial ways, it not only has no sustainable solutions to these problems but instead continues to exacerbate them. In the particular case of the global food system, far from offering the way out, a number of the specific ways in which capitalism has evolved now make renovating that system far more difficult than might have been the case in the mid-twentieth century, barring, that is, some very radical, systemic transformation that would impose serious limits on capitalism's freedom to operate more or less as it sees fit— curbs that it has not had to accept since the Franklin Roosevelt era in the United States and the post–World War II social-democratic compromise in Western Europe.

The New Alliance for Food Security and Nutrition initiative, launched by President Obama at the 2012 G8 summit and reaffirmed at the US-Africa summit in 2014, is a good illustration of this. In the words of an August 2014 White House press release, by bringing together donor governments, African governments, the African Union, and multinational corporations and generating large-scale new private investment in agriculture by the multinationals, the program would "lift 50 million people out of poverty in Sub-Saharan Africa by 2022."[36] By the end of the US-Africa summit, ten African countries[37] and 180 multinational companies had signed on, and $10 billion of what the press release called "socially responsible private sector commitments"[38] had been secured. Rajiv Shah boasted that this was proof of concept that USAID had "pioneered a new model of development that is transforming agriculture and accelerating Africa's impressive growth and potential." And he declared that "by harnessing the skills, resources and expertise of the private sector, we can build on our investments to power the markets of the future and lift millions of people out of extreme poverty."[39]

The problem with these claims is that while all the participants insisted that the welfare of smallholder farmers was one of their main priorities—Shah has insisted that the program would create 650,000 jobs and help five million smallholders in the ten countries that had already agreed to participate—so too, it seemed, were

African countries changing their laws to facilitate large-scale investment by global agribusiness firms. That the White House chose to
describe this as "country-led and country-right reforms"[40] could not
disguise that the basic thrust of the program's actions, though not of
its promises of the benefits that would soon accrue to smallholder
farmers, was removing constraints on multinationals. To be sure,
some of these big firms were African, which, along with the fact that
the leaders of the ten African countries had voluntarily signed on to
the initiative, was adduced as proof of "African ownership" of the
initiative. But as George Monbiot pointed out in a fiery retort to the
ONE Campaign's attack on criticisms he had made in his *Guardian*
column, there was no reason to suppose African-based companies
were "any more representative of the needs and aims of small farmers and the rural poor"[41] than Western multinationals. As for national leaders voluntarily signing on, Monbiot's argument was that
the same could be said of African leaders' acceptance of the World
Bank's Structural Adjustment Program and many other policies imposed on them from abroad that in some cases they were simply not
in a position to resist and in others found that these policies entirely
suited their interests.

That the New Alliance reforms gave global agribusiness a good
deal of what it, along with USAID and DFID, had been putting
forward was a *sine qua non* for them to make major new investments
in Africa. For example, Ethiopia was hailed for having "liberalize[d]
its seed sector,"[42] which in practice meant replacing state control and
the central role of small and medium-sized local enterprises with
international agribusiness, which was held to be capable alone of
managing Ethiopia's agricultural "value chain." For its part, Nigeria
was praised for committing to reform its "inefficient fertilizer sector."[43] And Tanzania was complimented for having removed bans on
the exports of certain foodstuffs and for facilitating imports of seeds
and agricultural chemicals from outside East Africa. Finally, a number of participating African countries, notably Malawi, Mozambique

(where Cargill leased some 40,000 hectares in 2012), and Ghana, had amended their land laws to encourage long-term leasing by corporations and in several cases set aside land for that purpose.

Taken together, the new agricultural landscape of Africa could be summed up as one in which tax laws had been amended in corporations' favor, control over seed markets and distribution channels had at least in part been passed from governments to agribusiness (the government of Mozambique even promised to "systematically cease distribution of free and unimproved [*sic*] seeds")[44], and property laws had been amended to make it easier for the agriculture multinationals to invest in land. The mainstream view was that this was, in the jargon, a win-win situation for everyone; for their part, the critics saw it as a catastrophe for the poor, above all for smallholder farmers. But even were one to grant the mainstream view, it begged to question the power relations at the heart of the New Alliance initiative. For as Monbiot pointed out, "Any constraints on the behavior of corporate investors remain[ed] voluntary, while the constraints on host nations [became] compulsory." This is not to say that the New Alliance was claiming it could function with a governance structure. But as a brilliant investigative piece in the *Guardian* written by Claire Provost, Liz Ford, and Mark Tran revealed,[45] the New Alliance was, as one of its internal documents put it, conceived from the start as relying on the "top level leaders" who were to make up its leadership council, that is to say, its governing body. And that council was exclusively composed of the leaders of African governments, the heads of the major Western donor agencies, notably USAID and DFID, and the CEOs of major seed, fertilizer, and food-producing firms including Unilever, Syngenta, Yara, and Cargill.

It certainly came as no surprise that while the New Alliance included three African farming organizations in its deliberations (though not on the leadership council), it did include representatives from those important farmers' groups and consumer associations that took the view that, as the head of the World Development

Movement, Nick Dearden, once put it, " 'market knows best' policies have not delivered food to the hungry [in the past]"[46] and will not do so in the future should have come as no surprise. As Olivier de Schutter told the *Guardian* reporters, governments had been making promises to investors "completely behind the screen, with no long-term view about the future of smallholder farmers"[47] and without their participation. Moreover, the *Guardian* investigation concluded that contracts multinational corporations had already signed with African governments by the time the Africa-US summit had gotten underway included dozens of investments in nonfood crops. At the summit, whose subtitle was "investing in the next generation," President Obama spoke of the meeting's purpose as discussing ways of "stimulating growth, unlocking opportunities, and creating an enabling environment for the next generation."[48] But well-intentioned though those sentences undoubtedly were, they fell into precisely the trap that de Schutter had cautioned against in the 2012 *Guardian* piece he wrote in response to the enthusiasm the recently announced New Alliance initiative was already generating. In it, he cautioned that privatizing aid was a dangerous strategy. "Opportunities," he wrote, "should not be mistaken for solutions."[49]

Unfortunately, taking that possibility seriously simply no longer seems to make sense in an era in which the development consensus is precisely the reverse. And when all is said and done, the debate between the New Alliance initiative and its critics ends where it begins, at the question of whether international business has or has not been transformed by the "values revolution," as the advertising executive whom I quoted earlier in this chapter had insisted, or whether they were no more benign in the second decade of the twenty-first century than they had been fifty years earlier. And where you stand on this is likely to depend on where you stand on globalization generally. The food security versus food sovereignty paradigms are a perfect illustration of this. In the food-security model, as long as poor people get enough nutritious food to eat and the price of that food is affordable, it does not matter much whether that food is grown in a particular region or country or it is imported from somewhere else, any more than it would for a citizen of a country in the rich world. For food activists, though, the poor of the Global South badly need the protections sovereignty affords, even if the rich, whether North or South, do not. More broadly, these campaigners see the vision of food security being put forward by the mainstream food establishment as one that integrates poor farmers into a global agrifood system, which, even if their incomes and nutrition levels are improved, something most activists do not believe will happen in any case, will still leave them in a state of perpetual subordination and dependency, at the mercy of a system that is and will remain rigged against them. And in the process, as Harriet Friedmann has put it, poor farmers will be forced to give up "the particularities of time and place in both agriculture and diets."[50]

If one takes globalization in *its current form* to be a fait accompli, then any effort to resist the mainstream model will seem quixotic at best and more often something very much worse and more destructive. Why harp on preserving the culture of the past, this argument goes, when the future promises to be so much better for everyone? In an important sense, equating "escaping poverty," to use a term one often encounters in the development world, with escaping the past has something curiously Marxist about it;[51] at the very least it seems to contain echoes of Bertolt Brecht's maxim from *The Threepenny Opera*, "First comes eating, then morality." But if one believes that preserving both history and culture in all their particularity is a moral and social imperative, then being included, even very successfully, as the food-security paradigm promises to do, in some global value chain in which what is produced is decided not according to local or national requirements but global ones, that paradigm becomes much more problematic. It is true that to a man and woman, officials of Western donor agencies, the World Bank, and the key NGO and philanthropic actors now claim, as Sam Dryden, the former head of the Gates Foundation's agriculture development programs, once put it, not to be imposing programs but instead to be "humbly listening to farmers and their families, learning and respecting their cultures, ways of living, and knowledge of place and home."[52]

But even if one accepts that this is the intention, even the most successfully consultative of these programs do not exist in the benign tabula rasa that Dryden's words evoke. To the contrary, they exist in the context of wildly lopsided relations of force in which virtually all the power and money is controlled by Western donors or Western-dominated international institutions, notably the World Bank, where the macroeconomic rules of the game, particularly as they affect the poor world, are still largely set. As the Princeton development economist Angus Deaton has put it, while the language of the development world "has moved toward an emphasis on partnership . . . it is not clear what sort of partnership is sustainable when one side has all the money."[53] And, one should add, when engaging or disengaging is entirely at the discretion of the donors.

If Sam Dryden or his successor, Pamela K. Anderson, or, for that matter, Bill and Melinda Gates themselves choose to listen, they will do so. But should they no longer wish to do so, they are at perfect liberty not to. There is no contract between philanthropist and grantee, social or otherwise; no enforceable one, anyway. And yet just as Angus Deaton is right when he writes that "economic development cannot take place without some sort of contract between those who govern and those who are governed,"[54] it is difficult to understand how it can take place successfully unless there is one between aid donors and aid recipients as well. As for the (largely Western-owned) multinational corporations, they may trumpet their corporate social responsibility, and, as George Monbiot wrote of Unilever, "if you blotted out its name while reading its web pages, you could mistake it for an agency of the United Nations"; their investment decisions are theirs alone to make, and of course they are free to wind up such investments whenever they choose to do so. Is it possible that in one more "first," for the first time in human history the powerful are irrevocably committed to empowering the powerless? Yes, it is possible. But the fact that they seem to assume they can do this without giving up their own power or changing anything basic to the liberal capitalist order as it now exists makes it seem highly unlikely.

The mainstream generally treats such skepticism—on the rare occasions, that is, when it confronts it at all—with responses that range from fury, above all in the case of pro-GMO scientists such as Nina Fedoroff, Robert Paarlberg, and the founder of the US Food and Drug Administration's Office of Biotechnology, Henry I. Miller, to pained forbearance of the kind Jeffrey Sachs exhibits in his pages on the antiglobalization movement in *The End of Poverty*. Neocolonialism? Ancient history, or so the mainstream view generally suggests; "surely we're beyond all that, and just need to work together to 'solve the problem' of hunger." A global economic system stacked in favor of the rich world, in which multinational corporations increasingly can do as they like? Nonsense, say the corporate CEOs who now believe it falls on them to take the lead role in development. Why, they ask, is there so much skepticism about business when corporations have now transformed themselves and are absolutely committed to running their businesses along socially responsible lines that will benefit not only their shareholders but their stakeholders too? As for the motives of the governments of Britain and France, which for so long ruled the world, and whose wealth was in large measure the product of the labor and natural resources of the poor world; or of the United States, that, BRICS or no BRICS, in large measure still does so? They, too, have transformed themselves. To think otherwise is to fall into the trap of the old left-right divide, to ensnare oneself in arguments from the past that are long past their sell-by date. Is it not more important to "Feed the Future," as US-AID's program for global agricultural development is called, than wallow in the grievances of the past?

I have not the slightest doubt that officials of Western European and North American governments, philanthropies such as Gates and Rockefeller, and NGOs that have come to accept the mainstream consensus believe this and feel themselves, again, quite sincerely, to be the victims of a fundamental injustice when, as they see it, their critics refuse to give them a fair hearing. Certainly, the fact that those in power dislike talking about power relations and prefer to talk about corporate responsibility or about how optimistic they are about the future, or preach empathy, as Bill and Melinda Gates did in their Stanford commencement speech, should hardly come as surprise. But however humanly understandable such responses are, it is only in a world shorn of its skepticism and in which the moral and intellectual default position is one that takes as a given the fundamental irrelevance of the past that it could seem reasonable to be genuinely surprised when many still decline to take such claims at face value.

·16·

Doing Everything to End Hunger
except Thinking Politically

To expect the powerful to question the legitimacy of the system in which they gained their power would be a utopian absurdity. It would be an act of class suicide, and no matter how diverse Gates's philanthropic portfolio may become in the future, that is one arena it is a safe bet to say the foundation will never be tempted to venture into. But that these philanthrocapitalists, social entrepreneurs, and CEOs so badly misunderstand how that system actually functions *is* unexpected. After all, who knows it better in all its intricacies than they do? Peter Buffett's explanation seems to be that what he calls the "charitable-industrial" complex is in some form of collective psychological denial about the contradiction between its social commitments and the norms according to which they operate their businesses. My own view is that the current mainstream consensus is simply too broad and too deep-seated for this to be the case any longer, assuming, that is, that the psychological explanation was correct in the first place.

Gilbert Rist, I think, comes closer to the mark with his concept of development having been transformed over the decades into a "global faith," one "shared by every national leader (and therefore all the international organizations), as well as by nearly all the economic technocrats and the immense majority of the population."[1] But let me propose a counterfactual: were these CEOs, social entrepreneurs, philanthropists, and aid officials to look at how global corporations actually function as if seeing them for the first time, would what they see ratify the reigning consensus that the new, private-sector-led development paradigm would usher in a world finally freed from extreme poverty and hunger? Or might they see such programs as the acts of what Cambridge economist Ha-Joon Chang has called "bad Samaritans," who "do not even realize that they are hurting the developing countries with their policies?"[2]

The most obvious place for them to start would be taxation, at home as well as abroad. American multinationals complain, accurately enough, that the United States has one of the highest corporate tax rates in the developed world. What they usually omit when doing so is the fact that for many businesses such rates only apply to 50 percent of their profits or less and that the American tax liabilities of some of the largest and best-known US corporations amount to only a small fraction of that. According to US government statistics, eighty-three of the one hundred biggest corporations have subsidiaries in tax havens through which they cycle the majority of their profits.[3] They do this—and, to be clear, it is perfectly legal under the US tax code—in part by domiciling foreign operations in low-tax jurisdictions such as the Republic of Ireland, the Netherlands, Luxembourg, Singapore, and the British Virgin Islands. These accounting schemes have lowered the effective tax rates of the companies that make use of them to a small fraction of what they would otherwise have to pay, For example, according to a 2013 report to the European Parliament, Google had an effective tax rate of 2.4 percent on its non-US profits, Adobe Systems paid below 7 percent, and Apple around 2 percent.[4]

This has been particularly true of Silicon Valley and other "new technology" companies, that is, those firms that are generally considered to have pioneered the corporate responsibility movement and whose alumni, Bill Gates first and foremost but by no means Gates alone, have been most associated with philanthrocapitalism, social entrepreneurship, and "impact investing." For example, despite Apple CEO Tim Cook's claim in testimony before a US congressional committee in 2013 that "we don't depend on tax gimmicks," and that Apple paid "all the taxes we owe,"[5] in 2012, Apple was able legally to allocate 70 percent of its worldwide profits to overseas subsidiaries. By refraining from repatriating those profits to the United States, not only could Apple defer ad infinitum any US tax bill, but it was entitled to use the money for any transaction except for direct investment in the company's US operations or payouts to shareholders. And even this was largely a fiction, since the existence of these funds, which as of this writing are deposited in New York banks, could not help but drive down the interest payments that potential bond buyers could demand, thus allowing the parent company to access funds at a very low cost more or less whenever it needed to. By 2014, Apple's nonrepatriated profits were reliably estimated to have reached the sum of $102 billion. For its part, Microsoft had amassed $60 billion.

Apple pioneered a version of this tax strategy, which involved using an accounting technique known as the "Double Irish"; the California-based company set up two subsidiaries in Ireland, the first of which is a tax resident of a Caribbean tax haven. Apple shifts its non-US intellectual property rights to the first Irish company, which in turn licenses it to the second Irish company. That second company collects royalties around the world and then transfers them back to the first company. Facebook now uses this strategy as well, so successfully, in fact, that in 2013, 50 percent of the company's profits were booked in Ireland. The figure for Microsoft Ireland was 24 percent of its profits, which obviously had nothing to do with the company's economic activity in the Republic of Ireland, including products exported from it. As for Google, it employs a variant called a "Double Irish with a Dutch Sandwich," in which profits collected by the second Irish company pass through a company in the Netherlands before being transferred to the first company back in Ireland and then on to the Caribbean. According to the *New York Times*, literally hundreds of other firms now use this technique.[6] This is not the only way that US corporations avoid paying taxes. There are also so-called "inversion deals" in which American companies buy smaller non-US corporations and then legally reincorporate in the lower tax country in which the foreign company is domiciled, thus acquiring the nationality of the subsidiary.

To state the obvious, while they might have been profitable anyway, many of the multinationals that have been most vociferous in insisting that they could do well and do well at the same time, were far more profitable than they would otherwise have been. On an infinitely smaller scale, such gimmicks have also been employed by many of the leading celebrities known for their commitments to social causes, which in 2013 prompted the Advocacy Hub, a respected British consultancy specializing in advising campaigning groups, to warn that "although not explicitly vocalized, the issue of tax [could possibly make] some celebrities nervous about the potential for having their own tax affairs in the public and media spotlight."[7]

The case of Bono is interesting in this regard. Hailed by Jeffrey Sachs in *The End of Poverty* (to which Bono wrote the forward) as "having opened the eyes of millions of fans and citizens to the shared struggle for global equality and justice,"[8] in 2005, Bono and his group U2 moved their tax domicile from Ireland, where their tax rate on their global earning was 25 percent, to a so-called letter-box company in the Netherlands, which lowered their tax obligation to 1.5 percent. Pressed on this by the *Irish Times* and mocked by left-wing members of the Irish Parliament, one of whom, Claire Daly, took to referring to him as Ireland's "Mr. Tax Exile himself," Bono defended the decision by saying U2 was acting in "a tax-efficient manner," like any other business. And yet, wearing his activist's hat, Bono has indignantly rebuked extractive companies such as ExxonMobil and Chevron for suing to block proposed US financial regulations aimed at forcing them to report publicly on what royalties, taxes, and other payments they make to African governments for the oil, gas, and mineral rights they hold throughout the continent, framing the issue as one of corruption and transparency on the part of some of the extraction companies and some African leaders. As Bono said in a speech in Addis Ababa in 2013, "Capital flight is always at night, in the dark."[9]

The issue of whether Bono and U2's company had pursued some capital flying of their own arose during a public conversation organized by the Clinton Global Initiative during its 2013 annual meeting. On the dais with Bono was the Anglo-Sudanese telecom billionaire Mo Ibrahim, himself a major philanthropist and a powerful advocate for what he refers to as good governance (rather than, say, democracy) in Africa and a member of the board of the ONE Campaign that Bono cofounded. Unlike Bono, Ibrahim's focus was squarely on taxes in a global context, excoriating what he called the broken international tax system and, to Bono's clear annoyance, singling out Ireland as an example of this dysfunction, so much so, in fact, that the singer interrupted and launched into a ringing defense of Ireland's tax system that was later widely derided by many antipoverty campaigners. Ibrahim, however, stuck to his guns. Asked how multinationals could help African communities, Ibrahim responded by saying that they first of all needed to pay their taxes. It was an idea Ibrahim elaborated on the following year in a speech he gave at Chatham House, where he was categorical. "Multinationals don't pay taxes in Africa," he said flatly, "we all know that." And Ibrahim went on to argue that while business was now global, "taxes need to be paid where profit arises."[10]

It is easy to exaggerate the affront of socially committed celebrities themselves engaging in tax avoidance. And even assuming Bono is indeed the hypocrite his detractors consider him to be, there are far greater moral affronts than hypocrisy. And lest it be forgotten, while Ibrahim and Bono may have been at loggerheads over the rectitude of countries "shopping" for low-tax domiciles, despite that Ibrahim's foundation is in London, he himself is legally domiciled in Monaco, another tax haven. Moreover, however one judges Bono's conduct, while doubtless the Irish Treasury would welcome getting the millions of euros that U2 would have had to pay had it not scampered off to the Netherlands, the sums in question are not significant in terms of even a small nation's annual budget. In contrast, as Ibrahim rightly emphasized in his Chatham House speech, for corporations not to pay taxes in the countries where they sell their products or services is morally odious and economically harmful to the economy of any nation but immensely dangerous and destructive to the economies of poor countries. One by no means unrepresentative example illustrating Ibrahim's point were five mining deals concluded between 2010 and 2012 between the government of the Democratic Republic of the Congo (DRC) and a number of Western extraction companies. According to a report issued in 2013 by the Africa Progress Panel chaired by Kofi Annan, in aggregate these assets were sold for $275 million even though their estimated commercial market value was $1.63 billion,[11] in other words for one-sixth of what they were worth. The differential of $1.36 billion was double that of the DRC's health and education budget, this in a country where seventeen out of every one hundred children do not reach their fifth birthday, where 43 percent of all children under five suffer from moderate to severe stunting, and more than seven million children between the ages of six and eleven do not attend school.[12]

The Africa Progress Panel report points out that in developed and developing countries alike, "Globalization has made it increasingly difficult to ensure that companies operating across borders provide their fair share of [tax] revenues." At the core of the problem is the multinationals' "extensive use of offshore companies, the high level of intra-company trade and the commercial secrecy surrounding foreign investment activity." To put the matter starkly, while Bill Gates would have been a vastly rich man under any tax regime, he is a very much richer man because of what the Africa Progress Panel report rather chastely refers to as "sophisticated but aggressive 'tax planning.' "[13] This is why, while it is perfectly reasonable to praise him for devoting so much of his money to his philanthropy, it is equally reasonable to point out that the reason Gates has had so much money with which to endow his foundation in the first place—Gates has transferred $28 billion to it between 2000 and 2013,[14] with the rest of the endowment coming from Warren Buffett's transfer of $15.1 billion to the Gates Foundation between 2006 and 2013 as part of his commitment to leave the bulk of his fortune to the foundation[15]—was because of the value of his Microsoft stock, of which, by a tiny margin (330 to 333 million shares in the spring of 2014), he remains the second largest shareholder after his successor as CEO, Steve Ballmer.[16]

In contrast to Bono's case, it is hard to argue that this is merely hypocrisy on a grander scale. The British tax campaigner Richard Murphy has calculated that through legal tax-avoidance schemes, Microsoft avoided paying $4.68 billion in taxes in 2012. Murphy added that since the total global aid budget is approximately $133.5 billion per year, Microsoft avoids paying approximately 3.5 percent of that budget.[17] He might have added that in the same year, 2012, the Gates Foundation spent a little over $2.6 billion on international programs. Of course, to free-marketeers who believe the state needs to be downsized still further than it already has been since the 1990s, this is all to the good. Tim Worstall, a fellow at the Adam Smith Institute in London, a *Forbes* columnist, and a self-described opponent of corporate income tax (though not, in fairness, of mining companies having to pay very high fees on their concessions), exemplifies this view. Writing on his blog, Worstall, who advised the

United Kingdom Independence Party on some of its tax proposals, readily acknowledged that "if Microsoft had paid more tax then the shares Bill Gates own[s] would be worth less." But Worstall went on to argue that this was a good thing since Gates "keeping the money out of the hands of the politicians and their plans, and spending it instead directly on aid to the poor would seem to be increasing the amount of money spent on said poor."[18]

Unsurprisingly, given the fact that while he is a capitalist he is anything but a free-market absolutist, Gates himself does not seem to agree with Worstall's view, at least not consistently. For example, he was a strong supporter of the Enough Food for Everyone campaign of the IF Coalition of two hundred British development NGOs, church groups, and other antipoverty and environmental organizations, which joined together in 2013 to put pressure on the British government and other major donor countries to do more to end global hunger. The coalition believed that Western leaders had to do four important things to fix what they described as a "broken [global] food system." The first was providing more aid, the second was putting an end to farmers being forced off their land and the use of crops for fuel rather than food, the third was getting honest communication from governments and corporations about their role in the world's food system, and the fourth was stopping "big companies dodging taxes in poor countries, so that millions of people can free themselves from hunger."[19]

Gates not only agreed to attend but was a featured speaker at IF's largest rally, held in Trafalgar Square in London in the spring of 2013. But as Ian Birrell of the *Guardian* pointed out in a fine critical piece, while Gates "loves to lecture nations on how they should give away more of their taxpayers' money [in foreign aid] . . . he sees nothing wrong in tax avoidance schemes" of companies such as Microsoft. Birrell quotes Gates as justifying this by saying, "if people want taxes at certain levels, great, set them at those levels," but that it is not "incumbent on those companies to take shareholder money and pay huge sums that aren't required."[20] What might at best be called such two-track thinking would seem to bear out Peter Buffett's charge that his fellow philanthropists were engaged in trying to solve problems they themselves either had caused or at least had exacerbated, since as the holder of 4.5 percent of Microsoft stock, apart from Steve Ballmer the shareholder whose pocketbook would have taken the biggest hit was Gates himself. As Birrell noted, it is difficult to see any principled basis for claiming that tax avoidance by Microsoft is perfectly legitimate while at the same time reproaching donor governments for not spending more of the taxes they are able to collect on development assistance—a situation made more egregious by the fact that the share of tax revenue derived from corporate income taxes has fallen steadily—in the United States from 32.1 percent to 8.9 percent between 1952 and 2009—thus imposing, in Birrell's words, "a far bigger burden on to other taxpayers."[21]

Gates and most of his fellow philanthrocapitalists have seemed more ready to dismiss objections to their accountants' having found legal ways to pay the lowest tax possible in the developed world than they are complaints about global corporations' massive tax avoidance in developing countries. And it is certainly true that the situation of poor and disenfranchised people in the developing world is objectively orders of magnitude worse than that of their opposite numbers in the rich world. Nonetheless, has caused tremendously damaging social effects on the majority of citizens if not most OECD countries,[22] a tax system that concentrates wealth in the hands of the very rich, who in turn, through their funding of candidates, have a decisive say (especially in the US) on who can attain high political office. Ironically, the activities of the Gates Foundation in the United States in such fields as education and health would seem to bear out Peter Buffett's accusation that philanthrocapitalists are in many cases endeavoring to repair problems created by the system that has made them so rich. Or to put it another way, if gaming the system *is* the system for multinationals where tax liabilities are concerned, then what is the basis for thinking that their claims that making profits and doing social good are now indivisible, exemplified by Monsanto's claim that "we're all in this together" and that it is "striv[ing] to find collective solutions to help feed our planet while protecting the earth for generations to come," should be taken at face value?[23]

But assume for the sake of argument that, having concluded, as Bill Gates seems to have done, that tax avoidance by corporations is more destructive in the poor world than anywhere else, and that the big multinationals bow to pressure from campaigners and from billionaires such as Gates and Ibrahim, really do start paying their taxes in, say sub-Saharan Africa, even while continuing to find 'creative' ways to minimize or even avoid them in the Global North. Even so, surely all but the most convinced of free-market absolutists would accept that a global system in which the richest people and the most powerful companies can pick and choose their societal obligations, whether in the case of individuals by endowing foundations whose focus and, indeed, whose perrenity at their founders' discretion,[24] and in the case of corporations, through commitments to social responsibility that are entirely voluntary and can be retracted at any time is not likely to prosper for long. The answer that is most frequently advanced in rebuttal is that philanthrocapitalists have not only good intentions but good ideas as well—many more good ideas, not to mention a far greater capacity to put them into practice, than government. But such a view is really only sustainable if one takes the "this time is different" view—that is, that in the era of philanthrocapitalism, extreme economic inequality is no longer a moral solecism and that extreme wealth concentration will not lead to the "capture of government" by the rich elite, who will then bend the rules, especially the tax code, in favor of themselves. Is this possible? In theory, I suppose it is. But surely it is far more likely that the famous remark commonly attributed to US Supreme Court justice Louis Brandeis that "we may have democracy, or we may have wealth concentrated in the hands of a few, but we can't have both," is as valid in the early twenty-first century as it ever was. As a 2011 Council of Europe report put it, "massive tax cheating by wealthy individuals and enterprises" throughout the world "not only penalizes ordinary tax payers, public finances and social spending, but also threatens good governance, macroeconomic stability and social cohesion."[25]

Surely it is only in an age when the consensus not just in the corporate world itself but among mainline development NGOs as well, and within the UN system, is that only transformative power of liberal capitalism in combination with science and technological innovation can end hunger and extreme poverty and also at least mitigate the worst effects of climate change, that issues of wealth and power could be presented as being of secondary importance. As for what would seem to be nothing more than commonsense skepticism about accepting the assurances of the inordinately rich people who are the principal beneficiaries of the global status quo that they are sincerely committed to radically altering through their philanthropy the very status quo that allowed them to get so rich in the first place, that too is deemed unfair or just ignorant—yet another example of the critics unable to understand the essential win-win character of twenty-first-century capitalism. A standard put-down of "old-fashioned" political activism by people in Silicon Valley and other futurists is its supposed failure to understand what has come to be known as "systems thinking," one conventional definition of which is that the component parts of a system can only be properly understood in the context of relationships between those parts and with other systems. But this is just what the philanthrocapitalism/public-private partnership model of development in general, and ending extreme poverty and hunger in particular, *fails* to do. To the contrary, the current paradigm depends on an engineering model in which a problem is defined, the best minds apply themselves to it, after honest and open debate a solution is arrived at, it is tried, and its success or failure is then quantified and measured.

Sir Gordon Conway's *One Billion Hungry*, which I discussed earlier, is one of the ablest expressions of this worldview.[26] In it, he uses his great expertise to argue that global food security can be attained through scientific discovery and its technological applications, which will allow what is commonly described as sustainable intensification of agriculture to occur—producing greater yields with less water and fewer chemicals and without having to increase the amount of arable land. In fairness, Conway does emphasize that for the "Doubly Green Revolution" he is calling for to succeed, there will have to be fair, not just open, markets and enlightened political leadership in the rich and poor worlds alike. But as the head of Food First, Eric Holt-Giménez, wrote in a respectful but highly critical review, Conway's chapter on "Political Economy" "avoids asking 'who owns what? who does what? who gets what? what do they do with it?' "[27] In other words, instead of subjecting the public-private partnership model for ending hunger to a proper systems analysis, Conway instead sees no reason not to take the conventional wisdom as an unassailable paradigm and make his recommendations without any serious effort to widen the frame. But had he done so, it would have produced some very damning results.

A good place for Conway to have started would have been "Honest Accounts? The True Story of Africa's Billion Dollar Losses,"[28] a 2014 report produced by Health Poverty Action, a coalition of campaigning groups that investigates what it calls "aid and its (mis) representations."[29] The section comparing inflows and outflows to Africa is devastating. According to the report, the continent receives approximately $37.9 billion in official OECD aid,[30] $0.4 billion in official aid from non-OECD countries, $9.9 billion in net private grants from Western NGOs and philanthropies, $23.4 billion in World Bank, IMF, donor government, and private lender loans to the national governments of African countries, $8.3 billion in loans from all non-African sources to the private sector in Africa, and $16.2 billion in purchases of shares and other financial instruments in African markets by non-African investors. The outflows include $21 billion in debt servicing by both the public and private sector in Africa to Western banks and international institutions, $46.3 billion in profits made in Africa by international corporations, $35.3 billion in illicit financial transactions, $17 billion in illegal logging, and $1.3 billion in illegal fishing in West Africa alone. More controversially, the report also includes outflows such as climate change mitigation and adaptation; sets (rather questionably) a figure on the losses to Africa from the migration of its professionally trained cadres to Europe and North America; and factors in the reserve in foreign currencies that African governments are obliged to hold so as to be able to import goods and services from abroad and service their debts should their own exports not provide sufficient funds for doing so. But even if one does not factor these figures in, this amounts to inflows of $96.1 billion versus outflows of $120.9 billion.

This alone should radically alter the received wisdom in the West of an Africa that is the beneficiary of generous aid from the Global North. To take only one example, if Mo Ibrahim is correct (and no one has seriously challenged him on the matter) that multinationals pay no taxes in Africa, then were companies to pay even the lowest European corporate tax rate, which is Ireland's 12.5 percent, they would owe approximately $5 billion on their declared revenues. And were tax haven countries in Europe or the Caribbean no longer to provide cover for illicit financial transactions and allow the proceeds from them to be deposited in their banks, it would add another $3.6 billion. Taken together, that figure is only a little more than a billion dollars less than the $9.9 billion in net grants from all private sources, including, of course, the Gates Foundation. Substitute the United Kingdom's corporate tax rate of 21 percent for Ireland's 12.5 percent, and the revenues for African governments would be over $17 billion. Throw in the debt, which even most people in the mainstream development world would concede was to a considerable extent a burden imposed on African countries by the World Bank, the IMF, and the major donors during the heyday of Structural Adjustment, and the figure outstrips the total of all annual official development aid from OECD countries. Finally, add the revenues Africa would receive were it properly remunerated for the illegal logging and fishing that is the work almost entirely of Asian and Western European countries, and the picture that Peter Buffett painted in his *New York Times* piece looks like an understatement. Indeed, he could have been far more severe. I am no admirer of the Slovenian Marxist provocateur Slavoj Žižek, but he is not always wrong. And surely he was onto something when, in the same vein, though of course far more harshly than Buffett, he described international development as "repairing with the right hand what [it] ruined with the left hand."[31]

Something, but not everything. In his review of *One Billion Hungry*, Eric Holt-Giménez speculates that the "arc of Dr. Conway's experience has drawn him into the technocratic vortex of the Green Revolution's episteme in which conventional assumptions regarding agriculture and society are accepted as fact."[32] If you view capitalism as a *consciously* brutal system, rather on the model of colonialism, then you are likely to view philanthropy, which, in its current philanthro-capitalist/public-private partnership paradigm, historically springs from it (no matter how loath the development world is to concede the point) and more proximately from the technocratic model (no matter how ready the development world is to insist on this), then the idea that a Rajiv Shah or a Justine Greening, or, for that matter, a Bill Gates, a Jeffrey Sachs, or a Jim Yong Kim could be drawn into the same vortex will appear naïve and far-fetched. But while it is obviously the case that the rich and the powerful are uniquely positioned to shape conventional wisdom, what is less commonly remarked upon is the degree to which they themselves are shaped by it. Silicon Valley prides itself on being a place for cutting-edge, future-oriented thought, not for repackaging conventional wisdom. And yet what could be more conventional than the view that business is creative and dynamic and government ponderous and ineffective, that technology will solve the world's problems (a fantasy that goes at least as far back as the nineteenth century), or that we live in a postideological world?

For all their claims of being focused on the promise of the future rather than limited in what they can imagine by the past, advocates of business taking the lead to end extreme poverty and hunger seem to find transcending their past just as difficult as anyone else does. Thus Gates, one of the leading monopolists of his era, sees no great problem with monopoly, whether held by Microsoft or by his foundation. As he has put it, "Microsoft is not about greed. It's about innovation and fairness."[33] In that, Gates is no different from the monopolists of the past. John D. Rockefeller once said of Standard Oil that the company was "an angel of mercy, reaching down from the sky, and saying 'Get into the ark. . . . We'll take all the risks."[34] If one believes as Gates does, then there is indeed no reason to be troubled by the fact that three agrichemical firms—Monsanto, Syngenta, and DuPont—now control 53 percent of the global commercial seed market and that the one market over which they do not yet exercise this degree of control is in sub-Saharan Africa. Even when Roger Thurow, a journalist specializing in hunger issues, now at the Chicago Council on Global Affairs, and whose book, *The Last Hunger Season*, was warmly praised both by Bill and Melinda Gates, called Africa "agriculture's final frontier,"[35] is there any reason to hear colonial echoes in that description? As for wondering whether putting one's faith in multinational corporations' professions of their good intentions is a safe and sensible thing to do, given the fact no one has ever shown that global agribusiness firms are a shining exception to Mo Ibrahim's rule that foreign multinationals in Africa generally do not pay anything like what they owe in taxes to the governments of the countries in which they operate, well, that, too, is excluded from the debate the mainstream food establishment and its donors—whether governments, the UN system, or the major philanthropies—are willing to engage in.

And for a man who continually insists on the need for metrics and data—in a piece he wrote for the *Wall Street Journal* in 2013, he described how "important measurement is to improving the human condition"[36]—Gates's view of measurement seems to be one in which anything can be analyzed critically and open-mindedly in the global food system but the system itself. Were it to be undertaken, whether by the Gates Foundation or any other part of the mainstream food establishment, such a comprehensive systems analysis would begin by posing a great many hard questions regarding the pluses and minuses of structuring the rural economy of the poor world around value chains controlled by quasi-monopolistic agribusiness multinationals. And it would then have to go on to confront the issue of whether the food security paradigm being put forward was actually fit for purpose, above all in its assumption that a globalized food system largely organized by private companies and individual entrepreneurs was the only sure way to ensure food security for the world's poor. It would also have to come to grips with the fact that while commodities markets for most of their history served an important purpose in what economists call price discovery and also in the transfer of price risk from producers to investors based on information about supply and demand, this is no longer the case. Commodities markets began to be deregulated in the United States during the Clinton administration in the 1990s, a process that culminated in the Commodities Futures Modernization Act of 2000. By the beginning of the twenty-first century, these markets were dominated by major banks such as Barclays and Deutsche Bank, hedge funds, and above all, investment banks, most notably Goldman Sachs and Morgan Stanley. As Olivier de Schutter has argued, these new financial investors were interested purely in short-term financial gains, the result being a "financialization of the commodities market [in which] the prices of products respond increasingly to a purely speculative logic."[37] In de Schutter's view, the sharp price rises of the 2007–2008 crisis could in part be explained because prices were "less and less determined by the real match between supply and demand" that had historically had been the organizing principle of commodities markets.

A proper systems analysis would have addressed all these questions. Given that the Gates Asset Trust has investments in Barclays and Deutsche Bank and, through its Berkshire Hathaway stockholdings, a much more substantial position in Goldman Sachs, it does not seem unreasonable to have expected the foundation to have seriously considered pressuring all these companies to modify their policies and to have actually applied that pressure in at least some instances. As the headline on the home page of the foundation's "What We Do" section of its website puts it, "Our job is to get results. We know that our results depend on the quality of our partnerships."[38] But for "impatient optimists," the Gates Foundation look, more like "resigned pessimists" when confronted by suggestions that its shareholdings give it the ability to influence the corporate policies of the companies in which it has major positions, whether with regard to the commodity speculation that has at least some effect on the poor farmers Gates has made it its mission to help or, given that the foundation's largest single focus is still on global health, with regard to companies whose products cause health problems for consumers throughout the world.

A look at the trust's holdings is instructive in this regard. According to its 2012 tax filing, the trust owned $871 million in shares of McDonald's, $312 million in British Petroleum, $661 million in ExxonMobil, and $2 billion in Coca-Cola, which, at 7 percent of its total assets, is the trust's largest holding after the Berkshire Hathaway shares donated by Warren Buffett. And given the heavy weighting of Coca-Cola in Berkshire's portfolio, this means that as Buffett's shares are transferred to the foundation, it will soon be the largest single shareholder in Coca-Cola. Given the foundation's central focus on health and nutrition and the fact that widespread obesity and rising rates of diabetes that can be correlated with the consumption of sugary drinks are now among the main threats to global public health, especially in developing countries, it hardly seems unreasonable to have expected the Gates Foundation to have foregone such investments as a matter of principle.

The case of Mexico is a paradigmic one. In 2013, 71 percent of the Mexican population was either obese or overweight, overtaking the United States, where the figure was 68 percent. Of the Mexican population, 14 percent now suffers from diabetes.[39] On average, Mexicans consumed 665 servings of Coke products per year, more than the average American (399), British (202), Chinese (32), and Indian (9) combined.[40] Obviously, correlation is not causation, but the link was so troubling to Mexican public health officials that in 2014, the new Mexican administration of President Enrique Peña Nieto slapped a 10 percent surtax per liter on sugar-sweetened drinks.

Coca-Cola's response has been to attempt to position itself as a friend of public health and to emphasize its commitments to corporate social responsibility. Though soft-drink manufacturers campaigned hard against the tax through advertisements in the media, with the spokesman of the beverage companies trade group, Jorge Romo, even at one point saying it wasn't soft drinks that were to blame for Mexico's obesity epidemic, but a "Latin gene," the head of Coca-Cola Latin America, Brian Smith, even took a seat on the dais with President Peña Nieto when the 10 percent tax was announced. Did the Gates Foundation endorse this self-portrayal? Given the Gates Foundation Trust's decision to forego investments in tobacco stocks, taking the same stance with regard to soft-drink companies would not have required a huge stretch. The obesity epidemic is estimated to have killed 2.8 million people in 2013, and according to a report issued in June 2014 by Anand Grover, the UN special rapporteur for the right to health, most of these deaths are caused by sugary drinks and snacks full of empty calories.[41] By contrast, the foundation's health programs have spent a great deal of money on combatting measles, which is thought to kill 1.2 million people per year, and on fighting other diseases, such as yellow fever, that kill many fewer people. But for years the foundation ignored what on the face of things seems a core contradiction at the heart of its health projects. Were this not the case, surely it would not have been systematically deepening and broadening its ties to Coca-Cola, most notably in a partnership in East Africa with the goal of "empower[ing] farmers in Uganda and Kenya as they sell their fruit for use in locally produced Coca Cola juices."[42] Other collaborations have included a library project in Indonesia and supply chain training expertise in Tanzania and Ghana.

The foundation's long-held view of Coca-Cola had always been irenic and was outlined in Melinda Gates's 2010 TED talk, "What Nonprofits Can Learn From Coca-Cola."[43] Despite the fact that one of her foundation's main priorities has always been public health, nowhere in her speech did Gates make any mention of the harmful effects of sugary drinks on public health. Instead, she focused on Coca-Cola's success in marketing itself. "Ultimately," she said, "Coke's success depends on one crucial fact and that is that people want a Coca-Cola." Gates then went on to discuss the way Coke's marketing campaign was tailored to local audiences and at one point played a video of a Somali hip-hop artist performing the song the company had commissioned from him for the World Cup. In contrast, she argued, in development "we make a fundamental mistake—we make an assumption that we think that, if people need something, we don't have to make them want it." What was needed, Gates concluded, was that if "we can learn lessons from the innovators in every sector, then in the future we make together, happiness can be just as ubiquitous as Coca Cola."

In 2015, the Gates Foundation did finally sell its holdings in Exxon Mobil, McDonald's, and Coca Cola, though without making clear whether this was in response to the criticisms leveled against it or was a strictly financial decision. Such pressure had been mounting. Already in 2007, the *Los Angeles Times* had published a detailed investigation[44] that found that its endowment had invested and continued to invest in firms that had contributed in major ways to the "human suffering in health, housing and social welfare that the foundation is trying to alleviate" with its grant-making activities.[45] The foundation did not dispute the facts. Instead, its then-CEO, Patty Stonesifer, responded to the *Times* stories by saying, "The stories you told of people who are suffering touched us all. But it is naïve to suggest that an individual stockholder can stop that suffering. Changes in our investment practices would have little or no impact on these issues."[46]

The kindest thing that can be said about Stonsifer's response is that it was disingenuous of her in the extreme to claim that the Gates Foundation cannot influence the policies and practices of the companies in which it holds major positions when for years it has successfully sought and then gone on to play a major role in setting the agenda of governments, academic research institutions, international organizations, and relief and development NGOs on vaccines, public health, and farming practices and technologies. Even a hint to the markets that the trust or Buffett's Berkshire Hathaway was thinking of selling its position in a company is enough to drive the company's share price down, just as word that such important investors have bought it is often enough to drive the price up, which, with apologies to Samuel Johnson, tends to concentrate the collective mind of a corporate board wonderfully. Since Bill and Melinda Gates are the trust's sole trustees, accountable to no one except themselves, Warren Buffett, and, of course, the US tax authorities, it is presumably safe to assume that it has been at their direction that the trust's money managers have always operated on the principle that again, with the very American exception of tobacco stocks,[47] their job is to invest in any company they think will add to the value of the endowment, without regard to whether the activities of these corporations conflict with the foundation's goals.[48] In an interview that was featured in the *Los Angeles Times*, American environmental activist Paul Hawken called this the "dirty secret" not just of the Gates Foundation but of many of the largest philanthropies. "Foundations donate to groups trying to heal the future," he said, "but with their investments they steal from the future."[49]

Michel Foucault once wrote that, "Power is tolerable only on condition that it mask a substantial part of itself." While this seems right to me as far as it goes, it misses the essential corollary, which is that power is tolerable only on condition that it mask a substantial part of itself *from itself*. The public-private partnership model of development, particularly with regard to agriculture, has succeeded in doing this to a degree that is historically unprecedented. But this does not mean it will have the staying power its advocates are so confidently predicting that it will have. This is not only because, as Dominican blogger Br. Clement Dickie O.P. has observed, "the promise of technology and human might is always shorter-lived than we think,"[50] though I believe this to be true. Nor, despite the correctness of Angus Deaton's diagnosis when he wrote that "the technical, anti-political view of development assistance has survived the inconvenient fact that apparently clear technical solutions [keep] changing," is it because its future prospects of survival are all that good. In my view, they are not, though if I had to bet now (I will not be alive to see it), I'd wager that will only become clear when the promise to end extreme poverty and hunger by 2030 or 2040 proves to be illusory. The most important reason is its refusal or inability to think politically, and, worse, to imagine that it doesn't have to. Trotsky famously declared, "You may not be interested in war, but war is interested in you." The same can be said about the development world's indifference to ideology.

Conclusion

I f conventional wisdom is correct and there really are no great deeds without there first being great dreams, then those charged with developing the so-called Sustainable Development Goals (SDGs), which are intended to take up the baton from the Millennium Development Goals (MDGs) when these expire in 2015, have been dreaming even grander dreams than those who formulated the MDGs ever dared. And those were grand enough—"the world's biggest promise," as David Hulme, the director of the Brooks World Poverty Centre at the University of Manchester, once called them. Compared to the promises contained in the SDGs, however, the eight MDGs almost appear modest. For among the seventeen goals and 169 "associated targets" enunciated in the so-called "zero draft" of the SDGs—which was first circulated for comment in early June 2014 by the UN working group charged with formulating the final document—were "end[ing] poverty in all its forms everywhere," "end[ing] hunger, achiev[ing] food security and adequate nutrition for all, and promot[ing] sustainable agriculture,"

316

"attain[ing] a healthy life for all at all ages," "protect[ing] and restor[ing] terrestrial ecosystems and halt[ing] all biodiversity loss," and "ensur[ing] sustainable consumption and production patterns."[1] The explicitly political goals of the zero draft were every bit as ambitious. The SDGs would pave the way for "peaceful and inclusive societies, rule of law, [and] effective and capable institutions."[2]

It is anything but clear why the framers of the zero draft were so determined to set the aspirational bar so high. After all, by the time the draft was issued, it had become clear not only that while there had undoubtedly been progress, a number of the MDGs were not going to be met but also that at least forty poor countries lacked sufficient data to track their performance on meeting the first Millennium Development Goal of eradicating extreme poverty and hunger, and there was an ongoing controversy over the World Bank's very drastic revision downward of how many people in the world actually were living on less than $1.25 per day. Jeffrey Sachs does not seem to have been at all shaken by this, which was significant, because his voice has continued to count for a great deal from the time that work on formulating the MDGs began in 1998, through the period of his service as special advisor to the UN secretary general for the MDGs, and finally, in 2013, when Sachs was named also to head the UN's newly founded Sustainable Development Solutions Network (SDSN). In an article he published in the *Lancet* in 2012, Sachs wrote that it was entirely reasonable to believe the SDGs "could help finally to move the world to a sustainable trajectory." And when the zero draft of the SDGs was released to the public, Sachs declared himself "very happy" with it, declaring that he considered it to be "on a very good track" even if it was "important to narrow the number of goals down significantly . . . to ten or under."[3]

Sachs's confidence reflected what, at least on the basis of the number of major development institutions and campaigning groups that had greeted the zero draft warmly though by no means uncritically, appeared to be the majority view in development circles. The British development economist and former Oxfam researcher Kate Raworth typified this response when, in a guest post on the From Poverty to Power blog run by Duncan Green of Oxfam, she called them "humanity's best chance to envision a shared and lasting prosperity for all."[4] To be sure, when the zero draft appeared, a number of important mainstream voices registered strong dissent. For example, Charles Kenny, himself an ardent believer in the idea that it is realistic to believe extreme poverty can be reduced to "absolute zero" by 2030, was nonetheless highly skeptical. "We all knew the point of the MDGs (or least how they were mostly used)," he wrote, "[It was] setting a framework for global aid discussions." In contrast, Kenny described the SDG draft as being "essentially useless for prioritizing anything, goes far beyond global public goods (and excludes key ones), is very weak on 'how do we get there,' is full of unrealistic targets, and yet fails as a complete vision of where we'd love to see the world in 2030."[5] And the editor of the *Lancet*, Richard Horton, was scathing. "Sustainable development?" he asked. "Try utopia instead." The SDGs, Horton concluded, are a "negotiated wish list . . . fairy tales, dressed in the bureaucratese of intergovernmental narcissism, adorned with the robes of multinational paralysis and poisoned by the acid of nation-state failure. Yet this is served up to us as our future."[6]

But if Horton is right, as (unsurprisingly) I believe him to be, then what is to be done? Throughout most of this book, I have focused on why I do not think either the public-private partnership model, with its emphasis on business-led development, nor the radical critique of the current food system offers a viable way forward to end extreme poverty in general and, more specifically, the chronic malnutrition and undernutrition on which this book has largely focused. I will not recapitulate those arguments at length in this conclusion, but my view remains that for all the insistence on "evidence-based" initiatives, the solutions offered by the mainstream food establishment suffer collectively from an overreliance verging on mystical faith on the application of scientific breakthroughs that will give farmers in the poor world the technological inputs and market savvy needed to grow enough food to feed comfortably the nine or ten billion human beings who will be alive on this earth by 2050 if not considerably sooner. Is it possible that the technological and scientific breakthroughs will keep on coming, which is another way of saying that unlike all the development silver bullets that have come before, this time really is different in that historical restrictions on what human beings could expect have been lifted? Of course it is. And this confidence goes a long way toward explaining why the mainstream view in the era of public-private partnerships has increasingly morphed from cautious optimism into a seemingly unshakeable conviction that no countervailing perspective need be taken seriously and thus that there is no need for any "Plan B."[7]

But as I have tried to illustrate throughout this book, this view makes sense only if it rejects the pertinence of the experience of human beings throughout all but the last two centuries of recorded history and instead is presented as being as predictively reliable as some all-but-immutable physical law. In contrast, it seems reckless in the extreme if one believes instead that the future may well hold not only the pleasant surprises afforded by innovations in science and technology but unpleasant surprises as well—black swan events, to use Nassim Taleb's well-known formulation—that will be much more than just tragic interruptions in the ever-upward movement of the economy and of society, which is the context in which Bill Gates has often presented the historical catastrophes of the past two hundred years. In the Gospel of Wealth 2.0, as Bishop and Green dub it in their book, rich philanthropists are put forward as uniquely effective because they are applying the business methods that made them rich to their charitable work. And yet surely a money manager who advocated an investment portfolio based entirely and permanently on "one-way bets," as the Wall Street expression goes, would be fired by any philanthrocapitalist who wanted to hold on to his or her money in order to continue doing so.

Jaron Lanier, the Microsoft Research scientist and best-selling author, thinks the biggest change in America is that "technology's never had to shoulder the burden of optimism all by itself."[8] Perhaps it is a burden that development can bear. Bill Gates certainly seems convinced of it. The problem is that the mainstream view depends on the assumption that the political, social, and cultural challenges to a world of decent livelihoods for smallholder farmers and food security for all can be relatively easily overcome, assuming, that is, enough money, intelligence, and commitment can be mustered. Part of this, as I tried to show at the beginning of this book, is the result of the continuing authority of Francis Fukuyama's idea of the End of History and, more specifically, his argument that now that its ideological rivals have so plainly failed to provide alternative models for successful societies, liberal capitalism is the only viable model left. But there is another element that needs to be taken into account, one whose importance is far too often ignored. For accompanying this type of technocratic antipolitics is a blindness to the centrality of culture and the often irrational, subjective, and largely unquantifiable nature of human beliefs, impulses, and desires. Since, historically, development has always largely been a subset of economics, it is hardly surprising that the mainstream view would reflect the standard view within that profession that, as John Gray has put it, "the economy can be understood in the same way we understand the workings of a machine."[9]

Bill Gates, who can appear at one moment like the conscience and at the next like the id of the current development paradigm, unsurprisingly typifies this. In an entry on his blog at the end of 2013 about the best books he had read that year, Gates mentioned that while he enjoyed fiction ("I've read *Catcher in the Rye* a bunch of times," he wrote), "I read mostly nonfiction because I always want to learn more about how the world works."[10] This is far more revealing than it may at first appear. Its relevance lies in what the implications are of the fact that it simply does not seem to occur to Gates that there might be something to learn from music, or from culture in general, about how the world works and that more to the point, it might be something you can't learn anywhere else. To be sure, if "learning about how the world works," means, as Gates goes on to say, reading books that teach him "something I didn't know," by which he evidently means facts and facts alone, then obviously fiction or poetry isn't likely to seem to have anything to contribute to his understanding of how the world "works." After all, one doesn't need to read *Anna Karenina* to know people are unfaithful to each other or Kafka to understand that many sons have complicated relations with their fathers. The same tropism toward believing that anything that can't be measured probably isn't all that central or important lies at the heart of Gates's philanthropy and more generally at the heart of the current development paradigm that its supporters promise will put an end to extreme poverty and hunger. As Gates wrote in his 2013 foundation letter, "You can achieve amazing progress if you set a clear goal and find a measure that will drive progress toward that goal."[11]

In his book, *The Great Escape*, Angus Deaton has dubbed this "the 'hydraulic' approach" to development aid, in which "fixing world poverty and saving the lives of dying children is seen as an engineering problem."[12] As he describes it, the solution then offered is to identify problems that "need to be fixed in agriculture, in infrastructure, in education, and in health,"[13] and come up with the cost of fixing each one. Contra Jeffrey Sachs, however, Deaton, insists that money is not the central problem. As he puts it, "You cannot develop other people's countries from the outside with a shopping list for Home Depot, no matter how much you spend."[14]

For Deaton, though the "hydraulic approach" is flawed in many crucial ways, its greatest flaw is what he calls its technical, antipolitical view. In this, Deaton both updates and broadens the analysis that was made brilliantly by anthropologist James Ferguson in his 1985 study (it was his dissertation), *The Anti-Politics Machine:*

Development, Depoliticization, and Bureaucratic Power in Lesotho.
Deaton calls it "one of the greatest books [ever written] about aid
and development,"[15] and he is absolutely right to do so. Ferguson's
argument was twofold. The first was that most development agencies preferred to screen out or ignore most of the historical and
political facts about the countries in which they operated. It would
have been one thing had development been a success. But as Deaton comments acerbically, "The technical, anti-political view of
development assistance has survived the inconvenient fact that the
apparently clear technical solutions [have] kept changing," even if
this "[has done] nothing to imbue the developers with humility or
uncertainty."[16]

Of course, if anything, it has been just the opposite. But how
has this confidence been renewed with the advent of each new development paradigm? In their own fine book, *Development Confronts
Politics*, Thomas Carothers and Diane de Gramont suggest that part
of the explanation is to be found in what they call the "temptation
of the technical." As they point out, "while economics appears as a
rational, scientific domain, politics seems to imply inevitable entan-
glement with the irrational side of human affairs—with ideological
fervor, nationalistic impulses, and other volatile passions. Economics
emphasizes consensual ideas, like the universal appeal of prosperity
and the tragedy of poverty. In contrast, politics is all about conflicting visions and objectives."[17]

Of course, historically there have been many political systems
across the ideological spectrum in which it was imagined that
whether through legislation, education, or force, rationality could be
imposed or inculcated. Maoism is the extreme, horrific example of
this. Mao Zedong actually spoke of the Chinese people as being "a
blank page." Che Guevara expressed a similar view when he insisted
that "to build communism a new man must be created." But even the
most benign modern societies make what are in reality quite radical
claims about human plasticity. One influential variant of this is the

so-called "libertarian paternalism" developed by the American legal scholars Cass Sunstein and Richard Thaler, and put into practice to a very limited extent by the billionaire Michael Bloomberg during his twelve years as mayor of New York City. Unlike the Gates/Sachs "hydraulic approach," it fully accepts the reality of human irrationality. But it posits that the new science of behavioral economics allows the (bad) choices that are so often the consequence of such irrationality to be accurately predicted, and, assuming the social environment can be changed, that people can be "nudged" toward more rational behavior and into changing the panoply of "self-destructive" behaviors such as too many sugary drinks or junk food to which so many human beings are prone.

That such ideas are far closer to Huxley's *Brave New World* than to Orwell's *1984* should be obvious. As the "Controller" says in Huxley's novel, "Our ancestors were so stupid and short-sighted that when the first reformers came along and offered to deliver them from those horrible emotions, they wouldn't have anything to do with them."[18] Sunstein and Thaler are trying to tame rather than stamp out what they view as human beings' intuitive and emotional side, the side that can't resist temptation, and will always, to use one of their concrete examples of this, "eat a delicious brownie,"[19] even though a person knows that, rationally, he or she should eat something healthier instead.

But whether it is because Bill Gates genuinely thinks most people view the world essentially in the way he does or because the question does not interest him, the radicalism of Gates's perspective is that he does not seem to think he has to nudge anyone, let alone more forcefully impose anything on anyone. He certainly does think that he is imposing capitalism, since he takes it as read that it is the only rational way of successfully ordering international society. In any case, there is no need. Technology changes people; it is as simple as that. From what he has said, Gates seems to see himself as a kind of master problem solver, an antipoverty engineer getting down to the hard, demanding, but also exhilarating and noble business of figuring out how, as he has put it, successfully to "deliver tools and services to everyone who will benefit."[20] It is an understanding that is almost entirely binary, in which there are problems and their solutions, with the greatest challenge, as Gates has said on numerous occasions, being in what time frame these solutions can be arrived at. As he once put it, the crucial things in his foundation's work are "setting clear goals, picking the right approach, and then measuring results to get feedback and refine the approach continually."[21]

Missing from all this is the understanding that people often make choices that may seem incomprehensible from an econometric point of view (Gates) or irrational from the perspective of those who believe the state exists in part to mitigate human beings' propensity to make choices that are against their long-term interests (Sunstein and Thaler) but that make eminent good sense to them and that they are unlikely to be "nudged" into relinquishing. The work of Esther Duflo and Abhijit Banerjee, the codirectors of MIT's Jameel Poverty Action Lab, is particularly relevant here. For example, they have shown through numerous case studies that what in the development world is called the "nutrition trap," that is, the condition in which many of the world's poorest people are too malnourished and physically weak to work as productively as they would if their diets were better, is unlikely to be solved "hydraulically," by simply making more money available to them. For as Banerjee and Duflo's studies illustrate, when the incomes of very poor people increase, instead of buying better food or spending more on health and education, the poor often choose instead to spend money on buying televisions and mobile phones, alcohol, tobacco, and more flavorful but not necessarily more nutritious food. Duflo and Banerjee attribute this to "the basic human need for a pleasant life,"[22] something which is unquantifiable, thus defying both Gates's hyperrationality and Sunstein and Thaler's insistence that in making such decisions, people are acting against their own interests.

For Duflo and Banerjee, this quest for a pleasant life helps explain why, as more consumer goods become available, food spending actually declines in many poor communities. They also make the essential point that given that prosperous people routinely make choices not in their long-term interest (were this not the case, after all, there would be no need for Sunstein and Thaler's nudges), the true irrationality lies in expecting the poor dependably to do so. This is not to say these behaviors affect rich and poor in the same way. More generally, behavioral economists emphasize that because the poor have narrower margins of error in the choices they make than do the rich, the consequences of any mistaken choice are likely to be far more harmful to them.[23]

Duflo and Banerjee have illustrated this with evidence from the field work they did in 2005 in Udaipur District in the Indian state of Rajasthan, where they estimate 47 percent of the population lives on less than $1 per day and 86 percent on less than $2 per day. Only a little more than half of the extremely poor households reported that they had enough to eat throughout the year, and malnutrition and undernutrition are rampant. And yet even in the context of such horrific deprivation, they calculated that "the typical poor household could spend up to 30% more on food than it actually does if it completely cut expenditures on alcohol, tobacco, and festivals,"[24] but instead these households choose not to. Duflo and Banerjee's assertion that in fact, not just in India but globally, the extremely poor are for the most part not going hungry has been bitterly challenged in the development world. Equally if not more controversial is their suggestion that assuming they are correct, extreme poverty and hunger may not be linked as they certainly have been in both the MDGs and the SDGs. What seems undeniable, though, is their contention that the rationalist expectations of the development world founder on the shoals of culture, custom, and human psychology. As Duflo and Banerjee put it, if, for example, extremely poor families often spend "so lavishly on funerals that they [have to] skimp on food for months afterwards,"[25] this is often because this is what is expected of them culturally, just as they expect it of their neighbors.

There is nothing new about such choices, nor are they emblematic of some moral flaw or greater degree of ignorance among the poor of the contemporary Global South. To the contrary, as Duflo and Banerjee point out, George Orwell observed the same patterns of behavior in *The Road to Wigan Pier*, his book on the lives of poor British workers, published in 1937. Working-class families, Orwell observed, had "an appalling diet." Would it not be better, he asked rhetorically, if instead they spent their money on "wholesome things like oranges and wholemeal bread?" His answer was simple: "Yes, it would, but the point is that no ordinary human being is ever going to do such a thing. . . . When you are unemployed . . . you don't want to eat dull wholesome food. You want something a little bit 'tasty.' [And] there is always some cheaply pleasant thing to tempt you."[26]

What the mainstream development world and more specifically most of the major institutions of the current global food system have never been willing to face up to is what Jaron Lanier has aptly called their own "missionary reductionism." And just as there is simply no room in the Gates Foundation's view of the world for thinking hard about culture and belief (although, good multiculturalists that foundation officials are, they of course pay lip service to it), nor is there room in their cosmos filled with inputs and outputs for so unquantifiable a phenomenon as simple human boredom. As Duflo and Banerjee put it, "We often see the world of the poor as a land of missed opportunities and wonder why they don't invest in what would really make their lives better." But, they add, "don't underestimate the power of factors like boredom. Life can be quite dull in a village. There is no movie theater, no concert hall. And not a lot of work, either."[27] Given the fact that smallholder farming is such brutally hard work, the first thing many smallholder farmers in the Global South are likely to do, *precisely* if the current schemes for improving their livelihoods and providing them with the means to increase their crop yields are as successful as the current development orthodoxy insists they will be, is to move to the cities of their own countries and, where possible, emigrate to the Global North.

Whatever the current developmentalist orthodoxy may be, the fundamental problems of the world have always been moral, not technological. The reigning cliché in the development world is that institutions like the Gates Foundation, the World Economic Forum, and the Clinton Global Fund are hardheaded realistic pragmatists, while the Right to Food movement and other dissidents are dreamers. But the debate about how to make the global food system work to feed the nine billion is not simply a scientific question, no matter how many times researchers who favor GMOs argue that it is, any more than building the atomic bomb was simply a technical question. In reality, despite the current pro-GMO mantra ("everything must be tried if the world of nine billion is to be fed") and denials of the Gates Foundation, USAID, and, of course, the agribusiness multinationals themselves, the question of GMOs has always been intensely political on both sides, not just on the anti-GMO campaigners' side. Anyone doubting this should read the 2007 cable written to the State Department by then–US ambassador to France Craig Stapleton about possible US responses to French moves to ban a particular Monsanto-developed GMO corn seed. Stapleton describes Paris's effort to implement bureaucratic processes that, as he puts it, will "circumvent science-based decisions in favor of an assessment of the 'common interest,'" words that revealingly, unlike "science-based," he puts in quotation marks. Stapleton recommends "a retaliation list" of European companies "that causes some pain across the EU since this is a collective responsibility." Such a move, he concludes, "could help strengthen European pro-biotech voices."[28]

In any case, to reiterate a point I made earlier in this book, even if one chooses to ignore Washington's thuggish behavior on behalf of Monsanto in particular and for GMOs in general, not just in France but globally, and assumes that GMOs do indeed work just as well and are just as safe as their proponents say they are, it should not be up to only scientists, the US State Department (including USAID which, lest it be forgotten, is the department's development arm), and philanthropies issuing from and relying on the practices of the business world, and buttressed by the best public relations campaign money can buy, to decide whether or not GMOs are adopted.[29] The usual rebuttal to the argument I am making here is to say that those who oppose GMOs are just as bad as those who deny that anthropogenic climate change is occurring. Both sets of "refusers" are condemned for irrationally rebuffing what is by now a wide consensus among scientists on the safety of the former and the reality of the latter. What this misses is that, unlike the ice caps melting and the temperature rising by somewhere between 2 and 5 degrees Celsius, farming is a culture, not just a means of production. Again, assume GMOs are safe. The fact still remains that the system by which these GMO seeds will be distributed, even if, as in the case of Golden Rice, companies forego their profits, will for the first time fully integrate smallholder farming into the global economy. This is not a controversial statement. To the contrary, it is an analysis on which the global food establishment and its critics absolutely concur. The difference, of course, lies in where one stands on the question of whether this signals the advent at long last of a much more prosperous and healthier future for smallholder farmers and by extension for the poor of the Global South, or instead presages an economic, social, political, and environmental catastrophe.

The answer to that question is one that can be answered in no other way except in moral and political terms. But to the extent that the development project remains Angus Deaton's and James Ferguson's "anti-politics machine," such a debate cannot take place. But while their analysis accurately sums up how much of the development world sees itself, it does not accurately encompass its underlying reality. To begin with, when Carothers and de Gramont describe the aid world's reconsideration of development's "apolitical framework"[30] with regard to goals and "technocratic outlook"[31] with regard to methods, in favor of a more political understanding of development whose goal was to fuse political and socioeconomic goals, they ignore that this fusion existed from the beginning. Early in their book, they actually all but concede the point, noting that aid organizations, most of which had been set up by Western governments in the first place, "initially hoped that economic growth in poor countries would produce political development which they defined primarily as liberal democracy."[32] Where Carothers and de Gramont go badly wrong is in their subsequent claim that the failure of this to occur led to efforts to "keep development aid away from politics."[33] In reality, there was nothing apolitical or, more properly, postideological about this. All that actually happened is that the expectation that economic development would ineluctably lead to democratic capitalist societies of the Western European or North American type was not realized, and in the wake of this failure, the Western development establishment settled instead for a purely technocratic approach in terms of the nuts and bolts of aid and, in many cases, for collaboration with autocratic regimes friendly to the West.

In fairness, Carothers and de Gramont do make some concession to this reality when they note that some critics have charged that "while aid providers often talk about market reforms in politically neutral terms [such] as maximizing economic goods or rationalizing state authority, market approaches grow out of a broader ideological framework with deeply embedded values and norms." They also observe, even more noncommittally, that these critics "feel that market reforms should be treated as a contestable choice, not an objective good"—a formulation that amply bears out Gilbert Rist's argument that from the beginning in the development world, "you don't argue about the obvious; the most you can do is try to improve it."[34] But when, in the conclusion to their book, Carothers and de Gramont say that "the road to politics in development aid—the journey away from early apolitical mindsets and approaches toward the incorporation of political thinking and action into both the goals and methods of assistance—has turned out to be remarkably long,"[35] they are fundamentally misdescribing the history of development. For it has not deviated from that road from the day President Truman first enunciated "Point Four," and the era of postcolonial development got under way.

When Carothers and de Gramont argue that "the opening to politics in development aid gained impetus from the optimistic international political, economic, and strategic landscape that emerged in the early 1990s and seemed to point to an emergent liberal world order,"[36] they are not so much talking about politics in the traditional sense between genuinely conflicting visions of how society should be ordered. Whether this is because they agree with Fukuyama that such debates have been settled once and for all is unclear. But their use of the word "optimistic" to describe the immediate post–Cold War political and strategic landscape certainly suggests that this is their view. If so, to borrow Dorothy Parker's wisecrack that the acting of Katherine Hepburn ran the gamut of emotions from A to B, the idea that technocratic development is apolitical and that the sole legitimate role of politics in development consists of fostering, or at least playing an important role in, the creation of democratic capitalist societies is, to put it charitably, an extremely narrow view. And yet when in their conclusion Carothers and de Gramont speak of the need for Western aid providers to "up their game politically, both in terms of seriously pursuing their values and genuinely understanding local processes of political change,"[37] it is difficult to see how they could mean anything else. While dismaying, this is not surprising. Herbert Marcuse had already anatomized this mind-set in the early 1960s when he wrote that "modern rationalism, in its speculative as well as empirical form, shows a striking contrast between extreme critical radicalism in scientific and philosophic method on the one hand, and an uncritical quietism in the attitude toward established and functioning social institutions."[38]

If anything, things have grown far worse in the half century since Marcuse wrote these lines. For when he wrote about the ideological underpinnings of advanced industrial societies, he was still able to put the state at its center. But what has happened since the Reagan-Thatcher era has been the rise of global markets that as John Gray has put it, "work to fracture societies and weaken states."[39] What has replaced them in much of the rich world has been what Gray has identified as transnational corporations whose vision of a functioning world order is a "universal free market."[40] Gray does not believe this effort can possibly succeed. I am less confident, but even assuming that he is right, this universal free market is already at the heart of the mainstream vision of twenty-first-century development. For Jeffrey Sachs, this does not pose a problem because, he argues, the state is still strong enough to set the rules under which the private sector will be allowed to operate. But while this is theoretically possible in the sense that states have the legal authority to do this, a world in which both states and international institutions not only increasingly defer to multinational corporations but take it for granted that their interests largely coincide is not one in which such rigorous oversight is likely to be pursued. To the contrary, the basic neoliberal claim, which George Monbiot has characterized as the view that "unrestricted competition, driven by self-interest, leads to innovation and economic growth, [thus] enhancing the welfare of all,"[41] now so dominates the thinking of political and economic elites both in the Global North and in the Global South that it is difficult to see on what intellectual and moral basis states would be motivated to reassert their primacy.

Assuming they could, that is. In his brilliant book *Governing the World*, historian Mark Mazower argues that in the early twenty-first century, "politicians have become policymakers, who listen in the first place to private interests and their lobbyists and try to adjudicate among them." And as he puts it, "Time will show whether they are any longer capable of governing." As for the future, it has been "privatized, monetized, and turned into a source of profit . . . has crowded out an older vision of what the public good might look like."[42] As recently as the 1970s, it would have been inconceivable that the great cause of trying to mitigate extreme poverty and hunger would to a very considerable extent have been subcontracted by the most powerful governments in the Global North and by the UN system to multinational corporations and to those people belonging to the richest 1 percent of the population, from Bill Gates down, who have decided that they want to be philanthrocapitalists—in other words to the most undemocratic and least accountable institutions and individuals in the world. This of course is where the blurring of the lines between advertising and reality has been so useful. For as Mazower points out, the weakening of the state has been "moralized and turned into something virtuous."[43] As I write this in 2015, things have gotten to the point where even to suggest that one does not admire a Bill Gates, a Jeffrey Sachs, or a Jim Yong Kim is to cast oneself out of the mainstream conversation, as if not accepting their account of themselves and doubting the feasibility of what they claim to be able to accomplish means that you are somehow "for" the persistence of extreme poverty and hunger.

As I have said repeatedly in this book, I do not doubt the good intentions of people such as Bill and Melinda Gates and Warren Buffett, though I am far less persuaded by the sincerity and commitment of the corporate as opposed to the philanthropic sector, especially when agribusiness is involved. There, the interface between companies such as Monsanto and the Gates Foundation does seem very problematic, and that is putting it very mildly indeed. But to me, their lack of accountability trumps those good intentions. After all, one can recognize the fact that there have been good tsars without accepting the proposition that monarchy is a morally acceptable form of government. The most cogent response to this is often made not by the Gates Foundation's admirers, many of the most vocal of whom turn out to be either grantees or former officials, but rather by well-informed, intelligent skeptics such as Nathanael Johnson, a professor at UC Berkeley who is also a widely admired writer on food issues, mainly for the magazine *Grist*. As Johnson put it to me in an e-mail exchange, "Better to have a democratic society making decisions for itself . . . than having the ultimate decider be Bill and/or Melinda [Gates]. And yet, we also have to make the best of the situation where tremendous wealth is centered in one place." Of course, he added, "better still to tax or redistribute it, if we could muster the political will."

From his tone, it did not appear that Johnson thought that last possibility very likely. I certainly don't. That should naturally align me with the radical critics, all the more because for the most part I find their evaluation of the global food system far more persuasive than the mainstream view, above all in its hostility to the global free market that John Gray anatomized and in its emphasis on the centrality of justice, of culture, and of diversity in the serious rather than in the consumerist sense of the word. Do these social movements have their fanatics? Of course they do. But there does not seem to me to be anything excessive or unreasonable about advancing the proposition that peasants' land rights should trump the rights of foreign investors to buy land, or that a seed system controlled by multinational corporations because of their control over the patents on these could well prove to be a poisoned chalice for poor smallholder farmers *even if* those seeds live up to their (as yet largely unfulfilled) promise of dramatically raising crop yields and by extension incomes. And some of their specific suggestions for coping with the crisis of the global food system seem to me to be morally impeccable, as, for example, in the case of the argument made by food activist José Luis Vivero Pol that since food is a common good, a human need rather than a human want, speculating on it in the commodities markets—which causes price swings that has put the nutrition of literally hundreds of millions of the world's poorest people at risk—is unacceptable and should be entirely prohibited.

In *The Rise and Fall of Development Theory*, Colin Leys observed of the Marxist development theorists of the 1970s such as Giovanni Arrighi, Bill Warren, and Geoffrey Kay that contrary to much of the conventional wisdom of that era, they "maintained a rather objective stance, relative to the various other [development] schools, helped by the broad historical perspective and understanding of capitalist dynamics that they drew from Marx." As far as I can see, much the same can be said of the analysis of the radical food rights groups of the early twenty-first century. Unfortunately, it seems to me that the withering critique Leys went on to level at those theorists is also just as applicable to today's activists. The problem, he wrote, was that "there were too few people in the Third World for whom the political and moral standpoint of their analysis made sense." As he put it dryly, "Their perspective was, to say the least, very long-term, and offered no plausible line of immediate political action to improve matters."[44]

Food rights campaigners would bitterly dispute this, of course. Indeed, Eric Holt-Giménez and Raj Patel's book, *Food Rebellions*, ends with a powerful call to arms: "As more and more people see alternatives on the ground, and as more people hear the voices of others demanding and obtaining transparency, accountability, equity and sustainability, hope and action will overcome fear—the root cause of fatalism, cynicism and apathy. They will join the food sovereignty movement, and drag their elected officials with them, along the people's pathway out of poverty and hunger."[45]

I wish I could believe this, but I cannot. This is not to say that food sovereignty campaigners have not had successes. To the contrary, radical peasant groups have won victories in many parts of the world, from India to Latin America. But to me, although I welcome them, those successes pale by comparison to the speed with which the public-private philanthrocapitalist model of development is transforming agricultural systems around the world. Is this fatalism? I suppose that depends on whether one thinks that the early twenty-first century is a revolutionary moment. Obviously, I do not think so, or rather, I am convinced that the truly powerful revolution that is occurring today is not to be found in the insurrectionary episodes that Holt-Giménez and Patel chronicle and derive hope from, nor in the promise of science and technology, but rather in what John Gray has called "the emancipation of market forces from social and political control." And I entirely agree with Gray that, "by allowing that freedom to world markets we ensure that the age of globalization will be remembered as another turn in the history of servitude."[46]

Where does this leave us? I wish I had a better answer, but it seems to me the only feasible one is to be found in the strengthening of the state and in the promise and the burden of democratic politics. Given how systematically the coherence and authority of the state have been undermined and our politics have been corrupted by money and advertising, this will be immensely difficult at best and very possibly will fail. And yet we also know that when states are serious about reducing poverty or hunger, great things can be achieved. For example, while hardly without its problems, the Zero Hunger (*Fome Zero*) program the Brazilian government began in 2003 dramatically reduced malnutrition and undernutrition. The underlying reason for such success was that the government made it a priority from the beginning and never wavered in that commitment. And apart from a $200 million loan from the World Bank, neither the private sector, either in Brazil or internationally, nor the global development establishment played a major role. The most important point, however, is that the issue of hunger was framed in political rather than technical terms. In other words, it was presented not as a matter of improved seeds or streamlined value chains or of foreign or, indeed, of domestic corporate social responsibility, but rather as a matter of social justice and a state's obligations to its citizens. To put it another way, *Fome Zero* could claim the legitimacy that only democratic politics can confer. That is why, if there is a viable model for reducing the number of malnourished and undernourished people in the world, it is to be found neither in technoutopian promises nor in revolutionary ones. Locke said of reason that it was a "dim candle," but that it was all we had. The same can be said about the state in the twenty-first century.

Acknowledgments

Any book, but particularly one that has taken as long to write as this one has, involves the accumulation of debts that, once accrued, can never properly be discharged.

Just as in the expression of condolence, in the expression of gratitude one comes up hard against the limits of language. But let me at least name some names.

Over the six years it took me to write *The Reproach of Hunger*, I was blessed to have interlocutors who became friends, and friendly acquaintances who became friends of the heart. In this latter camp, it is my honor to include Biraj Patnaik and Harsh Mander in Delhi, Paul Durcan, Rosemary Byrne, Kevin O'Rourke, Tom Arnold, Gillian Davidson, Cormac Ó Gráda, Máire Ní Chiosáin, and Bernard Treacy in Dublin, and Jim Fahy in Galway. Cormac Ó Gráda has far, far better things to do with his time, but he nonetheless devoted what I fear was too much of it to reading this book in draft; his comments were invaluable. And Tom Arnold paid me the ultimate compliment of holding steadfast to the brotherly love and loyalty we share despite the fact that there is much in this book he could not but find wrongheaded, and, indeed, more than wrongheaded.

I also want to thank David Singh Grewal, and the members of his seminar group at Yale, for reading and commenting on a draft of this book. And I am fortunate to have Talli Somekh for a friend. Over the years, our many conversations on the subjects treated in this book were not only humanly sustaining but time and time again challenged me to reconsider my own views.

Finally, I could quite simply never have written *The Reproach of Hunger* without Megan Campisi's help. She is a peerless researcher, a superb logistician, and a determined fact-checker. My debt to her is incalculable.

I am now in my sixties and it is no exaggeration to say that I could not have had the career I've had without the love and support of Alice Mayhew, Andrew Wylie, and Tracy Bohan. Meister Eckhart wrote somewhere that, "If the only prayer you ever say in your whole life is 'thank you,' that would suffice." I wish I could believe that. But what I do believe is that it's a start.

Notes

INTRODUCTION

1. Rajiv Shah, "Foreword," in Gordon Conway, *One Billion Hungry: Can We Feed the World?* (Ithaca, NY: Cornell University Press, 2012), ix.

2. "The Cost of Food: Facts and Figures," BBC News, October 16, 2008, news.bbc.co.uk/2/hi/7284196.stm.

3. Some environmental activists believed at the time that Nargis was an example of the kind of extreme weather caused by global climate change.

4. World Bank, "World Bank Warns Against Complacency amid High Food Prices and Hunger," press release, November 29, 2012, www.worldbank.org/en/news/press-release/2012/11/29/world-bank-warns-against-complacency-amid-high-food-prices-hunger.

5. Could this conventional wisdom prove mistaken in the way that the conventional wisdom of the last part of the twentieth century had proved to be in error? It is theoretically possible, of course, but the early assumptions were based in large measure on not paying enough attention to the realities of the global food system—one thing that one can say with confidence is not so today.

6. Charles Kenny, *Getting Better: Why Global Development Is Succeeding—And How We Can Improve the World Even More* (New York: Basic Books, 2011), 11.

7. Shah, "Foreword," ix.

8. Michael Pollan, "How to Feed the World," *Newsweek*, May 19, 2008.

9. Timothy Wise, "If We Want Food to Remain Cheap We Need to Stop Putting It in Our Cars," *Guardian*, September 5, 2012.

10. John Vidal, "UN Warns of Looming Worldwide Food Crisis in 2013," *Guardian,* October 13, 2012.

11. Obesity and its baneful effects on health were once thought to have been the exception—a problem of plenty from which the poor were spared. But this is no longer the case.

12. Cormac, Ó Gráda, *Eating People is Wrong and Other Essays on Famine, its Past, and its Future* (Princeton: Princeton University Press, 2015).

13. "Growing Influx: Germany Caught Off Guard by Surge in Refugees," *Spiegel* Online, July 7, 2014, www.spiegel.de/international/germany /surge-in-refugees-catches-german-leaders-off-guard-a-979633.html.

14. Branko Milanovic, *The Have and the Have-Nots: A Brief and Idiosyncratic History of Global Inequality* (New York: Basic Books, 2011), 124.

15. Andrew Shepherd et al., "The Geography of Poverty, Disasters and Climate Extremes in 2030." Overseas Development Institute, research report, October 2013, www.odi.org/publications/7491-geography -poverty-disasters-climate-change-2030.

16. This is in stark contrast to the general public's considerably less sanguine view, suggested by polling data, about what can realistically be done.

17. Francis Fukuyama, "The End of History," *The National Interest*, summer 1989.

CHAPTER ONE: A BETTER WORLD FINALLY WITHIN REACH?

1. Eric Holt-Giménez, "The World Food Crisis: What's Behind It and What We Can Do About It," Food First policy brief no. 16, October 1, 2008, foodfirst.org/publication/the-world-food-crisis-whats-behind -it-and-what-we-can-do-about-it.

2. Bill Gates, "Gates to Students: Don't Try to Be a Billionaire, It's Overrated," GeekWire, October 27, 2011.

3. One of the stranger aspects of development rhetoric, particularly at the bank and in the UN system, is its implacable optimism regarding the end of poverty in virtually all its public pronouncements *except* those concerned with climate change: these tend to a deep alarmism. Reconciling these two discourses is virtually impossible.

4. Olivier de Schutter, "The Transformative Potential of the Right to Food," Final Report of the Special Rapporteur on the Right to Food, UN Human Rights Council, A/HRC/25/57, January 24, 2014, ap.ohchr.org/documents/dpage_e.aspx?si=A/HRC/25/57.

5. Olivier de Schutter, "Democratizing the Millennium Development Goals," Online.Syndicate. 18 Session at University of Washington-rary. 2000.Project Syndicate, September 18, 2010, www.project-syndicate.org/commentary/democratizing-the-millennium-development-goals.

6. Jeffrey Sachs, *The End of Poverty: Economic Possibilities for Our Time* (New York: Penguin, 2005), 352.

CHAPTER TWO: THE WAGES OF OPTIMISM

1. Josué de Castro, *The Geography of Hunger* (Boston: Little, Brown, 1952), 139.

2. Lillian M. Li, *Fighting Famine in North China: State, Market, and Environmental Decline, 1690s–1990s* (Stanford, CA: Stanford University Press, 2007), 2.

3. Li, *Fighting Famine in North China*, 6. Although Lillian Li has argued that unlike in early modern Europe where food riots were frequent, "food did not become the subject of political struggle until the twentieth century."

4. This is the backstory to the fact that the UN's food agencies are all based in Rome, including of course the Food and Agriculture Organization (FAO), of which the IIA was a precursor.

5. "United Nations Food Conference Convenes in Hot Springs, Virginia," *Life*, May 31, 1943, 15.

6. In 1965, the Economic Research Service of the US Department of Agriculture forecast a famine in Bihar in 1966, and the Johnson administration later took credit for having averted it. The Indian government dismissed this claim, though it did acknowledge a very substantial food deficit. In any case, no famine occurred.

7. Amartya Sen, "The Truth about the Bengal Famine," *New York Review of Books*, March 24, 2011.

8. Sen, "Truth about the Bengal Famine."

9. Cormac O'Grada, "The End of Hunger," *Foreign Policy*, June 20, 2011.

10. Walter Isaacson, "In Search of the Real Bill Gates," *Time*, January 13, 1997.

11. Bill Gates, "Dream with a Deadline: The Millennium Development Goals," *Gates Notes*, September 18, 2013, www.gatesnotes.com /Development/MDGs-Dream-with-a-Deadline.

12. Bono, "Bringing the Statistics of Death to Life," World Association of Newspapers, May 1, 2004, www.atu2.com/news/bringing-the -statistics-of-death-to-life.html.

13. Kate Nash, "Global Citizenship as Show Business: The Cultural Politics of Make Poverty History," *Media Culture Society* 30, no. 2 (March 2008): 167–81.

14. As Duncan Green, a senior advisor to Oxfam UK, put it on his "Poverty Power" blog, "in come tax dodging, biofuels, agriculture, and nutrition, out go trade and debt."

15. Kate Nash, "Global Citizenship as Show Business."

16. Daphne Eviatar, "Spend $150 Billion Per Year to Cure World Poverty," *New York Times*, November 7, 2004.

CHAPTER THREE: MALTHUS ONLY NEEDS TO BE WRONG ONCE

1. Kofi Annan, "How to Achieve Millennium Development Goals," *Korea Times*, September 2010, kofiannanfoundation.org/newsroom /news/2010/09/how-to-achieve-millennium-development-goals.

2. Roy Porter, ed., *Cambridge History of Medicine* (New York: Cambridge University Press, 2006), 214.

3. Sachs, *End of Poverty*, 3.

4. John Maynard Keynes, "Economic Possibilities for Our Grandchildren," *Essays in Persuasion* (London: Macmillan, 1935).

5. In 1950, the population of Europe was twice that of Africa's. By 2050, the position will have been reversed.

6. Sachs, *End of Poverty*, 326.

7. Nina Munk, *The Idealist: Jeffrey Sachs and the Quest to End Poverty* (New York: Random House, 2013).

8. Peter Gill, *Famine and Foreigners: Ethiopia Since Live Aid* (Oxford: Oxford University Press, 2010).

9. Melinda Gates, "Celebrating Women and the Dignity of Family Planning," *Huffington Post*, November 11, 2013.

10. Sachs, *End of Poverty*, 1.

11. Sabine Alkire, Jose Manuel Roche, and Andy Sumner, "Where Do the World's Multidimensionally Poor People Live?" Oxford Poverty & Human Development Initiative Working Paper No 61, March 2013, 12, www.ophi.org.uk/wp-content/uploads/ophi-wp-61.pdf.

12. Andy Sumner, "Where Do the Poor Live? An Update," Institute of Development Studies, University of Sussex, July 2011.

13. Sachs, *End of Poverty*, 3.

14. John Maynard Keynes, *The Economic Consequences of Peace* (New York: Harcourt, Brace and Howe, 1919), I.3.

15. Sylvia Nasar, *Grand Pursuit: The Story of Economic Genius* (New York: Simon and Schuster, 2011), 309.

16. John Gray, *Gray's Anatomy: Selected Writings* (London: Penguin, 2009), chap. 19.

17. John Gray, "The Atheist Delusion," *Guardian*, March 14, 2008.

18. Sachs, *End of Poverty*, 78.

19. Sachs, *End of Poverty*, 75.

20. Munk, *Idealist*.

21. Gary Finnegan, "We Can Beat Polio," *Vaccines Today*, October 21, 2013, www.vaccinestoday.eu/vaccines/we-can-beat-polio.

22. Sumner, "Where Do the Poor Live?"

23. World Bank, "Unfinished Business: Mobilizing New Efforts to Achieve the 2015 Millennium Development Goals," September

2010, background paper prepared for the United Nations Millennium Development Goals Summit, www.worldbank.org/mdgs/MDG PaperFINALSeptember102010.pdf.

24. MDG Gap Task Force, "The Global Partnership for Development: Making Rhetoric a Reality," United Nations, 2012, www.un.org /millenniumgoals/2012_Gap_Report/MDG_2012Gap_Task_Force _report.pdf.

25. United Nations, "The Millennium Development Goals Report," 2011, www.un.org/millenniumgoals/pdf/(2011_E)%20MDG%20 Report%202011_Book%20LR.pdf.

26. Dani Rodrik, "After the Millennium Development Goals." Project Syndicate, September 10, 2012, www.project-syndicate.org/commentary /after-the-millennium-development-goals-by-dani-rodrik.

27. William Easterly, "A Modest Proposal," review of *The End of Poverty* by Jeffrey Sachs, *Washington Post*, March 13, 2005.

28. Rodrik, "After the Millennium Development Goals."

29. Hans Magnus Enzensberger, *Critical Essays: Hans Magnus Enzensberger* (New York: Continuum, 1982), 233.

30. Walden Bello, *La fabrique de la famine* (Paris: CarnetsNord, 2012), introduction.

CHAPTER FOUR: THE FOOD CRISIS OF 2007–2008: A TURNING POINT?

1. Like Margaret Sanger, the founder of Planned Parenthood, both Vogt and Osborn were profoundly influenced by the racist pseudoscience of eugenics, which, much to the discomfiture of contemporary environmentalists, was also hugely influential in the creation of the environmental movement.

2. Norman Borlaug, "The Green Revolution, Peace, and Humanity," Nobel Lecture, December 11, 1970, www.nobelprize.org/nobel _prizes/peace/laureates/1970/borlaug-lecture.html.

3. Norman Borlaug, "The Green Revolution Revisited and the Road Ahead," thirtieth anniversary lecture, Norwegian Nobel Institute, Oslo, September 8, 2000, www.nobelprize.org/nobel_prizes/peace /laureates/1970/borlaug-lecture.pdf.

4. "The Future We Want," outcome document adopted at Rio+20, United Nations Conference on Sustainable Development, Rio de Janeiro, June 22, 2012, www.uncsd2012.org/content/documents /727The%20Future%20We%20Want%2019%20June%201230 pm.pdf.

5. Jean-Hervé Bradol, "Malnutrition au Sahel: Les grandes avancées dans le domaine de la santé n'ont jamais été obtenues aux conditions initiales du marché," interview in *Issues de secours, un blog participative, animé par trois membres de Médecins Sans Frontières*, July 9, 2012. The original quote is "Ces messages amalgament 'ceux qui ont faim' et 'ceux qui meurent de faim.'"

6. Pedro Olinto and Hiroki Uematsu, "The State of the Poor: Where Are the Poor and Where Are the Poorest?," Poverty Reduction and Equity Department, World Bank, April 17, 2013, www.worldbank .org/content/dam/Worldbank/document/State_of_the_poor_paper _April17.pdf.

7. Steve Wiggins, "Pro-Poor Growth and Development," Overseas Development Institute briefing paper no. 33, January 2008, www.odi .org/sites/odi.org.uk/files/odi-assets/publications-opinion-files/825 .pdf.

8. Jim Yong Kim, "Warmer World Will Trap Millions in Poverty," video interview, World Bank, June 13, 2013, YouTube, www.youtube.com /watch?feature=player_embedded&v=REFEgy6jUVU.

9. Jim Yong Kim, "Remarks on Climate Change," YouTube, November 19, 2012, www.youtube.com/watch?v=YO9uGejvS3Q.

10. Jim Yong Kim, "Let's Be the Generation That Ends Poverty," *Huffington Post*, September 27, 2013. See also "The End of Poverty. Really? Jim Yong Kim in an Interview with CNN's Richard Quest," World Bank Online, October 9, 2013, live.worldbank.org/the-end -of-poverty-jim-kim-richard-quest-cnn.

11. World Food Programme, "How High Food Prices Affect the World's Poor," September 4, 2012, www.wfp.org/stories/how-high-food-prices -affect-worlds-poor.

12. Economic Research Service, United States Department of Agriculture, Food Expenditures data set, Table 7, "Food Expenditures by

Families and Individuals as a Share of Disposable Personal Income," December 1, 2014, www.ers.usda.gov/datafiles/Food_Expenditures /Food_Expenditures/table7.xls.

13. Derek Headey and Shenggen Fan, "Global Food Crisis. How Did It Happen? How Has It Hurt? And How Can We Prevent the Next One?," International Food Policy Research Institute research monograph 165, 2010, 101, www.ifpri.org/sites/default/files/publications /rr165.pdf.

CHAPTER FIVE: THE GLOBAL FOOD SYSTEM AND ITS CRITICS

1. Sachs, *End of Poverty*, 351,
2. Sachs, *End of Poverty*, 368.
3. Gilbert Rist, *The History of Development from Western Origins to Global Faith*, 3rd ed. (London: Zed Books, 2008), 33.
4. Sachs, *End of Poverty*, 355.
5. Sachs, *End of Poverty*, 357.
6. Sachs, *End of Poverty*, 357.
7. Joachim von Braun and Eugenio Diaz-Bonilla, "Globalization of Food and Agriculture and the Poor," IFPRI Issue Brief 52, September 2008, 6, www.ifpri.org/sites/default/files/publications/ib52.pdf. In fairness, a minority of mainstream voices were open to a more wide-ranging dialogue. As Joachim von Braun, the director general of IFPRI, and Eugenio Diaz-Bonilla of the Inter-American Development Bank put it in their book *Globalization of Food and Agriculture and the Poor*, "Economic analyses of the realities of poverty and food insecurity and their causes must be coupled with ethical reflection on current social and economic structures."
8. Olivier de Schutter, "Report Submitted by the Special Rapporteur on the Right to Food, Olivier de Schutter," United Nations Human Rights Council, December 26, 2011, www.ohchr.org/Documents /HRBodies/HRCouncil/RegularSession/Session19/A-HRC-19-59 _en.pdf.
9. De Schutter, "Report Submitted by the Special Rapporteur."
10. De Schutter, "Report Submitted by the Special Rapporteur on Food."

11. Sachs, *End of Poverty*, 358.
12. David Cleveland, *Balancing on a Planet: The Future of Food and Agriculture* (Berkeley: University of California Press, 2014), 207.
13. Right to Food and Nutrition Watch, "Alternatives and Resistance to Policies That Generate Hunger," October 2013, 10, www.fian.org /fileadmin/media/publications/Watch_2013_eng_WEB_final.pdf.
14. "Declaration of Nyéléni," Declaration of the Forum for Food Sovereignty, February 27, 2007, nyeleni.org/spip.php?article290.
15. Right to Food and Nutrition Watch, "Alternatives and Resistance to Policies that Generate Hunger," 10.
16. Walden Bello, "Foreword," in Eric Holt-Giménez and Raj Patel, *Food Rebellions: Crisis and the Hunger for Justice* (Cape Town: Food First Books, 2009).
17. Jeffrey Sachs, "Global Food Systems: Their Impact on Nutrition and Health for All," Earth Institute, Columbia University, September 16, 2008, web.archive.org/web/20100614015015/http://earth.columbia .edu/flashvideos/Food_09-08/?id=33.
18. Right to Food and Nutrition Watch, "Alternatives and Resistance to Policies that Generate Hunger," 92.
19. Tira Foran et al., "Taking Complexity in Food Systems Seriously: An Interdisciplinary Analysis," *World Development* 61 (September 2014): 85–101.
20. Sachs, "Global Food Systems."
21. Steve Wiggins, Sharada Keats, and Edward Clay, "International Rapid Responses to the Global Food Crisis of 2007/08," Overseas Development Institute, London, 2011, 7, www.odi.org/sites/odi.org .uk/files/odi-assets/publications-opinion-files/7632.pdf.
22. Alex Evans, "The Feeding of the Nine Billion: Global Food Security for the 21st Century," Chatham House, London, January 22, 2009, www .globaldashboard.org/2009/01/26/the-feeding-of-the-nine-billion.

CHAPTER SIX: PROMISES TO THE POOR

1. Colin Leys, *The Rise and Fall of Development Theory* (Oxford: James Currey, 1977), 141.

2. Sachs, "Global Food Systems."

3. Judith Dean, S. Desai, and J. Riedel, "Trade Policy Reform in Developing Countries since 1985: A Review of the Evidence," World Bank Discussion Paper No. 267, 1994, 97, quoted in Jeffrey Sachs and Andrew Warner, "Sources of Slow Growth in African Economies," *Journal of African Economies* 6, no. 3 (December 1997): 27.

4. "Free Trade, Loss of Support Systems Crippling Food Production in Africa," News and Research Communications, Oregon State University, February 15, 2010, oregonstate.edu/ua/ncs/archives/2010/feb /free-trade-loss-support-systems-crippling-food-production-africa, quoting William Moseley, Judith Carney, and Laurence Becker, "Neoliberal Policy, Rural Livelihoods and Urban Food Security in West Africa: A Comparative Study of the Gambia, Côte d'Ivoire, and Mali," *Proceedings of the National Academy of Sciences* 107, no. 13 (2010): 5774–5779.

5. Ha-Joon Chang, response to Martin Wolf's review of Chang's *Bad Samaritans*, August 3, 2007, www.cepr.net/documents/publications /FT_HaJoon.pdf.

6. Manitra Rakotoarisoa, Massimo Iafrate, and Marianna Paschali, "Why Has Africa Become a Net Food Importer? Explaining Africa Agricultural and Food Trade Deficits," Trade and Markets Division, Food and Agriculture Organization, Rome, 2011, 1, www.fao.org /docrep/015/i2497e/i2497e00.pdf.

7. Rakotoarisoa, Iafrate, and Paschali, "Why Has Africa Become a Net Food Importer?," 1.

8. Rakotoarisoa, Iafrate, and Paschali, "Why Has Africa Become a Net Food Importer?," 52.

9. Roger Riddell, *Does Foreign Aid Really Work?* (Oxford: Oxford University Press, 2007).

10. Nora McKeon, "Global Governance for World Food Security: A Scorecard Four Years after the Eruption of the 'Food Crisis,'" report for Heinrich-Böll-Stiftung, Berlin, October 2011, 4, www.boell.de /sites/default/files/Global-Governance-for-World-Food-Security .pdf.

11. Gilles van Kote, "Prix agricoles: le G20 envisage de convoquer le

Forum de réaction rapide," *Le Monde*, August 13, 2012. The original quote is: " 'Le Forum doit permettre aux pays de se parler pour éviter de prendre des décisions individuelles qui soient collectivement non rationnelles,' résume-t-on au ministère français de l'agriculture, où l'on reconnaît toutefois s'interroger sur les effets que pourrait avoir sur les marchés l'annonce d'une telle convocation." The communiqué is at "Full Text—G20 Cannes Summit Communiqué," Reuters, November 4, 2011, www.reuters.com/article/2011/11/04/g20 -communique-idUSP6E7K902Z20111104.

12. Van Kote, "Prix agricoles."

13. Terence Corcoran, "The UN Carbon Fiasco," *Financial Post*, October 4, 2010.

14. CGIAR, "History of CGIAR," www.cgiar.org/who-we-are/history -of-cgiar.

15. Ammar Siamwalla and Alberto Valdés, "Food Insecurity in Developing Countries," *Food Policy* 5, 4, November 1980.

16. "Alden Winship 'Tom' Clausen," Archives, World Bank, go.worldbank .org/DG1E29A900.

17. Stuart Corbridge, ed., *Development: Critical Concepts in the Social Sciences* (London: Routledge, 2000), 3:356.

18. Walden Bello and Shalmali Guttal, "The Limits of Reform: The Wolfensohn Era at the World Bank," Focus on the Global South, focusweb.org/node/604. The authors note that much of their report is drawn from Walden Bello, *Dilemmas of Domination: The Unmaking of the American Empire* (New York: Henry Holt, 2005).

19. Dambisa Moyo, *Dead Aid: Why Aid Is Not Working and How There Is a Better Way for Africa* (New York: Farrar, Straus and Giroux, 2009), 20.

CHAPTER SEVEN: CASSANDRA AND DOCTOR PANGLOSS

1. Rist, *History of Development*, 76.

2. Rist, *History of Development*, 76.

3. Rist, *History of Development*, 77.

4. Rist, *History of Development*, 77.

5. Leys, *Rise and Fall of Development Theory*, 117.

6. World Bank, *Adjustment in Africa: Reforms, Results, and the Road Ahead* (Oxford: Oxford University Press, 1994), 77.

7. Agriculture and Natural Resources Team, UK Department for International Development, "Official Development Assistance to Agriculture," November 2004, 3, dfid-agriculture-consultation.nri.org /summaries/wp9.pdf.

8. Jean Ziegler, *Destruction massive: Géopolitique de la faim* (Paris: Éditions du Seuil, 2011).

9. Vandana Shiva, *Soil Not Oil: Environmental Justice in an Age of Climate Crisis* (Brooklyn, NY: South End Press, 2008).

10. Joachim Von Braun and Eugenio Diaz-Bonilla, eds., *Globalization of Food and Agriculture and the Poor* (New Delhi: Oxford University Press, 2007), 296.

11. Arun Gupta, e-mail to David Rieff, August 24, 2012.

12. World Bank, *Adjustment in Africa*, xi.

13. World Bank, *Adjustment in Africa*, 17.

14. World Bank, *Adjustment in Africa*, 43.

15. World Bank, Pro-Poor Growth, econ.worldbank.org/external/default /main?theSitePK=477894&contentMDK=20292184&menuPK =545573&pagePK=64168182&piPK=64168060.

16. Max Planck, quoted in a letter to Wilhelm Wien, February 27, 1909, in J. L. Heilbron, *The Dilemmas of an Upright Man: Max Planck as Spokesman for German Science* (Berkeley: University of California Press, 1986), 8.

17. Nick Cullather, *The Hungry World* (Cambridge, MA: Harvard University Press, 2010), 1.

CHAPTER EIGHT: IS REFORMING THE SYSTEM ENOUGH?

1. Robert W. Herdt, "The Life and Work of Norman Borlaug, Nobel Laureate," speech in College Station, Texas, January 14, 1998, www .rockefellerfoundation.org/uploads/files/40e4f901-005d-425b -bd36-7c5913a5ac4d-98borlaug.pdf.

2. Borlaug, "Green Revolution, Peace, and Humanity."

3. The same revolving door between government and top-tier philanthropy can be seen at the Gates Foundation today, where Rajiv Shah moved from running the Gates agriculture programs to USAID and Sylvia Matthews could go from being CEO of the foundation to President Obama's choice as Secretary of Health and Human Services.

4. Lambert Mbom, "World Bank: 'Structural Adjustment Programmes Worked in Africa,'" *Think Africa Press*, May 7, 2013, thinkafricapress .com/development/world-bank-devarajan.

5. Sarah K. Lowder and Brian Carisma, "Financial Resource Flows to Agriculture: A Review of Data on Government Spending, Official Development Assistance and Foreign Direct Investment," ESA working paper no. 11–19, Food and Agriculture Organization, December 2011, www.fao.org/3/a-an108e.pdf.

6. Shantayanan Devarajan, "This Is How Structural Adjustment Policies Worked in Africa—a Rejoinder to Carlos Lopes," *Think Africa Press*, November 29, 2013, www.thinkafricapress.com/economy /structural-adjustment-programmes-and-africa-rejoinder-shantanayan -devarajan.

7. Anup Shah, "Structural Adjustment—A Major Cause of Poverty," Global Issues, last updated March 24, 2013, www.globalissues.org /article/3/structural-adjustment-a-major-cause-of-poverty.

8. De Schutter, "Report Submitted by the Special Rapporteur on the Right to Food," 4.

9. Gates Foundation, "Agricultural Development: Strategy Overview," 2011, 2, www.gatesfoundation.org/agriculturaldevelopment /Documents/agricultural-development-strategy-overview.pdf.

10. One of the most frustrating aspects of the pro-GMO argument is its utter lack of respect for culture and tradition. In a lab, one can establish that a new process or refinement of a process is an unqualified improvement. What the pro-GMO camp doesn't understand is that culture doesn't work (in both senses of the word) that way, that its values, and, for that matter, its *value*, are not quantifiable.

11. "Stiglitz: Time to Snuff the IMF?," edited version of interview with Joseph Stiglitz, conducted by Doug Henwood, WBAI, New York,

August 15, 2002, reprinted in *Left Business Observer* 102 (September 2002), www.leftbusinessobserver.com/Stiglitz.html.

12. Franco Moretti and Dominique Pestre, "World Bankspeak," *New Left Review* 92, March–April 2015, 81.

13. Easterly believes that this was not just a function of the SAP but of the development project as it was (to him, wrongly) conceived from the beginning. Whether his own preferred solutions would achieve better outcomes today at least is impossible to know. What is clear is that both in their conception and in the way they would have to be implemented, they are almost wholly incompatible with the Gates-style technocratic fixes plus good governance that constitutes the current conventional wisdom among donors.

14. International Fund for Agricultural Development, "Food Prices: Smallholder Farmers Can Be Part of the Solution," www.ifad.org/operations/food/farmer.htm.

15. Saleemul Huq, "Climate Impacts Are Here. Time to Talk?," Thomson Reuters Foundation, May 12, 2014, www.trust.org/item/20140512132633-cnx8t.

16. Ban Ki-moon, "Secretary-General's Remarks to the Climate Change Conference (UNFCCC COP19/CMP9) High-Level Segment," Warsaw, November 19, 2013, www.un.org/sg/statements/index.asp?nid=7290.

17. Jim Yong Kim, "Tackling the Most Difficult Problems: Infrastructure, Ebola and Climate Change," speech at the IMF/World Bank Annual Meetings 2014, Washington, DC, October 10, 2014.

18. Larry Elliot, "Climate Change Will 'Lead to Battles for Food,' Says Head of World Bank," *Guardian*, April 3, 2014.

19. Sachs, *End of Poverty*, 364.

20. Changhua Wu, "The Coming Heat Age," Project Syndicate, November 28, 2013, www.project-syndicate.org/commentary/changhua-wu-recommends-three-measures-to-limit-global-warming-by-2100.

21. World Economic Forum, "Global Risks 2014: Ninth Edition," Geneva, 2014, 13.

22. World Economic Forum, "Global Risks 2014: Ninth Edition," 9.

23. Joshua Kurlantzick, *Democracy in Retreat: The Revolt of the Middle Class and the Worldwide Decline of Representative Government* (New Haven, CT: Yale University Press, 2014), 29.

CHAPTER NINE: THE CASE FOR OPTIMISM

1. Swaziland, Lesotho, and some areas of South Africa are partial exceptions to this general conclusion. But while HIV/AIDS has and continues to have a catastrophic effect on people's lives in many countries, and has made the interlinked problems of poverty and ill health much worse wherever its prevalence has been significant, in terms of reducing overall population it has been comparatively insignificant. Since the 1980s, some 20 million people are thought to have died of AIDS. But this world-historical tragedy represents less than a third of the population rise expected in 2013 alone.
2. George Monbiot, "The Poor Get Stuffed," *Guardian*, December 24, 2002.
3. David C. Taylor-Robinson et al., "Re: Child Poverty and Malnutrition Rise in Spain as Austerity Measures Bite," *British Medical Journal* 347 (2013): f5261, doi: dx.doi.org/10.1136/bmj.f5261.
4. Bread for the World, "About U.S. Hunger," www.bread.org/hunger /us.
5. Bread for the World, "Hungry for Change: Vote to End Hunger," fact sheet, 2014, files.bread.org/elections2014/National.pdf.
6. A few American political figures, notably former New York City mayor Michael Bloomberg, have tried to impose very mild constraints on the sales of these drinks. These commonsense efforts have been widely derided in America as impingements on liberty (as if the advertising juggernaut behind this consumption did not exist). The reaction is almost as perverse as the seeming impossibility in the United States of imposing any serious limits on the private possession of firearms.
7. Alan Berg, "Sliding toward Nutrition Malpractice: Time to Reconsider and Redeploy," *American Journal of Clinical Nutrition* 13 (1993): 3, 5.

8. Alan Berg, "New and Noteworthy in Nutrition (No. 7)," memorandum, World Bank International Finance Corporation, November 3, 1989, www-wds.worldbank.org/external/default/WDSContentServer /WDSP/IB/2013/06/13/000442464_20130613144758/Rendered /INDEX/783710NEWS0New00Box377317B00PUBLIC0.txt.

9. One of the signature conceits of democratic capitalism is to be the only major ideology in the history of the world not to concede it is an ideology at all but just common sense—a stance one of its most important variants, the human rights movement, takes to an astonishing extreme.

10. Sachs, *End of Poverty*, 347.

11. Berg, "Sliding toward Nutrition Malpractice," 3.

12. Alan Berg, "The Nutrition Factor: Its Role in National Development," Brookings Institution, Washington, DC, 1973.

13. Sally Grantham-McGregor et al., "Developmental Potential in the First 5 Years for Children in Developing Countries," *Lancet* 369, no. 9555 (2007): 60–70.

14. Grantham-McGregor et al., "Developmental Potential in the First 5 Years."

15. Tom Arnold, "Too Much at Stake: The G8's Responsibility to Tackle Child Hunger," *Huffington Post*, May 16, 2012.

16. Jamie Drummond, "Scrutinizing ONE's 'Secret Sauce' for Global Social Change," *Stanford Social Innovation Review*, May 16, 2012, www.ssireview.org/blog/entry/scrutinizing_ones_secret_sauce_for _global_social_change.

17. Drummond, "Scrutinizing ONE's 'Secret Sauce' for Global Social Change."

CHAPTER TEN: SCIENCE TO THE RESCUE?

1. Sachs, *End of Poverty*, 368.

2. Concern Worldwide, "The Time Is Now: Improving Food Security and Nutrition for the Poorest," 2012, 1, www.concernusa.org /media/pdf/2011/06/FINAL_Hunger_Broch.pdf.

3. Concern Worldwide, "The Time Is Now."

4. Since the turn of the century, the issue of the role of business in general, and multinational corporations in particular, has come to the fore as one of the central issues in the debate over what needs to be done to end extreme poverty and hunger, and I shall return to examine it in detail further in this book.

5. Nick Cullather, "The Foreign Policy of the Calorie," *American Historical Review* 112, no. 2 (2007): 337–364.

6. Cullather, "The Foreign Policy of the Calorie."

7. Cullather, "The Foreign Policy of the Calorie."

8. Donald McLaren, "The Great Protein Fiasco," *Lancet* 304, no. 7872 (1974): 93–96.

9. Ted Greiner, "Vitamin A Wars: the Downside of Donor-Driven Aid," *Independent Science News.* September 24, 2012, www.independent sciencenews.org/health/vitamin-a-wars-the-downsides-of-donor -driven-aid/.

10. The controversy over both the safety and utility of GMOs plays a role in the debates over the reform of the global food system that is entirely out of proportion to the modest role GMOs now play in it, and for the moment represent the hopes of those who support them and the fears of those who do not about what their eventual effect will be.

11. Justus Wesseler, Scott Kaplan, and David Zilberman, "The Cost of Delaying Approval of Golden Rice," *Agricultural and Resource Economics Update* 17, no. 3 (January/February 2014).

12. International Rice Research Institute, "What Is the Status of the Golden Rice Project Coordinated by IRRI?," irri.org/golden-rice/faqs /what-is-the-status-of-the-golden-rice-project-coordinated-by-irri.

13. 2008 SUN movement draft policy document, private communication to author.

14. Ban Ki-moon, "In World of Plenty, No One Should Be Malnourished, Secretary-General Tells Meeting on Nutrition, Recalling His Own Pledge to End 'Hidden Disgrace of Stunting,'" press release, United Nations, September 27, 2012, www.un.org/press/en/2012 /sgsm14549.doc.htm.

15. A case in point is British Petroleum, which in 2010 made the corporate decision to "re-brand" itself as dedicated "to bringing brilliant

minds together with technology at a massive scale to meet the world's energy needs"—a catchphrase that, if you substitute "ending poverty" for "meet[ing] the world's energy needs," encapsulates the mission of the Gates Foundation as it itself defines it.

16. Tom Arnold, "Passing the Torch of Political Commitment to Reduce Hunger," Concern USA, August 10, 2012, blogs.concernusa.org /category/1000-days.

17. "UN Chief Hails Progress in Scaling Up Maternal and Child Nutrition Worldwide," press release, UN News Centre, September 27, 2012, www.un.org/apps/news/story.asp?NewsID=43084#.VPP nEo6iQYE.

18. United Nations, "Millennium Development Goals: 2012 Progress Chart," www.un.org/millenniumgoals/pdf/2012_Progress_E.pdf.

19. Sachs, *End of Poverty*. 1.

20. Lawrence Haddad, "The African Nutrition Congress: Declare the End of the 22nd Century Mindset," IFPRI Development Horizons, October 3, 2012, www.developmenthorizons.com/2012/10/the-african -nutrition-congress-declare.html.

21. Borlaug, "Green Revolution, Peace, and Humanity."

22. In a later chapter, I try to analyze in more depth Gates's "solutionism," to use the critic Evgeny Morozov's term for the reigning ideology of Silicon Valley.

23. Gordon Conway and Jeff Waage, *Science and Innovation for Development* (London: UK Collaborative on Development Sciences, 2010), 363.

24. Conway and Waage, *Science and Innovation for Development*, 363.

25. Gordon Conway, *The Doubly Green Revolution* (London: Penguin, 1997).

26. One can only hope that with the projections of population increase being what they are, the development world will be compelled to think seriously about demography sooner rather than later. Europe's nonresponse in other than immediate humanitarian terms to the exodus of sub-Saharan Africans from Libya to Sicily in the summer of 2014 was an emblem of the rich world's inability to think through the implications of demographically fueled mass immigration; it is not a hopeful sign.

27. Here Stein is quoting a phrase from one of my e-mails to him.
28. Jon Butterworth, "Science Is Not Political, Except When It Is," *Guardian*, December 26, 2012.
29. Ian Scoones, "GM Crops: Continuing Controversy," *Zimbabweland* blog, June 9, 2012, zimbabweland.wordpress.com/2014/06/09/gm -crops-continuing-controversy.
30. Scoones, "GM Crops: Continuing Controversy."
31. Dominic Glover, "Undying Promise: Agricultural Biotechnology's Pro-poor Narrative, Ten Years On." Social, Technological and Environmental Pathways to Sustainability Centre working paper 15, 2009, 43.
32. Glover, "Undying Promise," 43.
33. Glover, "Undying Promise," 43.

CHAPTER ELEVEN: FALLING IN LOVE WITH THE PRIVATE SECTOR

1. Shenggen Fan, "Food Policy in 2013: Nutrition Grabs the Spotlight as Hunger Persists," in Andrew Marble and Heidi Fritschel, eds., *2013 Global Food Policy Report* (Washington, DC: IFPRI, 2014), 1–14.
2. The United States was something of an exception to this rule. There, most of the major NGOs had developed much deeper links with the American government than their Western European counterparts had done with theirs. In Vietnam, for example, the International Rescue Committee (IRC), one of the biggest US development NGOs, was often sardonically referred to by journalists as IRCIA, and not without reason.
3. Elizabeth Ferris, "Faith-Based and Secular Humanitarian Organizations," *International Review of the Red Cross* 87, no. 858 (June 2005): 317.
4. Rajiv Shah and Karen Turner, "2010 VOLAG Report of Voluntary Agencies," USAID, 2010, pdf.usaid.gov/pdf_docs/PNADT627.pdf.
5. Michael Edwards, "Have NGOs Made a Difference? From Manchester to Birmingham with an Elephant in the Room," Global Policy Research Group, GPRG-WPS-028, 2005, www.gprg.org/pubs /workingpapers/pdfs/gprg-wps-028.pdf.

6. David Lewis, "Development Policy and Development NGOs: The Changing Relationship," *Social Policy and Administration* 32, no. 5 (December 1998): 501–512.

7. Lewis, "Development Policy and Development NGOs," 502.

8. World Bank, "Involving Nongovernmental Organizations in World Bank–Supported Activities," Operational Directive 14.70, August 28, 1989, World Bank Operating Manual, www.gdrc.org/ngo/wb -ngo-directive.html.

9. Michael Edwards and David Hulme, eds., *Making a Difference: NGOs and Development in a Changing World* (London: Earthscan, 1992), 20.

10. David Hulme and Michael Edwards, "Conclusion: Too Close to the Powerful, Too Far from the Powerless?," in David Hulme and Michael Edwards, eds., *NGOs, States and Donors: Too Close for Comfort?* (New York: St. Martin's Press, 1997), 275–284.

11. Edwards, "Have NGOs Made a Difference?"

12. Erinch Sahan, "Aid and the Private Sector: A Love Story," *Oxfam Blogs,* February 11, 2013, oxfamblogs.org/fp2p/aid-and-the-private -sector-a-love-story.

13. Paul Polak, *Out of Poverty: What Works When Traditional Approaches Fail* (San Francisco: Berrett-Koehler, 2008).

14. Michael Edwards, "When Is Civil Society a Force for Social Transformation?," *Transformation,* May 30, 2014, www.opendemocracy.net /transformation/michael-edwards/when-is-civil-society-force-for -social-transformation.

15. Oxfam America, the Coca-Cola Company, and SABMiller, "Exploring the Links between International Business and Poverty Reduction: The Coca-Cola/SABMiller Value Chain Impacts in Zambia and El Salvador," 2011, 12–13, www.oxfamamerica.org/explore /research-publications/exploring-the-links-between-international -business-and-poverty-reduction.

16. Pete Dauvergne and Genevieve LeBaron, *Protest Inc.: The Corporatization of Activism* (Cambridge: Polity Press, 2014).

17. Bill Gates, blurb for C. K. Prahalad, *The Fortune at the Bottom of the Pyramid* (Upper Saddle River, NJ: Pearson Education, 2010), front matter.

18. Steven Lawrence and Reina Mukai, "Foundation Growth and Giving Estimates," Foundation Center, New York, 2008, 1, foundationcenter .org/gainknowledge/research/pdf/fgge08.pdf.

19. Steven Lawrence, "Foundation Growth and Giving Estimates," Foundation Center, New York, 2012, 1, foundationcenter.org/gain knowledge/research/pdf/fgge12.pdf.

20. Tara Siegel Bernard, "Making a Difference in This Season of Giving," *New York Times*, December 6, 2013.

21. Interestingly, as Bishop and Green underscore in *Philanthrocapitalism: How Giving Can Save the World*, which is by far the best statement of this view (it has a preface by Bill Clinton), Gates was "relatively slow to join the movement." Matthew Bishop and Michael Green, *Philanthrocapitalism: How Giving Can Save the World* (New York: Bloomsbury, 2008), 5.

22. Thomas Frank and Matt Weiland, *Commodify Your Dissent: Salvos from the Baffler* (New York: W. W. Norton, 1997).

23. Larry Page and Sergey Brin, "2004 Founders' IPO Letter: From the S-1 Registration Statement "'An Owner's Manual' for Google's Shareholders," 2004 Founders' IPO Letter, investor.google.com /corporate/2004/ipo-founders-letter.html.

24. Unilever USA, "Unilever Looks to Young Entrepreneurs to Make Sustainable Living Commonplace," press release, September 2, 2013, www.unileverusa.com/media-center/pressreleases/2013/Unilever lookstoentrepreneursmakesustainablelivingcommonplace.aspx.

25. Paul Polman, "The Remedies for Capitalism." McKinsey & Company, www.mckinsey.com/features/capitalism/paul_polman.

26. Polman, "Remedies for Capitalism."

27. Bill Gates, remarks at World Economic Forum, "A New Approach to Capitalism in the 21st Century," Davos, Switzerland, January 24, 2008, www.weforum.org/sessions/summary/new-approach-capitalism -21st-century.

28. Gates, remarks at World Economic Forum.

29. Samuel Loewenberg, "Interview: A Business-Like Approach to Foreign Aid," *Foreign Policy*, May 3, 2012.

30. Bishop and Green, *Philanthrocapitalism*, 3.

31. Marc van Ameringen, "Can the Private Sector Help Combat Hunger and Malnutrition?," Global Alliance for Improved Nutrition, February 5, 2014, www.gainhealth.org/knowledge-centre/can-private-sector-help-combat-hunger-malnutrition.

32. Bishop and Green, *Philanthrocapitalism*, 6.

33. Justine Greening, "Smart Aid: Why It's All About Jobs," speech at the London Stock Exchange, January 27, 2014, www.gov.uk/government/speeches/smart-aid-why-its-all-about-jobs.

34. Greening, "Smart Aid."

35. "USAID Administrator Highlights Private Sector Partnerships to Reduce Hunger and Poverty at the World Economic Forum," press release, USAID, January 28, 2011, www.usaid.gov/news-information/press-releases/usaid-administrator-highlights-private-sector-partnerships-reduce.

36. Raj Shah, "Embracing Enlightened Capitalism," USAID blog, October 25, 2011, blog.usaid.gov/2011/10/embracing-enlightened-capitalism.

37. USAID, "Bilateral Donors' Statement in Support of Private Sector Partnerships for Development," press release, September 22, 2010, www.usaid.gov/news-information/press-releases/bilateral-donors-statement-support-private-sector-partnerships.

38. An analogous argument is routinely made in appealing to food activists to drop their opposition to GMOs on the grounds that if China, Brazil, Canada, and the United States are all going ahead with them, further resistance is simply futile.

39. Lawrence Haddad, "Hunger Strikes for Malnutrition?," *Development Horizons* blog, September 3, 2011, www.developmenthorizons.com/2011/09/hunger-strikes-for-malnutrition.html.

40. Haddad, "Hunger Strikes for Malnutrition?"

41. "The Contribution of the Private Sector and Civil Society to Improve Nutrition," online discussion September 4–October 2, 2013, Global Forum on Food Security and Nutrition, FAO, www.fao.org/fsnforum/forum/discussions/CS-PS-Nutrition?page=7.

42. Author interview with Raj Shah, summer 2008.

43. Pete Dauvergne and Genevieve LeBaron, "Not Just about the

Money: Corporatization Is Weakening Activism and Empowering Big Business," Open Democracy, March 14, 2014, www.open democracy.net/transformation/genevieve-lebaron-peter-dauvergne /not-just-about-money-corporatization-is-weakening-a.

44. Dauvergne and LeBaron, *Protest Inc.*
45. Gates, remarks at World Economic Forum, January 24, 2008.
46. Olivier de Schutter, "Food for All," Project Syndicate, January 28, 2011, www.project-syndicate.org/commentary/food-for-all.
47. Robert Zoellick, "Free Markets Can Still Feed the World," *Financial Times*, January 5, 2011.
48. A. Haroon Akram-Lodhi, "Modernising Subordination? A South Asian Perspective on the *World Development Report 2008*: *Agriculture for Development*," *Journal of Peasant Studies* 36, no. 3 (2009): 611–619.
49. Michael Edwards, "Money: In Terms of Social Change, It's Both 'Beauty and the Beast,'" Open Democracy, February 18, 2014, www.opendemocracy.net/transformation/michael-edwards/money -in-terms-of-social-change-it's-both-'beauty-and-beast'.
50. Dauvergne and LeBaron, "Not Just about the Money."
51. Bishop and Green, *Philanthrocapitalism*, 6.
52. Right to Food and Nutrition Watch, "Alternatives and Resistance to Policies that Generate Hunger," 22.
53. Even a cursory look at the websites of these firms will offer a wealth of examples of this rhetorical strategy.
54. *The Usual Suspects*, dir. Bryan Singer (MGM, 1995). Rephrasing of Charles Baudelaire's "The finest trick of the devil is to persuade you that he does not exist."
55. William Leuchtenberg, *Franklin D. Roosevelt and the New Deal* (New York: Harper Collins, 1963).
56. Gates, remarks at World Economic Forum, January 24, 2008.

CHAPTER TWELVE: PHILANTHROCAPITALISM: A [SELF-]LOVE STORY

1. Cullather, *Hungry World*, 134.
2. Gates, remarks at World Economic Forum, January 24, 2008.

3. David Rieff, "A Green Revolution for Africa?," *New York Times,* October 10, 2008.

4. Herbert Marcuse, *The Essential Marcuse: Selected Writings of Philosopher and Social Critic Herbert Marcuse* (Boston: Beacon Press, 2007), 56.

5. Even writers as entirely pro-Gates as Bishop and Green are have to concede in *Philanthrocapitalism* that "Microsoft may [*sic*] have enjoyed some monopoly," though they go on to insist that this was of secondary importance because the company had always been exposed to "dynamic competitors."

6. Fidel Castro, "Words to Intellectuals," speech, June 30, 1961, www.min.cult.cu/loader.php?sec=historia&cont=palabrasalosintelectuales.

7. Michael Kanellos, "Newsmaker: Gates Taking a Seat in Your Den," CNET, January 5, 2005, news.cnet.com/Gates-taking-a-seat-in-your-den/2100-1041_3-5514121.html.

8. Moyo has been careful to exempt emergency relief aid from her critique of development aid.

9. "An Audience with Bill Gates," video, Australian Broadcasting Corporation, May 28, 2013, www.abc.net.au/tv/qanda/txt/s3761763.htm.

10. Bill and Melinda Gates, "Text of the 2014 Commencement Address by Bill and Melinda Gates," Stanford University, June 15, 2014, news.stanford.edu/news/2014/june/gates-commencement-remarks-061514.html.

11. Castro, "Words to Intellectuals."

12. "Audience with Bill Gates."

13. Jeffrey Sachs, "Foreign Aid Skeptics Thrive on Pessimism," *Los Angeles Times,* May 7, 2006.

14. Jeffrey Sachs on Twitter, May 28, 2014, twitter.com/jeffdsachs/status/471774898730201089.

15. Sachs, *End of Poverty,* 368.

16. Bishop and Green, *Philanthrocapitalism,* 50.

17. Fact Up on Twitter, August 7, 2013, twitter.com/factup/status/365110811720556544.

18. Bishop and Green, *Philanthrocapitalism,* 263.

19. Bishop and Green, *Philanthrocapitalism,* 283.

20. Bill Gates, "2009 Annual Letter from Bill Gates: The Role of Foundations," Bill and Melinda Gates Foundation, 2009, www.gates foundation.org/Who-We-Are/Resources-and-Media/Annual-Letters -List/Annual-Letter-2009.

21. David Rieff interview.

22. John Ralston Saul, *Reflections of a Siamese Twin: Canada at the End of the Twentieth Century* (Toronto: Penguin, 1998).

23. Rajiv Shah, "Ending Extreme Poverty with a New Model of Development," USAID blog, April 14, 2014, blog.usaid.gov/2014/04 /ending-extreme-poverty-with-a-new-model-of-development.

24. Raj Shah, "Remarks by USAID Administrator Dr. Raj Shah at the 'DRG 2.0: Promoting Democracy, Human Rights, and Governance in 2011' Conference in Arlington, Virginia," June 20, 2011, www .usaid.gov/news-information/speeches/remarks-usaid-administrator -dr-raj-shah-drg-20-promoting-democracy-human.

25. European Commission, "Taking Stock of the Europe 2020 Strategy for Smart, Sustainable, and Inclusive Growth," Brussels, March 19, 2014, ec.europa.eu/europe2020/pdf/europe2020stocktaking_en.pdf, 2.

26. Independent Commission for Aid Impact, "DFID's Private Sector Development Work," London, May 2014, 33.

27. Tom Murphy, "A Peaceful and Food-Secure Africa Is Not Just a Dream," Humanosphere, June 25, 2014, www.humanosphere.org /basics/2014/06/peaceful-food-secure-africa-just-dream.

28. Human Rights Watch, "Ethiopia," World Report 2014, www.hrw .org/world-report/2014/country-chapters/ethiopia.

29. The HRW report could have legitimately added the benefits the Ethiopian dictatorship derives from having such influential supporters, which, while obviously unquantifiable, are anything but inconsequential.

30. Erik Solheim, "Three Lessons from Rwanda," *Global Policy*, April 4, 2014, www.globalpolicyjournal.com/blog/04/04/2014/three-lessons -rwanda. The Rwandan case is just as extreme. To cite only one example of the unqualified support Rwanda has received from major figures in the development world, experienced Norwegian diplomat Erik Solheim, who took the helm of the OECD's influential Disaster

Assistance Committee, praised Rwanda's dictatorial president, Paul Kagame, insisting that effective development cooperation required donors to "align behind the priorities of recipient governments and use the existing country systems."

The fact that Kagame's priorities included a long history of wreaking havoc in the neighboring Democratic Republic of Congo and standing accused of having several exiled dissidents murdered did not seem to give Solheim much pause. He does not even allude to it in his May 2014 essay, "Four Lessons from Rwanda."

31. John Tasioulas, "The Moral Reality of Human Rights," paper presented at the UNESCO Poverty Project philosophy seminar "Ethical and Human Rights Dimensions of Poverty: Towards a New Paradigm in the Fight Against Poverty," All Souls College, Oxford, March 2003, 1.

32. Joseph Raz, "Human Rights Without Foundations," University of Oxford Faculty of Law Legal Studies Research Paper Series, working paper no. 14/2007, March 2007.

33. Tom Paulson, "Philanthrocapitalists Propose a Social Progress Index," Humanosphere, April 15, 2013, www.humanosphere.org/basics /2013/04/philanthrocapitalists-propose-a-social-progress-index.

34. Sachs, *End of Poverty*, 354.

35. Jeffrey Sachs, "The End of Poverty, Soon," *New York Times*, September 24, 2013.

36. By this I mean his overall approach, of course. For all his confidence, Gates has always been at pains to emphasize that many particular projects undertaken by his foundation are bound to fail.

37. Rist, *History of Development*, 77.

38. Rist, *History of Development*, 77.

39. Sachs, *End of Poverty*, 352.

40. Paul Krugman, "The Fall and Rise of Development Economics," in *Development, Geography and Economic Theory* (Cambridge, MA: MIT Press, 1995).

41. Garry W. Jenkins, "Who's Afraid of Philanthrocapitalism?" *Case Western Reserve Law Review*, Volume 61:3, 65, law.case.edu/journals /LawReview/Documents/Jenkins.pdf.

CHAPTER THIRTEEN: THE END OF HUNGER?

1. Bill Gates, "2010 Annual Letter from Bill Gates: The Role of Foundations," Bill and Melinda Gates Foundation, www.gatesfoundation.org /Who-We-Are/Resources-and-Media/Annual-Letters-List/Annual -Letter-2010.

2. "Bill Gates on Innovation," video, USAID, March 19, 2013, www .usaid.gov/news-information/videos/bill-gates-innovation.

3. Bill and Melinda Gates, "Text of the 2014 Commencement Address by Bill and Melinda Gates."

4. "Innovation: Transforming the Way Business Creates Includes a Global Ranking of Countries," Economist Intelligence Unit, 2007, 7, graphics.eiu.com/upload/portal/ciscoinnosmallfile.pdf.

5. Jeff Madick, "Innovation: The Government Was Crucial After All," *New York Review of Books,* April 24, 2014.

6. Mariana Mazzucato, *The Entrepreneurial State: Debunking Public vs. Private Sector Myths* (London: Anthem Press, 2014), 88.

7. Patrick Gallagher, "Innovation as a Key Driver of Economic Growth and Competitiveness," Remarks at FedScoop's U.S. Innovation Summit, Newseum, Washington, DC, June 20, 2012, www.nist.gov /director/speeches/innovation-summit.cfm.

8. Nestor Osorio, "Opening Statement at 2013 AMR Regional Meeting for Africa," Dar es Salaam, Tanzania, March 14, 2013, www .un.org/en/ecosoc/president/statement_2013/wipo_ecosoc_amr _dar_13_g_osorio.pdf.

9. Workshop program, "Farmer First Revisited: Farmer Participatory Research and Development Twenty Years On," Institute of Development Studies, University of Sussex, December 12–14, 2007, www .future-agricultures.org/farmerfirst/files/Farmer_First_Revisited _Preliminary_Programme.pdf.

10. Ian Scoones, John Thompson, and Robert Chambers, "Farmer First Revisited: Innovation for Agricultural Research and Development, Workshop Summary, April 2008," 17, www.future-agricultures.org /farmerfirst/files/Farmer_First_Revisited_Post_Workshop_Summary _Final.pdf.

11. Scoones, Thompson, and Chambers, "Farmer First Revisited," 17.

12. *Agriculture Innovation Systems: An Investment Sourcebook* (Washington, DC: World Bank, 2012), 1, openknowledge.worldbank.org /handle/10986/2247.

13. Jeffrey Sachs, "The Global Innovation Divide," in Adam B. Jaffe, Josh Lerner, and Scott Stern, eds., *Innovation Policy and the Economy*, vol. 3 (Cambridge, MA: MIT Press, 2003), 131–141.

14. UN Millennium Project, *Innovation: Applying Knowledge in Development* (London: Earthscan, 2005), xiv.

15. UN Millennium Project, *Innovation*, 16.

16. Antonio Guarino and Maurizio Iacopetta, "A Conversation with William J. Baumol on Capitalism, Innovation, and Growth," *Rivista Internazionale di Scienze Sociali* 111, no. 1 (January-March 2003): 3.

17. Guarino and Iacopetta, "Conversation with William J. Baumol," 6.

18. Guarino and Iacopetta, "Conversation with William J. Baumol," 6.

19. Guarino and Iacopetta, "Conversation with William J. Baumol," 6.

20. Sachs, *End of Poverty*, 315. The issue of dictatorship not only did not trouble Sachs in terms of diminishing poor nations' prospects for successful economic growth, but as far as he was concerned was largely irrelevant even to governance issues. As he put it in *End of Poverty*, "the charge of authoritarian rule as a basic obstacle to good governance is *passé*."

21. Sachs, *End of Poverty*, 358.

22. UN Millennium Project, *Innovation*, 16.

23. Deepak Lal, "The Third World and Globalization," *Critical Review*, 14, no. 1 (2000): 35–46.

24. Gates's framing of the broad outlines of the history of the past three hundred years as one of inexorable material progress is entirely defensible. But to the extent he was claiming that this progress from the eighteenth century to the twenty-first had been linear, it is not wholly correct. For as Baumol has pointed out, in the nineteenth century the life expectancy of an average English person went down, not up.

25. Jeff Goodell, "Bill Gates: The *Rolling Stone* Interview," *Rolling Stone*, March 13, 2014.

26. Gates, "Text of the 2014 Commencement Address."

27. Michael Kinsley and Conor Clarke, *Creative Capitalism: A Conversation with Bill Gates, Warren Buffett, and Other Economic Leaders* (New York: Simon & Schuster, 2009), 21.

28. Jill Lepore, "The Disruption Machine," *New Yorker*, June 23, 2014.

29. Goodell, "Bill Gates: The *Rolling Stone* Interview."

30. Bill Gates, "Innovating to Zero!," TED talk, February 2010, www .ted.com/talks/bill_gates?language=en.

31. Rob Cox, "Silicon Valley's Undeserved Moral Exceptionalism," Reuters, March 12, 2012.

32. Jaron Lanier, *You Are Not a Gadget* (New York: Alfred A. Knopf, 2010), 48.

33. Lepore, "Disruption Machine."

34. Lepore also makes the interesting point that until the late 1930s, the words "innovate" and "innovation" had "chiefly negative connotations."

35. Vinod Khosla, "Fireside Chat with Google Co-founders, Larry Page and Sergey Brin," Khosla Ventures, July 3, 2014, www.khoslaventures .com/fireside-chat-with-google-co-founders-larry-page-and-sergey -brin.

36. Goodell, "Bill Gates: The *Rolling Stone* Interview."

37. "Q&A: CGIAR Consortium Head on Agriculture in Africa," SciDev.Net, June 20, 2014, www.scidev.net/sub-saharan-africa/food -security/feature/agriculture-in-africa.html.

38. L. Antonaci, M. Demeke, and A. Vezzani, "The Challenges of Managing Agricultural Price and Production Risks in Sub-Saharan Africa," ESA Working Paper no. 14–09, June 2014, Agricultural Development Economics Division, Food and Agriculture Organization, www.fao.org/3/a-i3907.pdf.

39. Alliance for a Green Revolution in Africa, *The Africa Agriculture Status Report 2013: Focus on Staple Crops* (Nairobi: AGRA, 2013), 164, agra-alliance.org/our-results/agra-status-reports.

40. Gerald C. Nelson, "Advancing Global Food Security in the Face of a Changing Climate," Chicago Council on Global Affairs, May 2014, www.thechicagocouncil.org/sites/default/files/ClimateChangeFood Security(1).pdf.

41. "Advancing Global Food Security: The Power of Science, Trade, and

Business," Chicago Council on Global Affairs, May 2013, 18, www
.thechicagocouncil.org/sites/default/files/2013_Advancing_Global
_Food_Security%283%29.pdf.

42. "Advancing Global Food Security: The Power of Science, Trade, and Business," 1.

43. Food and Agriculture Organization, *Climate-Smart Agriculture Sourcebook* (FAO, 2013), 7, www.fao.org/docrep/018/i3325e/i3325e.pdf.

44. Evans, "Feeding of the Nine Billion," 49.

45. The economist Angus Deaton, who has generally been every bit as optimistic about the condition of the poor as Gates has been, nonetheless has pointed out that aid undermines the connection between governments and people, as governments worry more about what their donors think than what their people think. Seeing as their donors in the main do not insist on democratic accountability as a *sine qua non* for aid, these would seem to be self-evident. But Gates retorted on his blog that he found Deaton's views "strange" and that he overemphasized the importance of institutions—which of course is just what one would expect of someone interested in disruptive innovation to conclude, which is of course corrosive of institutions.

46. World Food Programme website, www.wfp.org/hunger.

47. Norman E. Borlaug, "From the Green to the Gene Revolution—A 21st Century Challenge," *Science in Parliament* 63, no. 1 (Spring 2006): 14–15.

48. Amartya Sen, *Development as Freedom* (New York: First Anchor Books, 1999), 3.

49. Sen, *Development as Freedom*, 36.

50. Stuart Gillespie and Marie Ruel, "G8, Build Political Will to Overcome Malnutrition," *Guardian*, June, 18 2013.

51. Francis Fukuyama, "Second Thoughts: The Last Man in a Bottle," *National Interest*, summer 1999, 2.

52. John Gray, "The Atheist Delusion," *Guardian*, March 14, 2008.

53. Maureen Dowd, "Who Do We Think We Are?," *New York Times*, July 4, 2014.

54. Bill Gates Quotes on Twitter, September 13, 2014, twitter.com /gatesquotes13/status/510821579630977025.

55. There is even a parallel between, to put it charitably, Gates's tolerance for dictatorial regimes such as those in Ethiopia and Rwanda and modern utilitarianism's founder Jeremy Bentham's belief that much of the world could only be effectively ruled by enlightened despots.

56. Robert Gordon, "Is US Economic Growth Over? Faltering Innovation Confronts the Six Headwinds," Center for Economic Research Policy Insight no. 63, September 2012, www.cepr.org/sites/default/files/policy_insights/PolicyInsight63.pdf.

57. Andrew Carnegie, *An Employer's View of the Labor Question* (New York: J. J. Little, 1886), 118.

58. Goodell, "Bill Gates: The *Rolling Stone* Interview."

59. Goodell, "Bill Gates: The *Rolling Stone* Interview."

CHAPTER FOURTEEN: "FERTILIZING THE LAND WITH MONEY"

1. M. S. Swaminathan, "Making Globalization Work for the Poor: Technology and Trade," in Joachim von Braun and Eugenio Diaz-Bonilla, eds., *Globalization of Food and Agriculture and the Poor* (New York: Oxford University Press, 2007), 84.

2. Swaminathan, "Making Globalization Work for the Poor," 84.

3. M. S. Swaminathan, "Looking Back at the Green Revolution," Third Annual Governor's Lecture, 2006 Norman E. Borlaug/World Food Prize International Symposium, "The Green Revolution Redux: Can We Replicate the Single Greatest Period of Food Production in All Human History?," Des Moines, Iowa, October 19–20, 2006, 6, www.worldfoodprize.org/documents/filelibrary/images/borlaug_dialogue/2006/transcripts/SWAMINATHAN_7AACA4D65A650.pdf.

4. M. S. Swaminathan, "Ever-Green Revolution and Sustainable Food Security," in *Agricultural Biotechnology: Finding Common International Goals*, NABC Report 16, 2004, 72, nabc.cals.cornell.edu/Publications/Reports/nabc_16/16_2_4_Swaminathan.pdf.

5. Swaminathan, "Making Globalization Work for the Poor," 94.

6. Kinsley and Clarke, *Creative Capitalism*, 1.

7. Eric Schmidt, speaking at SXSW Interactive, Austin, Texas, March 7, 2014.

8. John Adams, letter to Thomas Jefferson, February 2, 1816, www .thefederalistpapers.org/founders/john-adams.

9. Bill Gates, "Remarks of Bill Gates, Harvard Commencement 2007," June 7, 2007, news.harvard.edu/gazette/story/2007/06/remarks-of -bill-gates-harvard-commencement-2007.

10. Andre Beteille, "Poverty and Inequality," *Economic and Political Weekly*, October 18, 2003.

11. There is, however, no consensus among economists on the question of whether this income inequality is actually a precondition for economic growth or if instead, where growth has yet to occur, it is an impediment to it.

12. Kenneth M. Cleaver and W. Graeme Donovan, "Agriculture, Poverty, and Policy Reform in Sub-Saharan Africa," March 1995, elibrary .worldbank.org/doi/abs/10.1596/0-8213-3189-2.

13. Gordon Conway, *One Billion Hungry: Can We Feed the World?* (London: Comstock, 2012).

14. Conway, *One Billion Hungry*, 333.

15. Conway, *One Billion Hungry*, 334.

16. Richard Horton, "Why the Sustainable Development Goals Will Fail," *Lancet* 383, no. 9936 (2014): 2185–268.

17. Horton, "Why the Sustainable Development Goals Will Fail"; Sudhir Anand and Amartya Sen, "Human Development and Economic Stability," *World Development* 28, no. 12 (2000): 2031.

18. Beteille, "Poverty and Inequality." Amartya Sen has made a similar point with regard to development. Amartya Sen, *Development as Freedom* (New York: Random House, 1999).

19. Michael Edwards, *Small Change: Why Business Won't Save the World* (San Francisco: Berrett-Koehler, 2008), 17.

20. Edwards, *Small Change*, 18.

21. Dennis Weller, "Remarks by USAID Ethiopia Mission Director Dennis Weller," Ethiopia New Alliance for Food Security and Nutrition Meeting, Addis Ababa, September 12, 2012, www.usaid.gov/ethiopia/speeches /ethiopia-new-alliance-food-security-and-nutrition-meeting.

22. Right to Food and Nutrition Watch, "Alternatives and Resistance to Policies That Generate Hunger."

23. As does Raj Patel who, to put it mildly, is no friend of the World Bank. Recalling his time there, he said of those he had worked with, "No one [working there] wakes up every morning and wonders how they're going to crush a Third World Economy. Everyone there has a sort of view of actually contributing to the global economy." David Zlutnick, "Raj Patel: Food Rebellions and Political Accountability," Truth-Out.org, July 15, 2012, truth-out.org/news/item/10338-raj-patel-food-rebellions-and-political-accountability#.

24. Stephen Greenberg, "The Modernisation Agenda in African Agriculture: Responding to AGRA's Africa Agriculture Status Report 2013," Future Agricultures, December 18, 2013, www.future-agricultures.org/blog/entry/the-modernisation-agenda-in-african-agriculture-responding-to-agras-africa-agriculture-status-report-2013.

25. Suma Chakrabarti and Jose Graziano da Silva, "Hungry for Investment: The Private Sector Can Drive Agricultural Development in Countries That Need It Most," *Wall Street Journal*, September 6, 2012.

26. Laura Ries, "BP Has a Brand Problem," Ries' Pieces, May 2010. ries.typepad.com/ries_blog/2010/05/bp-has-a-brand-problem.html.

27. Commonly attributed to Howard Schultz: www.brandingstrategyinsider.com/2006/09.

28. D. B. Holt, *How Brands Become Icons: The Principles of Cultural Branding* (Boston: Harvard Business School Press, 2013). Quoted in the publisher's synopsis.

29. Holt, *How Brands Become Icons.*

30. Syngenta, "Good Growth Plan," www.syngenta.com/global/corporate/en/goodgrowthplan/home/Pages/homepage.aspx.

31. Monsanto, "Who We Are," www.monsanto.com/whoweare/pages/default.aspx.

32. Monsanto, "Agent Orange: Background on Monsanto's Involvement," www.monsanto.com/newsviews/pages/agent-orange-background-monsanto-involvement.aspx; Edith Piaf, "Non, Je Ne Regrette Rien," 1960 recording. In original French: "Je repars à zero." Composed by

Charles Dumont. Lyrics by Michel Vaucaire. The company's own statements on the matter that are posted on its website are legalistic in the extreme. The most significant of these entries speaks of Agent Orange "continu[ing] to be an emotional [*sic*] subject for many people," and says that "a causal connection linking Agent Orange to chronic diseases in humans has not been established," even though it concedes that "governments and non-governmental humanitarian organizations have increased funding of environmental and health-care services to help address potential [*sic*] problems that may [*sic*] exist in Vietnam" from its use. It's over and done with. The prevailing attitude seems to be, Why should one accord it anymore importance than, say, technology before 1700 or medicine before the mid-twentieth century? In the words of one of Edith Piaf's greatest songs, "I start again from zero."

33. World Economic Forum, "Achieving the New Vision for Agriculture: New Models for Action," New Vision for Agriculture Initiative, report prepared in collaboration with McKinsey & Company, 2013, 1, www3.weforum.org/docs/IP/2013/NVA/WEF_IP_NVA_New _Models_for_Action_report.pdf.

34. World Economic Forum, "Achieving the New Vision for Agriculture," 2.

35. World Economic Forum, "Achieving the New Vision for Agriculture," 2.

36. "USAID Administrator Shah Travels to Arkansas," press release, September 9, 2013, www.usaid.gov/news-information/press-releases /usaid-administrator-shah-travels-arkansas.

37. "USAID Administrator Shah Travels to Arkansas."

38. Charles Kenny, "Give Sam Walton the Nobel Prize," *Foreign Policy*, April 29, 2013.

39. Loewenberg, "Business-Like Approach to Foreign Aid."

40. Loewenberg, "Business-Like Approach to Foreign Aid."

41. "Walmart Announces Global Responsible Sourcing Initiative at China Summit," press release, October 22, 2008, news.walmart.com /news-archive/2008/10/21/walmart-announces-global-responsible -sourcing-initiative-at-china-summit.

CHAPTER FIFTEEN: OPTIMISM AS MORAL VICTORY, PESSIMISM AS MORAL AFFRONT

1. Gates Poverty on Twitter, July 22, 2014, twitter.com/gatespoverty /status/491635974037065728.

2. There have also been a number of "interviews" in a similar vein with Raya, Elmo, and other *Sesame Street* characters on the Gates Foundation's website, Impatient Optimists.

3. Andrea Cornwall, "Deconstructing Development Discourse: Buzzwords and Fuzzwords," *Development in Practice* 17, nos. 4–5 (August 2007): 1056.

4. Andrea Cornwall and Karen Brock, "What Do Buzzwords Do for Development Policy? A Critical Look at 'Participation,' 'Empowerment,' and 'Poverty Reduction,'" *Third World Quarterly* 26, no. 7 (2005): 1056.

5. Cornwall and Brock, "What Do Buzzwords Do for Development Policy?," 1056.

6. One.org "2015 Action Pledge," www.one.org/us/2015-action-pledge/.

7. Cornwall and Brock, "What Do Buzzwords Do for Development Policy?," 1055.

8. "My World," United Nations Development Programme, May 5, 2014, www.undp.org/content/rbap/en/home/presscenter/articles/2014 /05/05/myworld-vote-for-the-change-you-want-to-see-in-the-world.

9. "Why Does My Vote Matter?," United Nations Global Survey for a Better World, vote.myworld2015.org.

10. "Emily McKhann: The Motherhood," ONE Campaign, www.one .org/us/person/emily-mckhann.

11. "Emily McKhann: The Motherhood."

12. Ralph, Stuart, "Lifting Lives for Good the Oxfam Way," Morally Marketed, December 27, 2013, www.morallymarketed.com/case -studies/lifting-lives-for-good-the-oxfam-way.

13. Cornwall and Brock, "What Do Buzzwords Do for Development Policy?," 1055.

14. Oxfam UK, "Corporate Engagment," www.oxfam.org.uk/get-involved /how-your-company-can-partner-with-us/corporate-engagement.

15. "Honest Accounts? The True Story of Africa's Billion Dollar Losses," Health Poverty Action briefing, July 2014, 3, www.healthpoverty action.org/wp-content/uploads/downloads/2014/07/Honest -Accounts-BRIEFING-v4-web.pdf.

16. In fact, it is not even clear that Invisible Children was ever all that discredited in the minds of mainstream figures in the development and human rights worlds. For example, the first speech Samantha Power gave after being confirmed as US permanent representative to the UN was to a conference the group had organized.

17. Gabrielle Fitzgerald, "Global Campaigns in the Clicktivist Era," Skoll World Forum, May 29, 2014, skollworldforum.org/2014/05/29 /global-campaigns-clicktivist-era.

18. Micah White, "Clicktivism: The Pollution of Activism with the Logic of Silicon Valley," www.micahmwhite.com/clicktivism.

19. White, "Clicktivism."

20. "About," Change.org, www.change.org/about.

21. Ironically, this is one claim about which clicktivism's advocates and its detractors would agree.

22. Sinead O'Carroll, "Clicktivism Isn't a Replacement for Boots-on-the-Ground Activism—but It Does Work," *TheJournal.ie*, May 20, 2012.

23. John Prendergast, participation in the session "A Changing Dynamic: Africa's Image and U.S. Perceptions in the 21st Century," session 2 of the Brookings Institution forum The Game Has Changed: The New Leadership for Innovation and Business in Africa, Washington, DC, August 4, 2014, 52.

24. Steve Tibbett and Chris Stalker, "Enough Food for Everyone IF Campaign Evaluation," 36, www.bond.org.uk/data/files/IF_campaign _evaluation_report.pdf.

25. Neil McMahon, "Recycling Issue Brewing in George Clooney's Nespresso Campaign," *Sydney Morning Herald*, April 20, 2014.

26. One can interpret Amartya Sen's argument in *Development and Freedom* that because, in his view, successful development also requires political liberty and civil freedoms, these are needs as well.

27. Stuart Ralph, "Marketers Are the New Vicars, Imams and Rabbis?!"

Morally Marketed, June 26, 2014, www.morallymarketed.com /marketing-ethics/marketers-are-the-new-vicars-imams-and-rabbis/.

28. Oliver Balch, "The Rise of 'Sadvertising': Why Social Good Marketing Works," *Guardian*, July 18, 2014.

29. Alex T. Williams, "The Growing Pay Gap between Journalism and Public Relations," Pew Research Center, August 11, 2014, www .pewresearch.org/fact-tank/2014/08/11/the-growing-pay-gap -between-journalism-and-public-relations.

30. "Guardian Labs Officially Launches with Unilever Sustainable Living Partnership," press release, Guardian News Media, February 13, 2014, www.theguardian.com/gnm-press-office/guardian-launches-guardian -labs-with-unilever-partnership.

31. Chris O'Shea, "WSJ Launches Native Advertising," *Adweek*, March 10, 2014.

32. Quoted with permission.

33. Balch, "The Rise of 'Sadvertising.'"

34. John Hilary, *The Poverty of Capitalism*. (New York: Palgrave Macmillan, 2013) 74; Gerard Hanlon, "Rethinking Corporate Social Responsibility and the Role of the Firm—On the Denial of Politics," in Andrew Crane, Abigail McWilliams, Dirk Matten, Jeremy Moon and Donald S. Siegel, eds., *The Oxford Handbook of Corporate Social Responsibility* (Oxford: Oxford University Press, 2008), 167.

35. Peter Buffet, "The Charitable-Industrial Complex," *New York Times*, July 26, 2013.

36. Office of the Press Secretary, White House, "Fact Sheet: Food Security in Sub-Saharan Africa," June 28, 2013, www.whitehouse .gov/the-press-office/2013/06/28/fact-sheet-food-security-sub -saharan-africa.

37. Ghana, Benin, Ivory Coast, Senegal, Nigeria, Burkina Faso, Malawi, Mozambique, Tanzania, and Ethiopia.

38. White House, "Fact Sheet: U.S.-African Cooperation on Food Security," press release, August 4, 2014, www.whitehouse.gov/the-press -office/2014/08/04/fact-sheet-us-african-cooperation-food-security.

39. USAID, "U.S. and African Leaders Announce Progress, New Partnerships to Help Millions of Farming Families through Agriculture,"

press release, August 5, 2014, www.usaid.gov/news-information /press-releases/aug-5-2014-us-and-african-leaders-announce -progress-new-partnerships-help-farming-families.

40. USAID, "U.S. Government Initiative Reduces Hunger and Poverty for Millions: Feed the Future Reaches Nearly 7 Million Farmers and 12.5 Million Children Globally," fact sheet, May 22, 2014, www .usaid.gov/news-information/fact-sheets/us-government-initiative -reduces-hunger-and-poverty-millions.

41. Molly Kinder and Nachilala Nkombo, "New Alliance as Imperialism in Another Guise? Monbiot Should Know Better," *Guardian*, June 12, 2013.

42. USAID, "U.S. Government Initiative Reduces Hunger and Poverty for Millions."

43. USAID, "U.S. Government Initiative Reduces Hunger and Poverty for Millions."

44. G8 New Alliance for Food Security and Nutrition, "Cooperation Framework to Support the New Alliance for Food Security & Nutrition in Mozambique," 4, feedthefuture.gov/sites/default/files/resource /files/Mozambique%20Coop%20Framework%20ENG%20FINAL %20w.cover%20REVISED.pdf.

45. Claire Provost, Liz Ford, and Mark Tran, "G8 New Alliance Condemned as New Wave of Colonialism in Africa," *Guardian*, February 18, 2014.

46. Nick Dearden, "G8 Needs Reminding the Market Doesn't Know Best When It Comes to Hunger," *Guardian*, June 9, 2013.

47. Quoted in Provost, Ford, and Tran, "G8 New Alliance Condemned."

48. White House, "U.S. Africa Leaders Summit," August 4–6, Washington, DC, 2014, www.whitehouse.gov/us-africa-leaders-summit.

49. Olivier de Schutter, "Privatizing Aid Is a Dangerous Strategy," *Guardian*, December 11, 2012.

50. Harriet Friedmann, "The Political Economy of Food: The Rise and Fall of the Postwar International Food Order," *American Journal of Sociology* 88 (1982); Harriet Friedmann, "The Political Economy of Food: A Global Crisis," *New Left Review* 1; 197 (January-February 1993).

51. Francis Fukuyama, "After Neoconservatism," *New York Times*, February 19, 2006. Fukuyama has actually described his "End of History?" thesis as "a kind of Marxist argument for the existence of a long-term process of social evolution, but one that terminates in liberal democracy rather than communism."

52. Quoted in John Vidal, "Sam Dryden: The Most Powerful Figure in the Global South's Agriculture?," *Guardian*, July 6, 2012.

53. Angus Deaton, *The Great Escape: Health, Wealth, and the Origins of Inequality* (Princeton, NJ: Princeton University Press, 2013), 303.

54. Angust Deaton, "The Great Escape: Health, Wealth, and the Origins of Inequality," lecture, London School of Economics, October 15, 2013.

CHAPTER SIXTEEN: DOING EVERYTHING TO END HUNGER EXCEPT THINKING POLITICALLY

1. Rist, *History of Development*, 255.

2. Ha-Joon Chang, *Bad Samaritans: The Myth of Free Trade and the Secret History of Capitalism* (London: Bloomsbury, 2007), xxiii.

3. U.S. Government Accountability Office, "International Taxation: Large U.S. Corporations and Federal Contractors with Subsidiaries in Jurisdictions Listed as Tax Havens or Financial Privacy Jurisdictions," report to congressional requesters, December 2008, 4, www.gao.gov/assets/290/284522.pdf.

4. Christopher Needham, "Corporate Tax Avoidance by Multinational Firms," Library of the European Parliament briefing, September 23, 2013, 4, www.europarl.europa.eu/RegData/bibliotheque/briefing/2013/130574/LDM_BRI(2013)130574_REV1_EN.pdf.

5. Connie Guglielmo, "Apple, Called a U.S. Tax Dodger, Says It's Paid 'Every Single Dollar' of Taxes Owed," *Forbes*, May 21, 2013.

6. Charles Duhigg, "How Apple Sidesteps Billions in Taxes," *New York Times*, April 28, 2012.

7. Tibbett and Stalker, "Enough Food for Everyone IF Campaign Evaluation," 36.

8. Sachs, *End of Poverty*, x.

9. "Senior Advice: Bono," *New Africa,* November 9, 2013, www.the newafrica.info/senior-advice-bono.

10. Luke Balleny, "Europe Must 'Walk the Walk' on Corruption—Mo Ibrahim," Thomson Reuters Foundation, February 4, 2014, www .trust.org/item/20140204210848-fyo5a.

11. Africa Progress Panel, "Equity in Extractives: Stewarding Africa's natural resources for all," report, 2013, 56, www.africaprogresspanel .org/wp-content/uploads/2013/08/2013_APR_Equity_in_Extractives _25062013_ENG_HR.pdf.

12. Africa Progress Panel, "Equity in Extractives," 57.

13. Africa Progress Panel, "Equity in Extractives," 65.

14. "Bill and Melinda Gates Foundation," Wikipedia, en.wikipedia.org /wiki/Bill_%26_Melinda_Gates_Foundation.

15. Alex Crippen, "Buffett's Gift to Gates Foundation is Biggest Ever," CNBC, July 15, 2014, www.cnbc.com/id/101838746.

16. Bill Rigby and Andre Grenon, "Bill Gates on Track to Own No Microsoft Stock in Four Years," Reuters, May 2, 2014.

17. Richard Murphy, "Microsoft's Tax Avoidance Represents 3.5% of the World Aid Budget," Tax Research UK, December 10, 2012, www .taxresearch.org.uk/Blog/2012/12/10/microsofts-tax-avoidance -represents-3-5-of-the-world-aid-budget.

18. Tim Worstall, "On Bill Gates and Microsoft's Taxes," Tim Worstall. com, January 6, 2014, www.timworstall.com/2014/01/06/on-bill -gates-and-microsofts-taxes/?utm_source=twitterfeed&utm_medium =twitter&utm_campaign=Feed%3A+timworstall%2FKTZv+%28 Tim+Worstall%29.

19. Action Aid, "Enough Food for Everyone IF," press release, January 23, 2103, www.actionaidusa.org/news/press-release-enough-food -everyone-if#sthash.VVeyQ1U1.dpuf.

20. Ian Birrell, "Bill Gates Preaches the Aid Gospel, But Is He Just a Hypocrite?," *Guardian,* January 6, 2014.

21. Birrell, "Bill Gates Preaches the Aid Gospel."

22. According to a 2013 UN report, between the mid-1980s and the late 2000s, income inequalities rose in 17 out of 22 OECD countries and between the early 1990s and 2008 increased significantly in

emerging economies as well, Brazil being an exception to this general trend.

23. Monsanto website, discover.monsanto.com.

24. Andy Beckett, "Inside the Bill and Melinda Gates Foundation," *Guardian,* July 12, 2010. A 2010 piece in the *Guardian* on the Gates Foundation quoted one unnamed official there as saying, "If you can capture [Gates's] imagination, he will listen to any idea." This was presumably meant to be an emblem of Gates's open-mindedness but surely was at least as much if not more an emblem of his lack of accountability quite literally to anyone.

25. Council of Europe, Parliamentary Assembly, "Promoting an Appropriate Policy on Tax Havens," document 12894, April 5, 2012, assembly.coe.int/ASP/Doc/XrefViewPDF.asp?FileID=18151& Language=en.

26. Conway, *One Billion Hungry*.

27. Henry Bernstein, *Class Dynamics of Agrarian Change* (Halifax, NS: Fernwood, 2010); Eric Holt-Giménez, "Can We Feed the Green Revolution?," review of Gordon Conway's *One Billion Hungry*, Amazon .com, October 16, 2013, www.amazon.com/review/RWNDXNNT7 RL0K/ref=cm_cr_pr_perm?ie=UTF8&ASIN=0801478022.

28. Natalie Sharples, Tim Jones, and Catherine Martin, "Honest Accounts? The True Story of Africa's Billion Dollar Losses," report by Health Poverty Action et al., July 2014, www.francophonie.org /IMG/pdf/honest-accounts_final-version.pdf.

29. Sharples, Jones, and Martin, "Honest Accounts?," 29.

30. The report actually gives the total as $44 billion, but in deference to the mainstream view, I have added back in the $6.1 billion that the report deducts on the grounds that this aid never makes it to Africa, though I have deducted the almost $9 billion in loans that the OECD categorizes as an element of its official aid but which the report includes elsewhere in its calculation of inflows.

31. Slavoj Žižek, "First as Tragedy, then as Farce," speech to the Royal Society for the Encouragement of Arts, London, November 2009, 3–4, www.thersa.org/globalassets/pdfs/videos/2010/08/rsa-animate -first-as-tragedy-then-as-farce-/rsa-lecture-slavoj-zizek-transcript.pdf.

32. Holt-Giménez, "Can We Feed the Green Revolution?"

33. "Bill Gates on Microsoft," *Financial Times*, June 15, 2006.

34. Ron Chernow, *Titan: The Life of John D. Rockefeller, Sr.* (New York: Random House, 1998), 150.

35. Roger Thurow, "The Fertile Continent: Africa, Agriculture's Final Frontier," *Foreign Affairs*, November/December 2010.

36. Bill Gates, "Bill Gates: My Plan to Fix the World's Biggest Problems," *Wall Street Journal*, January 25, 2013.

37. Grace Livingstone, "The Real Hunger Games: How Banks Gamble on Food Prices—and the Poor Lose Out," *Independent*, April 1, 2012.

38. Gates Foundation, "What We Do," www.gatesfoundation.org/what -we-do.

39. Juan Carlos Perez Salazar, "¿Realmente superó México a EE.UU. en adultos obesos?," BBC Mundo, July 9, 2013, www.bbc.co.uk /mundo/noticias/2013/07/130709_mexico_mas_obeso_que_eeuu _no_jcps.shtml.

40. Sarah Boseley, "Mexico Enacts Soda Tax in Effort to Combat World's Highest Obesity Rate," *Guardian*, January 16, 2014.

41. Kim Bhasin, "15 Facts About Coca-Cola That Will Blow Your Mind," *Business Insider*, June 9, 2011.

42. Anand Grover, "Unhealthy Foods, Non-Communicable Diseases and the Right to Health," Final Report of the Special Rapporteur on the Right of Everyone to the Enjoyment of the Highest Attainable Standard of Physical and Mental Health, UN Human Rights Council, A/HRC/26/31, April 1, 2014, www.ohchr.org/EN/Issues /Health/Pages/AnnualReports.aspx.

43. "The Coca-Cola Company, Technoserve and the Gates Foundation Partner to Boost Incomes of 50,000 Small-Scale Farmers in East Africa," press release, Technoserve, January 20, 2010, www.technoserve .org/press-room/detail/the-coca-cola-company-technoserve-and-the -gates-foundation-partner-to-boost.

44. Melinda Gates, "What Nonprofits Can Learn from Coca-Cola," TED talk, September 2010, www.ted.com/talks/melinda_french _gates_what_nonprofits_can_learn_from_coca_cola?language=en.

45. Charles Piller and Doug Smith, "Unintended Victims of Gates Foundation Generosity," *Los Angeles Times,* December 16, 2007.
46. Charles Piller, "Gates Foundation to Keep Its Investment Approach," *Los Angeles Times,* January 14, 2007.
47. Patty Stonesifer, "A Foundation States Its Case," *Los Angeles Times,* January 14, 2007.
48. There is also at least one known case of divestment on moral grounds, though not one in any obvious way related the foundation's activities. In 2014, in the wake of protests held outside its Seattle headquarters, the foundation did sell its position in the British firm G4S, the largest private military and security company in the world, apparently because of G4S's contracts with the Israeli Prison Authority.
49. Charles Piller, Edmund Sanders, and Robyn Dixon, "Dark Cloud over Good Works of Gates Foundation," *Los Angeles Times,* January 7, 2007.
50. Clement Dickie, "End of the Empire," *Dominicana,* July 21, 2014, www.dominicanablog.com/2014/07/21/end-of-the-empire.

CONCLUSION

1. End Poverty 2015 Millennium Campaign, "Zero Draft: Sustainable Development Goals," UN Millennium Campaign, www.endpoverty 2015.org/en/2014/06/04/zero-draft-sustainable-development-goals.
2. End Poverty 2015 Millennium Campaign, "Zero Draft."
3. Jeffrey Sachs, "From Millennium Development Goals to Sustainable Development Goals," *Lancet* 379 (2012): 2206.
4. Kate Raworth, "Will These Sustainable Development Goals Get Us into the Doughnut (aka a Safe and Just Space for Humanity)? Guest Post from Kate Raworth," Oxfam Blogs, August 11, 2014, oxfamblogs.org/fp2p/will-these-sustainable-development-goals -get-us-into-the-doughnut-aka-a-safe-and-just-space-for-humanity -guest-post-from-kate-raworth.
5. Charles Kenny and Casey Dunning, "What's the Point of the Post-2015 Agenda?," Center for Global Development, August 13, 2014, www.cgdev.org/blog/what's-point-post-2015-agenda.

6. Richard Horton, "Offline: Why the Sustainable Development Goals Will Fail," *Lancet* 383, no. 9936 (2014), 2196.

7. Without pushing the comparison, the history of America's wars, from Vietnam to the overthrow of Saddam Hussein, is a textbook example of what happens when powerful people refuse to take seriously anything but best-case scenarios.

8. Dowd, "Who Do We Think We Are?"

9. John Gray, *False Dawn: The Delusions of Global Capitalism* (New York: New Press, 1998), 197.

10. Bill Gates, "The Best Books I Read in 2013," *Gates Notes*, December 12, 2013, www.gatesnotes.com/About-Bill-Gates/Best-Books-2013.

11. Bill and Melinda Gates Foundation, "Annual Letter 2013," www.gatesfoundation.org/who-we-are/resources-and-media/annual-letters-list/annual-letter-2013.

12. Deaton, *Great Escape*, 272.

13. Deaton, *Great Escape*, 314.

14. Deaton makes an exception in the cases of health and emergency relief.

15. Deaton, *Great Escape*, 304.

16. Deaton, *Great Escape*, 305.

17. Thomas Carothers and Diane de Gramont, "Development Aid Confronts Politics: The Almost Revolution," Carnegie Endowment for International Peace, Washington, DC, 2013, 3–4, carnegieendowment.org/files/development_aid_politics_ch_1.pdf.

18. Aldous Huxley, *Brave New World* (New York: Rosetta Books, 1932), 45.

19. Cass Sunstein, *Why Nudge?: The Politics of Libertarian Paternalism* (New Haven, CT: Yale University Press, 2014), 26.

20. Bill and Melinda Gates Foundation, "Annual Letter 2013."

21. Bill and Melinda Gates Foundation, "Annual Letter 2013."

22. Abhijit Banerjee and Esther Duflo, *Poor Economics: A Radical Rethinking of the Way to Fight Global Poverty* (Philadelphia: Public Affairs, 2011), 37.

23. Aneel Karnani, *Fighting Poverty Together* (New York: Palgrave Macmillan, 2011).

24. Abhijit Banerjee and Esther Duflo, "More Than 1 Billion People Are Hungry in the World," *Foreign Policy*, April 25, 2011.

25. Bannerjee and Duflo, "More Than 1 Billion People Are Hungry in the World."

26. George Orwell, *The Road to Wigan Pier* (New York: Harcourt, 1937), 95–96.

27. Bannerjee and Duflo, "More Than 1 Billion People Are Hungry in the World."

28. Quoted in Marion Nestle, "Wikileaks Plays Food Politics: US vs. EU Agbiotech Policies," *Food Politics*, January 6, 2011, www.foodpolitics .com/2011/01/wikileaks-plays-food-politics-us-vs-eu-agbiotech -policies.

29. Throughout this book, I have consciously chosen not to take a position on the scientific controversy itself. The reason is quite simple: I am not competent to do so. But by the same token, I do not believe that the pro-GMO scientists involved in this debate have shown themselves to have understood even the basics of its cultural and social aspects, none of which can be fully addressed simply by reiterating that there is no basis for worrying about the safety of GMOs.

30. Carothers and de Gramont, "Development Aid Confronts Politics," 256.

31. Carothers and de Gramont, "Development Aid Confronts Politics," 15.

32. Carothers and de Gramont, "Development Aid Confronts Politics," 3.

33. Carothers and de Gramont, "Development Aid Confronts Politics," 4.

34. Rist, *History of Development*, 77.

35. Carothers and de Gramont, "Development Aid Confronts Politics," 255.

36. Carothers and de Gramont, "Development Aid Confronts Politics," 273.

37. Carothers and de Gramont, "Development Aid Confronts Politics," 283.

38. Herbert Marcuse, *One-Dimensional Man: Studies in the Ideology of Advanced Industrial Society* (Boston: Beacon Press, 1964), 15.

39. Gray, *False Dawn*, 196.

40. Gray, *False Dawn*, 194.

41. George Monbiot, "Sick of This Market-Driven World? You Should Be," *Guardian*, August 5, 2014.

42. Mark Mazower, *Governing the World: The History of an Idea, 1815 to the Present* (New York: Penguin, 2012).

43. Mazower, *Governing the World.*
44. Leys, *Rise and Fall of Development Theory,* 113.
45. Eric Holt-Giménez and Raj Patel, *Food Rebellions* (Oxford: Pambazuka Press, 2009), 181.
46. Gray, *False Dawn,* 208.

Index

Index

Index

Index

Daly, Claire, 298
Danida, 199
Danone, 207
Dauvergne, Peter, 191, 201, 204, 229
Davis, Mike, 24
Davos meeting, 143, 193, 198, 211, 233, 261
Dead Aid (Moyo), 213
Dean, Judith, 96
Dearden, Nick, 290
Deaton, Angus, 292, 315, 321–22, 328, 368n45
De Castro, Josué, 19–20
Decolonization, 92–95, 113
"Deconstructing Development Discourse: Buzzwords and Fuzzwords" (Cornwall and Brock), 272
De Gramont, Diane, 322, 328, 329–30
Democracy, xxvii, 41, 329, 335–36
in retreat, 143–44
SAP's disregard of, 136–37
World Bank barred from use of term, 11, 136
Democracy in Retreat (Kurlantzick), 143
Democratic Party (U.S.), 187
Democratic Republic of the Congo (DRC), 13, 300
Department for International Development (DFID), xxiv, 41, 74, 79, 94, 113, 137, 144, 192, 197–98, 199, 202, 223, 234, 264, 288, 289
Department of Defense, U.S., 243
Dependency theory, 117, 228
De Schutter, Olivier, 16–17, 75, 83–84, 115, 132, 137–38, 142, 144, 290, 310–11
Desertification, xix, 89
Deutsche Bank, 310, 311
Devarajan, Shantayanan, 130, 131–32
Development as Freedom (Sen), 246
Development Confronts Politics (Carothers and De Gramont), 322
DFID. *See* Department for International Development
Diabetes, 311, 312
Diaz-Bonilla, Eugenio, 116
Dickie, Clement, 315
Dictatorships. *See* Authoritarian regimes
Diouf, Jacques, 101
"Discovering Development: The Dreams and the Damage" (blog), 274–75

Donor countries, 109
agriculture and, 91, 92, 112–14, 126
NGOs and, 185–87, 188, 197
private sector and, 197–200
"Double Irish" (accounting technique), 297–98
"Double Irish with a Dutch Sandwich" (accounting technique), 298
Doubly Green Revolution, The (Conway), 177
Drayton, Bill, 195
Droughts, xiv–xv, xx, 7, 24, 27, 52, 155
Drummond, Jamie, 160, 161
Dryden, Sam, 291–92
Duflo, Esther, 13, 324–26
Dunant, Henri, 22
DuPont, 200, 309

Earth Institute, 81
Earth Summit, 59
Easterly, William, 11, 15, 41, 50, 58, 136, 137, 216, 226, 254, 352n13
Economic and Social Council (ECOSOC), 233
Economic Consequences of Peace, The (Keynes), 43
"Economic Possibilities for Our Grandchildren" (Keynes), 38, 43
Economist, 27, 232
Ecuador, 139
Edwards, Michael, 185–86, 188–89, 191, 193, 204, 253, 260, 261, 263
Egalitarian Moment, The (Low), 93
Egypt, xii, 7, 150
Ehrlich, Anne, 57, 146, 177
Ehrlich, Paul, xiii, 57, 146, 177
Einstein, Albert, 175
Eisenhower, Dwight, 85, 133
El-Erian, Mohammed, 85
El Niño Southern Oscillation, 24, 138
El Salvador, 223
"Embracing Enlightened Capitalism" (Shah), 199
End of History, 82, 163, 167, 168, 181, 247, 320
End of Poverty, The: Economic Possibilities for Our Time (Sachs), 37–44, 50, 73, 74, 79, 141, 172, 215, 226, 230, 293, 298
"End of Poverty, Soon, The" (Sachs), 226
End Poverty 2015 Millennium Campaign, 29

Index

Index

Hanlon, Gerard, 283–84
Hansen, James, 65
Hanyang University, 164
Harvard Business School, 225, 232
Harvard University, 253
*Haves and the Have-Nots, The: A Brief
  and Idiosyncratic History of Global
  Inequality* (Milanovic), xxiii
Hawken, Paul, 314–15
Headey, Derek, 70
Health Poverty Action, 274, 306
Hegemony, 34, 110–11
Hepburn, Katherine, 330
High Level Ministerial Meeting on Food
  Security for All, 83
Hilary, John, 283–84
Hinduism, 30
Hiroshima bombing, 175, 180
Hirschman, Albert, 228
History of Development, The (Rist), 110,
  227
Hobbes, Thomas, xxiv
Hoddinott, John, 69
Holodomor, 26
Holt, Douglas, 265
Holt-Giménez, Eric, 85, 88, 264, 306,
  308, 334, 335
Honduras, 223, 269
"Honest Accounts? The True Story
  of Africa's Billion Dollar Losses"
  (report), 306
Horn of Africa, xiv, 27, 52, 154
Horton, Richard, 259–60, 318
Hot Springs conference, 23–24
*How Brands Become Icons: The Principles
  of Cultural Branding* (Holt), 265
Hulme, David, 185–86, 188, 316
"Human rightism," 204
Human rights, xxiv, xxv, 3, 13, 64,
  83–84, 142, 171, 202
  Ethiopian record on, 48, 224, 225–26
  philanthrocapitalism and, 224–26
  quasi-religious aspects of movement,
    29–30
  Walmart record on, 270
Human Rights Watch, 224, 276
Humphrey, Hubert, 148
Hunger Winter (1944–1945), 26
*Hungry World, The: America's Cold
  War Battle against Poverty in Asia*
  (Cullather), 126–27
Huq, Saleemul, 139

Huxley, Aldous, 265, 323
Hydraulic approach to aid, 321, 323,
  324
Hyperagents, 216, 217, 229

Ibrahim, Mo, 299–300, 304, 307, 309
IFAD. *See* International Fund for
  Agricultural Development
IF Campaign, 32, 33
IF Coalition, 302
IFPRI. *See* International Food Policy
  Research Institute
Ignatieff, Michael, xxiv, 29, 30, 32,
  282–83
IMF. *See* International Monetary Fund
"Impatient Optimists" (blog), 226
Imperialist famines, 24, 25, 26
Imports, 98, 99, 101, 123, 124
Income inequality, 63–64, 142–44,
  253–61
  lack of consensus on issue of, 260–61
  morality and, 260
  poverty and, 254–55, 258
Independent Commission for Aid
  Impact, 222
Independent University, Bangladesh, 139
India, xiv, xvii, xix, xx, 17, 47, 64, 113,
  116, 118, 119, 182, 265, 271, 325
  capitalist development in, 58
  famine disappearance in, 25, 153
  famine in, 20, 24
  global warming and, 140
  Green Revolution in, 250
  population growth in, 42
  poverty decline in, 50
  SUN movement in, 205–8
Indiana University, 194
Indian Biscuit Manufacturers Association,
  208
"India Shining" campaign, 265
Indonesia, xvi, 88, 116, 122, 313
Industrialization, 111–12
Innovation. *See* Science and technology
"Innovation with Impact: Financing 21st
  Century Development" (report), 55
Innovator's Dilemma, The (Christensen),
  232
Inspire, 283
Institute for Advanced Study (Princeton
  University), 50
Institute of Development Studies (Sussex
  University), 42, 51, 200, 234

Index

Index

Vietnam, xvii, 50, 58, 88, 116, 221, 222
Vietnam War, 121, 210, 266
Vitamin A, 164–65
Vivero Pol, José Luis, 333
Vogt, William, 56, 344n1
"Vote for the World You Want to See" (online campaign), 273

Waage, Jeffrey, 175, 176–77
Wall Street Journal, 282, 310
Walmart, 196, 200, 264, 266–70
Walmart de México, 269
Walton, Sam, 268
Warner, Andrew, 95–96
War on Want, 283
Warren, Bill, 334
Washington Consensus, 106, 229
Water supplies, xxv, 47, 117–18
Watkins, Anna, 282
Weather, problems caused by, xiv–xv, xviii, xx
Wesleyan University, 164, 177
West Bengal, 24, 25
WFP. *See* World Food Programme
WhatsApp, 252
Wheat, xii, xv, 56, 88, 102
White, Micah, 275–76
WHO. *See* World Health Organization
WIC (Women, Infants, Children) program, 148
Wiggins, Steve, 64, 86
Williams, Alex T., 281
Williamson, John, 106
Wise, Timothy, xix–xx
Wolf, Martin, 97
Wolfensohn, James, 11, 12, 72, 107–8, 130, 136, 234, 257
Wolfowitz, Paul, 5
Women, 9, 28, 40, 83, 141, 150
"Words to the Intellectuals" (Castro speech), 212–13
World Bank, xvi, xxiv, 15, 45, 62, 91, 95, 103, 105–8, 109, 122–23, 130–37, 202, 223, 257, 292, 306, 307, 317, 335
    agriculture and, 92, 93, 204
    American monopoly in, 105–6
    apolitical stance of, 11–12, 99
    catchphrases used by, 134–36
    on climate change, 65, 66

"democracy" as forbidden word in, 11, 136
"Fifty Years Is Enough" campaign and, 107, 130
    food crisis and, 5, 8, 9
    global food system and, 72–73, 86
    on MDGs, 47, 48, 49
    new slogan of, 11, 107
    NGOs defined by, 187–88
    SAP of (*see* Structural Adjustment Program)
    on scientific innovation, 234–35
    trade liberalization and, 98
World Development Movement, 262, 289–90
World Economic Forum, 143, 198, 200, 261, 266, 327
World Food Conference, 30
World Food Programme (WFP), 1, 2, 3, 5, 34, 102, 104, 212, 245
World Health Organization (WHO), 34, 192, 212, 284
World Trade Organization, 226
World Vision, 11, 91, 159
World War II, 22–23, 25–26, 145
World We Want Foundation, The, 29
World Wildlife Federation, 191
Worstall, Tim, 301–2
Wu, Changhua, 141

Yale University, 278
Yara International, 78, 200, 289
Yellow fever, 312
Yemen, 47, 87
Yom Kippur War, 99
Young Entrepreneurs Sustainable Living Awards, 195
Young & Rubicam, 283
Yousafzai, Malala, 273
YouTube, 275

Zakaria, Fareed, 143–44
Zero draft of the SDGs, 316, 317–18
Zero Hunger program, 335
Zero-sum game perspective, 4, 82, 84, 109, 183, 206, 238
Ziegler, Jean, 17, 75, 114, 116, 117, 122
Žižek, Slavoj, 308
Zoellick, Robert, 5, 130, 202–3
Zuckerberg, Mark, 233

About the Author

David Rieff is the author of eight previous books, including *Swimming in a Sea of Death*, *At the Point of a Gun: Democratic Dreams and Armed Intervention*, *A Bed for the Night: Humanitarianism in Crisis*, and *Slaughterhouse: Bosnia and the Failure of the West*. He lives in New York City.